FINANCIAL ACCOUNTING

Alan Melville

FCA, BSc, Cert. Ed.

M&E PITMAN PUBLISHING

London · Hong Kong · Johannesburg · Melbourne · Singapore · Washington DC

PITMAN PUBLISHING
128 Long Acre, London WC2E 9AN
Tel: +44 (0)171 447 2000
Fax: +44 (0)171 240 5771

A Division of Pearson Professional Limited

First published in Great Britain 1997

ISBN 0 7121 1428 9

British Library Cataloguing in Publication Data
A CIP catalogue record for this book can be obtained from the British Library.

10 9 8 7 6 5 4 3 2 1

Printed and bound in Great Britain by Bell and Bain Ltd, Glasgow

CONTENTS

PREFACE

The main aim of this book is to explain financial accounting as clearly and concisely as possible for the benefit of those who are studying the subject for the first time. The book has not been written with any specific syllabus in mind but should be suitable for students on a wide variety of introductory accounting courses. In particular, the book will be of value to those preparing for the financial accounting examinations of the professional accounting bodies and to students on foundation courses in accounting at universities and colleges. Non-accountants who are studying accounting as part of a wider course in business or management studies (or any other subject) will also find the book useful.

Every effort has been made to strike the right balance between practical work and theoretical concepts. Of course it is vital that accounting students should learn *how* to prepare accounts but it is also important to understand *why* accounting works as it does. For this reason, the role of accounting conventions is stressed throughout the book and several pages are devoted to the ASB Statement of Principles. Accounting standards are covered in some detail, with an emphasis on those standards which are most likely to be of interest to the foundation level student.

Each chapter of the book concludes with a set of exercises. Solutions to many of these exercises can be found at the back of the book but solutions to the exercises which are marked with an asterisk (*) are provided in a separate Instructor's Manual.

Alan Melville
January 1997

1

INTRODUCTION TO ACCOUNTING

Chapter objectives

When you have finished this chapter, you should be able to:

- **Define the term "accounting".**
- **Explain the purpose of accounting.**
- **Identify the main users of accounting information.**
- **Contrast financial accounting with other branches of accounting.**
- **Identify the main professional accountancy bodies in the UK.**
- **List the qualitative characteristics of financial information.**

1. INTRODUCTION

This book is concerned with an important branch of accounting known as *financial accounting*. Subsequent chapters of the book describe financial accounting in great detail but the purpose of this first chapter is to discuss accounting in general terms and to explain how financial accounting fits into the overall picture.

A sensible starting point is to offer a definition of the term "accounting". Although there is no universally agreed definition, it is generally accepted that accounting consists of the following activities:

(a) collecting and recording economic data relating to a business enterprise

(b) processing this data to produce useful economic information (often referred to as *accounting information*)

(c) communicating or reporting this accounting information to interested parties and, if necessary, interpreting it for their benefit.

The economic data referred to in this definition is data which relates to the business activities of the enterprise and which can be measured in quantitative, usually monetary, terms. Typically, this will consist of data about goods bought and sold, payments made, money received and so forth.

As an example of accounting work, consider the task of determining the amount of profit made by a business in the course of a year. This task will involve:

(a) collecting and recording data about the income and expenditure of the business during the year

(b) processing this data to calculate the profit for the year

(c) reporting this information to the owner of the business and to others who need to be aware of it (e.g. the tax authorities).

The purpose of accounting

The purpose of accounting is to assist the users of accounting information to make *better economic decisions*. There would be no point in spending time and money on the production, communication and interpretation of accounting information if the people for whom it was produced then did nothing with the information when they received it. To understand the purpose of accounting more fully, therefore, we need answers to the following questions:

(a) Who are the users of accounting information?

(b) What economic decisions do they have to make?

(c) What accounting information do they need to help them make these decisions?

These questions are considered below.

2. THE USERS OF ACCOUNTING INFORMATION

The users of accounting information can be classified into a number of categories or groups. Each group has different types of economic decision to make and so each group has different information needs. This makes it difficult, if not impossible, for a single set of accounting information to satisfy the needs of all users. The principal users of accounting information are identified below.

Owners and Investors

The owner of a business is faced with a number of economic decisions. These might include:

(a) deciding whether to keep the business, sell it or close it down completely

(b) deciding whether to invest more money in the business

(c) deciding how much money can safely be withdrawn from the business, without damaging its financial stability.

Similarly, people who do not own a business outright but who have invested their money in one (e.g. the shareholders of a limited company) must decide whether to maintain, increase or reduce the size of their investment. Owners and investors who have delegated the day-to-day running of a business to managers acting on their behalf will also need to decide whether the managers should remain in office. This decision will usually depend upon how well the business has performed under the stewardship of the manager(s) concerned. When making all of these decisions, owners and investors will probably find the following information useful:

(a) information about the recent financial *performance* of the business, showing how well or badly the business has done
(b) information about the current financial *position* of the business, showing its assets (the things that it owns) and its liabilities (the amounts of money that it owes).

Forecasts relating to the future financial performance and position of the business would also be useful in many cases, not only to owners and investors but also to potential owners/investors and to the investment analysts who advise them.

Management

The managers of a business are responsible for its day-to-day operations. Their main role is to make plans for the business and then to ensure that these plans are carried out. This planning and control work involves a great many decisions. These might include:

(a) deciding what goods or services should be offered for sale by the business and determining selling prices
(b) deciding sales targets and deciding on the action to be taken if these targets are not met
(c) deciding on planned levels of income and expenditure (i.e. establishing a budget) and deciding what to do if actual results differ from the budget
(d) deciding between investment opportunities
(e) deciding how much money the business needs to borrow and deciding where the money should be borrowed from.

The managers making these decisions will require frequent, detailed accounting information relating to the past and present activities of the business, together with projections or forecasts for the future.

Banks and other lenders

The main concern of a bank (or other lender) when deciding whether to lend money to a business is the ability of the business to keep up interest payments during the course of the loan and to repay the loan at the end of its term.

In the case of short-term loans, the required accounting information will relate to the current financial position of the business and its expected financial position in the near future. For loans over a longer period, the required information will probably extend to a more general analysis of the financial prospects of the business in the long term.

Suppliers

Suppliers of goods or services on credit terms are in a similar position to lenders. They have to decide whether to offer credit to a business and, if so, how much credit to offer. Information about the financial position of the business will help them to make this decision.

Customers

A customer needing a secure source of supply may require accounting information from potential suppliers before deciding where to place a long-term contract. For example, a motor manufacturer will need to be sure that its supplier of gearboxes is financially stable and is not likely to cease trading in the foreseeable future.

Employees

An employee's main requirements from an employer are job security and fair pay. Information about the employer's financial performance and position will help employees (or trade unions acting on their behalf) to decide whether the employer is likely to continue in business and whether the remuneration offered is fair.

Competitors

Competing businesses may study the accounting information produced by their rivals in the hope of finding ways of improving their own financial performance. For this reason, businesses are usually keen to keep their accounting information as private as possible. However, if a business operates as a limited company it is obliged by law to make certain information public (see Chapter 14).

The Government

One obvious purpose for which the Government uses accounting information is the assessment of taxes (this is the work of the Inland Revenue and the Customs and Excise). Other purposes include the regulation of business and the production of national economic statistics.

The general public

The activities of some businesses (especially big, powerful businesses) are of interest to the general public. For example, a large company which has a monopoly over the supply of a certain product may be suspected of charging excessive prices for that product. A study of the accounting information published by the company may help the public to decide whether or not this suspicion is well-founded.

3. TYPES OF ACCOUNTING

As mentioned above, it is not usually possible for a single set of accounting information to satisfy the needs of all users. In particular, the needs of managers are very different from those of most other user groups. As a consequence, two quite distinct branches or types of accounting have emerged. These are *management accounting* and *financial accounting*.

Management accounting

Management accounting is concerned with the provision of accounting information to support the planning and control decisions made by managers. Typical examples of the information provided by a management accounting system might be:

(a) a report on the costs of manufacturing a particular product

(b) a report on the costs of running a particular department

(c) a monthly analysis of expenditure, comparing actual and planned expenditure over a variety of budget headings

(d) a projection of sales volumes over the next 6 months, analysed by product group

(e) a forecast of income and expenditure for each month of the year ahead, highlighting months in which the business might run into financial difficulties.

The main features of management accounting information are as follows:

(a) The information is much more detailed than the information used by other user groups and is required much more frequently.

(b) The information is often confidential and is intended for internal use only, not for external publication.

(c) There is no legal obligation to produce any management accounting information at all and the information actually produced will differ widely from one business to another. It is entirely up to management to specify the information that they require and to ensure that the cost of producing this information is justified.

(d) The information often incorporates forecasts and projections. This predictive information helps managers to make plans for the future of the business.

Financial accounting

Financial accounting is concerned with the provision of accounting information to owners, investors and other external users who are not involved in the day-to-day running of the business. The accounting information provided for these users consists of a number of *financial statements* which are usually prepared once a year. The two most important financial statements are:

(a) the *profit and loss account*, which summarises the financial performance of the business during the past year and reveals the profit or loss for that year

(b) the *balance sheet*, which shows the financial position of the business at the end of the year.

The task of recording the data on which the financial statements are based is often referred to as *book-keeping*, since the data is traditionally recorded in books of account (see Chapter 5). In many businesses, however, routine book-keeping work is now carried out by computer, in which case the books of account are replaced by computer files. The main features of financial accounting information are as follows:

(a) The information is provided in summarised form at annual intervals and lacks the detail associated with management information.

(b) There is a legal obligation to produce at least a minimum amount of financial accounting information (if only for the benefit of the tax authorities). A business which operates as a limited company is also subject to regulations concerning the format and content of its financial statements (see Chapter 14). The cost of keeping the necessary financial records and preparing the financial statements is therefore unavoidable.

(c) The information is mainly historical in nature. It is usually restricted to a review of past financial performance and a statement of the current financial position.

Limitations of financial statements

It is worth noting at this point that financial statements are subject to a number of limitations and so cannot provide all of the information which users might require. Some of these limitations are described below.

(a) Firstly, the information contained in financial statements is limited to information which can be expressed in quantitative terms. Matters such as the skill of the management team and the morale of the workforce are not included at all. Yet these matters could be of great concern to certain decision-makers (e.g. to a bank trying to assess the viability of a business before granting a loan).

(b) Secondly, financial statements are largely confined to an analysis of past events, whereas many users are much more interested in what is likely to happen in the future. Financial forecasts might occasionally be supplied to banks or to other lenders in support of a loan application, but businesses are usually reluctant to make forecast information more widely available. This is partly because of the unreliability of such information and partly because it might be of help to competitors.

    The historical information provided in the financial statements might be used as a guide to the future performance of the business, but in a rapidly changing world there can be no guarantee that such projections will prove accurate.

(c) Another problem is that accounting is not an exact science. The preparation of financial statements nearly always involves the exercise of *judgement* and this is bound to make the statements less reliable than users would wish. For example, it may be necessary to estimate the remaining useful life of a machine owned by a business or judge the likelihood that a customer who owes money to the business will ever pay up. The situations in which it is necessary to make estimates and form judgements are explained fully in later chapters of this book.

(d) It is also important to remember that most of the information given in financial statements is expressed in money terms and that the monetary unit (the pound sterling in the UK) is constantly changing in value. This introduces a number of problems, especially in times of high inflation (see Chapter 20).

Despite these limitations, financial statements do serve a useful purpose. They provide a great deal of vital information and for many users they constitute the only available guide to the financial performance and position of a business.

Other types of accounting work

As well as management accounting and financial accounting, people who work in the accounting profession may undertake other types of accounting-related work. The main types of work involved are as follows:

(a) **Auditing**. Auditors are responsible for checking the accuracy of accounting information. They may be external auditors or internal auditors.

- External auditors are appointed by the owners of a business to perform an independent review of the financial statements of the business and to express an opinion on the truth and fairness of the information given in those statements. This is a critically important function in cases where the owners take no part in the management of the business and is a legal requirement for limited companies with a turnover exceeding £350,000 per annum.
- Internal auditors work for a business (usually a fairly large one) and carry out checks on the accounting records and procedures of that business. They are appointed by management and report their findings to management.

(b) **Taxation**. This involves calculating the amount of tax payable by a client, negotiating with the tax authorities on his or her behalf and offering advice on ways in which the client's tax burden can legally be minimised. An accountant specialising in this field requires a great deal of detailed tax knowledge.

(c) **Financial management**. Financial management is the task of ensuring that a business obtains sufficient financial resources to meet its needs, that these resources are obtained as cheaply as possible and that any spare financial resources are invested as lucratively as possible.

4. THE ACCOUNTING PROFESSION

Qualified accountants in the UK belong to one of the following professional accountancy bodies:

(a) The Institute of Chartered Accountants in England and Wales (ICAEW)
(b) The Institute of Chartered Accountants in Scotland (ICAS)

(c) The Institute of Chartered Accountants in Ireland (ICAI)
(d) The Chartered Institute of Management Accountants (CIMA)
(e) The Association of Chartered Certified Accountants (ACCA)
(f) The Chartered Institute of Public Finance and Accountancy (CIPFA).

To become a member of any of these bodies it is necessary to pass a series of rigorous examinations and to undergo a prolonged period of training and relevant experience.

Chartered accountants work mainly in accounting practice, offering a variety of accounting, auditing and taxation services to their clients. Most CIMA members occupy management accounting posts in industry or commerce. Members of the ACCA are found both in practice and in industry or commerce, whilst CIPFA members work almost exclusively in the public sector.

Another important accountancy body is the Association of Accounting Technicians (AAT). Members of the AAT occupy technician-level posts and often work as assistants to professionally qualified accountants. The Association is sponsored by the main professional bodies and AAT membership can be used as the first step towards becoming a fully qualified accountant.

5. THE QUALITATIVE CHARACTERISTICS OF FINANCIAL INFORMATION

If financial information is going to be useful to the people for whom it is produced, it must possess a number of qualities or *qualitative characteristics*. The Accounting Standards Board (a body which seeks to improve the quality of financial accounting in the UK) has suggested that the following characteristics are especially important:

(a) **Relevance**. Financial information cannot be useful unless it is relevant to the needs of users and helps them to make economic decisions. Information which has *predictive relevance* helps users to make decisions about the future, whilst information with *confirmatory relevance* helps users to evaluate their past decisions.

(b) **Reliability**. Information is reliable if users can depend upon it to be *complete* and free from error or bias. Reliable information is prepared and presented in a *neutral* way, not in a way which seeks to influence the decisions which will be made by users.

Total reliability is usually difficult to achieve since (as mentioned earlier) the preparation of financial information nearly always involves the exercise of judgement. However, as far as possible, financial information should possess the quality of *objectivity*, consisting of definite facts rather than subjective opinions.

(c) **Comparability**. Users may need to compare the financial information produced by a business with:

- information produced by the same business in previous years, or

- information produced by other businesses.

Such comparisons will be valid only if all the information has been prepared and presented in a *consistent* manner, so that similar transactions and events are dealt with in a similar way.

(d) **Understandability**. An obviously desirable quality of financial information is that users should understand it. The degree of financial sophistication of the intended users should be taken into account when preparing and presenting information for their use.

These desirable qualities may seem very straightforward at first but it is often difficult to achieve them all in practice. The main difficulties are as follows:

(a) **Timeliness**. If financial information is needed quickly, it may be necessary to estimate figures which could have been established with certainty if more time had been available. This introduces an element of judgement or subjectivity into the information and reduces its reliability.

(b) **Cost**. Improving the quality of the financial information provided to users will cost money. For instance, a business could carry out research into user needs and then produce a different set of information for each user group, targeted at the needs of that group and taking into account the level of financial understanding possessed by the members of the group. This would improve relevance and understandability but the cost of the exercise might outweigh its benefits.

(c) **Conflict between the characteristics**. It may not be possible to achieve all of the qualitative characteristics simultaneously since some of them might be incompatible with others. In particular, information which is more relevant may be less reliable and vice-versa.

For example, some users may be keen to know the current market value of the land and buildings owned by a business. If an estimate of this value is included in the financial information provided to those users, this will increase relevance but reduce reliability. In circumstances such as these, the aim should be to achieve a balance between the characteristics, as appropriate to user needs.

6. SUMMARY

- Accounting is the task of collecting and recording economic data relating to a business, processing this data to produce useful economic information and then communicating this information to those who need it.
- The purpose of accounting is to help the users of accounting information to make better economic decisions.
- The main users of accounting information are owners/investors and managers. Other users include lenders, suppliers, customers, employees, competitors, the government and the general public.

- The role of management accounting is to provide information which supports the planning and control activities of managers.
- The role of financial accounting is to provide information for owners, investors and other external users. This information takes the form of financial statements which describe the financial performance and the financial position of the business.
- Qualified accountants in the UK belong to one of six professional accountancy bodies.
- Useful financial information should possess a number of qualities. These include relevance, reliability, comparability and understandability.

EXERCISES 1

1.1 List the users of accounting information. Describe the kinds of information needed by each user group. Explain why one set of accounting information is unlikely to satisfy the needs of all users.

1.2 The two main branches of accounting are management accounting and financial accounting.

(a) Explain the purpose of each of these branches of accounting.

(b) Contrast the distinguishing features of the accounting information produced by each branch.

1.3 List the desirable qualities that should be possessed by accounting information. Is there any reason why accounting information might not possess all of these qualities?

***1.4** Imagine that you are trying to decide whether or not to invest in the shares of a large company. To help you make this decision you have obtained the company's published financial statements for the last five years.

(a) What are the two main types of information that you would expect to find in these financial statements?

(b) Do you think that the statements will provide you with all of the information that you need? If not, why not?

***1.5** Consider the list of qualitative characteristics which accounting information ought to possess. If you had to choose the single most important characteristic, which one would it be? Give reasons for your answer.

***1.6** What services might a firm of practising accountants provide to:

(a) a small business?

(b) a large company?

2

FINANCIAL ACCOUNTING CONVENTIONS

Chapter objectives

When you have finished this chapter, you should be able to:

- **Explain the need for accounting conventions.**
- **Identify and describe the most important accounting conventions.**
- **Apply accounting conventions to practical accounting problems.**
- **Outline the progress made to date towards the development of a conceptual framework for financial accounting.**

1. INTRODUCTION

The first chapter of this book introduced accounting in general terms, explained the purpose of accounting and identified the users of accounting information. In that chapter, we saw that there are two main branches of accounting. These are:

(a) management accounting, which exists to satisfy the needs of managers

(b) financial accounting, which serves the needs of owners, investors and other external users.

Management accounting is considered no further in this book. From now on, we will concentrate exclusively on *financial accounting* and the first step is to consider some important accounting conventions on which financial accounting is based.

2. THE NEED FOR ACCOUNTING CONVENTIONS

We saw in Chapter 1 that the aim of financial accounting is to provide information about the financial performance and financial position of a business. This information takes the form of a number of financial statements which are usually produced once a year and which are often referred to as the *annual accounts* of the business. The main financial statements are:

(a) the profit and loss account, which summarises the revenue and expenses of the business for the year and shows the resulting profit or loss

(b) the balance sheet, which shows the assets and liabilities of the business at the end of the year.

The task of producing these statements is not as straightforward as it might seem and is *not* a mere mechanical exercise. If it were it could be delegated to computer systems and there would be no need for accountants. The problem is that the correct treatment of many of the items which appear in financial statements would appear to be a matter of *judgement*. Some simple examples will illustrate this point:

(a) A business owns a building which was bought 10 years ago for £1 million. The building now has a market value of an estimated £3 million. Should the building be listed in the balance sheet as a £1 million asset or a £3 million asset?

(b) A business sells some goods to a customer a few days before the end of the year. The customer is not expected to pay for several weeks. Should the income from the sale be shown as revenue in this year's profit and loss account or in next year's?

(c) A business is being sued by a customer and will have to pay damages and costs estimated at £100,000 if it loses the case. The case will not be decided until the middle of next year. Should the £100,000 be shown as a liability in the balance sheet drawn up at the end of this year?

The need to make judgements in situations like these makes financial accounting much more difficult than it would otherwise be. More importantly, it also introduces an undesirable element of subjectivity into financial accounting, so reducing the reliability of financial statements.

It will never be possible to eliminate judgement from financial accounting entirely, but it would be helpful if the number of situations in which judgement is required could be minimised. It would also be helpful if some guidelines could be provided to help accountants to form judgements when these are unavoidable. Such help is forthcoming in the form of *accounting standards* and *accounting conventions*.

The role of accounting standards

Accounting standards are devised and published in the UK by the Accounting Standards Board (ASB). Each standard addresses a different financial accounting problem and provides advice on how accountants should deal with that problem. In the case of limited companies, it is usually compulsory to follow this "advice", since compliance with most of the accounting standards is obligatory for most companies.

The first accounting standard was issued in 1971 and over thirty standards have been issued since. Standards issued before 1991 are known as *Statements of Standard Accounting Practice* (SSAP's). Standards issued since 1991 are known as *Financial Reporting Standards* (FRS's). Accounting standards are considered in detail in Chapter 15 of this book.

The role of accounting conventions

Financial accounting as we know it today is the result of several centuries of evolution. Accounting has developed to cope with an increasingly complex business world and it has been necessary over the years to devise practical solutions to many new accounting problems. One result of all this experience has been the emergence of a number of accounting *conventions* (sometimes known as accounting *concepts*, accounting *principles* or accounting *rules*) which accountants now use to guide them in their work.

It is important to realise that these conventions have arisen entirely from practical experience. They are the distillation of centuries of accounting practice and they represent nothing more than the accepted, time-honoured, conventional approach to financial accounting.

At the end of this chapter we will consider the disadvantages of basing financial accounting on a set of pragmatic conventions. We will also examine some attempts to build a sound theoretical foundation for the subject.

3. THE MAIN ACCOUNTING CONVENTIONS

There are many accounting conventions in existence. It would not be feasible to list every known convention here but the conventions listed below are generally agreed to be especially important.

Business entity

This convention states that, for accounting purposes, a business is to be treated as an independent entity, distinct from its owner (or owners). The financial statements of a business should provide information about the business only and should not provide information about the owner's private financial affairs. It is important to note the following points:

(a) Since owner and business are treated as separate entities, it is possible for one of them to owe money to the other. In fact it is very likely that a business will owe money to its owner (see Chapter 3).

(b) If a business is owned by just one person (a sole trader) or by a small group of people (a partnership), then the law recognises no distinction between the business and its owner(s). On the other hand, a business which operates as a limited company is a legal person in its own right and is legally distinct from the shareholders who own it. Nonetheless, for accounting purposes, a business is *always* treated as an independent entity, regardless of its legal status.

Money measurement

This convention states that financial accounting is concerned only with items which can be quantified and expressed in monetary terms. The main effect of this convention is that business assets to which a monetary value cannot reasonably be attributed (e.g. the skill of the workforce) are normally ignored in the financial statements, even though those assets might be of great worth to the business concerned.

Duality

As Chapter 3 of this book will make clear, every business transaction has two effects on the financial position of the business concerned. For example, if a business buys a motor vehicle and pays by cheque, this transaction results in an increase in the value of the motor vehicles owned by the business but a decrease in its bank balance. The duality convention (also known as the *dual aspect* convention) requires that the financial statements of a business should reflect the twofold effect of each business transaction.

Historic cost

The historic cost convention states that assets should be shown in the balance sheet at their historic cost to the business (i.e. their original cost) or at a value which is based upon historic cost. The current market value of assets is ignored. For example, if a building which was bought for £150,000 five years ago has now increased in value to £200,000, the historic cost convention requires that the building should continue to be shown on the balance sheet at its original cost of £150,000.

The main advantage of this convention is that the historic cost of an asset is a fact, whilst any other valuation is only an estimate or an opinion. The historic cost convention increases the objectivity (and therefore the reliability) of financial statements but may reduce their relevance to some users.

Stable monetary unit

When preparing financial statements, it is assumed that the monetary unit of measurement (the pound sterling in the UK) has a constant value. Changes in the purchasing power of money are ignored. This certainly makes accounting easier but it introduces a number of problems. One obvious problem is the difficulty of making meaningful comparisons between financial statements prepared in different years, especially at a time of rapid inflation. The accounting problems caused by changes in the purchasing power of money are discussed more fully in Chapter 20, together with some alternatives to the stable monetary unit convention.

Going concern

Under the going concern convention, it is assumed that a business will continue to operate for the foreseeable future unless there is good reason to think otherwise. If a business is a going concern, some of its assets may have useful lives stretching into future years and the going concern convention allows the treatment of those assets in the financial statements to take into account the length of their useful lives (see Chapter 6).

Accounting year

It is conventional to produce financial statements at yearly intervals. There is no compelling reason why a shorter or longer accounting period should not be adopted but it would be expensive to produce accounts more frequently and experience suggests that annual accounts are acceptable to most users.

The practice of producing annual accounts is also supported by the tax system and (for businesses which are limited companies) by company law.

Note that there is no need for an accounting year to coincide with the calendar year. Some businesses do choose 31 December as their year-end but many others choose different dates. For example, a business which is normally very busy during the winter months might choose 30 June as its annual accounting date, so ensuring that the task of preparing the annual accounts can be carried out at a comparatively quiet time of the year.

Realisation

The realisation convention states that a sale of goods or services should be shown or *recognised* in the profit and loss account when:

(a) the goods concerned have been passed to the customer (or the services concerned have been rendered), and

(b) the obligation to pay for the goods or services has been accepted by the customer.

This means that the revenue shown in a profit and loss account will include all of the sales made during the accounting period, even though sales made towards the end of the period may not yet have been paid for. The realisation convention requires a similar treatment of goods or services purchased by the business.

If this convention were not adopted (and sales/purchases were recognised only on a cash basis) profit and loss accounts could give a misleading picture. For example, it might appear that a business had made a large loss in one year, followed by a large profit in the next, simply because of the timing of payments and receipts.

A disadvantage of the realisation convention is that it does not cope well with bad debts. If a customer fails to pay for goods or services, the anticipated profit on the sale will never be received, yet this profit might already have been recognised in the financial statements. The problem of bad debts is considered further in Chapter 7 of this book.

Matching

The matching convention states that expenses should be matched against the revenue to which they relate. In other words, revenue and the expenses incurred so as to earn that revenue should be recognised in the *same accounting period*. Some of the practical consequences of this convention are listed below (others will be explained in the next few chapters of this book):

(a) **Unsold goods**. Any revenue derived from selling goods must be matched against the expense of purchasing *those goods only*. The cost of any goods bought during an accounting period but remaining unsold at the end of that period should be matched against the *following* period's sales (assuming that the goods are sold in the following period).

(b) **Accruals**. Expenses which relate to an accounting period must be shown in that period's profit and loss account, whether or not they are paid in that period. For example, if the most recent electricity bill paid by a business is dated 15 February and accounts are being prepared for the year to 31 March, the cost of the electricity consumed in the last six weeks of the year must be estimated and this *accrual* must be included in the electricity figure shown in the profit and loss account.

(c) **Prepayments**. Similarly, expenses which are paid in one accounting period but which relate to the following period (*prepayments*) must be recognised in the following period's profit and loss account.

It should be clear that the combined effect of the realisation convention and the matching convention makes it most unlikely that the profit for an accounting period will be equal to the difference between total cash received and total payments made during that period. It should also be clear that the matching convention requires accountants to make certain estimates (e.g. the amount of an accrual) and that this is bound to reduce the reliability of financial statements.

Substance over form

This convention states that the accounting treatment of an item should reflect its economic substance rather than its legal form. For example, if a business buys a motor vehicle on hire purchase terms, the legal position is that the business does not become the owner of the vehicle until the last instalment has been paid. The substance of the transaction is that the business owns the asset from the outset, and this is the way that the transaction will be represented in the financial statements of the business.

Materiality

Rigorous application of the accounting conventions to trivial or immaterial items might involve a disproportionate amount of accounting effort. In these circumstances, the materiality convention allows the other conventions to be ignored and a simpler accounting treatment to be adopted.

For example, if a business buys a £1 jar of coffee for office use and some of the coffee remains unused at the end of the accounting period in which it is bought, strict observance of the matching convention requires that part of the £1 should be regarded as a prepayment and should be shown in the following period's profit and loss account. The materiality convention would overrule this and allow the entire £1 to be shown as an expense in the profit and loss account of the period in which the coffee is bought.

Consistency

Despite the guidance provided by accounting standards and conventions, there is often a choice of accounting treatments available in relation to a financial item. Once the choice has been made, the consistency convention requires that the chosen treatment should be applied consistently to all items of the same type in the same accounting period and in future periods. Consistency aids comparability which (as we saw in Chapter 1) is a desirable characteristic of accounting information.

Objectivity

The objectivity convention requires that financial statements should be produced as objectively as possible. The statements should be free of personal bias and should be based on facts rather than opinions. Ideally, two or more accountants each faced with the same body of financial data should produce identical financial statements but, as we have already seen, this is unlikely to happen in practice. The element of judgement is always present and this is bound to make financial statements less objective and, therefore, less reliable than users would wish.

Prudence

The need to make estimates and form judgements when preparing financial statements inevitably introduces an element of doubt into the accounting process. For example, an accountant who is estimating the amount of an accrued expense at the end of an accounting period may have a choice between several estimates, any one of which might be correct. In these circumstances, the prudence convention states that the accountant should "err on the side of caution". In other words, a prudent accountant will tend to:

(a) *understate* revenue, profits and assets
(b) *overstate* expenses, losses and liabilities.

This is not pessimism but conservatism. The prudence convention ensures that financial statements do not give an over-optimistic view of the financial performance and position of a business. If there is a clash between prudence and one of the other conventions, prudence will usually take precedence.

4. A CONCEPTUAL FRAMEWORK FOR FINANCIAL ACCOUNTING

The accounting conventions listed above are simply a summary of the conventional approach to financial accounting. Accountants are trained to follow these conventions and few practising accountants have either the time or the inclination to question them. However, it has been suggested in recent years that the conventions do not provide an adequate foundation for financial accounting and that they should be replaced by something better. Some of the perceived drawbacks of the accounting conventions are as follows:

(a) The conventions tell accountants *what* to do and *how* to do it without necessarily telling them *why*. The only justification for the conventions is that they seem to work reasonably well in practice.

(b) One convention may sometimes be in conflict with another. For example, the matching convention might require a cost to be spread over several accounting periods whilst prudence suggests that the entire cost should be written off immediately. Prudence will usually win arguments like these, but a set of accounting rules which occasionally pull in opposite directions is obviously flawed.

(c) The conventions are not the only ones that could be devised, nor are they necessarily the best. They are what accountants *do*, but this may be different from what accountants *ought to do*.

Those who support these arguments have called for the development of a *conceptual framework* for financial accounting i.e. a set of basic theoretical principles to provide a solid foundation for the subject. Such a framework would:

(a) guide accountants to the theoretically correct way of dealing with new accounting problems

(b) provide a theoretical basis for the work of those who set accounting standards (see Chapter 15)

(c) ensure that financial accounting develops in a logical, consistent way.

The ASB Statement of Principles

Over the last twenty years, a considerable effort has been made (both in the UK and abroad) to develop a conceptual framework for financial accounting. The lead in the UK is now being taken by the Accounting Standards Board, which has published a draft of a document known as the *Statement of Principles*. The main aims of the Statement are to:

(a) identify the users of financial statements and their information needs

(b) specify the qualitative characteristics which financial information should possess

(c) specify the elements of financial statements (i.e. the items which a set of financial statements should contain)

(d) provide guidance as to when items should be recognised in the financial statements

(e) provide guidance as to how items should be measured and how they should be presented in the financial statements.

In summary, the Statement tries to explain *why* we are producing financial statements, *what* should be shown in those statements, *when* we should show an item in the statements and *how* each item should be measured and presented.

When finalised, the Statement of Principles will undoubtedly have some impact on financial accounting in the UK (if only because the ASB itself will presumably be guided by its own principles when it devises future accounting standards) but the full extent of that impact remains to be seen. The Statement of Principles is considered further in Chapter 15 of this book.

5. SUMMARY

- Guidance to accountants is provided in the form of accounting standards and accounting conventions.
- Accounting standards are devised by the Accounting Standards Board. Each standard provides guidance on how accountants should deal with a specific accounting problem.
- Accounting conventions are the product of centuries of accounting practice. They summarise the conventional approach to financial accounting work.
- The main accounting conventions are business entity, money measurement, duality, historic cost, stable monetary unit, going concern, accounting year, realisation, matching, substance over form, materiality, consistency, objectivity and prudence.
- Attempts have been made in recent years to develop a set of basic theoretical principles of accounting, often referred to as a conceptual framework. The ASB Statement of Principles is one such attempt.

EXERCISES 2

2.1 (a) Explain the role of accounting standards. Where do they come from?

(b) Explain the role of accounting conventions. Where do they come from?

2.2 Make a list of the principal accounting conventions. Briefly explain the effect that each convention has on the preparation of financial statements.

2.3 Consider each of the situations listed below. Identify the accounting convention(s) which would be used to determine the appropriate accounting treatment of each situation.

(a) A business is preparing accounts for the year ended 30 September. The most recent telephone bill paid by the business is dated 31 August. An insurance premium was paid in 1 January, covering the business until 31 December.

(b) A business has an excellent local reputation and enjoys the goodwill of many regular customers.

(c) A business bought a piece of land ten years ago for £10,000. Its market value has now increased to £20,000.

(d) A customer who owes the business £1,000 at the end of an accounting year appears to be in financial trouble and is in danger of going bankrupt. However, no-one knows for certain whether or not this will happen.

(e) A box of paper clips is bought towards the end of an accounting year. Some of the clips remain unused at the end of the year.

(f) The owner of a business pays for a holiday out of her personal bank account.

(g) The owner of a business pays for a holiday out of his business bank account.

(h) Goods are sold to a customer in one accounting period but are not paid for until the next accounting period.

(i) Goods are sold to a customer who never pays for them.

(j) A business repays a loan which has been outstanding for some time.

***2.4** Over the last thirty years a business has acquired a number of buildings. The latest balance sheet for the business (drawn up in accordance with the usual accounting conventions) shows one of the assets of the business as "Buildings £700,000".

(a) Explain what the figure of £700,000 represents.

(b) Discuss the extent to which this figure is relevant and reliable.

***2.5** The financial statements of a business show a profit of £10,000 for the year. The owner of the business is perplexed by this, since his business bank balance has increased by only £2,000 during the year. Explain how this difference might have arisen, referring to relevant accounting conventions.

3

THE BALANCE SHEET

Chapter objectives

When you have finished this chapter, you should be able to:

- **Explain the purpose of a balance sheet.**
- **Define the terms "asset", "liability" and "capital".**
- **State the balance sheet equation.**
- **Illustrate the effect of various financial transactions on the balance sheet of a business.**
- **Distinguish between fixed assets and current assets.**
- **Distinguish between long-term liabilities and current liabilities.**
- **Draw up a balance sheet in an accepted format.**

1. INTRODUCTION

We saw in Chapter 1 that the main aim of financial accounting is to provide information about the financial performance and financial position of a business. The statement which provides information about financial position is the *balance sheet*, which lists the assets and liabilities of the business on a specified date.

The purpose of this chapter is to show how balance sheets are drawn up and to explain how a balance sheet is affected by the financial transactions of the business concerned. The first step is to provide formal definitions of the terms "asset" and "liability" and to introduce the concept of the owner's "capital".

2. ASSETS, LIABILITIES AND CAPITAL

Assets

The ASB Statement of Principles (see Chapter 2) gives a formal definition of the term "asset". Assets are defined as "*rights or other access to future economic benefits controlled by an entity as a result of past transactions or events*". This definition is rather technical but it does make a number of important points:

(a) An item cannot be shown as an asset on a balance sheet unless it will be of some future value to the business. For example, a business might own an utterly obsolete piece of machinery which cannot be used in the future and which has no resale or scrap value. Even though this is something which the business owns, it cannot give rise to future economic benefits and so it will not appear as an asset on the balance sheet.

(b) The business must control the item for it to be regarded as an asset. Control is usually achieved through ownership and we will assume from now on that an item cannot be an asset unless the business owns it. However, certain types of leased item are included within the definition.

(c) An item can be an asset only if it has arisen as the result of some past transaction or event. In most cases, this past transaction/event comprises the purchase of the item.

Liabilities

The ASB Statement of Principles also defines the term "liability". Liabilities are defined as "*an entity's obligations to transfer economic benefits as a result of past transactions or events*". The main points to absorb from this definition are:

(a) Liabilities consist of the financial obligations of a business.

(b) A financial obligation will be shown in the balance sheet as a liability only if the transaction or event which gives rise to that obligation has already occurred by the balance sheet date. An obligation which might or might not arise, depending upon the outcome of some future event (a *contingent liability*) does not fall within this definition. Contingent liabilities are discussed in Chapter 15 of this book.

One further point to note is that the term liabilities refers to financial obligations to *external* parties only (e.g. amounts owed by a business to a bank or a supplier). The financial obligation of a business to its owner or owners is *not* included within the definition (see below).

Capital

One consequence of the business entity convention (see Chapter 2) is that a business can have a financial obligation to its owner or vice versa. In fact, a business will nearly always owe money to its owner. This debt arises as follows:

(a) The owner of a business usually puts some of his or her own money into the business to start it up and may put in more later to help the business to expand.

(b) This money has, in effect, been lent to the business and will eventually have to be repaid to the owner (if only when the business closes down).

(c) In the meantime, this "loan" is a financial obligation of the business.

The financial obligation of a business to its owner is usually referred to as the owner's capital or the owner's equity. The term "capital" is used more often in practice and is preferred in this book.

It is worth noting at this point that the external liabilities of a business and the owner's capital both represent financial *claims* against the business. For this reason, the word "claims" is sometimes used as a collective term for all of the financial obligations of a business.

3. THE BALANCE SHEET EQUATION

The only way in which a business can acquire assets is to use finance provided by the owner or finance obtained from external sources (e.g. money borrowed from banks, credit obtained from suppliers). It follows, therefore, that the sum of the assets shown in a balance sheet must at all times be equal to the sum of the claims against those assets. This is the *balance sheet equation* (sometimes known as the *accounting equation*). The equation is usually expressed as follows:

Assets = Liabilities + Capital

The ASB's definition of capital (or equity) makes this clear, stating that equity is "*the ownership interest in the entity; it is the residual amount found by deducting all of the entity's liabilities from all of the entity's assets*".

The fact that the balance sheet equation must hold good at all times means that a business transaction which changes the value of one item in a balance sheet must also change the value of another item. Otherwise, assets would no longer be equal to liabilities plus capital, and the balance sheet would not balance. It is this argument which gives rise to the duality convention (see Chapter 2).

EXAMPLE

Barbara starts her own business on 1 July 19X7. Her first five business transactions are as follows:

1 July Barbara opens a bank account for the business and pays £7,500 of her own money into this account.

2 July A further £2,500 is paid into the business bank account. This money has been borrowed from Colin, Barbara's brother.

3 July The business buys a motor van for £8,500, paying by cheque.

5 July The business buys a stock of goods for resale costing £3,000. These goods are bought on credit from J Brown Ltd on the understanding that they will be paid for within four weeks.

7 July A business cheque for £1,000 is sent to J Brown Ltd in part payment of the amount owing to the company.

Describe the effect of these transactions on the assets, liabilities and capital of the business and show the balance sheet as it will appear after all five transactions have been completed.

SOLUTION

The effect of each transaction is as follows:

1 July Bank balance increases by £7,500. Capital increases by £7,500.

2 July Bank balance increases by £2,500. Liabilities increase by £2,500.

3 July Motor vans increase by £8,500. Bank balance decreases by £8,500.

5 July Stock of goods increases by £3,000. Liabilities increase by £3,000.

7 July. Bank balance decreases by £1,000. Liabilities decrease by £1,000.

The balance sheet after all five transactions have been completed will appear as follows:

Barbara
Balance sheet as at 7 July 19X7

	£	£
Assets		
Motor van	8,500	
Stock of goods for resale	3,000	
Bank balance	500	12,000
		12,000
Capital		7,500
Liabilities		
Colin	2,500	
J Brown Ltd	2,000	4,500
		12,000

Notes:

1. The bank balance is £7,500 + £2,500 – £8,500 – £1,000 = £500.
2. The liability to J Brown Ltd is £3,000 – £1,000 = £2,000.
3. As expected, the balance sheet balances. Total assets are £12,000 and the total of capital and liabilities is also £12,000.
4. The balance sheet has been laid out with assets listed first and with capital and liabilities listed beneath. This is only one way of laying out a balance sheet. Other ways are considered later in this chapter.

4. FREQUENCY OF PRODUCING BALANCE SHEETS

In theory, balance sheets could be drawn up on a daily basis, showing the assets, capital and liabilities of a business at the close of each working day. In practice, however, balance sheets are prepared far less frequently. The reasons for this are fairly obvious:

(a) The amount of effort involved in preparing a balance sheet makes it impracticable to prepare one every day.
(b) The users of the information contained in a balance sheet do not require this information daily.

As we saw in Chapter 2, it is conventional to produce annual financial statements and therefore most businesses prepare only one balance sheet per year, showing the financial position of the business at the end of its accounting year.

We should remember that the balance sheet is intended for the eyes of owners, investors and other external users, whose needs are normally satisfied by an annual set of financial statements. By contrast, the managers of a business need to keep track of the financial position at all times and will require a continual flow of information on the subject. The content, format and frequency of the information required by management is the domain of management accounting, however, and is beyond the scope of this book.

5. TRANSACTIONS WHICH YIELD A PROFIT OR A LOSS

It is a basic rule of financial accounting that the balance sheet equation will always hold good, no matter what financial transactions a business performs. But some types of transaction seem to disobey this rule. As an example, consider the following series of transactions:

(a) A business begins with £5,000 in the bank, supplied by its owner.
(b) The business buys a stock of goods for £3,000, paying by cheque.
(c) The goods are all sold for £4,000 and this money is paid into the bank.

After the first two transactions, the business has total assets of £5,000 (stock £3,000, bank balance £2,000), no liabilities and capital of £5,000. The balance sheet equation is satisfied. But the problem arises with the third transaction. The bank balance of £2,000 is increased by a further £4,000 to £6,000 and this is now the only asset that the business owns. There are still no liabilities and capital appears to be unchanged at £5,000. We now seem to have assets £6,000, liabilities £nil and capital £5,000. The balance sheet does not balance.

This problem is caused by the fact that the business has bought goods for £3,000 and sold them for £4,000, so making a *profit* of £1,000. It is this £1,000 profit which is causing the balance sheet not to balance.

Profits and losses

The solution to the problem described above is straightforward. Any profit made by a business belongs to the owner of that business. Therefore the profit serves to increase the amount of money which the business owes to its owner and should be *added* to the owner's capital. In the example given above, the balance sheet after the third transaction should show assets £6,000 and capital £6,000 (the original £5,000 plus £1,000 profit). The balance sheet equation is now satisfied.

Similarly, any loss which a business sustains must be borne by the owner. A loss serves to decrease the amount of money which the business owes to its owner and should therefore be *deducted* from the owner's capital.

Revenue and expenses

Profit is the difference between *revenue* and *expenses*. In the example given above, the business had to sacrifice stock which had cost £3,000 (an expense) in order to generate revenue of £4,000 and so make a £1,000 profit.

For many businesses, the income derived from selling goods or services is the main or only source of revenue. But the cost of buying goods for resale is by no means the only expense. Other expenses might include wages paid to staff, the rent of business premises, the cost of running motor vehicles and so forth. Revenue and expenses are discussed in more detail in Chapter 4 of this book.

6. TRANSACTIONS WHICH AFFECT CAPITAL

In summary, the transactions which affect an owner's capital are as follows:

(a) Capital is *increased* by:

- any amounts of money paid into the business by the owner (often referred to as *capital injections* or *capital introduced*)
- any profits earned by the business.

(b) Capital is *reduced* by:

- any amounts of money drawn out of the business by the owner (often referred to as the owner's *drawings*)
- any losses sustained by the business.

It is important to note that *all* money drawn out of a business by the owner for his or her personal use should be regarded as drawings, no matter how the transaction is described in the accounting records of the business. Confusion sometimes arises over payments to the owner described as "owner's wages", "owner's salary" and so forth but these are still drawings, despite their description. There is a clear distinction between payments to employees and payments to owners:

(a) Employees earn wages and salaries in return for their work. Employees' wages and salaries are a business expense and are taken into account when calculating the profit of a business.

(b) Owners invest their money in a business and (possibly) work on behalf of the business. In return they are entitled to the profits, which are added to their capital. Owners cannot employ themselves and so cannot receive a wage or salary from their own business. All amounts paid to an owner (however described) are drawings and should be deducted from the owner's capital.

Capital introduced and drawings - further aspects

In most cases, capital introduced takes the form of money paid into the business by its owner. However, it is possible for the owner to introduce capital in other ways. For example:

(a) The owner might transfer an asset other than money to the business (e.g. a motor vehicle or an item of equipment).

(b) The owner might pay a business liability out of a personal bank account.

Similarly, drawings normally consist of money paid by a business to its owner, but it is possible for drawings to occur in other ways. For example:

(a) The business might transfer an asset other than money to the owner.

(b) The business bank account might be used to pay one of the owner's personal expenses.

Accounting for transactions like these is straightforward. All we have to do is to consider the effect of each transaction on assets, liabilities and capital and then adjust the balance sheet accordingly.

EXAMPLE

Describe the effect of the following transactions on the assets, liabilities and capital of the business concerned:

(a) When starting up in business, David transferred his own car (valued at £9,000) to the business, together with some tools (valued at £2,500).

(b) Elaine owns her own business. On one occasion last year the business owed £800 to a supplier and, because the business bank account was nearly empty, she paid the supplier out of her own private bank account.

(c) Frank, who owns his own business, took goods out of the business for his own personal use. The goods had cost the business £150.

(d) Gillian owns her own business. She paid for her annual holiday with a £1,200 cheque drawn on the business bank account.

SOLUTION

The effect of each transaction is as follows:

(a) Motor vehicles increase by £9,000 and tools increase by £2,500. The business now owes David £11,500 more than before, so capital increases by £11,500.

(b) Liabilities decrease by £800. The business is now indebted to Elaine for this amount, so capital increases by £800.

(c) Stock of goods decreases by £150. The business now owes Frank £150 less than before, so capital decreases by £150.

(d) The bank balance decreases by £1,200. The business now owes Gillian £1,200 less than before, so capital decreases by £1,200.

Presentation of capital in the balance sheet

A balance sheet may be useful to many user groups (see Chapter 1) but the principal user of the balance sheet is undoubtedly the owner of the business. The owner will probably be interested to know not only the amount of his or her capital on the balance sheet date, but also how that figure was arrived at. It is normal, therefore, to present this information on the face of the balance sheet.

EXAMPLE

The balance sheet of a business on 31 May 19X7 shows capital of £12,300. During the year to 31 May 19X8, the owner introduces further capital of £5,000 and draws £7,100 out of the business. The profit of the business for the year to 31 May 19X8 is £8,900.

(a) Calculate the owner's capital at 31 May 19X8.

(b) Show how this figure will be presented in the balance sheet for 31 May 19X8.

SOLUTION

(a) The owner's capital at 31 May 19X8 is £12,300 + £5,000 – £7,100 + £8,900 = £19,100.

(b) In the balance sheet drawn up for 31 May 19X8, this figure will probably be presented as follows:

	£	£
Capital:		
As at 31 May 19X7	12,300	
Capital introduced	5,000	
Profit for the year	8,900	
	26,200	
Less: Drawings	7,100	19,100

7. CLASSIFICATION OF ASSETS AND LIABILITIES

In principle, a balance sheet could list the assets of a business in any order. So long as assets are kept separate from liabilities, it would seem to make no difference which asset is shown first, which is shown second and so forth. A similar argument applies to liabilities. However, the users of the balance sheet will find it easier to assess the financial position of the business if the assets and liabilities are classified into groups and listed in a logical order.

Classification of assets

Assets are usually classified into two main groups. These are *fixed assets* and *current assets*:

(a) Fixed assets are those which are acquired with the intention that they should be retained within the business. They are used to help the business to generate profits, often over a period of several years. They are *not* acquired with the intention of immediate resale to a customer. Typical examples of fixed assets are a factory building, a delivery van and an office computer system. Note that:

- Although fixed assets are not acquired with immediate resale in mind, most fixed assets will eventually be sold at some time in the future i.e. when the business has no further use for them.
- Fixed assets are not usually shown individually on the balance sheet but are gathered together into categories. For example, all the factory machines owned by a manufacturing business might be aggregated into one figure on the balance sheet under the heading "Plant and machinery".
- Fixed assets are often subdivided into *tangible* fixed assets and *intangible* fixed assets. Tangible fixed assets are those which have a physical existence e.g. a building, a vehicle or a piece of equipment. Intangible fixed assets are those without a physical existence e.g. a patent or a copyright.
- Tangible fixed assets are usually listed in descending order of longevity. A typical order might be land and buildings, plant and machinery, motor vehicles.

(b) Current assets consist of cash in hand, cash held in a bank account and other assets which the business has acquired with the intention that they should be converted into cash within 12 months. Examples of current assets apart from cash and bank balances are stocks of goods for resale and amounts owed to the business by its customers. Note that:

- Customers who have bought goods or services from a business and have not yet paid for them are known as *debtors*. The amounts owed to the business are often shown on the balance sheet under the heading "Debtors" or "Trade debtors".
- Current assets (like fixed assets) are not usually shown individually on the balance sheet but are aggregated into categories. For example, all of the amounts owed to a business by its customers will normally be aggregated into just one debtors figure on the balance sheet.
- Current assets are usually listed with the least liquid assets first. (The liquidity of an asset is a measure of the length of time it will probably take to convert that asset into cash). The usual order is stock, trade debtors, cash at bank, cash in hand.

Classification of liabilities

Liabilities are also classified into two main groups. These are *long-term liabilities* and *current liabilities*:

(a) Long-term liabilities are defined as financial obligations which the business is not required to meet until at least 12 months after the balance sheet date. An example would be a loan due for repayment in five years' time.

(b) Current liabilities are those financial obligations which must be met within 12 months of the balance sheet date. Examples of current liabilities are short-term loans, amounts owed to suppliers of goods or services and bank overdrafts. Note that:

- Suppliers of goods or services to whom the business owes money are known as *creditors*. The total amount owed by the business to all its suppliers is often shown on the balance sheet under the heading "Creditors" or "Trade creditors".
- Technically, most bank overdrafts are repayable on demand. This makes them current liabilities, even though many businesses have a more or less permanent bank overdraft.
- Current liabilities are usually listed in such a way that the most imminent liabilities are shown at the bottom of the list. A typical order might be short-term loans, trade creditors, bank overdrafts.

8. FORMAT OF THE BALANCE SHEET

The example balance sheet given earlier in this chapter began by listing the assets of the business. Capital and liabilities were then shown beneath the list of assets. This way of laying out a balance sheet is known as the *vertical* format and (with some modifications) is used almost exclusively in practice. It is also used in this book.

It is worth noting, however, that there are alternative ways of laying out a balance sheet. For example, the horizontal format shows assets on one side of the page with capital and liabilities shown on the other side. This format was popular at one time but has now been replaced by the vertical format, which is generally thought to be more user-friendly.

EXAMPLE

A typical balance sheet, laid out in the variation on the vertical format which is normally used in practice, is shown on the facing page. Note the order in which items are shown and the places in which totals and sub-totals have been calculated.

A N Other
Balance sheet as at 31 December 19X8

	£	£
Fixed assets		
Land and buildings		80,000
Motor vehicles		21,200
		101,200
Current assets		
Stock of goods for resale	22,600	
Trade debtors	14,800	
Cash in hand	30	
	37,430	
Current liabilities		
Trade creditors	9,300	
Bank overdraft	7,700	
	17,000	
Net current assets		20,430
Total assets less current liabilities		121,630
Long-term liabilities		
Loan from J White		20,000
		101,630
Capital		
As at 31 December 19X7	98,300	
Profit for the year	37,400	
	135,700	
Less: Drawings	34,070	101,630
		101,630

Notes:

1. This variation on the vertical format shows the assets of the business first and then subtracts the liabilities. The total thus obtained is shown to be equal to the owner's capital. In effect, the balance sheet equation has been rewritten as:

   Assets – Liabilities = Capital

2. Assets are separated into fixed assets and current assets.
3. Liabilities are separated into current liabilities and long-term liabilities.
4. Current liabilities are subtracted from current assets to give a subtotal for net current assets. This subtotal is also known as *working capital.*
5. Fixed assets are added to net current assets to give a subtotal for total assets less current liabilities. Long-term liabilities are then subtracted.

COMPREHENSIVE EXAMPLE

Henry starts a business on 1 March 19X8. His business transactions for the first month of trading are as follows:

1 March Henry pays £35,000 of his own money into a business bank account. He also transfers his own motor car (valued at £18,750) to the business.

2 March Premises costing £120,000 are acquired for the business. £20,000 of this is paid by business cheque. The remaining £100,000 is borrowed and is due for repayment in 10 years' time.

5 March A stock of goods for resale is acquired at a cost of £24,600. These goods are bought on credit from R Black Ltd.

7 March Stock costing £8,700 is sold on credit to P Stevens for £11,300.

16 March Stock costing £9,700 is bought from a supplier and is paid for immediately by business cheque.

21 March A £200 cheque is drawn on the business bank account to purchase opera tickets for Henry and his wife.

23 March Stock costing £5,500 is sold on credit to K Jones for £7,850.

28 March Henry draws £1,000 out of the business bank account to cover personal living expenses. He also takes goods out of the business for his own use. These goods had cost the business £500.

31 March A cheque for £10,000 is sent to R Black Ltd in part payment of the amount owing to the company.

Describe the effect of these transactions on the assets, liabilities and capital of the business and show the balance sheet as at 31 March 19X8.

SOLUTION

1 March Bank balance increases by £35,000. Motor vehicles increase by £18,750. Capital increases by £53,750.

2 March Land and buildings increase by £120,000. Bank balance decreases by £20,000. Long-term loans increase by £100,000.

5 March Stock of goods for resale increases by £24,600. Trade creditors increase by £24,600.

7 March Stock of goods for resale decreases by £8,700. Trade debtors increase by £11,300. Capital increases by £2,600 (the profit on the transaction).

16 March Stock of goods for resale increases by £9,700. Bank balance decreases by £9,700.

21 March Bank balance decreases by £200. Capital decreases by £200.

23 March Stock of goods for resale decreases by £5,500. Trade debtors increase by £7,850. Capital increases by the profit of £2,350.

28 March Bank balance decreases by £1,000. Stock of goods for resale decreases by £500. Capital decreases by £1,500.

31 March Bank balance and trade creditors both decrease by £10,000.

Henry
Balance sheet as at 31 March 19X8

	£	£
Fixed assets		
Land and buildings		120,000
Motor vehicles		18,750
		138,750
Current assets		
Stock of goods for resale	19,600	
Trade debtors	19,150	
	38,750	
Current liabilities		
Trade creditors	14,600	
Bank overdraft	5,900	
	20,500	
Net current assets		18,250
Total assets less current liabilities		157,000
Long-term liabilities		
Loan		100,000
		57,000
Capital		
Capital introduced	53,750	
Profit for the month	4,950	
	58,700	
Less: Drawings	1,700	57,000
		57,000

Notes:

1. Stock of goods for resale is £24,600 – £8,700 + £9,700 – £5,500 – £500 = £19,600.
2. Trade debtors are P Stevens £11,300 + K Jones £7,850 = £19,150.
3. Trade creditors consist of R Black Ltd £24,600, less paid £10,000 = £14,600.
4. The bank balance is £35,000 – £20,000 – £9,700 – £200 – £1,000 – £10,000, giving an overdraft of £5,900.
5. The profit for the month consists of £2,600 on 7 March and £2,350 on 23 March, making a total of £4,950.
6. Drawings are £200 on 21 March and £1,500 on 28 March, making a total of £1,700.

9. SUMMARY

- The purpose of a balance sheet is to show the financial position of a business on the balance sheet date. The balance sheet lists the assets, the liabilities and the capital of the business.
- Assets are items from which the business will derive future economic benefits. They must be controlled by the business and they must have arisen as the result of a past transaction.
- Liabilities are financial obligations to external parties. Capital is the financial obligation of a business to its owner.
- The balance sheet equation states that the sum of the assets shown in a balance sheet must at all times be equal to the sum of the claims against those assets.
- Profits belong to the owner of the business and are added to capital. Losses must be borne by the owner and are deducted from capital.
- Assets are usually classified into fixed assets and current assets. Fixed assets may be further classified into tangible and intangible assets.
- Liabilities are usually classified into long-term liabilities and current liabilities.
- A balance sheet may be drawn up in a variety of formats. The vertical format is used almost exclusively in practice.

EXERCISES 3

3.1 Ian owns his own computer retailing business. For each of the following items, state whether or not the item should be included in Ian's balance sheet at 31 December 19X9 and, if so, under which classification and at what amount:

(a) A computer which cost £1,500 in late 19X9. The computer was bought for resale but had not been sold by 31 December 19X9. It is expected to be sold for £2,000 in the near future.

(b) A computer which has been hired from a computer manufacturer and which is used for display and demonstration purposes. The hire charge is £100 per month.

(c) A computer which was bought for £1,000 several years ago but which was never sold and is now worthless.

(d) A computer which Ian took from the business as a gift for his son. The computer cost the business £800 to acquire.

(e) Ian's business premises which cost £50,000 eight years ago. The premises are now worth at least £80,000.

(f) A 15-year bank loan which was used to finance the acquisition of the business premises. The amount outstanding on 31 December 19X9 is £37,000.

(g) Ian's own home, which cost him £75,000 originally but which is now worth £120,000.

(h) A debt of £27,400 which the business owed to one of its major suppliers on 31 December 19X9.

(i) A debt of £1,800 which was owed to the business by one of its customers on 31 December 19X9.

(j) The business bank overdraft, which stood at £13,750 on 31 December 19X9. The business has had an overdraft of roughly this size for many years.

3.2 A business has the following assets and liabilities on 30 September 19X7:

	£
Trade debtors	12,670
Trade creditors	17,850
Bank overdraft	4,800
Cash in hand	35
Stock of goods for resale	21,950
Land and buildings	54,000
Office furniture and equipment	3,500

How much is the owner's capital on 30 September 19X7?

3.3 On 1 May 19X7, a business had assets totalling £23,560 and liabilities totalling £11,650. On 30 April 19X8, assets were £25,880 and liabilities were £9,890. During the year to 30 April 19X8, the owner of the business made no capital injections but took drawings of £15,600. What was the profit of the business for the year to 30 April 19X8?

3.4 Jill started a business on 1 January 19X8. Her first few business transactions were as follows:

1 January Jill opened a business bank account and paid £20,000 of her own money into this account.

2 January A motor van costing £7,200 was paid for by business cheque.

2 January Goods for resale were acquired from J Green at a cost of £6,200. Half of this was paid by business cheque and it was agreed that the other half would be paid in a month's time.

3 January Jill paid £2,500 out of her own money to buy equipment for the business.

4 January Stock costing £2,200 was sold on credit to L Richards for £2,960.

6 January Stock costing £2,800 was sold for £3,880. The sale proceeds were received immediately and paid into the business bank account.

Required:

Draw up Jill's balance sheet as it would appear after all of these transactions have occurred.

***3.5** Explain the relationship (if any) between profit and drawings.

***3.6** (a) Why must the assets of a business be equal at all times to the claims on those assets? Isn't this tantamount to saying that the business can never improve its financial position?

(b) What important information should be included in the heading of a balance sheet?

(c) Is the good reputation of an established business an asset? If so, can this asset be shown on the balance sheet?

***3.7** Kevin started a business on 3 April 19X7. His first transactions were as follows:

3 April	Kevin paid £40,000 into a business bank account. He also transferred to the business a motor van valued at £11,500 and equipment valued at £9,000.
4 April	A loan from Kevin's father of £25,000 was paid into the business bank account. Kevin has agreed to repay the money in two year's time.
5 April	Retail premises costing £45,000 were paid for by business cheque.
7 April	Further equipment was acquired costing £12,500. This was paid for by business cheque.
8 April	Goods for resale were acquired on credit from P Thomas at a cost of £17,500.
17 April	Stock costing £11,200 was sold for £18,600. Half of this money was received immediately and was paid (by mistake) into Kevin's personal bank account. The other half was a sale of goods on credit to B Parsons.
19 April	Goods for resale were bought at a cost of £12,000 and were paid for by business cheque.
29 April	Stock costing £11,600 was sold on credit to F Davis for £19,100.
30 April	A business cheque for £8,750 was sent to P Thomas.
30 April	Kevin was paid £1,000 out of the business bank account as his salary for April.

Required:

Draw up Kevin's balance sheet as at 30 April 19X7.

4

THE PROFIT AND LOSS ACCOUNT

Chapter objectives

When you have finished this chapter, you should be able to:

- **Explain the purpose of a profit and loss account.**
- **Understand the terms "revenue" and "expenses".**
- **Account correctly for opening and closing stocks of goods.**
- **Account correctly for accruals and prepayments.**
- **Distinguish between capital expenditure and revenue expenditure.**
- **Draw up a trading, profit and loss account in an accepted format.**

1. INTRODUCTION

The financial statement which provides information about the financial performance of a business is the *profit and loss account*, which summarises the revenue and expenses of the business for an accounting period. The difference between total revenue and total expenses is the profit (or loss) for the period, which is then added to (or subtracted from) the owner's capital.

The examples given in Chapter 3 managed to account for profits without preparing a profit and loss account. This is because those examples contained very few transactions which gave rise to revenue or expenses and so it was easy to calculate the profit figure. In practice, however, a profit and loss account is essential for the following reasons:

(a) In a typical accounting period for a typical business, there may be thousands or even millions of transactions which give rise to revenue or expenses. In these circumstances, we need a systematic way of working out the profit or loss for the period. This is provided by the preparation of a profit and loss account.

(b) The balance sheet shows the total profit for the period as an addition to the owner's capital but users need more than this. They need to know *how* that profit was made. They need an analysis of revenue and expenses so that they can assess the financial performance of the business, make comparisons with other businesses (or with the same business in previous periods) and perhaps spot areas in which the financial performance of the business might be improved. The profit and loss account provides this analysis.

Frequency of producing profit and loss accounts

As we saw in Chapter 2, it is conventional to produce financial statements annually and so most businesses produce only one profit and loss account per year. This profit and loss account is, of course, intended for owners, investors and other external users. It is not intended for the managers of the business, who will make their own arrangements to ensure that they receive financial performance information much more frequently.

It is important to appreciate that a profit and loss account relates to a *period* of time and provides information on the financial performance of the business during that period. A balance sheet, on the other hand, relates to a single *moment* in time, providing a "snapshot" of the financial position of the business at the end of its accounting period.

2. REVENUE AND EXPENSES

Revenue

The most important (and possibly the only) source of revenue for most businesses is the income derived from the sale of goods or the sale of services. The realisation convention (see Chapter 2) states that this income should be shown or "recognised" as revenue in the profit and loss account only when:

(a) the goods concerned have been passed to the customer (or the services concerned have been rendered), and

(b) the obligation to pay for the goods or services has been accepted by the customer.

In the case of a sale of services, it may sometimes be difficult to determine exactly when a service has been performed and, therefore, to decide when the income derived from that service can be regarded as revenue. For example, if a business hires out some equipment to a customer on an annual contract, the service provided by the business is not performed on a single date but is spread over a 12-month period. In these circumstances, it is normal to recognise revenue on a time apportionment basis. If the annual accounting date of the business falls (say) three months after the start of the contract, 3/12ths of the income from the contract will be recognised as revenue in the current accounting year. The other 9/12ths will be recognised in the following year.

Apart from revenue relating to the sale of goods or services, other types of revenue which might appear in a profit and loss account include rents receivable, bank interest receivable, profits on the sale of fixed assets (see Chapter 6), bad debts recovered (see Chapter 7) and discounts received (see later in this chapter).

Expenses

If a business sells goods, one of its main expenses will be the cost of the goods that it sells. A retailer or wholesaler buys goods for resale from suppliers. A manufacturer buys raw materials from suppliers and incurs various production costs so as to turn these raw materials into finished goods. Other expenses which a business might typically incur include:

(a) **Selling and distribution expenses** e.g. salaries paid to sales managers and sales assistants, advertising costs, the costs of running a fleet of delivery vans.

(b) **Administrative expenses** e.g. salaries paid to office managers and staff, rent and rates of office premises, heating and lighting costs, insurance costs, postage and telephone costs, printing and stationery costs.

(c) **Finance charges** e.g. bank charges and interest, loan interest, discounts allowed (see later in this chapter).

The matching convention requires that expenses should be matched against the revenue to which they relate. This means that we must take account of unsold stocks of goods, accruals, prepayments and the gradual "using up" of fixed assets. All of these matters are considered later in this chapter.

EXAMPLE

Linda's balance sheet as at 30 September 19X8 and her transactions during the year to 30 September 19X9 are shown below. Describe the effect of the transactions on the assets, liabilities and capital of the business. Then prepare Linda's profit and loss account for the year to 30 September 19X9 and her balance sheet as at that date.

Linda
Balance sheet as at 30 September 19X8

	£	£
Fixed assets		
Freehold shop premises		40,000
Motor van		8,500
		48,500
Current assets		
Stock of goods for resale	12,400	
Trade debtors	2,600	
Cash at bank	1,730	
	16,730	
Current liabilities		
Trade creditors	4,900	
Net current assets		11,830
		60,330
Capital		
As at 30 September 19X8		60,330

Transactions (in total) during the year to 30 September 19X9:

(a) Stock costing £42,800 was purchased on credit from suppliers.

(b) Stock costing a further £3,150 was bought and paid for immediately by cheque.

(c) Linda paid herself a monthly salary of £1,000 out of the business bank account.

(d) Stock costing £43,190 was sold for £81,340. Of this sum, £73,870 represented sales on credit. The remaining £7,470 was received immediately and was paid into the bank.

(e) Cheques totalling £39,670 were sent to suppliers. Cheques totalling £69,650 were received from credit customers and paid into the bank.

(f) Expenses paid for by business cheque were staff wages £13,600, business rates £870, electricity £2,340, motor expenses £1,750, insurance £500 and sundry expenses of £820.

SOLUTION

(a) Stock increases by £42,800. Trade creditors increase by £42,800.

(b) Stock increases by £3,150. Cash at bank decreases by £3,150.

(c) Cash at bank decreases by £12,000. Capital decreases by £12,000. (Linda's "salary" must be treated as drawings).

(d) Stock decreases by £43,190. Trade debtors increase by £73,870 and cash at bank increases by £7,470. The profit on these transactions of £38,150 will eventually be added to Linda's capital but, in the first instance, the sales (£81,340) and the cost of the goods sold (£43,190) are recorded as revenue and expenses in the profit and loss account. Any other revenues and expenses arising during the year are also recorded in the profit and loss account and then the overall profit or loss for the year is added to or subtracted from Linda's capital.

(e) Cash at bank decreases by £39,670 and trade creditors decrease by £39,670. Cash at bank increases by £69,650 and trade debtors decrease by £69,650.

(f) Cash at bank decreases by a total of £19,880. Expenses of £19,880 are recorded in the profit and loss account.

Linda
Profit and loss account for the year to 30 September 19X9

		£	£
Sales			81,340
Less:	Cost of goods sold		43,190
Gross profit			38,150
Less:	Staff wages	13,600	
	Business rates	870	
	Electricity	2,340	
	Motor expenses	1,750	
	Insurance	500	
	Sundry expenses	820	19,880
Net profit for the year			18,270

Notes:

1. The profit and loss account includes a subtotal for *gross profit*, which is the difference between the sales revenue and the cost of goods sold. The last line shows the final *net profit* achieved by the business, after deduction of all expenses. This is the profit which is added to the owner's capital.
2. The profit and loss account has been laid out in a vertical format. Other formats are considered later in this chapter.

Linda

Balance sheet as at 30 September 19X9

	£	£
Fixed assets		
Freehold shop premises		40,000
Motor van		8,500
		48,500
Current assets		
Stock of goods for resale	15,160	
Trade debtors	6,820	
Cash at bank	4,150	
	26,130	
Current liabilities		
Trade creditors	8,030	
Net current assets		18,100
		66,600
Capital		
As at 30 September 19X8	60,330	
Profit for the year	18,270	
	78,600	
Less: Drawings	12,000	66,600
		66,600

Notes:

1. Stock is £12,400 + £42,800 + £3,150 – £43,190 = £15,160.
2. Trade debtors are £2,600 + £73,870 – £69,650 = £6,820.
3. Cash at bank is £1,730 – £3,150 – £12,000 + £7,470 – £39,670 + £69,650 – £19,880 = £4,150.
4. Trade creditors are £4,900 + £42,800 – £39,670 = £8,030.

3. FORMAT OF THE PROFIT AND LOSS ACCOUNT

The example profit and loss account given above began by showing the revenue derived from selling goods. The cost of those goods was then deducted, leaving the *gross profit*. Other expenses (sometimes known as *overheads*) were then listed, totalled and subtracted from the gross profit to give the *net profit*. This way of laying out a profit and loss account is known as the *vertical* format. It is used almost exclusively in practice and is also used in this book. Note the following points:

(a) The top part of the profit and loss account (which shows sales revenue, cost of goods sold and gross profit) is often referred to as the trading account. In this case the term "trading and profit and loss account" is used to refer to the entire financial statement.

(b) If a business provides a service rather than selling goods, it does not need a trading account. The profit and loss account of such a business will begin with the revenue derived from selling services. Expenses will then be listed, totalled and subtracted from sales revenue to give net profit. The term "gross profit" has no relevance to a non-trading business.

(c) If a business has other revenue apart from that which is derived from selling goods or services, it is conventional to list this revenue just after gross profit (for a trading business) or just after sales revenue (for a non-trading business). A subtotal is then calculated before overhead expenses are deducted to give the net profit.

An alternative way of laying out the profit and loss account is the *horizontal* format. In this format, expenses are listed on the left-hand side of the page and revenue is listed on the right. The difference between the two sides is then computed to give the profit or loss for the accounting period. This format was popular at one time and it arises naturally if a double entry book-keeping system is in use (see Chapter 5). However, it has now been replaced almost entirely by the vertical format.

4. OPENING AND CLOSING STOCKS

As we have seen, the matching convention requires that the revenue earned from the sale of goods should be matched against the expense of acquiring those goods. This expense, which is shown in the trading account, is usually referred to as the *cost of goods sold* but may be abbreviated to *cost of sales*. The cost of any stock remaining unsold at the end of an accounting period (the *closing stock*) is shown as a current asset in the balance sheet.

It should be obvious that the cost of the goods sold during an accounting period and the closing stock at the end of that period are related by the following formula:

Cost of closing stock = Cost of opening stock at the start of the period
+ Cost of goods purchased during the period
− Cost of goods sold during the period.

Using this formula, there are two ways of obtaining the required figures for cost of goods sold (shown in the trading account) and closing stock (shown on the balance sheet):

(a) Each time that goods are sold, the cost of acquiring those goods is determined and recorded on a list. At the end of each accounting period:

(i) The list is totalled to give the cost of all the goods sold during the period.

(ii) The cost of the closing stock is then deduced from the above formula.

This method is used mainly by large businesses which maintain detailed records of stock movements.

(b) When goods are sold, no attempt is made to determine or record the cost of those goods. At the end of each accounting period:

(i) The closing stock is physically counted and the cost of this closing stock is determined.

(ii) The cost of the goods sold during the period is then deduced from the above formula.

This method is used by the majority of businesses (especially smaller ones) and is assumed to apply throughout the remainder of this book unless stated otherwise.

EXAMPLE

(a) Business A had opening stock on 1 April 19X8 which cost £12,870. During the year to 31 March 19X9, the business bought goods costing £86,700 and sold goods for £129,650 which had cost £84,980. Calculate the cost of the closing stock at 31 March 19X9 and calculate the gross profit for the year ending on that date.

(b) Business B had opening stock on 1 April 19X8 which cost £5,840. During the year to 31 March 19X9, the business bought goods costing £42,090 and sold goods for £63,430. The cost of the closing stock on 31 March 19X9 was £6,130. Calculate the cost of the goods sold during the year to 31 March 19X9 and calculate the gross profit for that year.

SOLUTION

(a) Cost of closing stock = £12,870 + £86,700 – £84,980 = £14,590.
Gross profit = £129,650 – £84,980 = £44,670.

(b) Cost of goods sold = £5,840 + £42,090 – £6,130 = £41,800.
Gross profit = £63,430 – £41,800 = £21,630.

5. FORMAT OF THE TRADING ACCOUNT

For a business which buys and sells goods, the purpose of a trading account is to calculate the gross profit for the accounting period i.e. the difference between sales revenue and the cost of goods sold. It is conventional to provide a breakdown of the figure for cost of goods sold, showing the opening stock, cost of goods purchased and closing stock.

EXAMPLE

Prepare trading accounts for Business A and for Business B for the year to 31 March 19X9 (see above example).

SOLUTION

	Business A		Business B	
	£	£	£	£
Sales		129,650		63,430
Cost of goods sold:				
Stock as at 1 April 19X8	12,870		5,840	
Purchases	86,700		42,090	
	99,570		47,930	
Less: Stock as at 31 March 19X9	14,590	84,980	6,130	41,800
Gross profit		44,670		21,630

Note:

The term "purchases" is often used as an abbreviation for "purchases of goods for resale".

Carriage, returns and own consumption

The trading account format shown above may need amending so as to take account of the following matters:

(a) **Carriage inwards.** If a business pays to have goods delivered to its premises from its suppliers' premises, this expense is known as *carriage inwards* or *carriage in*. Carriage inwards is regarded as part of the cost of acquiring goods and is shown in the trading account. This should be contrasted with carriage *outwards* i.e. the expense of delivering goods to customers. This is a selling and distribution expense and is shown in the profit and loss account.

(b) **Returns inwards and outwards.** A *return inwards* (also known as a *sales return*) occurs when a customer who has bought goods from a business returns them, possibly because the goods are unsatisfactory in some way. Similarly, a *return outwards* (or *purchase return*) occurs if the business returns goods to a supplier. Returns inwards are deducted from the sales figure in the trading account and returns outwards are deducted from the purchases figure.

(c) **Own consumption.** If the owner of a business takes goods out of the business for his or her own personal use, this is known as *own consumption*. The goods in question have been bought from suppliers and are included in the purchases figure, but they have not been sold to customers. Therefore the cost of these goods must be shown as a deduction when calculating the cost of goods sold.

EXAMPLE

The cost of Martin's opening stock on 1 July 19X7 was £6,720. During the year to 30 June 19X8 he bought goods costing £34,150, paying carriage inwards of £730. He also achieved sales amounting to £57,350, paying carriage outwards of £1,290. Martin returned goods costing £690 to his suppliers and took goods costing £800 from the business for his own use. Customers returned goods which had been sold to them for £200. The cost of Martin's closing stock on 30 June 19X8 was £8,560.

Prepare Martin's trading account for the year to 30 June 19X8.

SOLUTION

Martin

Trading account for the year to 30 June 19X8

	£	£	£
Sales			57,350
Less: Returns inwards			200
			57,150
Cost of goods sold:			
Stock as at 1 July 19X7		6,720	
Purchases	34,150		
Carriage inwards	730		
	34,880		
Less: Returns outwards	690	34,190	
		40,910	
Less: Own consumption		800	
		40,110	
Less: Stock as at 30 June 19X8		8,560	31,550
Gross profit			25,600

Note:

Carriage outwards is shown in the profit and loss account, not the trading account.

6. DISCOUNTS

A business might obtain discounts from its suppliers and/or grant discounts to its customers. There are two main types of discount, as explained below.

(a) **Trade discounts**. A business might be able to buy goods from a supplier at a reduced price because the business is in the same trade as the supplier or because the business trades with that supplier frequently. For similar reasons, a business might offer reduced prices to some of its customers. The difference between the full price of the goods and the reduced price is known as a *trade discount*.

If goods are bought or sold at a trade discount, it is conventional to record only the reduced prices in the accounting records of the business concerned. As a consequence, the figures shown in the trading account for sales and cost of goods sold are automatically net of any trade discounts granted or obtained. For this reason, trade discounts are *not* shown separately anywhere in the trading and profit and loss account.

(b) **Cash discounts**. A *cash discount* is a discount for prompt payment. Cash discounts which are granted to customers are known as *discounts allowed* and cash discounts which are obtained from suppliers are known as *discounts received.*

If goods are bought or sold with the possibility of a cash discount, the purchase or sale is always recorded at the pre-discount price. Any cash discounts received are then shown as revenue in the profit and loss account and any cash discounts allowed are shown as finance charges. Note that the trading account (and therefore the gross profit) is *not* affected by cash discounts at all.

EXAMPLE

Norma started her own business on 1 October 19X8. During the year to 30 September 19X9, she bought goods from just one supplier. These goods would normally have cost £28,000 but Norma was granted a 5% trade discount. The supplier also granted Norma a cash discount of 2.5% of the amount owing if she paid within 30 days. Norma always took advantage of this discount. On 30 September 19X9 she owed the supplier £1,200 for goods purchased during September.

Show how these transactions will be reflected in Norma's trading and profit and loss account for the year to 30 September 19X9 and in her balance sheet on that date.

SOLUTION

The purchases figure in Norma's trading account will be £26,600 (i.e. £28,000, less 5%). Of this £26,600, £1,200 is still outstanding on 30 September 19X9 and will appear as a current liability in her balance sheet. The remaining £25,400 has been cleared by payments totalling £24,765 (i.e. £25,400, less 2.5%). The discount received of £635 will appear as revenue in Norma's profit and loss account.

7. ACCRUALS AND PREPAYMENTS

The matching convention requires that the expenses shown in the profit and loss account of a business for an accounting period must include all of the expenses which relate to that period. Any expenses which do not relate to the period must not be included. These requirements have the following consequences:

(a) If an expense is incurred during an accounting period but is not charged to the business until the period is over, the amount of the accrued expense (or *accrual*) must be included in the profit and loss account. It may be necessary to estimate the accrued amount. The accrual will also be shown in the balance sheet as a current liability.

(b) If an expense is paid during an accounting period but relates to a future period, the amount of the prepaid expense (or *prepayment*) must be excluded from the profit and loss account. The prepayment will be shown in the balance sheet as a current asset and will eventually appear in the profit and loss account of the future period to which it relates.

EXAMPLE

(a) Oliver began trading on 1 January 19X7. During the year to 31 December 19X7, he made the following payments for electricity and business rates out of his business bank account:

Electricity		*Business rates*	
Period covered	*Amount*	*Period covered*	*Amount*
	£		£
1.1.X7 to 28.2.X7	360	1.1.X7 to 31.3.X7	280
1.3.X7 to 31.5.X7	418	1.4.X7 to 31.3.X8	1,200
1.6.X7 to 31.8.X7	389		
1.9.X7 to 30.11.X7	430		
Totals	1,597		1,480

An estimated £175 worth of electricity was consumed during December 19X7.

Describe how these transactions will affect the profit and loss account for the year to 31 December 19X7 and the balance sheet on that date.

(b) During the following year, electricity bills totalling £1,680 were paid. Oliver also paid business rates of £1,440 covering the year to 31 March 19X9. The electricity accrual was estimated at £190 on 31 December 19X8.

Describe how these transactions will affect the profit and loss account for the year to 31 December 19X8 and the balance sheet on that date.

SOLUTION

(a) **Electricity**. The profit and loss account for the year to 31 December 19X7 will show an expense of £1,772 (£1,597 paid + £175 accrued). The balance sheet on 31 December 19X7 will show the accrual of £175 as one of the current liabilities.

Rates. The £1,200 payment includes £300 (£1,200 x 3/12) relating to the following year. Therefore the profit and loss account for the year to 31 December 19X7 will show an expense of only £1,180 (£1,480 paid – £300 prepaid). The balance sheet on 31 December 19X7 will show the prepayment of £300 as one of the current assets (because the business owns the right to occupy its premises for the next three months without any further rates payments).

(b) **Electricity**. The amount paid during the year to 31 December 19X8 includes £175 relating to the previous year. Therefore the profit and loss account for the year to 31 December 19X8 will show an expense of £1,695 (£1,680 paid – £175 relating to last year + £190 accrued). The accrual of £190 will be shown as a current liability in the 31 December 19X8 balance sheet.

Rates. The amount paid last year included £300 relating to the current year. Also, this year's payment of £1,440 includes £360 (£1,440 x 3/12) relating to the following year. Therefore the profit and loss account for the year to 31 December 19X8 will show an expense of £1,380 (£300 paid last year + £1,440 paid this year – £360 prepaid). The prepayment of £360 will be shown as a current asset in the 31 December 19X8 balance sheet.

Accrued revenue and prepaid revenue

Accruals and prepayments might also arise in relation to certain types of revenue. For example, if a business rents premises to a tenant, the tenant might owe the business some rent at the end of an accounting period (accrued revenue) or might have paid rent in advance (prepaid revenue). The treatment of accrued revenue and prepaid revenue in the financial statements is fairly obvious:

(a) Any accrued revenue is included as revenue in the profit and loss account and is shown as a current asset on the balance sheet.

(b) Any prepaid revenue is excluded from the revenue shown in the profit and loss account and is shown as a current liability on the balance sheet.

EXAMPLE

Paula owns a shop and prepares accounts to 31 May each year. On 1 June 19X7, she began renting out a flat above the shop at a rental of £200 per month. The following amounts of rent were received from her tenant:

during the year to 31 May 19X8	£2,200
during the year to 31 May 19X9	£2,800

Calculate the amount which should be shown for rent receivable in Paula's profit and loss account for each of these years. Describe the effect of these transactions on the balance sheets as at 31 May 19X8 and 19X9.

SOLUTION

On 31 May 19X8, the tenant owes £200 to Paula. Therefore the rent receivable figure shown in the profit and loss account for the year to 31 May 19X8 will be £2,400 (£2,200 received + £200 accrued). The accrued revenue of £200 is a type of debtor and will be shown as a current asset in the 31 May 19X8 balance sheet.

The £2,800 received during the year to 31 May 19X9 must consist of £200 to clear the amount owing from the previous year, £2,400 for the current year and a £200 prepayment for the following year. The rent receivable figure shown in the profit and loss account for the year to 31 May 19X9 will be £2,400 (£2,800 received – £200 relating to last year – £200 relating to next year). The prepaid revenue of £200 will be shown as a current liability in the 31 May 19X9 balance sheet (because Paula owes the tenant one month's occupation of the flat).

8. CAPITAL EXPENDITURE AND REVENUE EXPENDITURE

When a business incurs expenditure, that expenditure can be one of two types:

(a) **Capital expenditure**. Expenditure on fixed assets is known as *capital expenditure*. As we saw in Chapter 3, a fixed asset is one which is acquired with the intention that it should be retained within the business and used to help the business to generate income over a number of years (e.g. a factory building).

(b) **Revenue expenditure**. Expenditure on current assets or on the day-to-day running costs of the business (e.g. buying goods for resale, paying wages, telephone bills etc.) is known as *revenue expenditure*.

Both of these terms might be confused with other, similar terms. To avoid confusion, it is perhaps worth pointing out that capital expenditure and an owner's capital are two totally different concepts. Revenue expenditure and revenue are also completely distinct.

Accounting treatment of each type of expenditure

The need to distinguish between capital expenditure and revenue expenditure arises because of the very different way in which each type of expenditure is treated in the financial statements of a business. Capital expenditure results in a new fixed asset appearing on the balance sheet, whilst revenue expenditure is shown as an expense in the profit and loss account of the accounting period to which it relates. These different treatments make it extremely important that all expenditure is classified correctly.

Depreciation

Capital expenditure is not shown in the profit and loss account and therefore the purchase of a fixed asset would appear to have no effect on the profit of the business concerned. But most fixed assets have finite useful lives and are gradually "used up" over the years until they can offer no further economic benefits. This fact has the following consequences:

(a) The cost of acquiring a fixed asset should be regarded as an expense of running the business over the years of its use.

(b) This expense, like any other, should be matched against the revenue which it helps to generate. Therefore part of the cost of the asset should be shown as an expense in the profit and loss account for each accounting period in which the asset is used. This expense is known as *depreciation*.

(c) The asset should be shown in the balance sheet at its historic cost, less the depreciation which has occurred so far. In effect, the balance sheet shows the cost of the remaining economic benefits which the asset still has to offer. (A much more detailed explanation of depreciation and its accounting treatment is given in Chapter 6 of this book).

The distinction between capital expenditure and revenue expenditure is, in the end, a matter of timing. Virtually all expenditure is eventually shown as an expense in the profit and loss account. For revenue expenditure the transfer to the profit and loss account is usually immediate. For capital expenditure, this transfer may be prolonged over many years.

EXAMPLE

A fixed asset is acquired on 1 January 19X6 by a business which prepares accounts to 31 December each year. The asset costs £5,600 and is expected to have a useful life of four years. Describe how the asset should be treated in the financial statements of the business, assuming that an equal amount of depreciation is deemed to occur in each of the four years and that the asset will be entirely worthless at the end of that time.

SOLUTION

The treatment of the asset in the financial statements over the four years can be summarised as follows:

	Depreciation shown in profit and loss account	*Remaining cost shown on balance sheet*
	£	£
Year to 31 December 19X6	1,400	4,200
Year to 31 December 19X7	1,400	2,800
Year to 31 December 19X8	1,400	1,400
Year to 31 December 19X9	1,400	nil

COMPREHENSIVE EXAMPLE

Richard's balance sheet as at 30 April 19X8 and his transactions (in total) during the year to 30 April 19X9 are shown below. Prepare Richard's trading and profit and loss account for the year to 30 April 19X9 and his balance sheet as at that date.

Richard
Balance sheet as at 30 April 19X8

	£	£
Fixed assets		
Land and buildings		61,500
Tools and equipment		8,500
		70,000
Current assets		
Stock of goods for resale	9,290	
Trade debtors	15,300	
Prepayment	200	
Cash at bank	2,220	
	27,010	
Current liabilities		
Trade creditors	7,880	
Accruals	720	
	8,600	
Net current assets		18,410
		88,410
Capital		
As at 30 April 19X8		88,410

Notes:

1. The prepayment relates to an insurance premium.
2. Accruals are Electricity £480, Telephone £240.

Transactions during the year to 30 April 19X9:

(a) Stock costing £128,390 was purchased on credit from suppliers who charged a further £1,560 for postage and packing.

(b) Stock was sold to credit customers for £183,490.

(c) Stock costing £4,670 proved to be unsatisfactory and was returned to suppliers.

(d) Customers returned stock which had been sold to them for £2,310.

(e) Cheques totalling £120,520 were sent to suppliers. These cheques were in satisfaction of debts totalling £122,980, less cash discounts of £2,460.

(f) Cheques totalling £173,830 were received from customers. These cheques were in satisfaction of debts totalling £179,200, less cash discounts of £5,370.

(g) Richard took £24,000 out of the business bank account as his own salary and paid total staff wages of £15,000.

(h) Further expenses paid for by cheque were electricity £1,600, telephone £950, insurance £880, delivering goods to customers £7,490, sundry expenses £830.

(i) Equipment costing £500 was paid for by cheque. Depreciation of £2,250 should be accounted for in the year.

(j) Richard took goods costing £1,320 out of the business for his own use.

On 30 April 19X9, accrued electricity charges were £530 and accrued telephone charges were £270. Insurance premiums paid during the year included £220 relating to the following year. Closing stock at 30 April 19X9 was £10,750.

SOLUTION

Richard
Trading and profit and loss account for the year to 30 April 19X9

	£	£	£
Sales			183,490
Less: Returns inwards			2,310
			181,180
Cost of goods sold:			
Stock as at 1 May 19X8		9,290	
Purchases	128,390		
Carriage inwards	1,560		
	129,950		
Less: Returns outwards	4,670	125,280	
		134,570	
Less: Own consumption		1,320	
		133,250	
Less: Stock as at 30 April 19X9		10,750	122,500
Gross profit			58,680
Discounts received			2,460
			61,140
Carriage outwards		7,490	
Staff wages		15,000	
Electricity		1,650	
Telephone		980	
Insurance		860	
Sundry expenses		830	
Discounts allowed		5,370	
Depreciation		2,250	34,430
Net profit for the year			26,710

Notes:

1. Electricity is £1,600 – £480 + £530 = £1,650.
2. Telephone is £950 – £240 + £270 = £980.
3. Insurance is £880 + £200 – £220 = ££860.

Richard
Balance sheet as at 30 April 19X9

	£	£
Fixed assets		
Land and buildings		61,500
Tools and equipment		6,750
		68,250
Current assets		
Stock of goods for resale	10,750	
Trade debtors	17,280	
Prepayment	220	
Cash at bank	4,280	
	32,530	
Current liabilities		
Trade creditors	10,180	
Accruals	800	
	10,980	
Net current assets		21,550
		89,800
Capital		
As at 30 April 19X8	88,410	
Net profit for the year	26,710	
	115,120	
<u>Less</u>: Drawings	25,320	89,800
		89,800

Notes:

1. Tools and equipment are £8,500 + £500 – £2,250 = £6,750.
2. Trade debtors are £15,300 + £183,490 – £2,310 – £179,200 = £17,280.
3. Cash at bank is £2,220 – £120,520 + £173,830 – £24,000 – £15,000 – £1,600 – £950 – £880 – £7,490 – £830 – £500 = £4,280.
4. Trade creditors are £7,880 + £128,390 + £1,560 – £4,670 – £122,980 = £10,180.

9. SUMMARY

► The purpose of a profit and loss account is to provide information about the financial performance of a business. The profit and loss account matches the revenue realised during an accounting period against the expenses incurred so as to earn that revenue.

- A profit and loss account may be drawn up in various formats, but the vertical format is used almost exclusively in practice. For a business which buys and sells goods, the top part of the profit and loss account is known as the trading account and reveals the gross profit for the period.
- A trading account includes adjustments relating to opening and closing stocks, carriage inwards, returns and own consumption. Carriage outwards is shown as an expense in the profit and loss account.
- Trade discounts are not shown separately anywhere in the trading and profit and loss account. Cash discounts received and cash discounts allowed are shown as revenue and expenses respectively in the profit and loss account.
- Accrued and prepaid expenses must be taken into account when preparing the financial statements of a business.
- Capital expenditure is expenditure on fixed assets. Revenue expenditure is expenditure on current assets and on the day-to-day running costs of the business.
- If a fixed asset has a finite useful life, an appropriate part of its cost should be shown as an expense in the profit and loss account for each accounting period in which the asset is used. This expense is known as depreciation.

EXERCISES 4

4.1 A business had opening stock on 1 July 19X8 which had cost £2,950. During the year to 30 June 19X9, the business bought goods costing £23,870 (of which goods costing £560 were returned to suppliers) and sold goods for £37,850 (of which goods sold for £1,830 were returned by customers). The cost of carriage inwards and outwards during the year was £370 and £590 respectively. The cost of the closing stock on 30 June 19X9 was £3,190.

Required:

Prepare the trading account for the year to 30 June 19X9.

4.2 Sylvia owns her own business, preparing accounts to 31 December each year. In the year to 31 December 19X9 she sold goods to one of her regular customers for £2,800. She would normally have sold these goods for £3,000. Another customer who owed her £1,078 paid very quickly and therefore she accepted £1,000 in full satisfaction of the debt.

Required:

Show how these transactions would be reflected in Sylvia's accounts for the year to 31 December 19X9.

4.3 A business which prepares accounts to 31 December each year paid insurance premiums as follows:

Date paid	*Amount*	*Period covered*
1 December 19X6	£840	year to 30 November 19X7
2 January 19X8	£960	year to 30 November 19X8
4 December 19X8	£1,020	year to 30 November 19X9

Required:

Calculate the amount which should be shown for insurance in the profit and loss account for the years to 31 December 19X7 and 19X8. Also calculate the amount of any accruals or prepayments which should be included in the balance sheets as at 31 December 19X6, 19X7 and 19X8.

4.4 Terry began trading on 1 June 19X7. His transactions during the year to 31 May 19X8 included the following:

(a) He borrowed £5,000 from his bank, on the understanding that no repayments would be made during his first year of trading. The bank charged 10% per annum interest on this loan.

(b) He paid rent of £1,400 covering the period 1 June 19X7 to 31 December 19X7, and a further £3,000 covering the year to 31 December 19X8.

(c) He paid wages of £1,300 per month. This included £500 per month for himself.

(d) He bought stock from a single supplier costing £23,670. At the end of the year he still owed £2,570 to this supplier. The supplier offered a 1% discount for prompt payment and Terry always took advantage of this discount.

(e) He sold stock to customers for £34,990. At the end of the year, all except £1,820 of this had been received from the customers.

(f) Stock which had cost Terry £2,560 remained unsold on 31 May 19X8.

(g) He paid electricity bills of £1,740 and telephone bills of £1,130. Accrued expenses at 31 May 19X8 were estimated to be electricity £120 and telephone £80.

(h) He paid £1,200 to advertise his business in "Yellow Pages" for the 12-month period from 1 July 19X7 to 30 June 19X8.

(i) On 31 May 19X8 (the very last day of his accounting year) he bought a motor van for £6,900.

Required:

Prepare Terry's trading and profit and loss account for the year to 31 May 19X8.

*4.5 Vivienne's assets and liabilities on 1 January 19X8 were as follows:

Land and buildings £50,000; Equipment £10,000; Long-term bank loan £20,000; Trade debtors £4,600; Trade creditors £6,320; Bank overdraft £7,590; Prepaid business rates £400; Prepaid insurance £300; Accrued electricity £670; Accrued telephone £130; Stock of goods for resale £10,800.

In summary, her transactions for the year to 31 December 19X8 were as follows (all payments and receipts were via the business bank account):

(a) Stock with a list price of £54,800 was bought on credit from suppliers who gave Vivienne a 2.5% trade discount. Some of Vivienne's suppliers also offered a discount for prompt payment. As a result, suppliers' invoices totalling £52,330 were satisfied by payments of £49,560.

(b) Stock was sold on credit for £95,370. This includes a £1,000 sale which was made to a valued customer at a special low price (the normal price of the goods sold to the customer would have been £1,250). Vivienne offered her customers a 4% discount on the amount owing in return for prompt payment. Invoices totalling £45,800 were paid by customers who took advantage of this discount and invoices totalling a further £47,600 were paid by customers who were too late to enjoy the discount offered.

(c) Vivienne took stock costing £400 out of the business for her own use.

(d) The following payments (totalling £45,570) were made during the year:

- cost of having stock delivered from suppliers £2,670
- cost of having stock delivered to customers £3,200
- staff wages £11,800
- business rates (for the year to 31 March 19X9) £1,800
- insurance (for the year to 30 June 19X9) £700
- electricity £3,240
- telephone £1,630
- bank overdraft interest £790
- interest on long-term bank loan £1,240
- Vivienne's salary £10,000
- new business equipment £8,500.

(e) On 1 July 19X8, Vivienne began subletting a part of her premises at an annual rental of £2,000. The tenant paid the first year's rent in advance on 1 July 19X8.

The cost of the closing stock on 31 December 19X8 was £9,220. Accrued electricity and telephone charges at that date were estimated to be £760 and £150 respectively. Depreciation of business equipment for the year is estimated at £3,700.

Required:

Prepare Vivienne's trading and profit and loss account for the year to 31 December 19X8 and her balance sheet as at that date.

5

RECORDING FINANCIAL TRANSACTIONS

Chapter objectives

When you have finished this chapter, you should be able to:

- **Explain the principles of double entry book-keeping.**
- **Record financial transactions in ledger accounts.**
- **Balance ledger accounts and extract a trial balance.**
- **Account for end-of-period adjustments and prepare final accounts.**

1. INTRODUCTION

A profit and loss account and balance sheet cannot be produced at the end of an accounting period unless the business concerned has kept a record of its financial transactions during the period. There are two main ways of recording financial transactions:

(a) The transactions could be recorded manually in hand-written books of account, using a recording system known as *double-entry book-keeping*.

(b) The transactions could be input to a computer system and recorded in computer files.

The purpose of this chapter is to explain the principles of double-entry book-keeping and it is assumed throughout the chapter that a *manual* recording system is being used. However, this does not mean that computer-based systems are being ignored. It is important to appreciate that computer-based systems also work on double-entry principles and that a grasp of these principles is fundamental to an understanding of both manual and computer-based systems. The only significant distinction between the two approaches is that computer-based systems involve far less clerical effort than manual systems, particularly if the volume of transactions is high. This makes them especially attractive to larger businesses.

2. BASIC DOUBLE-ENTRY BOOK-KEEPING

In a traditional double-entry book-keeping system, financial transactions are recorded in an account book known as a *ledger*. The ledger contains a number of *accounts*, each consisting of a page (or pages) headed with the name of a financial item and used to record the transactions which affect that item. Accounts are needed for:

(a) the owner's capital
(b) each type of asset owned by the business
(c) each of its liabilities
(d) each type of revenue which the business receives
(e) each type of expense which the business incurs.

The recording system must be able to record increases and decreases in each of these items as financial transactions occur. This is achieved by recording increases on one side of the page and decreases on the other side.

The left-hand side of a page is known as the *debit* side and the right-hand side is known as the *credit* side. It is important to disregard any non-accounting meanings which might be associated with the words "debit" and "credit". From a book-keeping point of view they are simply a convenient (and conventional) way of referring to the two sides of a ledger account.

Double-entry rules

As we have already seen, every financial transaction has two effects on the financial position of the business concerned. This means that each transaction must be recorded *twice* in the books of account (hence the name "double-entry"). For example, if a business buys a motor vehicle and pays by cheque, an increase must be recorded in the account called "Motor vehicles" and a decrease must be recorded in the account called "Cash at bank". The basic rules of the double-entry system of book-keeping can be summarised as follows:

(a) If an account represents an asset or an expense, *increases* are recorded on the *debit* side of the account and *decreases* are recorded on the *credit* side.

(b) If an account represents a liability, a source of revenue or the owner's capital, *decreases* are recorded on the *debit* side of the account and *increases* are recorded on the *credit* side.

These rules may appear unnecessarily complicated at first but they ensure that each transaction results in one debit entry and one credit entry. As a consequence, the sum of all the debit entries made during an accounting period should equal the sum of all the credit entries and this provides a means of detecting book-keeping errors. For example, if the purchase of a motor vehicle by cheque is recorded in the "Cash at bank" account but not in the "Motor vehicles" account, the total debits made during the accounting period will not equal the total credits, indicating that a book-keeping error has been made.

EXAMPLE

Walter started his own business on 1 May 19X9. His first few business transactions were as follows:

1 May Walter opened a bank account for the business and paid £10,000 of his own money into this account.

2 May A further £5,000 was paid into the business bank account. This money had been borrowed from Walter's sister Yvonne.

3 May Machinery was bought for £4,750 and paid for by cheque.

4 May A £200 insurance premium was paid by cheque

7 May Walter withdrew £250 from the business bank account for his own use.

Record these transactions in ledger accounts.

SOLUTION

Capital

		£			£
7.5.X9	Bank	250	1.5.X9	Bank	10,000

Bank

		£			£
1.5.X9	Capital	10,000	3.5.X9	Machinery	4,750
2.5.X9	Loan from Yvonne	5,000	4.5.X9	Insurance	200
			7.5.X9	Drawings	250

Loan from Yvonne

		£			£
			2.5.X9	Bank	5,000

Machinery

		£			£
3.5.X9	Bank	4,750			

Insurance

		£			£
4.5.X9	Bank	200			

Notes:

1. The name of an account is separated from the entries in that account by a horizontal line. The debit side of an account is separated from the credit side by a central vertical line. These two lines form the shape of a letter "T" and, for this reason, ledger accounts are often referred to as "T" accounts.

2. Each entry in an account consists of the following data:
   - the date of the transaction which is being recorded
   - the name of the account which contains the other half of the double-entry for that transaction
   - the amount of the transaction.

   The word "bank" has been used rather than the more cumbersome "cash at bank".

3. Increases in assets (bank, machinery) and expenses (insurance) have been recorded on the debit side of the relevant accounts. Decreases have been recorded on the credit side.
4. Increases in liabilities (Yvonne's loan) and capital have been recorded on the credit side of the relevant accounts. Decreases have been recorded on the debit side.
5. As expected, the total of the debit entries equals the total of the credit entries (£20,200 in each case). This indicates that each debit entry has been matched by an equal and opposite credit entry, as required by double-entry rules.

3. RECORDING STOCK TRANSACTIONS

If a business buys and sells goods, it may seem obvious that its ledger should contain an account called "stock of goods" and that purchases and sales of stock should be debited and credited to this account. But purchases and sales of stock are not made at the same price and this causes a difficulty, as illustrated below.

EXAMPLE

On 1 January, a business commenced trading with capital of £1,500 and cash at bank of £1,500. A stock of goods costing £1,000 was bought immediately and paid for by cheque. On 7 January, part of this stock was sold for £1,100 and the sale proceeds were paid into the bank. Show how these transactions might be entered in ledger accounts.

SOLUTION

At first sight, the required entries would *seem* to be as follows:

Capital

		£			£
			Jan 1	Bank	1,500

Bank

		£			£
Jan 1	Capital	1,500	Jan 1	Stock of goods	1,000
Jan 7	Stock of goods	1,100			

Stock of goods

		£			£
Jan 1	Bank	1,000	Jan 7	Bank	1,100

On reflection, though, it is evident that these entries cannot be entirely right. The stock account shows that stock has increased by £1,000 and decreased by £1,100. Therefore the business appears to have a negative stock of goods. This illogical result has been caused by the fact that purchases of stock are recorded at cost price whilst sales are recorded at selling price.

Division of the stock account

The difficulty described above is usually resolved by dividing the stock of goods account into five separate accounts, as follows:

(a) **Purchases account**. The purchases account records purchases of stock from suppliers *at cost price*. This account is debited when stock is purchased (because stock has increased). The corresponding credit entry will depend upon whether the stock is bought for cash (credit the cash account), paid for by cheque (credit the bank account) or bought from a supplier on credit terms (credit the supplier's account).

(b) **Returns outwards account**. The returns outwards account records returns of stock to suppliers *at cost price*. This account is credited (because stock has decreased) when goods are returned to a supplier. The corresponding debit is in the supplier's account. The returns outwards account is also known as the *purchase returns* account.

(c) **Sales account**. The sales account records sales of stock to customers *at selling price*. This account is credited whenever stock is sold (because stock has decreased). If the customer pays immediately in cash or by cheque, the cash or bank account is debited. If the customer has bought the goods on credit terms, the customer's account is debited.

(d) **Returns inwards account**. The returns inwards account records returns of goods by customers *at selling price*. This account is debited whenever goods are returned by a customer (because stock has increased). The corresponding credit is in the customer's account. The returns inwards account is also known as the *sales returns* account.

(e) **Own consumption account**. If the owner of the business takes goods for his or her own personal use without paying for them, the *cost price* of the goods taken is credited to the own consumption account (because stock has decreased). The corresponding debit entry is made in the owner's capital account.

At the end of each accounting period, it will be necessary to determine the cost of the goods sold during the period and the closing stock figure. The relevant procedure is described later in this chapter.

EXAMPLE

Record the following transactions in ledger accounts:

5 November	Stock is bought for £2,000 and paid for by cheque
6 November	Stock costing £3,000 is bought on credit from A Pearson
9 November	Stock is sold for £1,150. The customer pays by cheque.
10 November	Stock costing £100 is returned to A Pearson
11 November	Stock is sold on credit to P Lowther for £2,130.
13 November	P Lowther returns stock which had been sold to him for £50.

SOLUTION

Bank

		£			£
Nov 9	Sales	1,150	Nov 5	Purchases	2,000

Purchases

		£			£
Nov 5	Bank	2,000			
Nov 6	A Pearson	3,000			

Returns outwards

		£			£
			Nov 10	A Pearson	100

Sales

		£			£
			Nov 9	Bank	1,150
			Nov 11	P Lowther	2,130

Returns inwards

		£			£
Nov 13	P Lowther	50			

A Pearson

		£			£
Nov 10	Returns outwards	100	Nov 6	Purchases	3,000

P Lowther

		£			£
Nov 11	Sales	2,130	Nov 13	Returns inwards	50

Notes:

1. A Pearson's account represents a trade creditor i.e. a liability.
2. P Lowther's account represents a trade debtor i.e. an asset.

4. ACCOUNT BALANCES AND THE EXTRACTION OF A TRIAL BALANCE

At the end of an accounting period, it is necessary to calculate the *balance* on every account in the ledger so as to derive the figures which are required for the profit and loss account and balance sheet. For each account, this involves the following procedure:

(a) The debit entries in the account are totalled.

(b) The credit entries in the account are totalled.

(c) The difference between the two totals is calculated, giving the account balance. If total debits exceed total credits, the account has a *debit balance*. If total credits exceed total debits, the account has a *credit balance*. If total debits equal total credits, the account has a *nil balance*.

We have already seen that the total of all the debit entries made in the ledger during an accounting period should equal the total of all the credit entries. Checking that this is the case provides a means of detecting book-keeping errors but involves the time-consuming and error-prone task of computing the necessary totals. Fortunately, there is an equivalent check which can be made much more easily. If all the debit balances in the ledger are listed and totalled and then all the credit balances are also listed and totalled, the two totals should agree. This procedure is known as *extracting a trial balance*. The following important points should be noted:

(a) A trial balance is usually extracted at the end of each accounting period *after* all of the routine transactions for the period have been recorded but *before* dealing with end-of-period adjustments such as accruals, prepayments and closing stock (see later in this chapter) and depreciation (see Chapter 6).

(b) If the trial balance totals do not agree, there has definitely been a book-keeping error. If the trial balance totals *do* agree, this is encouraging news but cannot be taken as definite proof that no book-keeping errors of any kind have been made. For example, the complete omission of both halves of a double-entry is certainly a book-keeping error but would not disturb the agreement of the trial balance totals. (See Chapter 9 for a more detailed discussion of book-keeping errors and means by which they may be detected).

EXAMPLE

Angela started a business on 1 August, operating from rented premises. Her first month's transactions were as follows:

1 August	Angela opened a business bank account and paid £12,000 of her own money into this account. From then on, all payments were made out of the business bank account.
	The first month's rent of £600 was paid by cheque.
5 August	A motor van was bought for £5,200 and paid for by cheque.
7 August	Fixtures and fittings costing £4,750 were paid for by cheque.
8 August	Stock costing £8,700 was bought on credit from T Johnson.
	Petrol was bought for £35 on credit from S Davies Garages Ltd.
13 August	Stock was sold on credit to W Findley for £4,880.
14 August	Stock costing £4,800 was bought on credit from T Johnson.
22 August	Stock was sold for £7,700. The customer paid by cheque.
25 August	Angela took stock costing £100 out of the business for her own use.

31 August Wages of £320 were paid to Angela's employees and a salary of £400 was paid to Angela herself.

A cheque for £2,000 was received from W Findley.

A cheque for £5,000 was sent to T Johnson.

Record these transactions in ledger accounts and extract Angela's trial balance as at 31 August.

SOLUTION

Capital

		£			£
			Aug 1	Bank	12,000

Motor van

		£			£
Aug 5	Bank	5,200			

Fixtures and fittings

		£			£
Aug 7	Bank	4,750			

Bank

		£			£
Aug 1	Capital	12,000	Aug 1	Rent	600
Aug 22	Sales	7,700	Aug 5	Motor van	5,200
Aug 31	W Findley	2,000	Aug 7	Fixtures and fittings	4,750
			Aug 31	Wages	320
			Aug 31	Drawings	400
			Aug 31	T Johnson	5,000

Purchases

		£			£
Aug 8	T Johnson	8,700			
Aug 14	T Johnson	4,800			

Sales

		£			£
			Aug 13	W Findley	4,880
			Aug 22	Bank	7,700

Own consumption

		£			£
			Aug 25	Drawings	100

Rent

		£			£
Aug 1	Bank	600			

Motor expenses

		£			£
Aug 8	S Davies Garages Ltd	35			

Wages

		£			£
Aug 31	Bank	320			

Drawings

		£			£
Aug 25	Own consumption	100			
Aug 31	Bank	400			

T Johnson

		£			£
Aug 31	Bank	5,000	Aug 8	Purchases	8,700
			Aug 14	Purchases	4,800

S Davies Garages Ltd

		£			£
			Aug 8	Motor expenses	35

W Findley

		£			£
Aug 13	Sales	4,880	Aug 31	Bank	2,000

Trial balance as at August 31

	Dr balances £	Cr balances £
Capital		12,000
Motor van	5,200	
Fixtures and fittings	4,750	
Bank	5,430	
Purchases	13,500	
Sales		12,580
Own consumption		100
Rent	600	
Motor expenses	35	
Wages	320	
Drawings	500	
T Johnson		8,500
S Davies Garages Ltd		35
W Findley	2,880	
	33,215	33,215

Notes:

1. Angela's drawings reduce her capital and could have been debited directly to her capital account. It is common practice, however, to debit all of the drawings for an accounting period to a drawings account and then to transfer the total drawings to the owner's capital account at the end of the period. This facilitates the calculation of total drawings (which might be an interesting piece of information) and avoids cluttering the capital account with detailed drawings figures. Similarly, own consumption has been debited to the drawings account rather than being debited directly to the capital account.
2. The balance on each ledger account has been calculated and all of the balances have been listed in the trial balance. Debit balances have been listed in one column and credit balances have been listed in another column.. The reader is advised to check that he or she agrees with each of the balances shown in the trial balance.
3. The trial balance is *not* a ledger account. It is merely a listing of account balances.
4. "Dr" and "Cr" (used in the column headings of the trial balance in this example) are abbreviations for "Debit" and "Credit".
5. The trial balance totals agree, as they must if no book-keeping errors have been made.

5. FROM TRIAL BALANCE TO FINAL ACCOUNTS

If a trial balance has been extracted and the trial balance totals agree, preparation of the final accounts (i.e. the trading and profit and loss account and the balance sheet) becomes very straightforward. Assuming that no end-of-period adjustments are required (see later in this chapter) the procedure is as follows:

The trading account

(a) The balance on the sales account is transferred to the trading account by debiting the sales account and crediting the trading account with the amount involved.

(b) The balance on the returns inwards account is transferred to the trading account by crediting the returns inwards account and debiting the trading account with the amount involved.

(c) Similarly, the balances on the purchases, returns outwards and own consumption accounts are transferred to the trading account.

(d) After these entries have been made, the purchases, sales, returns and own consumption accounts are all left with nil balances. The debit and credit sides are totalled and the accounts are ruled off. These accounts are now ready to be used again in the next accounting period.

(e) The trading account now contains all the figures required to calculate gross profit, apart from closing stock. Assuming that the business does not maintain detailed stock records, it will be necessary to physically count the closing stock and calculate its cost. The closing stock figure must then used in the calculation of the cost of goods sold (and hence gross profit) and must also shown as a current asset in the balance sheet. The desired effect is achieved by debiting an account called "stock of goods for resale" and crediting the trading account with the amount of the closing stock.

(f) The gross profit for the accounting period is carried down to the profit and loss account.

The profit and loss account

(a) The profit and loss account begins with the gross profit transferred from the trading account. If the business has any other sources of revenue, the balance on each revenue account is transferred to the profit and loss account by debiting the revenue account and crediting the profit and loss account with the amount involved.

(b) The balance on each expense account is transferred to the profit and loss account by crediting the expense account and debiting the profit and loss account with the amount involved.

(c) The revenue and expenses accounts are now left with nil balances. The debit and credit sides are totalled and the accounts are ruled off. These accounts are now ready to be used again in the next accounting period.

(d) The profit for the period is calculated in the usual way by subtracting total expenses from total revenue. The profit is then transferred to the owner's capital account by debiting profit and loss account and crediting capital account with the amount of the profit. (These entries are reversed if the business has incurred a loss).

It is important to appreciate that the trading account and the profit and loss account (as their names imply) are indeed ledger accounts, although for reasons of convenience they are usually drawn up on a separate sheet of paper rather than being written in the ledger itself. They have a debit side (on which expenses are shown) and a credit side (on which revenue is shown). The two-sided nature of the trading account and the profit and loss account becomes more obvious if they are laid out in horizontal format but the vertical format is almost always preferred in practice.

The balance sheet

(a) The only balances now remaining in the ledger are those relating to assets, liabilities and capital. These are used to draw up the balance sheet in the usual way. The balance sheet is *not* a ledger account and does not have a debit or credit side. It is merely a list of the balances that remain in the ledger at the end of an accounting period.

(b) Finally, the ledger is tidied up by ruling off the accounts relating to assets, liabilities and capital and carrying down the balances on these accounts to the start of the next accounting period. This procedure is illustrated in the following example.

EXAMPLE

Refer back to the previous example. Now prepare Angela's trading and profit and loss account for the month to 31 August and her balance sheet as at that date, showing the necessary entries in Angela's ledger. Assume that the cost of Angela's closing stock at 31 August was £3,830.

SOLUTION

Capital

		£			£
Aug 31	Drawings	500	Aug 1	Bank	12,000
Aug 31	Balance c/d	13,555	Aug 31	Profit for the month	2,055
		14,055			14,055
			Sept 1	Balance b/d	13,555

Motor van

		£			£
Aug 5	Bank	5,200	Aug 31	Balance c/d	5,200
Sept 1	Balance b/d	5,200			

Fixtures and fittings

		£			£
Aug 7	Bank	4,750	Aug 31	Balance c/d	4,750
Sept 1	Balance b/d	4,750			

Bank

		£			£
Aug 1	Capital	12,000	Aug 1	Rent	600
Aug 22	Sales	7,700	Aug 5	Motor van	5,200
Aug 31	W Findley	2,000	Aug 7	Fixtures and fittings	4,750
			Aug 31	Wages	320
			Aug 31	Drawings	400
			Aug 31	T Johnson	5,000
			Aug 31	Balance c/d	5,430
		21,700			21,700
Sept 1	Balance b/d	5,430			

Stock of goods for resale

		£			£
Aug 31	Trading a/c	3,830	Aug 31	Balance c/d	3,830
Sept 1	Balance b/d	3,830			

Purchases

		£			£
Aug 8	T Johnson	8,700	Aug 31	Trading a/c	13,500
Aug 14	T Johnson	4,800			
		13,500			13,500

Sales

		£			£
Aug 31	Trading a/c	12,580	Aug 13	W Findley	4,880
			Aug 22	Bank	7,700
		12,580			12,580

Own consumption

		£			£
Aug 31	Trading a/c	100	Aug 25	Drawings	100

Rent

		£			£
Aug 1	Bank	600	Aug 31	Profit and loss a/c	600

Motor expenses

		£			£
Aug 8	S Davies Garages Ltd	35	Aug 31	Profit and loss a/c	35

Wages

		£			£
Aug 31	Bank	320	Aug 31	Profit and loss a/c	320

Drawings

		£			£
Aug 25	Own consumption	100	Aug 31	Capital	500
Aug 31	Bank	400			
		500			500

T Johnson

		£			£
Aug 31	Bank	5,000	Aug 8	Purchases	8,700
Aug 31	Balance c/d	8,500	Aug 14	Purchases	4,800
		13,500			13,500
			Sept 1	Balance b/d	8,500

S Davies Garages Ltd

		£			£
Aug 31	Balance c/d	35	Aug 8	Motor expenses	35
			Sept 1	Balance b/d	35

W Findley

		£			£
Aug 13	Sales	4,880	Aug 31	Bank	2,000
			Aug 31	Balance c/d	2,880
		4,880			4,880
Sept 1	Balance b/d	2,880			

Notes:

1. The abbreviations "c/d", "b/d" and "a/c" have been used for "carried down", "brought down" and "account" respectively.
2. The act of carrying down a balance on an asset account obeys double-entry rules. The balance is entered on the credit side at the end of the accounting period (Aug 31) and then entered again on the debit side at the start of the new accounting period (Sept 1). There has been a debit and an equal and opposite credit, but both have been entered in the same account. This principle applies also to the carrying down of balances on liability accounts and on the capital account.

Angela
Trading and profit and loss account for the month to 31 August

	£	£
Sales		12,580
Cost of goods sold		
Purchases	13,500	
Less: Own consumption	100	
	13,400	
Less: Stock at 31 August	3,830	9,570
Gross profit		3,010
Rent	600	
Motor expenses	35	
Wages	320	955
Net profit for the month		2,055

Angela
Balance sheet as at 31 August

	£	£	£
Fixed assets			
Motor van			5,200
Fixtures and fittings			4,750
			9,950
Current assets			
Stock of goods for resale		3,830	
Trade debtors		2,880	
Cash at bank		5,430	
		12,140	
Current liabilities			
Trade creditors		8,535	
Net current assets			3,605
			13,555
Capital			
Capital introduced		12,000	
Net profit for the month		2,055	
		14,055	
Less: Drawings	400		
Own consumption	100	500	13,555
			13,555

Notes:

1. Trade debtors consists of the amount owed by W Findley.
2. Trade creditors consist of T Johnson £8,500 and S Davies Garages Ltd £35.
3. As usual, the balance on the capital account has been analysed on the face of the balance sheet. The drawings figure has been analysed into cash drawings and own consumption.

EXAMPLE

Carol began trading many years ago, preparing accounts to 30 June each year. Her balance sheet at 30 June 19X8 included the following balances:

	£
Stock of goods for resale	4,560
Trade debtors	11,630
Cash at bank	3,340
Trade creditors	13,890

Her summarised transactions for the year to 30 June 19X9 included the following:

	£
Cost of goods bought from suppliers (all on credit)	43,910
Cost of goods returned to suppliers	650
Selling price of goods sold to customers (all on credit)	69,110
Selling price of goods returned by customers	1,200
Payments made to suppliers (all by cheque)	41,230
Cheques received from customers	70,080

A physical stock-take performed on 30 June 19X9 revealed that the cost of Carol's stock on that date was £5,550.

Record these transactions in Carol's ledger and prepare her trading account for the year to 30 June 19X9.

SOLUTION

Bank

		£			£
1.7.X8	Balance b/d	3,340	30.6.X9	Trade creditors	41,230
30.6.X9	Trade debtors	70,080			

Stock of goods for resale

		£			£
1.7.X8	Balance b/d	4,560	30.6.X9	Trading a/c	4,560
30.6.X9	Trading a/c	5,550	30.6.X9	Balance c/d	5,550
1.7.X9	Balance b/d	5,550			

Purchases

		£			£
30.6.X9	Trade creditors	43,910	30.6.X9	Trading a/c	43,910

Returns outwards

		£			£
30.6.X9	Trading a/c	650	30.6.X9	Trade creditors	650

Sales

		£			£
30.6.X9	Trading a/c	69,110	30.6.X9	Trade debtors	69,110

Returns inwards

		£			£
30.6.X9	Trade debtors	1,200	30.6.X9	Trading a/c	1,200

Trade creditors

		£			£
30.6.X9	Returns outwards	650	1.7.X8	Balance b/d	13,890
30.6.X9	Bank	41,230	30.6.X9	Purchases	43,910
30.6.X9	Balance c/d	15,920			
		57,800			57,800
			1.7.X9	Balance b/d	15,920

Trade debtors

		£			£
1.7.X8	Balance b/d	11,630	30.6.X9	Returns inwards	1,200
30.6.X9	Sales	69,110	30.6.X9	Bank	70,080
			30.6.X9	Balance c/d	9,460
		80,740			80,740
1.7.X9	Balance b/d	9,460			

Notes:

1. The bank account cannot be balanced off because we are given no information about other receipts and payments during the year.
2. The opening balance on the stock account is the opening stock figure. This is transferred to the trading account so that it can take part in the calculation of the cost of goods sold during the year. The closing stock figure is debited to the stock account and credited to the trading account, as previously explained.

Carol

Trading account for the year to 30 June 19X9

	£	£	£
Sales			69,110
Less: Returns inwards			1,200
			67,910
Cost of goods sold:			
Stock as at 1 July 19X8		4,560	
Purchases	43,910		
Less: Returns outwards	650	43,260	
		47,820	
Less: Stock as at 30 June 19X9		5,550	42,270
Gross profit			25,640

6. ACCOUNTING FOR ACCRUALS AND PREPAYMENTS

We saw in Chapter 4 that expenses might be accrued or prepaid at the end of an accounting period. The book-keeping entries required to deal with accrued and prepaid expenses are as follows:

(a) **Accrued expenses.** The amount of the accrual is entered on the debit side of the relevant expense account (an expense has increased) and carried down to the credit side of the same account in the following accounting period. This credit balance is a current liability which is shown on the balance sheet.

(b) **Prepaid expenses.** The amount of the prepayment is entered on the credit side of the relevant expense account (a decrease in an expense) and carried down to the debit side of the same account in the following accounting period. This debit balance is a current asset which is shown on the balance sheet.

Similarly, any accrued revenue (an asset) is carried down as a debit balance on the relevant revenue account and any prepaid revenue (a liability) is carried down as a credit balance on the relevant revenue account.

EXAMPLE

Write up ledger accounts from the information given below.

	Accrued at 31.12.X8	*Prepaid at 31.12.X8*	*Paid during year to 31.12.X9*	*Accrued at 31.12.X9*	*Prepaid at 31.12.X9*
	£	£	£	£	£
Electricity	1,298	–	6,750	1,347	–
Insurance	–	500	6,200	–	700
Rent payable	–	1,000	9,000	1,000	–

SOLUTION

Electricity

		£			£
31.12.X9	Bank	6,750	1.1.X9	Accrual b/d	1,298
31.12.X9	Accrual c/d	1,347	31.12.X9	Profit and loss a/c	6,799
		8,097			8,097
			1.1.X0	Accrual b/d	1,347

Insurance

		£			£
1.1.X9	Prepayment b/d	500	31.12.X9	Profit and loss a/c	6,000
31.12.X9	Bank	6,200	31.12.X9	Prepayment c/d	700
		6,700			6,700
1.1.X0	Prepayment b/d	700			

Rent payable

		£			£
1.1.X9	Prepayment b/d	1,000	31.12.X9	Profit and loss a/c	11,000
31.12.X9	Bank	9,000			
31.12.X9	Accrual c/d	1,000			
		11,000			11,000
			1.1.X0	Accrual b/d	1,000

Notes:

1. For each of these expenses, the amount to be shown in the profit and loss account is derived by inserting whatever figure is required to make the relevant account balance after all of the other entries (including this year's accrual or prepayment) have been made.
2. The balance sheet at 31 December 19X9 will include accruals of £2,347 (a current liability) and prepayments of £700 (a current asset).

7. SUMMARY

- In a manual book-keeping system, financial transactions are recorded in a ledger which contains accounts for assets, liabilities, revenues, expenses and the owner's capital. The left-hand side of each account is known as the debit side and the right-hand side is known as the credit side. Ledger accounts are sometimes referred to as "T" accounts.
- If an account represents an asset or an expense, increases are recorded on the debit side of the account and decreases are recorded on the credit side. If an account represents a liability, a source of revenue or the owner's capital, decreases are recorded on the debit side of the account and increases are recorded on the credit side.
- Purchases of stock, returns outwards, sales of stock, returns inwards and own consumption are normally recorded in separate ledger accounts.
- A trial balance is extracted at the end of each accounting period when all the routine transactions for the period have been entered. This lists and totals all the debit balances and all the credit balances. If the two totals do not agree this is evidence that a book-keeping error has occurred.
- End-of-period adjustments may need to be made in the ledger to reflect accruals and prepayments.
- The balance on each revenue or expense account at the end of an accounting period is transferred to the profit and loss account. Balances on accounts representing assets, liabilities and the owner's capital are carried down to the next period.

EXERCISES 5

5.1 State which ledger account should be debited and which should be credited for each of the following transactions:

(a) Purchase of land and buildings, paid for by cheque.
(b) Rent paid in cash.
(c) Stock purchased on credit from J Calvert Ltd.
(d) Stock returned to J Calvert Ltd.
(e) Cheque sent to J Calvert Ltd
(f) Motor vehicle bought on credit from ABC Motors Ltd.
(g) Petrol paid for by cheque.
(h) Stock sold to customers for cash.
(i) Cheque received from D Bentley, who is a trade debtor.
(j) Stock sold on credit to D Bentley.
(k) Goods returned by D Bentley.
(l) Interest received on a bank account.

5.2 Damon started a business on 1 November. His first month's transactions were as follows:

1 November	Damon started the business with £10,000 in cash. He immediately put £9,500 of this into a business bank account.
	The first month's rent of his business premises, amounting to £350, was paid in cash.
2 November	Equipment costing £3,400 was paid for by cheque.
	Stock costing £8,950 was bought on credit from G McNab.
6 November	Stock was sold for £3,670. The customers paid by cheque.
9 November	Stock costing £100 was returned to G McNab
14 November	Stock was sold on credit to M Hall for £5,000 and to H Reynolds for £300.
16 November	Sundry expenses of £37 were paid in cash.
18 November	M Hall returned stock originally sold to him for £200.
24 November	The amount owing to G McNab was paid by cheque. Damon was given a 2% cash discount.
25 November	Stock costing £6,200 was bought on credit from K Shaw.
28 November	The amount owing by M Hall was received by cheque. Damon gave M Hall a 2.5% cash discount.
30 November	Wages of £1,750 were paid by cheque. This included £1,200 for Damon himself.

Required:

Record these transactions in Damon's ledger and extract a trial balance as at 30 November.

5.3 Following on from the previous example, the cost of Damon's closing stock at 30 November was £7,980. There were no accruals or prepayments and depreciation of the equipment may be ignored.

Required:

Prepare a trading and profit and loss account for the month to 30 November and a balance sheet as at that date, showing the necessary entries in Damon's ledger.

5.4 Emma prepares accounts to 31 March annually. Her trial balance at 31 March 19X9 is as follows:

	Dr balances	*Cr balances*
	£	£
Capital as at 1 April 19X8		8,000
Motor van	6,500	
Bank		3,777
Stock as at 1 April 19X8	2,445	
Purchases	11,510	
Sales		32,868
Returns outwards		50
Returns inwards	420	
Rent	1,100	
Heating and lighting	1,630	
Insurance	1,350	
Staff wages	6,540	
Bank overdraft interest	350	
Drawings	12,000	
Trade debtors	3,720	
Trade creditors		2,870
	47,565	47,565

Further information:

1. The cost of Emma's closing stock on 31 March 19X9 was £3,480.
2. Accrued expenses on 31 March 19X9 were heating and lighting £340, rent £100.
3. Insurance premiums of £210 had been prepaid on 31 March 19X9.
4. Depreciation is to be ignored.

Required:

Prepare Emma's trading and profit and loss account for the year to 31 March 19X9 and a balance sheet on that date. (Ledger accounts are not required).

*5.5 An inexperienced book-keeper has drawn up a trial balance as at 30 June 19X8 (see below) and cannot understand why the trial balance totals do not agree.

	Dr balances	*Cr balances*
	£	£
Capital as at 1 July 19X7		54,070
Land and buildings	50,000	
Fixtures and fittings	4,650	
Stock as at 1 July 19X7		3,480
Trade debtors		12,820
Trade creditors	14,590	
Bank overdraft	10,100	
Purchases	63,430	
Sales		95,360
Returns outwards	870	
Returns inwards		2,350
Carriage inwards		1,330
Carriage outwards	8,650	
Wages and salaries	12,670	
Heating and lighting	2,410	
Bank overdraft interest	920	
Repairs and renewals	3,880	
Discounts allowed		990
Discounts received		1,030
Drawings		8,440
	172,170	179,870

Required:

Prepare a corrected trial balance.

*5.6 The following information relates to a business which prepares accounts to 30 September each year:

	Accrued at 30.9.X7	*Prepaid at 30.9.X7*	*Paid/(received) during year to 30.9.X8*	*Accrued at 30.9.X8*	*Prepaid at 30.9.X8*
	£	£	£	£	£
Telephone	569	–	6,385	673	–
Business rates	–	4,200	8,850	–	4,425
Rent receivable	–	500	(5,300)	400	–

Required:

Write up ledger accounts from this information and calculate the amount which should be shown in the profit and loss account for each item for the year to 30 September 19X8.

***5.7** George's balance sheet at 31 May 19X8 and a summary of his transactions for the year to 31 May 19X9 are shown below:

George
Balance sheet as at 31 May 19X8

	£	£
Fixed assets		
Business premises		52,800
Tools and equipment		6,850
		59,650
Current assets		
Stock of goods for resale	6,430	
Trade debtors	7,650	
Prepayments	1,250	
	15,330	
Current liabilities		
Trade creditors	12,760	
Accruals	840	
Bank overdraft	7,990	
	21,590	
Net current liabilities		6,260
		53,390
Capital		
Balance as at 31 May 19X8		53,390

Notes:

1. Prepayments consist of Business rates £750 and Insurance premiums £500.
2. Accruals consist of Telephone £230 and Electricity £610.

Summarised transactions during the year to 31 May 19X9:

(a) Stock costing £71,210 was purchased on credit from suppliers. Stock costing a further £5,770 was purchased and paid for immediately by cheque.

(b) Stock costing £1,090 was returned to suppliers.

(c) Stock was sold to credit customers for £93,020. Sales amounting to a further £6,100 were made to customers who paid immediately by cheque.

(d) Stock originally sold for £4,380 was returned by customers.

(e) Cheques totalling £68,880 were sent to suppliers from whom stock had been bought on credit. Cash discounts received from these suppliers were £420.

(f) Cheques totalling £89,340 were received from customers to whom stock had been sold on credit. Cash discounts allowed to these customers were £1,070.

(g) George took stock costing £500 from the business for his own use.

(h) Tools and equipment costing £2,500 were paid for by cheque.

(i) Expenses paid for by cheque were salaries £29,000 (including £10,000 for George), business rates £4,700, electricity £3,760, telephone £1,540 and insurance £900. Bank interest of £2,400 was charged during the year.

Accruals at 31 May 19X9 were Telephone £260 and Electricity £690. Prepayments at 31 May 19X9 were Business rates £790 and Insurance premiums £520. The cost of George's closing stock at 31 May 19X9 was £6,190.

Required:

Write up George's ledger accounts for the year to 31 May 19X9. Also prepare a trading and profit and loss account for the year to 31 May 19X9 and a balance sheet as at that date. (Depreciation may be ignored).

6

ACCOUNTING FOR FIXED ASSETS AND DEPRECIATION

Chapter objectives

When you have finished this chapter, you should be able to:

- **Identify costs which can be regarded as capital expenditure.**
- **Define the term "depreciation".**
- **Recognise the need to provide for depreciation.**
- **Calculate depreciation using the straight-line method and the reducing-balance method.**
- **Record depreciation in ledger accounts.**
- **Record the disposal of a fixed asset in ledger accounts.**

1. INTRODUCTION

Fixed assets and the concept of depreciation were introduced in Chapters 3 and 4. The purpose of this chapter is to explain these ideas in more detail, beginning with a closer look at the definition of capital expenditure.

2. CAPITAL EXPENDITURE

As was explained in Chapter 4, capital expenditure is expenditure on the acquisition of fixed assets. The cost of a fixed asset is deemed to include the cost of acquiring the asset, bringing it to the required location and preparing it for use. Therefore the following costs can all be regarded as capital expenditure:

(a) the initial cost of acquiring a fixed asset

(b) other costs associated with the acquisition of a fixed asset (legal fees, delivery charges, installation costs etc)

(c) the cost of any *improvements* made to a fixed asset.

On the other hand, the following costs cannot be regarded as capital expenditure and must be treated as revenue expenditure:

(a) any loan interest or other finance charges paid in connection with the acquisition of a fixed asset

(b) the cost of any *repairs* made to a fixed asset.

The distinction between improvements and repairs is important. An improvement is something which enhances the future economic benefits to be derived from the ownership of a fixed asset. A repair merely maintains those benefits at their previously expected level.

EXAMPLE

Which of the following costs should be regarded as capital expenditure?

(a) The basic cost of acquiring a new factory machine.

(b) The Value Added Tax (VAT) charged on the purchase of the machine.

(c) The cost of transporting the machine to the factory where it is to be installed.

(d) The wages paid to the workmen who install the machine.

(e) The cost of maintaining the machine at regular intervals.

(f) The cost of replacing the machine's electromechanical control system with an electronic control system, thus increasing the quality of the output produced by the machine.

(g) The interest paid on a loan to acquire the machine.

SOLUTION

(a) The cost of acquiring a fixed asset is capital expenditure.

(b) Any VAT which the business cannot reclaim is part of the cost of the machine and is capital expenditure.

(c) Delivery costs are capital expenditure.

(d) Installation costs are capital expenditure.

(e) Maintenance costs are revenue expenditure.

(f) The cost of this improvement is capital expenditure.

(g) Interest and other finance charges are revenue expenditure.

3. DEPRECIATION - BASIC PRINCIPLES

Sooner or later, virtually all of the expenditure incurred by a business is shown as an expense in its profit and loss account. The allocation of expenditure to accounting periods is controlled by the matching convention, which requires that the revenue for an accounting period should be matched against all of the costs incurred so as to earn that revenue. This leads to the following rules:

(a) Expenditure on day-to-day running costs is shown in the profit and loss account of the accounting period to which the expenditure relates.

(b) Expenditure on stock for resale is shown in the profit and loss account of the accounting period in which the stock is sold.

(c) Expenditure on a fixed asset with a finite useful life is transferred to the profit and loss account over a number of accounting periods, as the economic benefits associated with ownership of the asset are gradually used up. The amount of expenditure which is transferred to the profit and loss account in each accounting period is known as *depreciation*. The remaining expenditure, which is shown as an asset in the balance sheet, is *not* the market value of the asset. It is the historic cost of the economic benefits which the asset still has to offer.

The only expenditure which will never find its way to the profit and loss account is expenditure on fixed assets with an infinite useful life. The one asset of this type which springs to mind is land, but even land may have a finite useful life in some circumstances (e.g. a coal mine or a quarry). It is worth noting that buildings, unlike the land on which they stand, usually do have finite useful lives and should therefore be depreciated. Note also that the term *amortisation* is sometimes used to refer to the depreciation of intangible assets such as leases and copyrights.

A definition of depreciation

Statement of Standard Accounting Practice 12 (see Chapter 15) defines depreciation as "*the measure of the wearing out, consumption or other reduction in the useful economic life of a fixed asset whether arising from use, effluxion of time or obsolescence through technological or market changes*". This definition makes two useful points:

(a) The purpose of depreciation is to spread the cost of a fixed asset over the accounting periods in which the asset is used. This process has nothing to do with the current market value of the asset and in fact the word "value" does not appear in the definition.

(b) Reductions in the useful economic life of a fixed asset are caused by a number of factors, which are often referred to as the *causes of depreciation*. These include use of the asset (e.g. a motor vehicle), the passage of time (e.g. a lease) and obsolescence.

Factors involved in depreciation calculations

The amount of depreciation which should be shown in the profit and loss account for each accounting period in which a fixed asset is used may be calculated in various ways (see later in this chapter). But depreciation calculations cannot begin until the following factors have been determined:

(a) The *historic cost* of the asset.

(b) The *residual value* of the asset i.e. the amount of money (if any) for which the asset can be disposed of at the end of its useful life.

(c) The length of the *useful life* of the asset to the business. Note that the useful life of an asset to a particular business may not be the same as the physical life of that asset. For instance, if a business replaces its motor vehicles every three years, the useful life of a vehicle to the business is only three years long, whilst the vehicles may have a physical life extending to ten years or more.

The historic cost of a fixed asset is of course an objective fact, but its residual value and useful life can only be estimated. This means that depreciation calculations are always approximate.

It is important to appreciate that the residual value and useful life of a fixed asset are generally assessed on the assumption that the business is a going concern. This is permitted by the going concern convention unless there is evidence that the business might cease trading in the near future. If such evidence exists, the useful life of the fixed assets owned by the business will have to be revised downwards and the residual value of those assets will have to be set to whatever sum could be obtained if all of the assets owned by the business were sold off.

EXAMPLE

A business buys a motor van on hire-purchase terms. The details of this purchase are as follows:

	£
Basic cost of new motor van (including VAT)	13,500
Hydraulic loading platform fitted to rear of van	1,200
Delivery charge	250
One year's road fund licence	300
Full tank of diesel fuel	40
	15,290
Less: Part-exchange allowance on old van	4,200
	11,090
Less: Deposit paid	1,090
	10,000
Hire-purchase interest	2,000
Balance to pay	12,000

The balance of £12,000 is payable in 24 monthly instalments of £500. The business expects to use the van for four years and then to sell it for approximately £5,000.

Calculate the historic cost, useful life and residual value of the van for depreciation calculation purposes, assuming that the business cannot reclaim the VAT which is included in the purchase price of the van.

SOLUTION

The van has an expected useful life of four years and a residual value estimated at £5,000. Its historic cost is £13,500 + £1,200 + £250 = £14,950. The other costs (i.e. licence, fuel and interest) are revenue expenditure. The part-exchange allowance will be taken into account in the calculations made on the disposal of the old van (see later in this chapter).

4. DEPRECIATION METHODS

Having ascertained the historic cost, useful life and residual value of an asset, it is then possible to calculate the amount of depreciation which should be charged in each accounting period in which the asset is used. There are several different methods of calculating depreciation but only two are used to any great extent in practice. These are the *straight-line* method and the *reducing-balance* method, both of which are described below.

The straight-line method

The straight-line method allocates an equal amount of depreciation to each accounting period in which an asset is used (assuming that accounting periods are all of the same length). The amount of depreciation charged to the profit and loss account in each accounting period is given by the following formula:

$$\frac{(HC - RV)}{L}$$

where HC is the historic cost of the asset, RV is its estimated residual value and L is the estimated length of its useful life. The balance sheet at the end of each accounting period shows the historic cost of the asset less the accumulated amount of depreciation to date.

EXAMPLE

An item of equipment costs £5,000, has a useful life of five years and a residual value of £750. The item is to be depreciated on the straight-line basis. Calculate the amount of depreciation charged to the profit and loss account in each of the five years and show how the item will be represented in the balance sheet at the end of the second year.

SOLUTION

The amount of depreciation charged in each of the five years will be (£5,000 – £750)/5 = £850. Since £850 is equal to 17% of the cost of the equipment, this could be described as straight-line depreciation at an annual rate of 17%. At the end of two years, the item will be shown in the balance sheet as follows:

	£	£
Equipment, at cost	5,000	
Less: Accumulated depreciation to date	1,700	3,300

The terms "written down value" (WDV) and "net book value" (NBV) are often used to describe the part of an asset's cost which remains after deducting the depreciation to date. As usual, it is important to stress that this is not necessarily any indication of the market value of the asset.

The straight-line method gives logical results so long as the benefits derived from the ownership of an asset are spread fairly evenly over its useful life.

But even if this is not the case, many businesses adopt the straight-line method simply because it is easy to use.

The reducing-balance method

In the first accounting period in which a fixed asset is used, the reducing-balance method calculates depreciation by applying a percentage to the asset's cost. In subsequent accounting periods, the same percentage is applied to the asset's written down value at the end of the previous period. The relevant percentage is obtained from the following formula:

$$\left(1 - \sqrt[L]{\frac{RV}{HC}}\right) \times 100\%$$

EXAMPLE

A machine costs £8,000, has a useful life of four years and a residual value of £500. The machine is to be depreciated on the reducing-balance basis. Calculate the percentage which should be used in the depreciation calculations and calculate the amount of depreciation which will be charged to the profit and loss account in each of the four years.

SOLUTION

The percentage to be used in the depreciation calculations is 50% per annum, computed as follows:

$$\left(1 - \sqrt[4]{\frac{500}{8{,}000}}\right) \times 100\% = 50\%$$

The amount of depreciation charged to the profit and loss account in each of the four years is:

		£
Year 1	Cost of machine	8,000
	Depreciation at 50% of cost	4,000
	Written down value	4,000
Year 2	Depreciation at 50% of WDV	2,000
	Written down value	2,000
Year 3	Depreciation at 50% of WDV	1,000
	Written down value	1,000
Year 4	Depreciation at 50% of WDV	500
	Written down value	500

The reducing-balance method gives a high depreciation charge in the early part of an asset's life and a lower charge as the asset ages. Although this method is more complex than the straight-line method, it may be more appropriate in situations where the benefits derived from the use of an asset gradually diminish in the course of its useful life.

It is sometimes argued that the reducing-balance method may be appropriate even if the benefits derived from the use of an asset are spread evenly over the accounting periods in which it is used. The theory is that the total cost charged to the profit and loss account in relation to a fixed asset is the sum of depreciation and maintenance costs. For certain types of asset (e.g. machines) maintenance costs tend to increase as the asset gets older. In these circumstances, use of the reducing balance method of depreciation will ensure:

(a) high depreciation and low maintenance costs in early accounting periods

(b) low depreciation and high maintenance costs in later accounting periods.

In this way, the total costs charged to the profit and loss account in each accounting period will remain more or less constant, matching the constant level of benefits derived from the use of the asset.

5. REVALUATIONS

Fixed assets with infinite useful lives

Fixed assets with infinite useful lives (e.g. freehold land) are usually not depreciated, because there is no cost associated with their use. The historic cost convention requires such assets to be shown in the balance sheet at cost, but some businesses disregard this convention and revalue the assets concerned so that they are shown in the balance sheet at their market value. It can be argued that this accounting policy makes the balance sheet more relevant to its users. Two possible situations might arise:

(a) The market value of an asset may exceed its cost, in which case the asset has *appreciated*. If the asset is shown at market value in the balance sheet, the difference between cost and market value (an unrealised profit) is added to the owner's capital.

(b) The market value of an asset may be less than its cost. In this case, prudence usually overrides the historic cost convention. The asset is shown at market value in the balance sheet and the difference between cost and market value is shown as an expense in the profit and loss account.

Fixed assets with finite useful lives

Fixed assets with finite useful lives are depreciated as described earlier and the market value of such assets is irrelevant to this process. However, the market value of assets which are being depreciated may actually exceed cost in certain cases (e.g. in the early years of a lease at a time of rising property prices). In these circumstances, some businesses disregard the historic cost convention and revalue the assets concerned, showing them at market value in the balance sheet. Depreciation in subsequent accounting periods is then based on the amount of the revaluation rather than on historic cost. It can be argued that this accounting policy makes the balance sheet more relevant to its users and ensures that the depreciation charge shown in the profit and loss account more accurately reflects the real cost of using the asset.

Of course, the market value of an asset which is being depreciated may sometimes be *less* than its written down value. This fact could justifiably be ignored (so long as the estimates of the asset's useful life and residual value are unaffected) but the prudence convention may override the matching convention here and the asset might be revalued downwards. In this case, the difference between written down value and market value would be shown as an expense in the profit and loss account and depreciation in subsequent accounting periods would be based on the amount of the revaluation.

6. RECORDING DEPRECIATION IN LEDGER ACCOUNTS

The usual way of recording the acquisition of fixed assets and their depreciation in ledger accounts is as follows:

(a) When a fixed asset is acquired, its cost is debited to the appropriate fixed asset account (e.g. motor vehicles, plant and equipment, fixtures and fittings etc). If the asset is paid for immediately, a corresponding credit entry is made in the cash at bank account. If the asset is bought on credit terms, the credit entry is made in the supplier's account.

(b) At the end of each accounting period, the required amount of depreciation is calculated, debited to the profit and loss account and credited to a *provision for depreciation* account. There is usually one such account for each class of fixed asset (e.g. provision for depreciation of motor vehicles).

(c) The balance on each provision for depreciation account represents the accumulated depreciation to date for that class of fixed assets. This balance is deducted from the cost of the relevant class of fixed assets in the balance sheet.

A *provision* is an amount set aside out of the profits of a business to provide for an expense, the amount of which cannot be determined with substantial accuracy.

EXAMPLE

Hermione starts a business on 1 January 19X6 and decides to prepare accounts to 31 December each year. On 1 January 19X6 she buys fixed assets as follows, paying by cheque:

	Cost	*Estimated useful life*	*Estimated residual value*
	£		£
Motor vehicle	8,000	5 years	2,500
Equipment	9,766	4 years	4,000

The motor vehicle is to be depreciated using the straight-line method. The equipment is to be depreciated at 20% per annum on the reducing-balance basis (working to the nearest £). Show the relevant ledger accounts for the years to 31 December 19X6, 19X7 and 19X8. Also show how these fixed assets will appear in the balance sheet as at 31 December 19X8.

SOLUTION

Motor vehicles

		£			£
1.1.X6	Bank	8,000			

Equipment

		£			£
1.1.X6	Bank	9,766			

Provision for depreciation of motor vehicles

		£			£
31.12.X6	Balance c/d	1,100	31.12.X6	Profit and loss a/c	1,100
31.12.X7	Balance c/d	2,200	1.1.X7	Balance b/d	1,100
			31.12.X7	Profit and loss a/c	1,100
		2,200			2,200
31.12.X8	Balance c/d	3,300	1.1.X8	Balance b/d	2,200
			31.12.X8	Profit and loss a/c	1,100
		3,300			3,300
			1.1.X9	Balance b/d	3,300

Provision for depreciation of equipment

		£			£
31.12.X6	Balance c/d	1,953	31.12.X6	Profit and loss a/c	1,953
31.12.X7	Balance c/d	3,516	1.1.X7	Balance b/d	1,953
			31.12.X7	Profit and loss a/c	1,563
		3,516			3,516
31.12.X8	Balance c/d	4,766	1.1.X8	Balance b/d	3,516
			31.12.X8	Profit and loss a/c	1,250
		4,766			4,766
			1.1.X9	Balance b/d	4,766

Hermione
Balance sheet as at 31 December 19X8 (extract)

	£	£
Fixed assets		
Motor vehicles at cost	8,000	
Less: Accumulated depreciation to date	3,300	4,700
Equipment at cost	9,766	
Less: Accumulated depreciation to date	4,766	5,000
		9,700

Notes:

1. The motor vehicle's annual depreciation is (£8,000 – £2,500)/5 = £1,100. This is equivalent to a depreciation rate of 13.75% of the cost of the vehicle per annum.
2. In this example (as is often the case) the percentage to be used in the reducing-balance calculations was given. If the percentage had not been given it could have been calculated using the formula shown earlier in this chapter.
3. The equipment depreciation in 19X6 is 20% x £9,766 = £1,953. This leaves a written-down value of £9,766 – £1,953 = £7,813 so the depreciation in 19X7 is 20% x £7,813 = £1,563 (and so forth).
4. Strictly speaking, the fixed asset accounts should be balanced off at the end of each year and a balance carried down to the following year. These balances have been omitted from the solution for the sake of clarity.

7. FIXED ASSET DISPOSALS

When a fixed asset is disposed of, its cost must be removed from the relevant fixed asset account and its accumulated depreciation must be removed from the relevant provision for depreciation account. It is also necessary to compare the disposal proceeds of the asset (if any) with its written down value and to calculate any profit or loss arising on the disposal. The fact that depreciation calculations are always estimates means that the disposal proceeds of an asset will rarely equal its written down value. The required book-keeping entries are as follows:

(a) The fixed asset account is credited with the cost of the asset and this is debited to a fixed asset disposal account.

(b) The provision for depreciation account is debited with the asset's accumulated depreciation and this is credited to the fixed asset disposal account.

(c) The disposal proceeds are debited to the cash at bank account (assuming that the proceeds are paid into the bank) and credited to the fixed asset disposal account.

(d) The balance on the fixed asset disposal account represents the profit (a credit balance) or loss (a debit balance) on the disposal and this is transferred to the profit and loss account.

EXAMPLE

Continuing from the previous example, Hermione sold her motor vehicle for £4,350 on 1 January 19X9. Show how this disposal would be recorded in her ledger accounts.

SOLUTION

Motor vehicles

		£			£
1.1.X9	Balance b/d	8,000	1.1.X9	Disposal a/c	8,000

Provision for depreciation of motor vehicles

		£			£
1.1.X9	Disposal a/c	3,300	1.1.X9	Balance b/d	3,300

Disposal of motor vehicle

		£			£
1.1.X9	Motor vehicles	8,000	1.1.X9	Prov'n for dep'n	3,300
			1.1.X9	Bank	4,350
			31.12.X9	Profit and loss a/c	350
		8,000			8,000

Note:

The loss on disposal is £350. This represents under-depreciation in previous accounting periods and is charged as an expense to the profit and loss account of the period in which the disposal takes place.

Acquisitions and disposals during an accounting year

If a fixed asset is acquired or disposed of part-way through an accounting year, a partial depreciation charge may be calculated for the year in relation to the asset, based on the proportion of the year for which the asset is in use. However, for the sake of simplicity, many businesses adopt the policy of providing:

(a) a full year's depreciation in the year of acquisition (regardless of how early or late in the year the asset is acquired), and

(b) no depreciation at all in the year of disposal (regardless of how early or late in the year the asset is disposed of).

Partial depreciation charges should always be calculated in the year of acquisition or disposal, unless it is made clear that the business in question has adopted the simpler policy described above.

EXAMPLE

James owns his own business and prepares annual accounts to 30 June. On 1 July 19X7 he had the following balances in his ledger:

	£
Office equipment	35,200
Provision for depreciation of office equipment	12,140

On 31 December 19X7, James acquired new office equipment costing £11,500 and sold for £2,000 office equipment which he had originally acquired on 1 August 19X5 for £3,600. He uses the reducing-balance depreciation method at an annual rate of 25% (working to the nearest £). He provides a full year's depreciation in the year of acquisition and none in the year of disposal. Show the relevant ledger accounts for the year to 30 June 19X8.

SOLUTION

Office equipment

		£			£
1.7.X7	Balance b/d	35,200	31.12.X7	Disposal a/c	3,600
31.12.X7	Bank	11,500	30.6.X8	Balance c/d	43,100
		46,700			46,700
1.7.X8	Balance b/d	43,100			

Provision for depreciation of office equipment

		£			£
31.12.X7	Disposal a/c	1,575	1.7.X7	Balance b/d	12,140
30.6.X8	Balance c/d	18,699	30.6.X8	Profit and loss a/c	8,134
		20,274			20,274
			1.7.X8	Balance b/d	18,699

Disposal of office equipment

		£			£
31.12.X7	Office equipment	3,600	31.12.X7	Prov'n for dep'n	1,575
			31.12.X7	Bank	2,000
			30.6.X8	Profit and loss a/c	25
		3,600			3,600

Notes:

1. The equipment disposed of on 31 December 19X7 was acquired during the year to 30 June 19X6 and therefore must have been depreciated in the year to 30 June 19X6 (25% of £3,600 = £900, leaving a WDV of £2,700) and in the year to 30 June 19X7 (25% of £2,700 = £675). This gives accumulated depreciation of £900 + £675 = £1,575.

2. Before charging depreciation for the year to 30 June 19X8, the balance on the provision for depreciation account is £12,140 – £1,575 = £10,565. Therefore the depreciation charge for the year to 30 June 19X8 is 25% x (£43,100 – £10,565) = £8,134.
3. There is a loss on disposal of £25 which is shown as an expense in the profit and loss account.

8. SUMMARY

- The cost of a fixed asset includes the cost of acquiring the asset, bringing it to the required location and preparing it for use.
- The purpose of depreciation is to allocate the cost of a fixed asset to the accounting periods in which the asset is used. The causes of depreciation include use of the asset, the passage of time and obsolescence.
- Depreciation calculations are based on the historic cost of the asset, its residual value and the length of its useful life.
- The two most popular depreciation methods are the straight-line method (which allocates an equal amount of depreciation to each accounting period in which an asset is used) and the reducing-balance method (which gives a high depreciation charge in the early years of an asset's life and a lower charge in later years).
- Despite the historic cost convention, some businesses show certain fixed assets at a valuation rather than at historic cost. If a depreciating asset is revalued, depreciation is based subsequently on the amount of the revaluation rather than on cost.
- It is customary to record the accumulated depreciation for each class of fixed asset in a provision for depreciation account.
- The disposal of a fixed asset involves transferring the cost of the asset and its accumulated depreciation to a disposal account and calculating a profit or loss on the disposal.

EXERCISES 6

6.1 Explain the relationship between expenditure, assets and expenses.

6.2 "Providing for depreciation ensures that funds will be available to replace fixed assets when this becomes necessary". Do you agree with this statement?

6.3 A fixed asset costing £138,600 is acquired on 1 October 19X5. The asset has an estimated useful life of four years and an estimated residual value of £50,000.

(a) Calculate the amount of depreciation which should be charged to the profit and loss account in relation to this asset for each of the four years to 30 September 19X6, 19X7, 19X8 and 19X9, assuming that the straight-line method is to be used.

(b) Repeat your calculations, this time assuming that the asset is to be depreciated at 22.5% per annum, using the reducing-balance method and working to the nearest pound.

(c) In your opinion, which of these methods is preferable?

6.4 Katherine prepares accounts to 31 May each year. On 1 June 19X8 her ledger included the following balances:

	£
Motor vehicles (all less than 4 years old)	18,320
Provision for depreciation of motor vehicles	11,540

On 1 September 19X8, Katherine bought a new motor vehicle for £9,400, paying by cheque. On the same day, she sold for £3,350 a vehicle which she had bought originally on 1 December 19X5 for £7,200. Katherine depreciates her motor vehicles at a rate of 20% per annum using the straight-line method.

Required:

Show the relevant ledger accounts for the year to 31 May 19X9.

***6.5** A Premiership football club pays a £4 million transfer fee to acquire the services of a new player, who signs a five-year contract with the club. With reference to appropriate accounting conventions, explain how the new player might be dealt with in the club's financial statements.

***6.6** What does the fixed assets section of a balance sheet represent? Is the information both relevant and reliable?

***6.7** On 1 April 19X1, a business which prepares annual accounts to 31 March acquires freehold property for £100,000 . The cost of the property can be divided into land £30,000 and buildings £70,000. The business estimates that the buildings have a useful life of 50 years with a residual value of £nil and it is decided to depreciation the buildings (but not the land) using the straight-line method.

On 1 April 19X8, the property is revalued at £140,000, which can be divided into land £75,000 and buildings £65,000. It is decided to incorporate this revaluation into the accounts of the business. The estimates of the buildings' useful life and residual value remain unchanged.

Required:

Calculate the depreciation charge which should be shown in the profit and loss account for the years to 31 March 19X2 through to 19X9.

***6.8** Leonard's trial balance at 30 June 19X9 is as follows:

	£	£
Capital as at 1 July 19X8		26,444
Equipment at cost	42,100	
Provision for dep'n of equipment at 1 July 19X8		26,765
Disposal of equipment		2,000
Trade debtors and creditors	7,666	4,549
Cash at bank	1,875	
Stock as at 1 July 19X8	5,870	
Purchases	31,756	
Sales		79,220
Carriage inwards	680	
Carriage outwards	420	
Rent of business premises	6,500	
Heating and lighting	1,340	
Wages and salaries	37,500	
Sundry expenses	1,146	
Discounts allowed and received	2,450	325
	139,303	139,303

Further information:

1. The balance on the equipment at cost account consists of £34,600 brought forward from the previous year, plus new equipment bought for £7,500 on 1 May 19X9.
2. Equipment which cost £5,000 on 17 November 19X5 was sold for £2,000 on 11 April 19X9. The only entries made so far in relation to this disposal are to debit cash at bank and credit the disposal of equipment account with the sale proceeds of £2,000.
3. Equipment is depreciated at 30% per annum on the reducing-balance basis, with a full year's charge in the year of acquisition and none in the year of disposal.
4. The cost of Leonard's closing stock on 30 June 19X9 was £6,210.
5. The only accrued expense on 30 June 19X9 was heating and lighting £120.
6. Rent of £500 had been prepaid on 30 June 19X9.
7. Wages and salaries include Leonard's salary of £1,500 per month.

Required:

(a) Write up ledger accounts for equipment, provision for depreciation of equipment and disposal of equipment (no other ledger accounts are required).

(b) Prepare Leonard's trading and profit and loss account for the year to 30 June 19X9 and a balance sheet as at that date.

7

ACCOUNTING FOR CURRENT ASSETS

Chapter objectives

When you have finished this chapter, you should be able to:

- **Value closing stocks of goods for accounting purposes.**
- **Contrast the FIFO, LIFO and AVCO methods of stock valuation.**
- **Account correctly for bad debts written off and bad debts recovered.**
- **Calculate the amount of a provision for doubtful debts.**
- **Make the necessary entries to establish and maintain a provision for doubtful debts.**
- **Perform a bank reconciliation.**

1. INTRODUCTION

The previous chapter of this book was concerned with accounting problems relating to fixed assets. In this chapter we turn our attention to current assets and consider some problems relating to stocks, debtors and bank balances.

2. THE VALUATION OF CLOSING STOCK

At the end of an accounting period, most businesses own stocks of goods which will appear on the balance sheet as current assets. Stocks may include:

(a) in the case of a retailer or wholesaler, stocks of goods bought for resale

(b) in the case of a manufacturing business:
   - stocks of raw materials
   - stocks of part-finished goods (often referred to as *work in progress*)
   - stocks of finished goods

(c) stocks of consumables such as stationery, heating oil, fuel etc. (though these stocks may be ignored if the amounts involved are small, as permitted by the materiality convention).

As explained in Chapter 4, many businesses do not maintain stock records and therefore need to perform a physical stock-take at the end of each accounting period to determine the amount of closing stock. The closing stock figure has a direct effect on the profit of the accounting period and so it is very important that closing stocks should be counted and valued correctly.

The cost of closing stock

The historic cost convention suggests that stocks should be valued at their original cost to the business. For this purpose, "cost" is defined as all expenditure incurred so as to bring the stock to its present location and condition. The expenditure involved may comprise:

(a) **Cost of purchase**. This is the cost of acquiring the stock, including any VAT or other duties payable in connection with the stock and not reclaimable by the business. Also included is the cost of having the stock delivered from suppliers' premises (carriage inwards) plus any further freight costs incurred in moving the stock to its present location.

(b) **Cost of conversion**. This is the cost of any work done on the stock so as to bring it to its present condition. Conversion costs occur largely in relation to manufacturing businesses which buy raw materials and convert them into finished goods. Conversion costs may include:

- the wages of factory employees who have carried out the conversion work on the stock
- any other expenses which are incurred during conversion and which can be directly attributed to the closing stock (e.g. a royalty payable per unit of production to the inventor of a process used during manufacturing)
- a fair proportion of general production overheads (e.g. factory rent and rates, factory heat and light, the salaries of factory supervisors and managers etc).

The accounts of manufacturing businesses are dealt with in Chapter 8 of this book.

EXAMPLE

A business which manufactures only a single product produces 50,000 units of the product in a certain accounting year. Production costs incurred during the year are:

	£
Purchase of raw materials	761,000
Wages of factory employees	500,000
Royalties payable (£2 per unit produced)	100,000
Factory rent and rates	104,000
Factory heating and lighting	57,500
Salaries of factory supervisors	53,200
Repairs to factory machines	17,600
Depreciation of factory machines	84,700

The opening and closing stocks of raw materials cost £42,000 and £53,000 respectively. At the end of the year, the business has 4,000 units of the product in stock and no work in progress. Calculate the cost of this stock of finished goods.

SOLUTION

The total cost of manufacturing 50,000 units is as follows:

	£	£
Raw materials:		
Opening stock	42,000	
Purchases	761,000	
	803,000	
Closing stock	53,000	750,000
Factory wages		500,000
Royalties		100,000
Factory overheads:		
Rent and rates	104,000	
Heating and lighting	57,500	
Supervisor salaries	53,200	
Machine repairs	17,600	
Machine depreciation	84,700	317,000
		1,667,000

Therefore the cost of the 4,000 units in stock at the end of the accounting year is 4,000/50,000 x £1,667,000 = £133,360.

Net realisable value

Although the historic cost convention requires closing stock to be valued at cost, this is overridden by the prudence convention, which requires closing stock to be valued at *the lower of cost and net realisable value.* Net realisable value (NRV) is defined as the selling price of the stock, less any costs which would have to be incurred in order to prepare the stock for sale, less any anticipated selling expenses. In other words, if the expected net sale proceeds of the stock are less than its cost, this loss should be accounted for immediately by valuing the stock at NRV. This view is supported by Statement of Standard Accounting Practice 9 (see Chapter 15).

The going concern convention allows NRV to be calculated on the assumption that the stock will be sold in the normal course of business, unless there is evidence that the business may soon cease trading. If the business is not a going concern, stock may have to be sold off in a forced sale of bankrupt stock and this will result in a much lower NRV figure.

Ideally, the cost and NRV of each stock item should be calculated individually and the lower figure taken in each case. If this would be too time-consuming or difficult, it is permissible to compare cost and NRV for groups of stock items.

EXAMPLE

Mark buys and sells second-hand motor cars. At the end of his accounting year, he has the following cars in stock:

	Cost	*Selling price*		*Cost*	*Selling price*
	£	£		£	£
Car 1	6,200	8,000	Car 4	11,700	11,000
Car 2	8,300	10,000	Car 5	5,900	7,000
Car 3	5,400	7,000	Car 6	8,900	9,000

Mark pays a 2% commission to his sales staff when they sell a car. Calculate the figure at which Mark's closing stock should be shown in his balance sheet.

SOLUTION

	Cost	*Selling price*	*NRV*	*Lower of cost and NRV*
	£	£	£	£
Car 1	6,200	8,000	7,840	6,200
Car 2	8,300	10,000	9,800	8,300
Car 3	5,400	7,000	6,860	5,400
Car 4	11,700	11,000	10,780	10,780
Car 5	5,900	7,000	6,860	5,900
Car 6	8,900	9,000	8,820	8,820
	46,400	52,000	50,960	45,400

The closing stock should be valued at £45,400. This is lower than the figure of £46,400 which would have been used if total cost had been compared with total NRV.

3. STOCKS WHICH ARE NOT UNIQUELY IDENTIFIABLE

We have assumed so far that it is possible to uniquely identify each stock item held at the end of an accounting period and to ascertain the cost of each item without difficulty. But this is not always the case, as illustrated below.

EXAMPLE

A business buys oil in bulk and stores it in a tank. On 1 January the tank contained 14,000 litres of oil which had cost the business 50 pence per litre. During January, the following purchases of oil were made:

	No of litres	*Cost per litre (pence)*
3 January	10,000	52
11 January	12,000	54
19 January	23,000	55
27 January	7,000	57

Sales of oil during the month consisted of 20,000 litres sold on 8 January, 10,000 litres sold on 15 January and 25,000 litres sold on 25 January. How many litres of oil were left in the tank on 31 January and what was the cost of this stock of oil?

SOLUTION

The opening stock of oil was 14,000 litres. Purchases totalled 52,000 litres and sales totalled 55,000 litres. Therefore the closing stock was 11,000 litres (14,000 + 52,000 – 55,000). However, it is not possible to state with any certainty *which* 11,000 litres were left in stock. And since the oil was purchased at various prices, it is also not possible to be certain about the cost of the closing stock.

In the above example, it is likely that the oil has all mixed together in the tank and that the closing stock is in fact a mixture of stock purchased at various times and at different prices. If the stock were of some other material (e.g. coal, gravel, wheat etc.) and were held in some other container (e.g. a bunker or silo) it might be more likely that the closing stock consisted of the newest stock or perhaps the oldest stock, depending upon the physical characteristics of the stock itself and its container. In practice, however, it is usual to neglect physical characteristics in situations like these and to use a standard stock valuation method for determining:

(a) the cost of any stock sold or used during an accounting period, and
(b) the cost of the closing stock held at the end of the accounting period.

The three most commonly used stock valuation methods are known as First In First Out (FIFO), Last In First Out (LIFO) and Weighted Average Cost (AVCO) respectively. Each of these is described below.

First In First Out (FIFO)

The FIFO stock valuation method assumes that stock is sold or used in the same order as that in which it is acquired. In other words, it is assumed that older stock is sold or used before newer stock. Applying this approach to the above example gives the following results:

	No of litres			*Cost (£)*
Sold 8 January	20,000	14,000 @ 50p	7,000	
		6,000 @ 52p	3,120	10,120
Sold 15 January	10,000	4,000 @ 52p	2,080	
		6,000 @ 54p	3,240	5,320
Sold 25 January	25,000	6,000 @ 54p	3,240	
		19,000 @ 55p	10,450	13,690
Cost of goods sold				29,130
Stock 31 January	11,000	4,000 @ 55p	2,200	
		7,000 @ 57p	3,990	6,190

Last In First Out (LIFO)

The LIFO stock valuation method assumes that stock is sold or used in the opposite order to that in which it is acquired. In other words, it is assumed that newer stock is sold or used before older stock. Applying this approach to the above example gives the following results:

	No of litres			Cost (£)
Sold 8 January	20,000	10,000 @ 52p	5,200	
		10,000 @ 50p	5,000	10,200
Sold 15 January	10,000	10,000 @ 54p		5,400
Sold 25 January	25,000	23,000 @ 55p	12,650	
		2,000 @ 54p	1,080	13,730
Cost of goods sold				29,330
Stock 31 January	11,000	7,000 @ 57p	3,990	
		4,000 @ 50p	2,000	5,990

Weighted Average Cost (AVCO)

The AVCO stock valuation method involves computing the weighted average cost of the stock held after each stock acquisition takes place. Any stock sold or used is then costed at this weighted average figure until another acquisition takes place, when a new weighted average cost is computed. Closing stock is valued at the weighted average cost in force on the last day of the accounting period. Applying this approach to the above example gives the following results:

	No of litres		Total cost (£)	Weighted average cost	Cost of stock sold (£)
Opening stock	14,000	@ 50p	7,000		
Bought 3 January	10,000	@ 52p	5,200		
	24,000		12,200	50.83p	
Sold 8 January	20,000	@ 50.83p	10,167		10,167
Balance 8 January	4,000		2,033		
Bought 11 January	12,000	@ 54p	6,480		
	16,000		8,513	53.21p	
Sold 15 January	10,000	@ 53.21p	5,321		5,321
Balance 15 January	6,000		3,192		
Bought 19 January	23,000	@ 55p	12,650		
	29,000		15,842	54.63p	
Sold 25 January	25,000	@ 54.63p	13,657		13,657
Cost of goods sold					29,145
Balance 25 January	4,000		2,185		
Bought 27 January	7,000	@ 57p	3,990		
Stock 31 January	11,000		6,175	56.14p	

Comparison of FIFO, LIFO and AVCO

The results of the above example enable us to draw a number of conclusions about the relative merits of FIFO, LIFO and AVCO:

(a) FIFO results in the highest closing stock figure (£6,190) and the lowest figure for cost of goods sold (£29,130). This will always occur at a time of rising prices and leads to the criticism that the use of FIFO is not prudent. On the other hand, the value of closing stock is calculated at the most recent prices available and it can be argued that this makes the balance sheet more relevant to users.

(b) LIFO results in the lowest closing stock figure (£5,990) and the highest figure for cost of goods sold (£29,330). Again, this will always occur at a time of rising prices and suggests that the use of LIFO is a prudent approach to stock valuation. However, the closing stock figure is calculated at outdated prices and this might make the balance sheet less relevant than users would wish. It is worth noting that the use of LIFO is not acceptable for UK taxation purposes. Nor is it approved by Statement of Standard Accounting Practice 9 (see Chapter 15).

(c) AVCO produces figures which fall in between those produced by FIFO and LIFO (closing stock £6,175, cost of goods sold £29,145). This may seem to be a good compromise but the method does involve a great deal of extra calculation. It might also be suggested that stock should be valued at one of the prices actually paid for the stock, rather than at an artificial average price.

In the long run, the choice of stock valuation method has no effect on the calculation of the total profits earned by a business during its entire lifespan. However, the choice of method *does* affect the distribution of profits between accounting periods. For this reason, it is important to choose an appropriate method and then to use it consistently unless there is very good reason to change. Changing the stock valuation method for no good reason makes it very difficult to compare the results of one accounting period with another and constitutes a breach of the consistency convention.

4. BAD DEBTS

The next current asset which gives rise to special accounting problems is the asset known as "debtors" or "trade debtors" and the main problem which arises is that of dealing with bad debts. When a business sells goods or services to customers on credit terms, it is almost inevitable that bad debts will arise from time to time (i.e. that customers will fail to pay their debts). The accounting consequences of a bad debt are as follows:

(a) The debt can no longer be regarded as an asset and must be removed from the balance sheet. In other words, the debt must be "written off".

(b) The amount of money lost as a result of the bad debt is an expense which, like all other expenses, must be shown in the profit and loss account.

It is normal to open a ledger account called "Bad debts" to record all the debts written off in the course of an accounting period. The required book-keeping entries are as follows:

(a) When a debt is written off, the bad debts account is debited (an expense has increased) and the customer's account is credited (an asset has decreased) with the amount being written off.

(b) At the end of each accounting period, the balance on the bad debts account is transferred to the profit and loss account in the usual way.

Note that these entries do *not* attempt to reverse the entries made when the goods or services were originally sold to the customer. The sale did take place and it would be wrong to obliterate it from the books simply because the customer fails to pay. The correct approach is to recognise sales revenue when a sale occurs (the realisation convention) and then to match this revenue against all expenses incurred so as to achieve the sale, including bad debts (the matching convention).

EXAMPLE

Nancy owns her own business, preparing accounts to 31 December each year. During the year to 31 December 19X8, her transactions included the following credit sales:

		£
12 March 19X8	S Coombes	500
23 July 19X8	A McKinlay	1,200

S Coombes paid £200 on account on 30 April 19X8 but failed to make any further payment. A McKinlay made no payment at all. After several unsuccessful attempts to recover these debts, Nancy has decided to write them off. Make the necessary entries in her ledger accounts.

SOLUTION

S Coombes

		£			£
12.3.X8	Sales	500	30.4.X8	Bank	200
			31.12.X8	Bad debts	300
		500			500

A McKinlay

		£			£
23.7.X8	Sales	1,200	31.12.X8	Bad debts	1,200

Bad debts

		£			£
31.12.X8	S Coombes	300	31.12.X8	Profit and loss a/c	1,500
31.12.X8	A McKinlay	1,200			
		1,500			1,500

Bad debts recovered

If a debt which has been written off as bad is subsequently recovered (in whole or in part), the amount recovered is recorded in a revenue account known as "Bad debts recovered". The required book-keeping entries are as follows:

(a) The appropriate customer's account is debited and the bad debts recovered account is credited with the amount which is now recoverable. This reinstates the debtor as an asset and records the recoverable amount as revenue.

(b) The money actually received from the customer is dealt with in the usual way i.e. the bank account is debited and the customer's account is credited.

EXAMPLE

During the year to 31 December 19X9, Nancy (see above) discovers that A McKinlay has been made bankrupt and that his affairs are in the hands of a receiver. On 23 May 19X9, Nancy receives £480 from the receiver in final settlement of the £1,200 owed to her by A McKinlay. Make the necessary entries in her ledger accounts.

SOLUTION

A McKinlay

		£			£
23.7.X8	Sales	1,200	31.12.X8	Bad debts	1,200
23.5.X9	Bad debts recovered	480	23.5.X9	Bank	480

Bad debts recovered

		£			£
31.12.X9	Profit and loss a/c	480	23.5.X9	A McKinlay	480

5. PROVISIONS FOR DOUBTFUL DEBTS

The matching convention requires that expenses should be shown in the same profit and loss account as the revenue to which they relate. However, it can be difficult to adhere to this convention in the case of bad debts. There may be insufficient evidence to write off a debt at the end of the accounting period in which the corresponding sale occurs but the debt may then be written off in a future period, so breaching the convention. This problem cannot be resolved completely, but a step in the right direction is to make a *provision for doubtful debts* at the end of each accounting period.

The idea is to estimate the amount of potentially bad debts existing at the balance sheet date and to set up a provision equal to this amount. (As explained in Chapter 6, a provision is an amount set aside out of profits so as to provide for an expense, the amount of which cannot be determined with substantial accuracy). The doubtful debts are *not* written off and they remain as part of the debtors figure, but the provision for doubtful debts is shown as a deduction from total debtors on the face of the balance sheet. As well as attempting to satisfy the matching convention, the establishment of a provision for doubtful debts is also in line with the prudence convention, making it less likely that debtors will be overstated. There are two ways of calculating the amount of a provision for doubtful debts:

(a) **Specific provisions.** A specific provision for doubtful debts is calculated by working through the list of debtors one by one and totalling those debtors which appear to be doubtful.

(b) **General provisions.** A general provision for doubtful debts is calculated by simply applying a percentage (based on experience) to the total debtors figure. A variation on this method is to classify debts by age and then to apply a different percentage to each age group, as illustrated below:

Age of debt	*Total amount of debtors*	*Percentage provision*	*Amount of provision*
	£	%	£
Up to 1 month	24,600	1	246
Over 1 month and up to 2 months	11,500	2	230
Over 2 months and up to 3 months	4,200	5	210
Over 3 months	1,500	10	150
General provision for doubtful debts			836

Accounting for a provision for doubtful debts

The book-keeping entries required in order to establish and maintain a provision for doubtful debts (whether specific or general) are as follows:

(a) When a provision for doubtful debts is first established, the amount of the provision is debited to profit and loss account and credited to the provision for doubtful debts account. The balance on this account is shown as a deduction from debtors in the balance sheet.

(b) In each subsequent accounting period, the amount of the required provision is calculated (as described above) and is then compared with the amount of the provision at the end of the previous period. If the provision now required is greater than before, the increase is debited to profit and loss account and credited to the provision account. If the provision now required is less than before, the decrease is credited to profit and loss account and debited to the provision account.

EXAMPLE

Owen prepares accounts to 30 June each year. He has never provided for doubtful debts before, but on 30 June 19X7 he decides to establish a provision of £750. On 30 June 19X8 he decides that the provision should be £820 and on 30 June 19X9 he calculates the provision as £795. Show the required book-keeping entries.

SOLUTION

Provision for doubtful debts

		£			£
30.6.X7	Balance c/d	750	30.6.X7	Profit and loss a/c	750
30.6.X8	Balance c/d	820	1.7.X7	Balance b/d	750
			30.6.X8	Profit and loss a/c	70
		820			820
30.6.X9	Profit and loss a/c	25	1.7.X8	Balance b/d	820
30.6.X9	Balance c/d	795			
		820			820
			1.7.X9	Balance b/d	795

Notes:

1. The profit and loss account shows an expense of £750 in the year to 30 June 19X7 and an expense of £70 in the year to 30 June 19X8. The £25 reduction in the provision made in the year to 30 June 19X9 is shown as revenue in the profit and loss account for that year.
2. The original provision of £750 is shown as a deduction from debtors in the balance sheet as at 30 June 19X7. Similarly, the provision of £820 is shown in the balance sheet as at 30 June 19X8 and the provision of £795 is shown in the balance sheet as at 30 June 19X9.

A common mistake is to debit profit and loss account with the full amount of the required provision in a second or subsequent year, rather than showing only the increase or decrease in the provision. In the above example, the profit and loss account for the year to 30 June 19X8 might mistakenly be debited with £820 rather than £70. The argument for the profit and loss account showing only the increase or decrease in the provision is as follows:

(a) By now, the doubtful debts included in the previous year's provision will either have been received or written off. In either case, the previous year's provision is no longer required.

(b) Therefore we need to remove or "write back" the previous year's provision and to establish the current year's provision instead.

(c) We could remove the previous year's provision by debiting the provision account and crediting profit and loss account with the full amount of the old provision. We could then establish the current year's provision by debiting profit and loss account and crediting the provision account with the full amount of the new provision. Exactly the same effect is achieved much more simply by either debiting (or crediting) profit and loss account with the increase (or decrease) in the provision.

EXAMPLE

Pauline prepares accounts to 30 September each year. On 30 September 19X7, she decides to establish a provision for doubtful debts equal to 1% of debtors and to maintain the provision at 1% of debtors in future accounting years. Her debtors and bad debts can be summarised as follows:

	Debtors at year-end (before writing off bad debts)	*Bad debts to be written off*
	£	£
30 September 19X7	22,400	1,300
30 September 19X8	21,700	800
30 September 19X9	25,900	2,100

Make the necessary book-keeping entries to record Pauline's bad debts and her provision for doubtful debts. Also, show relevant extracts from the profit and loss accounts for the years to 30 September 19X7, 19X8 and 19X9 and the balance sheets as at those dates.

SOLUTION

Bad debts

		£			£
30.9.X7	Sundry debtors	1,300	30.9.X7	Profit and loss a/c	1,300
30.9.X8	Sundry debtors	800	30.9.X8	Profit and loss a/c	800
30.9.X9	Sundry debtors	2,100	30.9.X9	Profit and loss a/c	2,100

Provision for doubtful debts

		£			£
30.9.X7	Balance c/d	211	30.9.X7	Profit and loss a/c	211
30.9.X8	Profit and loss a/c	2	1.10.X7	Balance b/d	211
30.9.X8	Balance c/d	209			
		211			211
30.9.X9	Balance c/d	238	1.10.X8	Balance b/d	209
			30.9.X9	Profit and loss a/c	29
		238			238
			1.10.X9	Balance b/d	238

Pauline
Profit and loss a/cs for the years to 30 September (extracts)

	£
19X7	
Bad debts written off	1,300
Provision for doubtful debts	211
19X8	
Bad debts written off	800
Decrease in provision for doubtful debts	(2)
19X9	
Bad debts written off	2,100
Increase in provision for doubtful debts	29

Pauline
Balance sheets as at 30 September (extracts)

	£	£
19X7		
Current assets		
Trade debtors	21,100	
Less: Provision for doubtful debts	211	20,889
19X8		
Current assets		
Trade debtors	20,900	
Less: Provision for doubtful debts	209	20,691
19X9		
Current assets		
Trade debtors	23,800	
Less: Provision for doubtful debts	238	23,562

Notes:

1. The provision for doubtful debts is calculated at 1% of the debtors remaining after bad debts have been written off.
2. The provision at 30 September 19X7 is 1% of (£22,400 – £1,300) = £211.
3. The provision at 30 September 19X8 is 1% of (£21,700 – £800) = £209.
4. The provision at 30 September 19X9 is 1% of (£25,900 – £2,100) = £238.

6. BANK RECONCILIATIONS

Virtually every business has a bank account. The balance on this account will be either a current asset (cash at bank) or a current liability (bank overdraft). From time to time the bank will send the business a *bank statement*, listing the transactions which have passed through the account since the previous statement and showing the account balance at the statement date.

A bank statement provides valuable external evidence of bank transactions and therefore it is important that the account balance shown in the statement should be reconciled with the balance shown in the books of the business. In practice, these two balances will rarely agree. Discrepancies will arise for the following reasons:

(a) The bank account in the books of the business may contain errors, which must be corrected.

(b) The bank statement may contain errors. These are fairly unlikely but the bank must be notified if such errors have occurred.

(c) The bank statement may show items which have not yet been recorded in the books of the business. These items could include:

- bank charges and interest (which are not usually known about until a statement arrives)
- payments made out of the account by direct debit or standing order
- amounts paid into the account by credit transfer (e.g. when a customer pays a debt by transferring money from his or her own bank account directly into the business bank account)
- dishonoured cheques (i.e. cheques which have been paid into the business bank account but which have then "bounced").

These items should be recorded in the bank account and an updated balance on that account should then be calculated.

(d) The bank account in the books of the business may show items which do not yet appear on the bank statement. These items could include:

- unpresented cheques (i.e. cheques which have been recorded in the books of the business and sent to their recipients but which have not yet been paid into the recipients' bank accounts)
- outstanding lodgements (i.e. amounts paid into the bank account just before the statement date and which are still passing through the bank's accounting system).

These timing differences require no adjustments in the books of the business but must be taken into account when performing a bank reconciliation.

EXAMPLE

The bank account of a business for the month of March 19X9 is shown below. Cheque numbers are recorded on the credit side of the account for identification purposes. The account has been totalled on both sides but a balance has not yet been calculated.

Bank

19X9 March		£	19X9 March		Cheque Number	£
1	Balance b/d	232.65	2	Wages	212	759.33
5	Sales	379.67	3	J Fox	213	1,220.76
8	B McDougal	1,212.98	5	Heat and light	214	295.67
9	C Sharpe	724.69	7	P Lowe	215	1,000.00
12	F Smith Ltd	3,665.00	9	Wages	216	758.27
19	Sales	222.99	16	Wages	217	772.89
29	T Walker Ltd	900.00	18	Cash	218	100.00
31	R Blake	341.49	23	Wages	219	773.43
			29	V Moore	220	1,100.00
			31	Wages	221	781.65
		7,679.47				7,562.00

The bank statement for March 19X9, which was received by the business in early April, is shown below. Write up the bank account as necessary and then prepare a bank reconciliation as at 31 March 19X9.

Statement of account

19X9		Debit	Credit	Balance
Mar 1	Balance brought forward			232.65 C
Mar 3	Cheque 212	759.33		526.68 D
Mar 6	Sundry credits		379.67	147.01 D
Mar 9	Cheque 214	295.67		442.68 D
Mar 10	Cheque 216	758.27		1,200.95 D
Mar 10	Cheque 213	1,220.76		2,421.71 D
Mar 10	Sundry credits		1,937.67	484.04 D
Mar 13	Sundry credits		3,665.00	3,180.96 C
Mar 17	Cheque 217	772.89		2,408.07 C
Mar 19	Cheque 218	100.00		2,308.07 C
Mar 20	Sundry credits		222.99	2,531.06 C
Mar 22	Credit transfer (B Davis)		213.76	2,744.82 C
Mar 24	Cheque 219	773.43		1,971.39 C
Mar 25	Direct debit (Gas Board)	150.00		1,821.39 C
Mar 30	Dishonoured cheque	1,212.98		608.41 C
Mar 31	Charges	33.75		574.66 C

Abbreviations: D = Debit C = Credit

SOLUTION

Bank

		£			£
31 March	Total b/f	7,679.47	31 March	Total b/f	7,562.00
	B Davis	213.76		Heat and light	150.00
	Balance c/d	1,065.50		B McDougal	1,212.98
				Bank charges	33.75
		8,958.73			8,958.73
			1 April	Balance b/d	1,065.50

Bank reconciliation as at 31 March 19X9

	£	£
Favourable balance, per bank statement		574.66
Add: Outstanding lodgements:		
T Walker Ltd	900.00	
R Blake	341.49	1,241.49
		1,816.15
Less: Unpresented cheques:		
Cheque 215 P Lowe	1,000.00	
Cheque 220 V Moore	1,100.00	
Cheque 221 Wages	781.65	2,881.65
Overdrawn balance, per bank account		1,065.50

Notes:

1. The bank statement is drawn up from the bank's point of view, not from the point of view of the business. Money paid into the account increases the bank's liability to the business and is therefore shown as a credit on the bank statement. Money taken out of the account reduces the bank's liability to the business and is therefore shown as a debit on the bank statement.
2. The amount of £1,937.67 shown on the bank statement as paid in on 10 March consists of the £1,212.98 received from B McDougal and the £724.69 received from C Sharpe. Presumably these two sums were paid into the bank on the same day.
3. The dishonoured cheque appears to be the cheque received earlier in the month from B McDougal.

7. SUMMARY

- The cost of closing stock is defined as all expenditure incurred so as to bring the stock to its present location and condition.
- Closing stock should be valued at the lower of cost and net realisable value.

- If stock items cannot be uniquely identified, it is normal to use a standard stock valuation method to determine the cost of closing stock. Methods in common use include FIFO, LIFO and AVCO, but LIFO is not acceptable for UK taxation purposes and is not approved by SSAP9.
- Bad debts must be written off to the profit and loss account. Debts which are written off and then subsequently recovered are shown as a revenue item in the profit and loss account.
- Doubtful debts may be provided for at the end of an accounting period. Such debts are not written off and they remain as part of the debtors figure, but the provision for doubtful debts is shown as a deduction from total debtors on the face of the balance sheet. A provision may be either specific or general.
- The bank balance shown in the books of a business will usually disagree with the balance shown by a bank statement. The discrepancy is often caused by timing differences but it is important to perform a bank reconciliation in case it reveals items which need to be entered in the books. The reconciliation might also reveal errors, either in the books or in the bank statement.

EXERCISES 7

7.1 A dealer in second-hand lorries has the following vehicles in stock on 31 December 19X9:

	Cost	*Expected cost of preparing the lorry for sale*	*Expected selling price*
	£	£	£
Lorry A	12,500	420	15,000
Lorry B	15,700	870	18,000
Lorry C	22,800	1,120	21,000
Lorry D	19,600	950	22,000

The dealer sells the lorries at auction and pays a 5% commission to the firm of auctioneers when a lorry is sold.

Required:

Calculate the value at which the above vehicles should be shown in the balance sheet as at 31 December 19X9.

7.2 A business buys and sells sand. On 1 April 19X8, the stock of sand was 1,200 tons, which had cost £8 per ton. During the month of April, the following purchases and sales were made:

3 April	Bought 500 tons at £8.50 per ton
10 April	Sold 900 tons
14 April	Bought 400 tons at £8.30 per ton
18 April	Bought 600 tons at £8.10 per ton
23 April	Sold 1,100 tons

Required:

Calculate the cost of the sand in stock on 30 April 19X8 using each of the following stock valuation methods:

(a) FIFO (b) LIFO (c) AVCO.

7.3 Ronald's provision for doubtful debts on 1 July 19X7 was £153. During the years to 30 June 19X8 and 19X9 he wrote off the following bad debts:

		£
21 November 19X7	P Gardiner	75
18 May 19X8	B Williams	102
29 October 19X8	F Scott	43
12 May 19X9	L Turner	66

After writing off these debts, Ronald's debtors at 30 June 19X8 and 19X9 were £7,950 and £7,300 respectively. It is Ronald's policy to maintain a general provision for doubtful debts equal to 2% of debtors.

Required:

Make the necessary book-keeping entries to record Ronald's bad debts and his provision for doubtful debts. Also, show relevant extracts from the profit and loss accounts for the years to 30 June 19X8 and 19X9 and the balance sheets as at those dates.

7.4 On 31 May 19X9, Susan's bank account shows an overdraft of £3,229. The bank statement dated 31 May 19X9 shows an overdraft of £1,351. Comparison of Susan's ledger and the bank statement reveals the following discrepancies:

(a) Unpresented cheques amount to £2,820.

(b) Outstanding lodgements amount to £450.

(c) Bank charges of £37 were made on 31 May 19X9. These charges have not been entered in Susan's ledger.

(d) A cheque for £500 received from J Giles and paid into the bank account was not honoured. The bank has debited Susan's account with the amount of the cheque.

(e) A cheque for £327 paid to P Jarvis was shown incorrectly as £372 in Susan's ledger.

Required:

Write up Susan's bank account as necessary and then prepare a bank reconciliation as at 31 May 19X9.

***7.5** A profit and loss account is usually drawn up in accordance with a number of accounting conventions. Identify the main conventions which have an effect on the profit and loss account and explain the likely effect of each convention on the reliability of the profit figure.

***7.6** Stock is generally valued at the lower of cost and net realisable value. Is this policy in accord with all of the commonly accepted accounting conventions?

***7.7** The bank account of P Watkinson & Co Ltd for the month of October 19X9 appears in the firm's ledger as follows:

Bank

19X9		£	19X9		Cheque Number	£
October			October			
3	Sales	483.42	1	Balance b/d		505.03
5	Sales	229.03	2	Petrol	314	37.20
9	D Reeves	2,887.77	4	Business rates	315	2,750.00
11	G Cotton	452.60	5	Bank charges (Sept)		12.50
14	P Jones Ltd	1,250.00	8	K Green	316	428.56
19	Sales	745.99	11	D Rivers	317	1,956.47
28	W Johnson	2,000.00	17	Cash	318	500.00
30	M Keane	110.78	22	S Stevens	319	280.00
			24	T Waugh	320	450.65
			30	Stationery	321	78.12
			31	Salaries	322	956.49
			31	Balance c/d		204.57
		8,159.59				8,159.59
November						
1	Balance b/d	204.57				

The bank statement for October 19X9, which was received on 5 November 19X9, is shown below.

Statement of account

19X9		Debit	Credit	Balance
Oct 1	Balance brought forward			579.23 C
Oct 1	Sundry credits		123.24	702.47 C
Oct 3	Cheque 312	1,000.00		297.53 D
Oct 6	Sundry credits		712.45	414.92 C
Oct 6	Cheque 315	2,750.00		2,335.08 D
Oct 7	Cheque 314	37.20		2,372.28 D
Oct 10	Direct Debit (B Telecom)	550.00		2,922.28 D
Oct 11	Cheque 316	428.56		3,350.84 D
Oct 12	Credit Transfer (L Thomas)		120.67	3,230.17 D
Oct 12	Sundry credits		3,340.37	110.20 C
Oct 15	Cheque 311	200.00		89.80 D
Oct 16	Sundry credits		1,250.00	1,160.20 C
Oct 18	Cheque 318	500.00		660.20 C
Oct 22	Sundry credit		745.99	1,406.19 C
Oct 23	Dishonoured cheque	452.60		953.59 C
Oct 26	Cheque 319	280.00		673.59 C
Oct 31	Bank charges	88.70		584.89 C

Abbreviations: D = Debit C = Credit

Required:

Write up the bank account as necessary and then prepare a bank reconciliation as at 31 October 19X9. Suggest reasons for any unexplained discrepancy between the bank account and the bank statement. (It may be helpful to begin by trying to reconcile the opening balances as at 1 October).

***7.8** Timothy's trial balance at 30 September 19X9 is as follows:

	£	£
Capital as at 1 October 19X8		89,840
Vans at cost	45,600	
Provision for dep'n of vans at 1 October 19X8		15,750
Trade debtors and creditors	57,540	62,650
Bank overdraft		9,540
Stock as at 1 October 19X8	35,780	
Purchases and sales	295,320	479,740
Returns inwards and outwards	14,650	12,480
Carriage inwards	3,510	
Carriage outwards	24,540	
Rent, rates and insurances	23,750	
Heating and lighting	11,830	
Wages and salaries	95,600	
Repairs and renewals	3,570	
Sundry expenses	7,690	
Discounts allowed and received	14,590	1,420
Bad debts written off	7,650	
Provision for doubtful debts at 1 October 19X8		2,320
Drawings	32,120	
	673,740	673,740

Further information:

1. The balance on the vans account comprises £29,600 brought forward from the previous year, plus £16,000 relating to the purchase of a new van on 1 January 19X9. The new van cost £21,000, less a part-exchange allowance of £5,000 in respect of a van which had been bought for £13,200 on 1 August 19X5.
2. Motor vans are depreciated at 20% per annum on the straight-line basis. All of the vans owned by Timothy on 1 October 19X8 were less than four years old on that date.
3. The cost of Timothy's closing stock on 30 September 19X9 was £45,760.
4. Rent of business premises costs £1,300 per month and is paid quarterly in advance on 1 March, 1 June, 1 September and 1 December each year. An insurance premium of £2,400 covering the year to 31 December 19X9 was paid on 2 January 19X9.
5. Accrued heating and lighting expenses are estimated to be £1,600.
6. Repairs and renewals include £2,300 for some building work carried out on Timothy's own home.
7. Sundry expenses include telephone charges. An £820 telephone bill was received on 7 October 19X9, consisting of £270 line rental for the three months to 31 December 19X9 and £550 for calls made during the three months to 30 September 19X9.
8. It has been decided to write off bad debts of £2,390 (in addition to those already written off during the year) and to set the provision for doubtful debts at 4% of the remaining debtors.

9. During the year to 30 September 19X9, Timothy took stock from the business for his private use. This stock cost £750 and had a selling price of £1,150. No entries were made in the books when Timothy took this stock.

Required:

(a) Write up ledger accounts for motor vans, provision for depreciation of vans, disposal of vans, bad debts and provision for doubtful debts (no other ledger accounts are required).

(b) Prepare Timothy's trading and profit and loss account for the year to 30 September 19X9 and a balance sheet as at that date.

8

MANUFACTURING ACCOUNTS

Chapter objectives

When you have finished this chapter, you should be able to:

- **Distinguish between direct and indirect costs of manufacture.**
- **Prepare a manufacturing account.**
- **Calculate the amount of a provision for unrealised profit.**
- **Make the necessary entries to establish and maintain a provision for unrealised profit.**

1. INTRODUCTION

Most of the businesses dealt with so far in this book have been engaged in *trading*. In other words, their principal activity has been the sale of goods purchased especially for that purpose. In this chapter we consider the accounting needs of *manufacturing* businesses. A manufacturing business is one which buys raw materials, converts those raw materials into a finished product and then sells the finished product to its customers.

The trading account of a manufacturing business matches the sales revenue of the business against the cost of producing the goods which have been sold. This *production cost* consists of the cost of the raw materials used in the manufacturing process, together with the costs of converting those raw materials into finished goods. It is normal to preface the trading account of a manufacturing business with an extra account known as a *manufacturing account*, which is used to calculate the production cost of the finished goods manufactured during the accounting period.

2. DIRECT COSTS AND INDIRECT COSTS

Manufacturing costs can be classified into two main categories:

(a) **Direct costs**. Direct costs are manufacturing costs which can be clearly linked to the manufacture of a specific product. They include direct materials, direct labour and direct expenses. An example of a direct expense would be a royalty payable per unit of production to the inventor of a manufacturing process. The total of the direct costs incurred by a manufacturing business during an accounting period is known as *prime cost*.

(b) **Indirect costs**. Indirect costs are manufacturing costs which cannot be linked to specific products. They are sometimes referred to as *factory overhead expenses*. Common examples of indirect manufacturing costs include:

- factory rent, rates and insurance
- factory power, heating and lighting
- factory repairs
- wages of factory managers, storekeepers, cleaners etc.
- depreciation of factory plant and machinery.

It is sometimes necessary to apportion costs which relate only partly to the manufacturing activities of a business. For instance, a single fire insurance premium might cover both factory and office premises, in which case only the portion of the premium relating to the factory would be shown as an indirect manufacturing cost.

Work in progress

The term *work in progress* is used to refer to any incomplete, part-manufactured goods which a manufacturing business has on hand at the end of an accounting period. Since these incomplete goods have not yet been transferred to the stock of finished goods, it would be wrong to include their cost in the trading account. Therefore the calculation of production cost in the manufacturing account must include an adjustment to take account of work in progress.

The treatment of opening and closing work in progress is in fact very similar to the treatment of opening and closing stocks. The cost of opening work in progress is added to the total manufacturing costs incurred during the accounting period and the cost of closing work in progress is subtracted. The result is the production cost of the goods which have been completed during the period. This figure is transferred to the trading account and the cost of closing work in progress is shown as a current asset on the balance sheet.

EXAMPLE

Murray Engineering is a manufacturing business which prepares accounts to 30 June each year. The following information relates to the year ended 30 June 19X9:

	£
Stock of raw materials as at 1 July 19X8	4,120
Stock of raw materials as at 30 June 19X9	5,200
Purchases of raw materials	41,750
Direct factory wages	92,340
Direct factory expenses	2,270
Salary of factory supervisor	18,130
Factory power, heat and light	4,890
Factory repairs and sundry expenses	1,580

	£
Rent, rates and insurances	16,900
Depreciation of factory machinery	2,400
Work in progress as at 1 July 19X8	8,750
Work in progress as at 30 June 19X9	9,140

Rent, rates and insurances are to be apportioned between the factory (70%) and administration (30%). Prepare a manufacturing account for the year to 30 June 19X9.

SOLUTION

Murray Engineering
Manufacturing account for the year to 30 June 19X9

	£	£
Stock of raw materials as at 1 July 19X8		4,120
Purchases of raw materials		41,750
		45,870
Less: Stock of raw materials as at 30 June 19X9		5,200
Direct materials consumed		40,670
Direct labour	92,340	
Direct expenses	2,270	94,610
Prime cost		135,280
Indirect manufacturing costs		
Indirect wages and salaries	18,130	
Power, heat and light	4,890	
Repairs and sundry expenses	1,580	
Rent, rates and insurance	11,830	
Depreciation of plant and machinery	2,400	38,830
Total manufacturing costs incurred during the year		174,110
Add: Work in progress as at 1 July 19X8		8,750
		182,860
Less: Work in progress as at 30 June 19X9		9,140
Production cost of goods completed (transferred to trading account)		173,720

3. TRANSFER OF FINISHED GOODS TO TRADING ACCOUNT AT MORE THAN PRODUCTION COST

It is fairly common for a manufacturing business to transfer finished goods from the manufacturing account to the trading account at a value which exceeds production cost. This policy might be adopted for the following reasons:

(a) The business may wish to allocate its gross profit between manufacturing and trading operations so that the extra profit earned as a consequence of making its own products (rather than buying them in) is clearly identified.

(b) The business may sell a mixture of manufactured goods and bought-in goods. In this case it is desirable to transfer manufactured goods between manufacturing and trading at their market value so that the trading account is prepared on a consistent basis.

The mark-up applied to production cost is shown in the manufacturing account as *manufacturing profit*. In precisely the same way as the gross profit on trading is calculated in the trading account and then credited to the profit and loss account, the profit on manufacturing is calculated in the manufacturing account and then credited to the profit and loss account.

Provision for unrealised profit

If finished goods are transferred from manufacturing at a value which exceeds production cost, the transfer value of the closing stock of finished goods will include an element of *unrealised profit*. This unrealised profit must be eliminated from the profit and loss account and the stock of finished goods must be shown in the balance sheet at the lower of cost and net realisable value. The usual procedure for dealing with this situation is as follows:

(a) The opening and closing stocks of finished goods are shown in the trading account at transfer value.

(b) The closing stock of finished goods is shown in the balance sheet at transfer value, less a *provision for unrealised profit*. The amount of this provision is equal to the amount of manufacturing profit included in the transfer value of the stock. (A further reduction is required if the net realisable value of the stock is less than its production cost).

(c) When a provision for unrealised profit is first established, the amount of the provision is debited to the profit and loss account. In subsequent accounting periods, only the increase (or decrease) in the provision is debited (or credited) to the profit and loss account. The accounting treatment of a provision for unrealised profit is very similar to that of a provision for doubtful debts (see Chapter 7).

EXAMPLE

McAllister Products is a manufacturing business which prepares accounts to 31 August annually. Finished goods are transferred between manufacturing and trading at production cost plus 10%. The following information relates to the year ended 31 August 19X8:

	£
Sales	244,390
Stocks as at 1 September 19X7	
Raw materials	4,330
Work in progress	3,150
Finished goods (at transfer value)	11,990
Stocks as at 31 August 19X8	
Raw materials	4,610
Work in progress	3,250
Finished goods (at transfer value)	12,320
Purchases of raw materials	61,270
Direct labour	51,400
Direct manufacturing expenses	3,450
Factory overhead expenses	29,860
Selling and distribution costs	14,290
Administrative expenses	25,600
Finance costs	2,340
Provision for unrealised profit as at 1 September 19X7	1,090

Write up the provision for unrealised profit account and then prepare a manufacturing, trading and profit and loss account for the year to 31 August 19X8.

SOLUTION

Provision for unrealised profit

		£			£
31.8.X8	Balance c/d	1,120	1.9.X7	Balance b/d	1,090
			31.8.X8	Profit and loss a/c	30
		1,120			1,120
			1.9.X8	Balance b/d	1,120

Note:

Since finished goods are transferred at production cost plus 10%, one-eleventh of the transfer value consists of manufacturing profit. The opening provision for unrealised profit was £11,990 x 1/11th = £1,090. The required closing provision is £12,320 x 1/11th = £1,120, an increase of £30.

McAllister Products
Manufacturing account for the year to 31 August 19X8

	£	£
Stock of raw materials as at 1 September 19X7		4,330
Purchases of raw materials		61,270
		65,600
Less: Stock of raw materials as at 31 August 19X8		4,610
Direct materials consumed		60,990
Direct labour	51,400	
Direct expenses	3,450	54,850
Prime cost		115,840
Factory overhead expenses		29,860
Total manufacturing costs incurred during the year		145,700
Add: Work in progress as at 1 September 19X7		3,150
		148,850
Less: Work in progress as at 31 August 19X8		3,250
Production cost of goods completed		145,600
Manufacturing profit		14,560
Transfer value of goods completed		160,160

McAllister Products
Trading and profit and loss account for the year to 31 August 19X8

	£	£
Sales		244,390
Cost of goods sold:		
Stock as at 1 September 19X7	11,990	
Completed goods transferred from manufacturing	160,160	
	172,150	
Less: Stock as at 31 August 19X8	12,320	159,830
Gross trading profit		84,560
Manufacturing profit	14,560	
Less: Increase in provision for unrealised profit	30	14,530
		99,090
Selling and distribution costs	14,290	
Administrative expenses	25,600	
Finance costs	2,340	42,230
Net profit		56,860

4. SUMMARY

- The trading account of a manufacturing business matches sales revenue for an accounting period against the production cost of the goods which have been sold.
- The function of a manufacturing account is to calculate the production cost of completed goods. The manufacturing account shows both direct and indirect manufacturing expenses.
- Work in progress consists of part-manufactured goods held by a manufacturing business at the end of an accounting period. The cost of opening and closing work in progress must be taken into account when calculating the production cost of completed goods.
- A manufacturing business might transfer finished goods to the trading account at a value exceeding cost. If any such goods remain in stock at the end of an accounting period, it is necessary to provide for the element of unrealised profit which is included in their valuation.

EXERCISES 8

8.1 Classify each of the following as either a direct manufacturing cost, an indirect manufacturing cost, a selling and distribution expense, an administrative expense or a finance cost:

(a) Factory supervisor's wages
(b) Carriage outwards
(c) Machinists' wages
(d) Carriage inwards
(e) Sales representatives' salaries
(f) Repairs to factory windows
(g) Cost of raw materials
(h) Depreciation of plant & machinery
(i) Cost of machine oil
(j) Computer running costs
(k) Interest paid on a loan to buy factory machinery
(l) Hire of plant and machinery needed for a special customer order.

8.2 Stewart owns a manufacturing business and prepares accounts to 31 March each year. The following figures relate to the year ended 31 March 19X8:

	£
Stocks as at 1 April 19X7	
Raw materials	53,210
Work in progress	11,650
Finished goods	49,420
Stocks as at 31 March 19X8	
Raw materials	55,190
Work in progress	13,220
Finished goods	47,150
Sales for the year	391,380
Expenditure during the year:	
Purchase of raw materials	151,490
Direct factory wages	68,220
Royalties payable (£1 payable per unit of production)	13,550
Factory power costs	11,500
Factory supervisor's salary	21,000
Factory repairs	1,170
Rent and rates	12,260
Depreciation of factory machines	4,500
Carriage outwards	6,230
Depreciation of office equipment	2,400
Office salaries	36,800
Office heating and lighting	2,540
Other office expenses	5,660

Rent and rates are to be apportioned equally between the factory and the offices.

Required:

Prepare Stewart's manufacturing, trading and profit and loss account for the year to 31 March 19X8.

8.3 Sean started a manufacturing business on 1 January 19X7, preparing accounts to 31 December each year. He decided to transfer finished goods from manufacturing account to trading account at production cost plus 20%. His closing stocks of finished goods (at transfer value) at the end of each of the first three accounting years were as follows:

	£
31 December 19X7	7,260
31 December 19X8	7,740
31 December 19X9	7,320

Required:

Write up Sean's provision for unrealised profit account for each of the three years to 31 December 19X9.

***8.4** The trial balance of McFadden Manufacturing at 30 September 19X9 is as follows:

	£	£
J McFadden's capital account as at 1 October 19X8		110,400
Factory machinery:		
Cost	91,400	
Provision for depreciation at 1 October 19X8		43,600
Delivery vans:		
Cost	41,100	
Provision for depreciation at 1 October 19X8		12,500
Office equipment:		
Cost	33,400	
Provision for depreciation at 1 October 19X8		17,520
Stocks as at 1 October 19X8		
Raw materials	4,250	
Work in progress	3,790	
Finished goods	15,280	
Provision for unrealised profit at 1 October 19X8		2,300
Trade debtors	13,400	
Provision for doubtful debts at 1 October 19X8		850
Cash in hand	220	
Bank balance		19,600
Trade creditors		11,950
Sales		389,400
Returns inwards	3,370	
Purchases of raw materials	66,220	
Carriage inwards on raw materials	2,830	
Returns outwards of raw materials		1,460
Purchases of finished goods	12,470	
Carriage outwards	12,700	
Wages and salaries:		
Direct factory wages	87,120	
Indirect factory wages	31,650	
Sales representatives' salaries	54,200	
Office salaries	28,770	
J McFadden's salary	50,000	
Rent, rates and insurances	23,790	
Heating, lighting and power	16,230	
Advertising	3,100	
General office expenses	8,660	
Bank interest	2,480	
Bad debts written off	3,150	
	609,580	609,580

Further information:

1. There were no disposals of fixed assets during the year.
2. All fixed assets are depreciated on the straight line basis with a full charge in the year of acquisition and none in the year of disposal. Residual values are always assumed to be nil. Annual depreciation rates are:

Factory machinery	10%
Delivery vans	20%
Office equipment	25%

None of the fixed assets had been fully depreciated by 30 September 19X8.

3. The business makes most of its own finished goods but also buys in some finished goods from outside suppliers. Finished goods are transferred from manufacturing to trading at production cost plus 25%.
4. Closing stocks on 30 September 19X9 were as follows:

	£
Raw materials, at cost	4,470
Work in progress, at cost	4,110
Finished goods:	
Manufactured, at transfer value	12,850
Bought in, at cost	3,540

The stock of finished goods at 1 October 19X8 included bought-in goods costing £3,780.

5. The provision for doubtful debts is to be adjusted to 5% of trade debtors.
6. On 30 September 19X9, prepaid rent, rates and insurances amounted to £2,150 and accrued heating, lighting and power amounted to £1,440.
7. One-half of rent, rates and insurances and two-thirds of heating, lighting and power are to be allocated to manufacturing.

Required:

Prepare a manufacturing, trading and profit and loss account for McFadden Manufacturing for the year to 30 September 19X9 and a balance sheet as at that date.

9

DIVISION OF THE LEDGER, ERRORS AND CONTROLS

Chapter objectives

When you have finished this chapter, you should be able to:

- **Explain why a manual ledger might be divided into several books.**
- **Identify the main account books which are normally used and explain the purpose of each book.**
- **Distinguish between errors which cause the trial balance totals to disagree and errors which have no effect on the agreement of the trial balance totals.**
- **Make journal entries and operate a suspense account.**
- **Explain the purpose of control accounts and resolve any discrepancy between a control account balance and the total of the balances extracted from the relevant ledger.**
- **Contrast the control aspects of manual accounting systems and computer-based accounting systems.**

1. INTRODUCTION

It has been assumed so far that a manual book-keeping system involves the use of a single account book known as the ledger. It has also been assumed that the trial balance extracted from this ledger at the end of each accounting period always yields total debit balances equal to total credit balances. In practice, however, the ledger is usually subdivided into a number of separate books and agreement of the trial balance totals is by no means guaranteed. The main purpose of this chapter is to explain why and how a ledger may be divided into several books and to consider ways of resolving any discrepancy which may arise between the trial balance totals.

2. THE NEED TO DIVIDE THE LEDGER

For any except the smallest of businesses, it is impracticable for all financial transactions to be recorded in a single account book. The reasons for this are fairly obvious:

(a) In a business of any size, the volume of transactions is such that is impossible for one book to hold them all or for one person to record them all in the time available. It is also impossible for two or more people to use a single account book at the same time, so the ledger must be divided into a number of separate books.

(b) It is essential that the accounting system should minimise opportunities for error and/or fraud. Division of the ledger into separate books, each handled by a different member of the book-keeping staff, prevents any one person from having exclusive control over the accounting system. This makes frauds more difficult to perpetrate and makes it more likely that any errors will come to light.

(c) Accurate and efficient book-keeping can occur only if those performing the work are skilled at their tasks. This expertise will develop if book-keeping staff specialise in one area of the work rather than attempting to record transactions of every conceivable type. If the ledger is divided into separate books, junior staff can be charged with the task of recording repetitive, routine transactions whilst experienced staff can be entrusted with the more advanced work.

Of course, many businesses (and especially those which need to record a great many transactions) now use computer-based accounting systems and so have no account books at all. However, as indicated in Chapter 5, computer-based systems work on very similar principles to manual systems and use much of the same terminology. An appreciation of the way in which manual accounting systems operate is essential, therefore, if the operation of computer-based systems is to be fully understood.

A set of manual account books could be organised in many ways. A fairly standard approach is to split the ledger into several books, each holding a different class of account, and to supplement these ledgers with a number of *subsidiary books*. The way in which such a system operates is described below.

Division of the ledger

A typical division of the ledger is as follows:

(a) **The cashbook**. This book contains the cash account and the bank account. The book is invariably known as the "cashbook" even if all receipts and payments are made via the bank and there is no cash account. If both cash and bank accounts exist, it is normal to organise the cashbook as a two-column cashbook with a pair of debit columns on the left (one for cash receipts and one for bank receipts) and a pair of credit columns on the right (one for cash payments and one for bank payments). The cashbook might be the responsibility of an official known as the *cashier*.

(b) **The petty cashbook**. Most business payments are now made by cheque or credit transfer and most business receipts are banked immediately. In these circumstances, the only use of cash is to pay for petty items such as postage stamps, office sundries etc. and so the cash account is often relegated to a book known as the *petty cashbook*. This book is usually maintained by a junior cashier who is provided with a float or *imprest* with which to make petty cash payments. The imprest is provided initially from the bank account. From time to time, the amount of cash spent is reimbursed (again from the bank account) so bringing the imprest back up to its previous level.

(c) **The sales ledger**. This book contains the personal accounts of customers who buy goods or services from the business on credit terms. The book is maintained by sales ledger clerks and is sometimes known as the debtors' ledger. If there are very many customer accounts, the sales ledger may be further sub-divided on an alphabetical or geographical basis.

(d) **The purchase ledger**. This book contains the personal accounts of suppliers from whom the business buys goods or services on credit terms. The book is maintained by purchase ledger clerks and is sometimes known as the bought ledger or creditors' ledger. The purchase ledger may also be sub-divided on an alphabetical or geographical basis if there are very many suppliers' accounts.

(e) **The nominal ledger**. This book contains all of the accounts remaining after the cash account, bank account, debtors' accounts and creditors' accounts have been transferred to the other books described above. The nominal ledger is usually maintained by the Chief Accountant or some other senior member of staff. Highly confidential accounts (e.g. the owner's capital account) might be held in a separate book known as the private ledger.

Subsidiary books

The number of detailed entries required in the nominal ledger can be reduced considerably if the ledger is supplemented by a set of subsidiary books. The purpose of these subsidiary books is to provide a place in which transactions of a similar type can be listed and totalled *before* being entered in the ledgers. The usual subsidiary books are as follows:

(a) **The sales daybook**. This book (which is also known as the sales journal) is used to record credit sales. When a credit sale occurs, the customer is sent a document called a sales invoice, giving details of the goods or services provided and showing the amount payable. Sales invoices are recorded initially in the sales daybook. Then, at convenient intervals, each sale recorded in the daybook is debited (or "posted") to the relevant customer's account in the sales ledger and the sales total is credited to the sales account in the nominal ledger. This arrangement has the following advantages:

- The actions of recording a sale in the sales daybook, debiting the customer's account in the sales ledger and crediting the sales account in the nominal ledger can be carried out by three different people. It is essential that a manual accounting system should allow work to be shared between several members of staff in this way if the volume of transactions is high.

- It is no longer necessary for the debit entry in the customer's account and the credit entry in the sales account to be made at the same time. This makes it less likely that two members of staff will need to use the same account book simultaneously. For example, one member of staff can be working through the sales daybook, posting sales to the sales ledger, whilst another member of staff can be using the nominal ledger for an entirely different purpose.
- The sales account in the nominal ledger will contain far fewer entries than it would have done if each sale had been credited to the account individually.

A typical format for the sales daybook is shown below.

Date	*Invoice No.*	*Customer name*	*Folio*	*Amount*
				£
1.4.X8	24001	A Dent	SL58	100.00
2.4.X8	24002	D Hall	SL74	1,390.00
4.4.X8	24003	R Johnson	SL81	20.00
5.4.X8	24004	H Maddocks	SL113	161.60
5.4.X8	24005	J Proctor	SL124	2,424.40
7.4.X8	24006	B Cooper	SL43	440.00
Total sales				4,536.00

Each sales invoice is listed, showing date, invoice number, customer's name and amount. The folio column shows the customer's account number in the sales ledger or the number of the page in the sales ledger where the customer's account is located. In this example, the task of posting the sales to the sales ledger will involve debiting A Dent's account with £100.00, debiting D Hall's account with £1,390.00 and so forth. The total sales for the week of £4,536.00 will be credited to the sales account in the nominal ledger.

(b) **The purchases daybook**. This book (also known as the purchases journal) is used to record purchases of stock on credit terms. When a purchase invoice arrives, it is recorded initially in the purchases daybook. At convenient intervals, each purchase is credited ("posted") to the relevant supplier's account in the purchase ledger and the purchases total is debited to the purchases account in the nominal ledger. The use of a purchases daybook offers similar advantages to those offered by the use of a sales daybook.

A purchases daybook is sometimes used to record *all* purchases of goods or services on credit terms, not just purchases of stock. In this case, the daybook must be provided with analysis columns, as illustrated below.

Date	*Creditor name*	*Folio*	*Total*	*Purchases of stock*	*Heat & light*	*Motor exp's*	*Office exp's*
			£	£	£	£	£
1.7.X9	A Allen	PL02	56.32	56.32			
4.7.X9	I Jones	PL55	42.21			42.21	
7.7.X9	W Green	PL42	85.00	85.00			
9.7.X9	D Dooley	PL34	145.89	145.89			
12.7.X9	E Fox	PL39	66.67			66.67	
18.7.X9	D Pym	PL69	12.65				12.65
21.7.X9	C Chan	PL23	433.65	433.65			
24.7.X9	T Hart	PL48	100.00				100.00
26.7.X9	Br. Gas	PL17	130.48		130.48		
31.7.X9	K Lane	PL61	17.77	17.77			
			1,090.64	738.63	130.48	108.88	112.65

The amount of each purchase invoice is recorded in the total column and extended into the appropriate analysis column. At a later stage, each invoice is posted to the credit of the relevant supplier's account in the purchase ledger. The total of each analysis column is debited to the relevant expense account in the nominal ledger. In the example given above (which, for the sake of simplicity, has only four analysis columns) the purchases account will be debited with £738.63, the heat and light account with £130.48 and so forth. The grand total of £1,090.64 should equal the total of all the analysis columns, so providing a check on the arithmetic accuracy of the analysis.

A further column which may be found in the purchases daybook is a column headed "invoice number" or "voucher number". Purchase invoices are often numbered sequentially on arrival and these numbers can then be recorded in the purchases daybook, so providing a cross-reference to the documentary evidence of each transaction.

(c) **Returns daybooks**. The sales returns daybook and the purchases returns daybook operate in the same way as the sales and purchases daybooks. These daybooks are also known as the returns journals.

It is very important to realise that the subsidiary books do *not* form part of the double-entry system. They do, however, provide a convenient means of recording and accumulating transactions prior to the necessary double-entry work. For this reason, they are often referred to as *books of prime entry* or *books of original entry*.

EXAMPLE

For each of the following transactions, identify the account book in which the transaction would be recorded initially and explain how the necessary double-entry would then be achieved:

(a) Goods are sold on credit for £1,000.

(b) Goods which had been sold on credit for £250 are returned.

(c) Goods are sold for £500, the customer paying immediately by cheque.

(d) Stock costing £800 is bought on credit.

(e) A cheque for £100 is received from a trade debtor.

(f) £50 is drawn out of the bank to provide a petty cash float.

SOLUTION

(a) The sale is recorded initially in the sales daybook. In due course, £1,000 will be debited to the customer's account in the sales ledger. The sales account in the nominal ledger will be credited with a sales total which includes this £1,000 sale.

(b) The return is recorded initially in the sales returns daybook. £250 will be posted to the credit of the customer's account in the sales ledger. The sales returns account in the nominal ledger will be debited with a total which includes this £250 return.

(c) This is a *cash sale* (i.e. a sale where the customer pays immediately, whether by cash or by cheque) and so the sales ledger is not involved. The initial entry is made in the cashbook, where £500 is debited to the bank account. The double-entry is completed by making a £500 credit entry in the sales account in the nominal ledger. If a number of cash sales occur on the same day, it is likely that the required entries will be made in total.

(d) The purchase is recorded initially in the purchases daybook. In due course, £800 will be posted to the credit of the supplier's account in the purchase ledger. The purchases account in the nominal ledger will be debited with a purchases total which includes this £800 purchase.

(e) The cheque is debited to the bank account (in the cashbook) and credited to the customer's account in the sales ledger.

(f) The bank account (in the cashbook) is credited with £50 and the cash account (in the petty cashbook) is debited with £50.

Value added tax (VAT)

If a business is VAT-registered and charges VAT to its customers at the standard rate (currently 17.5%) the VAT component of each sale must be recorded separately. This can be achieved for credit sales by adding further columns to the sales daybook, as illustrated below:

Date	*Invoice No.*	*Customer name*	*Folio*	*Amount before VAT*	*VAT*	*VAT-inclusive amount*
				£	£	£
1.4.X8	24001	A Dent	SL58	100.00	17.50	117.50
2.4.X8	24002	D Hall	SL74	1,390.00	243.25	1,633.25
4.4.X8	24003	R Johnson	SL81	20.00	3.50	23.50
5.4.X8	24004	H Maddocks	SL113	161.60	28.28	189.88
5.4.X8	24005	J Proctor	SL124	2,424.40	424.27	2,848.67
7.4.X8	24006	B Cooper	SL43	440.00	77.00	517.00
				4,536.00	793.80	5,329.80

The amount debited to each customer's account in the sales ledger is the amount which the customer has to pay i.e. the VAT-inclusive amount. The sales account in the nominal ledger is credited with the pre-VAT sales total of £4,536.00 and a VAT account in the nominal ledger is credited with the tax of £793.80. This amount is a creditor and is payable to HM Customs and Excise.

A VAT-registered business is able to recover the VAT charged when it buys goods or services. This means that the purchases daybook must also be equipped with a VAT column, so that the total VAT suffered can be accumulated and debited to the VAT account in the nominal ledger. Similarly, the returns daybooks must each include a VAT column.

If a VAT-registered business has cash sales, the debit side of the cashbook must include a VAT column so that the VAT charged on such sales can be accumulated and credited to the VAT account in the nominal ledger. Finally, the credit side of both the cashbook and the petty cashbook must also have VAT columns, so that the VAT element of any cash purchases (or other expenses) can be recorded and accumulated.

3. THE CASHBOOK - FURTHER ASPECTS

As explained above, receipts and payments are recorded initially in the cashbook. Each receipt or payment must then be posted to the appropriate account in another part of the ledger system so as to complete double-entry. For example, a cash sale is recorded initially on the debit side of the cashbook and is then posted to the credit side of the sales account in the nominal ledger. The cashbook has some features in common with the daybooks:

(a) It provides a location for the original entry of a transaction, without needing to complete double-entry at the same time. In fact the cashbook, like the daybooks, is often described as a book of prime entry or a book of original entry.

(b) Double-entry can be completed at some convenient future time, possibly by someone other than the person who made the original entry in the cashbook.

(c) If the cashbook is equipped with analysis columns (see below) some of the required entries in the nominal ledger can be made in total.

It is important to appreciate, however, that the cashbook is very different in nature to the daybooks. The cashbook holds the bank account and (possibly) the cash account. These are ledger accounts in their own right and so the cashbook forms part of the double-entry system. Once an entry has been made in the cashbook, only *one* further entry is required to complete the necessary double-entry. The daybooks, on the other hand, do not contain ledger accounts and are not part of the double-entry system. An entry in a daybook must be followed by *two* entries in ledger accounts so as to achieve double-entry.

Two-column and three-column cashbooks

As explained earlier, a two-column cashbook has a pair of debit columns (for cash receipts and bank receipts) and a pair of credit columns (for cash payments and bank payments). If discounts are allowed to customers or received from suppliers, these discounts need to be recorded along with the relevant receipts or payments and it is conventional to use a third pair of columns in the cashbook for this purpose. An extract from a typical three-column cashbook is illustrated below.

Cashbook

19X9		Disc. Allow'd	Cash	Bank	19X9		Disc. Rec'd	Cash	Bank
May		£	£	£	May		£	£	£
1	Balance b/d		27	542	3	S Caton	3		97
7	E Shaw	5		195	10	R Williams	2		48
18	A Barker		10		17	G Sullivan			57
					23	P Bench	7		193
					31	Balance c/d		37	342
		5	37	737			12	37	737
June									
1	Balance b/d		37	342					

It is important to realise that the discount columns are *not* debit and credit columns and do not form part of the double-entry system. They are simply a convenient place to list discounts allowed and discounts received, prior to double-entry. In a way, the discount columns form a kind of daybook which happens to be stored within the pages of the cashbook. The operation of a three-column cashbook is as follows:

(a) **Receipts**

(i) Receipts are recorded on the debit side of the cashbook in either the cash column or the bank column, as appropriate. If a discount has been allowed to the customer concerned, it is noted in the discounts allowed column.

(ii) The customer's account in the sales ledger is credited with the amount received and with the discount allowed (if any).

(iii) At convenient intervals, the total of the discounts allowed column is debited to the discounts allowed account in the nominal ledger.

(b) **Payments**

(i) Payments are recorded on the credit side of the cashbook in either the cash column or the bank column, as appropriate. If a discount has been received from the supplier concerned, it is noted in the discounts received column.

(ii) The supplier's account in the purchase ledger is debited with the amount paid and with the discount received (if any).

(iii) At convenient intervals, the total of the discounts received column is credited to the discounts received account in the nominal ledger.

As noted above, most business receipts and payments now pass through the business bank account and so the cash account may not exist (or may be relegated to a petty cashbook). In these circumstances, the three-column cashbook reduces to a two-column cashbook, with a discount column and a bank column on each side.

Analysed cashbooks

We have already seen that an analysed purchases daybook facilitates the accumulation of totals which can then be debited to the appropriate nominal ledger accounts. This avoids cluttering the nominal ledger with details of individual transactions. An analysed cashbook can perform the same service in relation to expenses which are paid immediately and which do not pass through the purchases daybook. The operation of an analysed cashbook (payments side only) is as follows:

(a) The cashbook has columns for payment date, payment details and amount paid, together with a number of analysis columns (e.g. wages, rent and rates, repairs and renewals, sundry expenses etc).

(b) Each payment is entered in turn and extended into the appropriate analysis column.

(c) Completion of double-entry is delayed until (when convenient) the total of each analysis column is debited to the appropriate account in the nominal ledger.

(d) Assuming that there is a purchase ledger in existence, one of the analysis columns will be headed "purchase ledger" and will show payments to suppliers whose invoices have passed through the purchases daybook. The double-entry for each of these payments is to debit the relevant supplier's account in the purchase ledger.

(e) If there is a petty cashbook, this will be analysed in a similar way to the main cashbook.

A business which has many sources of revenue might also employ analysis columns on the debit side of the cashbook.

4. THE JOURNAL

The cashbook, the sales daybook, the purchases daybook and the returns daybooks have all been identified as books of prime entry. These books provide an initial "home" for the majority of transactions but it is desirable that *every* transaction should pass through a book of prime entry. Therefore a further book, known simply as the *journal* is used to record non-routine transactions prior to double-entry. Some of the main items which might pass through the journal include:

(a) the purchase of fixed assets on credit terms (unless the purchases daybook has appropriate analysis columns for this purpose) the disposal of fixed assets and the depreciation of fixed assets

(b) bad debts written off and increases/decreases in the provision for doubtful debts

(c) accruals and prepayments

(d) adjustments relating to closing stock

(e) the correction of errors (see below)

(f) the entries required to open a set of books when a new business begins.

A *journal entry* identifies the accounts which are to be debited and credited, states the amounts involved and provides a narrative which explains why the entry is being made. If the journal did not exist, non-routine transactions would have to be entered directly into the ledger. The advantages of recording such transactions in the journal first are as follows:

(a) The accountant is required to write down all of the required ledger entries relating to a transaction before embarking upon any of them. Therefore the risk of a transaction being entered incorrectly, or only partially, is reduced.

(b) The need to provide an accompanying narrative makes it more likely that the ledger entries being made will be understood by any interested parties in the future (e.g. auditors).

EXAMPLE

Valerie maintains a provision for doubtful debts equal to 2% of total debtors. On 1 August 19X8 the provision was £375. Her total debtors on 31 July 19X9 were £22,300. Show the journal entry required so to adjust the provision to the required figure on 31 July 19X9.

SOLUTION

		Dr	Cr
		£	£
31.7.X9	Profit and loss account	71	
	Provision for doubtful debts		71
	Being an increase of £71 in the provision for doubtful debts, calculated at 2% of £22,300 less the opening provision of £375.		

5. ERRORS AND SUSPENSE ACCOUNTS

As explained above, one of the main uses of the journal is to record the entries required so as to correct book-keeping errors. Errors are of two main types:

(a) **Errors which do *not* cause the trial balance totals to disagree**. The main classes of error which fall into this category are as follows:

- the complete omission of both halves of a double-entry
- the reversal of an entry, so that the account which should have been debited is credited and vice-versa
- an error of commission, whereby an entry is made in the wrong account but is made in the right type of account (e.g. debiting a sale to the wrong customer's personal account)
- an error of principle, whereby an entry is made in entirely the wrong type of account (e.g. debiting the cost of a new fixed asset to the purchases account)
- recording an incorrect amount in a book of prime entry
- a pair of compensating errors, whereby an error in one account is exactly matched by an equal but opposite error in another account.

Errors such as these are not apparent when the trial balance is extracted but often come to light as the result of external evidence. For example, a bank statement may reveal errors in the cashbook, suppliers' statements may reveal errors in the purchase ledger and so forth. Alternatively, material errors may become obvious when draft accounts are prepared at the end of an accounting year. For example, a repairs figure which is ten times greater than usual may indicate that the cost of a fixed asset has been debited to the repairs account by mistake.

When one of these errors is discovered, appropriate ledger entries must be made so as to correct the error. The journal is used to record the required entries and to explain why they are necessary.

(b) **Errors which *do* cause the trial balance totals to disagree**. A wide range of errors will reveal their existence by causing the trial balance totals to disagree. Typical examples of errors of this type are as follows:

- making a debit entry without a corresponding credit entry (or vice versa)
- making a debit entry and a credit entry which are not equal in amount
- calculating the balance on a ledger account incorrectly
- calculating a total incorrectly in a book of prime entry
- entirely omitting a balance from the trial balance, or listing a debit balance as a credit balance (or vice versa).

If the trial balance totals disagree, it is necessary to locate the errors concerned and to correct them via the journal. However, if draft accounts are required as quickly as possible, the difference between the trial balance totals may be entered into a *suspense account* and held there temporarily, pending resolution of the problem at some more convenient time. Although the use of a suspense account allows draft accounts to be produced more rapidly, it is essential that all errors are corrected and that the suspense account balance is cleared before the accounts are finalised.

This discussion of errors has assumed that a manual accounting system is in force. If the system is computer-based, errors of type (a) above can still occur but errors of type (b) almost certainly cannot. The control aspects of computer-based accounting systems are considered later in this chapter.

EXAMPLE

A trial balance extracted from the books of a business on 31 August 19X9 showed total debit balances equal to total credit balances. However, the following errors were subsequently discovered:

(a) A £40 purchase invoice from G Smith had been credited to J Smith's account in the purchase ledger.

(b) A cheque for wages of £250 had been entirely omitted from the books of account.

(c) A £378 sales invoice relating to P Charles had been recorded as £738 in the sales daybook.

(d) The £8,500 cost of a new motor vehicle had been debited to motor expenses.

(e) A £30 discount allowed to V Baker had been debited to V Baker's account in the sales ledger and credited to discounts allowed account in the nominal ledger.

Show the journal entries required to correct these errors.

SOLUTION

			Dr	Cr
			£	£
(a)	31.8.X9	J Smith	40	
		G Smith		40
		Being the correction of an error. Purchase invoice entered in the wrong account in the purchase ledger.		
(b)	31.8.X9	Wages	250	
		Bank		250
		Being the correction of an error. Wages cheque for £250 entirely omitted from the books of account.		
(c)	31.8.X9	Sales	360	
		P Charles		360
		Being the correction of an error. £378 sales invoice entered in the sales daybook as £738.		
(d)	31.8.X9	Motor vehicles	8,500	
		Motor expenses		8,500
		Being the correction of an error. Purchase of motor vehicle entered in motor expenses account.		

			Dr	Cr
			£	£
(e)	31.8.X9	Discounts allowed	60	
		V Baker		60
		Being the correction of an error. Discount allowed of £30 incorrectly debited to V Baker's account and credited to discounts allowed.		

Note that the final journal entry is for double the amount of the original error. This has the effect of cancelling out the erroneous entries and then replacing them with the correct ones.

EXAMPLE

Ahmed's trial balance on 30 June 19X8 showed total debit balances of £94,659 and total credit balances of £95,349. The difference was placed in a suspense account and the books were searched for errors. The following errors were discovered:

(a) Bank charges of £25 had been credited to the bank account but had not been debited to the bank charges account.

(b) The sales daybook had been undercast by £10.

(c) A £75 purchase invoice received from H Patel had been recorded correctly in the purchases daybook but had been posted to the purchase ledger as £750.

Show the journal entries required to correct these errors and show how the balance on the suspense account is cleared by these entries.

SOLUTION

The difference between the trial balance totals is £95,349 – £94,659 = £690. An extra debit balance of £690 is required to make the trial balance totals agree and therefore a suspense account is opened and debited with £690. The journal entries needed so as to correct the errors are as follows:

			Dr	Cr
			£	£
(a)	30.6.X8	Bank charges	25	
		Suspense account		25
		Being the correction of an error. Bank charges of £25 shown in the cashbook but not posted to the nominal ledger.		
(b)	30.6.X8	Suspense account	10	
		Sales		10
		Being the correction of an error. Sales daybook undercast by £10 and therefore total sales understated by £10.		

			Dr	Cr
			£	£
(c)	30.6.X8	H Patel	675	
		Suspense account		675
		Being the correction of an error. Purchase invoice for £75 posted to H Patel's account as £750.		

In each case, the error affects only one ledger account. When the error is corrected, the balance on that account changes and so the difference between the trial balance totals also changes. Therefore the balance on the suspense account needs to be increased or decreased accordingly. For example, increasing bank charges by £25 increases total debit balances to £94,684 (£94,659 + £25) and reduces the suspense account balance to £665 (£95,349 – £94,684). This is why the suspense account is credited with £25 when the error is corrected. The suspense account is as follows:

Suspense account

		£			£
30.6.X8	Balance b/d	690	30.6.X8	Bank charges	25
30.6.X8	Sales	10	30.6.X8	H Patel	675
		700			700

6. CONTROL ACCOUNTS

We have seen that, if the trial balance totals do not agree, it is necessary to search through all of the books of account in order to find the errors which have caused this situation to occur. It would be very helpful if the sales ledger and the purchase ledger (which are often the largest account books in the system) could be eliminated from this search and this can be done if control accounts are used.

A *control account* is essentially a *summary* of all the individual accounts within the ledger to which it relates. A sales ledger control account provides a check on the internal accuracy of the sales ledger and a purchase ledger control account does the same for the purchase ledger.

The sales ledger control account

The figure for total debtors at the end of an accounting period may be obtained in one of two ways. The approach adopted so far in this book has been to balance off each customer's account in the sales ledger, produce a list of these balances and total the list. An alternative approach is to argue that total debtors at the end of an accounting period must be equal to:

(a) total debtors at the beginning of the period, *plus*
(b) total credit sales made during the period, *less*

(c) the total of all the amounts credited to customers' accounts during the period (e.g. total cash received, total sales returns, total discounts allowed, total bad debts etc).

The opening total debtors figure can be obtained from the opening balance sheet. The other totals can be extracted from the books of prime entry. It is, therefore, a fairly straightforward matter to use this approach to obtain a total debtors figure. The calculation is usually laid out in the form of a *sales ledger control account*, as shown below:

Sales ledger control account

	£		£
Total debtors b/d	x	Total sales returns	x
Total credit sales	x	Total cash received	x
		Total discounts allowed	x
		Total contras to the purchase ledger	x
		Total bad debts	x
		Total debtors c/d	x
	x		x
Total debtors b/d	x		

It is very important to appreciate that the figure shown for "total debtors c/d" is a *balancing figure*, deduced after all of the other figures have been entered. The whole point of preparing the control account is to generate this figure, which should then be exactly equal to the total obtained by listing and adding all of the individual account balances in the sales ledger. This provides a means of proving the accuracy of the sales ledger, as follows:

(a) If the control account balance *is* equal to the total of the individual account balances, this is evidence that the sales ledger contains no errors of the type which would cause a trial balance discrepancy. Any such discrepancy must be caused by an error somewhere else in the accounting system.

(b) If the control account balance is *not* equal to the total of the individual account balances, there must be a mistake somewhere in the sales ledger (or in the books of prime entry which support it) and there is no point in trying to reconcile the trial balance totals until this error has been traced.

Strictly speaking, a sales ledger control account is not a ledger account at all and does not form part of the double-entry system. It is merely a memorandum or working which is used to check the accuracy of the sales ledger. However, it is far quicker to generate a figure for total debtors by means of a control account than it is to extract a list of individual account balances from the sales ledger. Therefore, the trade debtors figure in the trial balance if often obtained from the sales ledger control account. This approach is especially useful if draft accounts are wanted as soon as possible at the end of an accounting period, or if interim accounts are being produced part-way through an accounting period.

Contras

A customer who is also a supplier will have an account in the sales ledger and an account in the purchase ledger. In these circumstances, it is common practice to offset or *contra* the account balances in the two ledgers, leaving a net balance which is then payable to or by the business. A contra consists of a credit in the customer's sales ledger account and a debit in the corresponding purchase ledger account. Since the sales ledger control account must show, in total, all of the entries made in the sales ledger, the total contras (if any) must be shown on the credit side of the sales ledger control account.

EXAMPLE

A business sells goods to XYZ Ltd on credit terms. The business also buys goods from XYZ Ltd, again on credit terms. The accounts for XYZ Ltd in the sales ledger and the purchase ledger for the month of April are as follows:

Sales ledger
XYZ Ltd

		£			£
April 1	Balance b/d	3,491	April 23	Sales returns	117
April 18	Sales	2,227			

Purchase ledger
XYZ Ltd

		£			£
			April 6	Purchases	1,150
			April 27	Purchases	900

Show the contra entry which could be made between these two accounts at the end of April. Would this entry be recorded in a book of prime entry? If so, which one?

SOLUTION

Sales ledger
XYZ Ltd

		£			£
April 1	Balance b/d	3,491	April 23	Sales returns	117
April 18	Sales	2,227	April 30	Contra to purchase ledger	2,050
			April 30	Balance c/d	3,551
		5,718			5,718
May 1	Balance b/d	3,551			

Purchase ledger
XYZ Ltd

		£			£
April 30	Contra to sales ledger	2,050	April 6	Purchases	1,150
			April 27	Purchases	900
		2,050			2,050

Contras should (like all other entries) be recorded in a book of prime entry. If contras are a frequent occurrence, a special contras book could be used for this purpose. Otherwise, contras should pass through the journal.

EXAMPLE

Joan's debtors on 1 July were R Gibson £845, P Roberts £1,256, J Lloyd £317 and D Riley £430. During the month of July, her transactions included the following:

		£
July 1	Goods sold on credit to D Riley	500
July 3	Cheque received from R Gibson (after £10 cash discount)	390
July 5	Goods sold on credit to P Roberts	1,110
July 8	Goods returned by D Riley	100
July 11	Goods sold on credit to R Gibson	217
July 15	Goods sold on credit to D Riley	40
July 17	Cheque received from D Riley (after £5 cash discount)	325
July 22	Cheque received from P Roberts	1,000
July 23	Goods returned by R Gibson	27
July 30	Goods sold on credit to P Roberts	600
July 31	Bad debts written off (J Lloyd)	317

All of these transactions were recorded correctly in the books of prime entry but the sale to P Roberts on July 5 was debited to his account incorrectly as £1,100.

Show how the above transactions were recorded in Joan's books of prime entry and in her ledger accounts. Prepare a sales ledger control account for the month of July and demonstrate that this control account would reveal the existence of the £10 error mentioned above.

SOLUTION

Sales daybook

Date	*Name*	*Amount*
		£
July 1	D Riley	500
July 5	P Roberts	1,110
July 11	R Gibson	217
July 15	D Riley	40
July 30	P Roberts	600
Total sales for the month		2,467

Sales returns daybook

Date	*Name*	*Amount*
		£
July 8	D Riley	100
July 23	R Gibson	27
Total returns for the month		127

Cashbook (debit side only)

		Disc. Allow'd	Cash	Bank	Disc. Rec'd	Cash	Bank
July		£	£	£	£	£	£
3	R Gibson	10		390			
17	D Riley	5		325			
22	P Roberts			1,000			
		15		1,715			

Journal

		Dr	Cr
		£	£
July 31	Bad debts	317	
	J Lloyd		317
	Being a bad debt written off.		

Sales ledger

R Gibson

		£			£
July 1	Balance b/d	845	July 3	Bank	390
July 11	Sales	217	July 3	Discounts allowed	10
			July 23	Sales returns	27
			July 31	Balance c/d	635
		1,062			1,062
Aug 1	Balance b/d	635			

P Roberts

		£			£
July 1	Balance b/d	1,256	July 22	Bank	1,000
July 5	Sales	1,100	July 31	Balance c/d	1,956
July 30	Sales	600			
		2,956			2,956
Aug 1	Balance b/d	1,956			

J Lloyd

		£			£
July 1	Balance b/d	317	July 31	Bad debts	317

D Riley

		£			£
July 1	Balance b/d	430	July 8	Sales returns	100
July 1	Sales	500	July 17	Bank	325
July 15	Sales	40	July 17	Discounts allowed	5
			July 31	Balance c/d	540
		970			970
Aug 1	Balance b/d	540			

Nominal ledger

Sales

		£			£
			July 31	Debtors	2,467

Sales returns

		£			£
July 31	Debtors	127			

Discounts allowed

		£			£
July 31	Debtors	15			

Bad debts

		£			£
July 31	J Lloyd	317			

Joan's closing debtors, according to her sales ledger, are R Gibson £635, P Roberts £1,956 and D Riley £540. This gives total debtors of £3,131. Her sales ledger control account is as follows:

Sales ledger control account

		£			£
July 1	Total debtors b/d	2,848	July 31	Total sales returns	127
July 31	Total sales	2,467	July 31	Total cash received	1,715
			July 31	Total discounts allowed	15
			July 31	Total bad debts	317
			July 31	Total debtors c/d	3,141
		5,315			5,315
Aug 1	Total debtors b/d	3,141			

The control account balance is £3,141, indicating that there must be a £10 error somewhere in the sales ledger or in one of the books of prime entry. If this error had not been detected by drawing up a sales ledger control account, there would have been a £10 discrepancy between the trial balance totals.

The purchase ledger control account

A purchase ledger control account performs precisely the same function in relation to the purchase ledger as does the sales ledger control account in relation to the sales ledger. The format of a purchase ledger control account is as follows:

Purchase ledger control account

	£		£
Total purchase returns	x	Total creditors b/d	x
Total payments	x	Total credit purchases	x
Total discounts received	x		
Total contras to the sales ledger	x		
Total creditors c/d	x		
	x		x
		Total creditors b/d	x

7. CONTROL IN COMPUTER-BASED SYSTEMS

So far, this chapter has been concerned exclusively with manual accounting systems and with ways of detecting and correcting the errors which are bound to occur when manual systems are used. An alternative approach, now adopted by many businesses, is to use a computer-based system. The reasons for using computer-based systems are given below, together with a brief review of the control aspects of such systems.

The disadvantages of manual systems

Manual accounting systems have been in use for several centuries and are still used extensively today (especially by smaller businesses) but it must be recognised that such systems do possess a number of disadvantages when compared with computer-based systems. The principal disadvantages of manual accounting systems are as follows:

(a) Manual systems involve substantial amounts of clerical effort. Much of this effort is expended on copying information from one place to another (e.g. posting invoices from a sales daybook to a sales ledger) and this is a slow, costly, error-prone activity.

(b) Tracking down the inevitable clerical errors takes time and adds to system costs.

(c) A manual system is not good at responding quickly to an unexpected request for accounting information (e.g. if a set of interim accounts is suddenly needed to support an application for a bank loan).

(d) Without a great deal of extra clerical work, it is impossible to obtain analyses of income and expenditure other than those provided by the analysis columns in the books of prime entry. From a management accounting point of view, this sets a limit on the flexibility and usefulness of a manual system.

(e) The cost of operating a manual system will increase in proportion to the volume of business transactions and will become ever more onerous as a business grows.

Computer-based systems do not suffer from these disadvantages. The capital cost of the necessary hardware and software may be high but running costs are low and a computer-based accounting system offers a degree of speed, accuracy and flexibility which a manual system cannot hope to match.

Control aspects of computer-based systems

Computer-based accounting systems are not prone to the data processing errors which occur regularly in manual systems. Unless there is a hardware or software failure (which is very unlikely) the trial balance totals will always agree and the balance sheet will always balance. But this does *not* mean that computer-based systems are error-proof. A system is only as good as the data which is fed into it and computer-based systems are especially vulnerable to data entry errors. Potential errors include:

(a) transactions not being input to the system at all
(b) the same transaction being input to the system more than once
(c) the amount of a transaction being input incorrectly
(d) a transaction being mis-coded on input, so that the software makes an entry in the wrong account or in the wrong type of account.

Once data has been input to the system, it is processed without any further human intervention. Therefore the main control emphasis in a computer-based system must be to ensure that all input data is both *complete* and *correct*. The following security matters are also important:

(a) The system must maintain a permanent record of all input data. This *audit trail* helps in the detection of data entry errors and provides valuable audit evidence (if the business is subject to an annual audit). It must be impossible to enter data without this being recorded on the audit trail.

(b) Access to the computer system must be limited to authorised persons only.

8. SUMMARY

- In a manual accounting system, the ledger is usually divided into a cashbook, a petty cashbook, a sales ledger, a purchase ledger and a nominal ledger. The ledger is supplemented by a number of subsidiary books, principally the sales daybook, the purchases daybook, the returns daybooks and the journal.
- The cashbook, the petty cashbook, the daybooks and the journal are often referred to as books of original entry or books of prime entry.

- Discounts allowed are noted on the debit side of a three-column cashbook. Each discount is posted to the credit of the relevant customer's account in the sales ledger. The total of the discounts allowed is then posted to the debit of the discounts allowed account in the nominal ledger. A similar but opposite arrangement applies to discounts received.
- The journal is used as a book of prime entry for non-routine transactions.
- If the trial balance totals disagree, the difference between the two totals may be held in a suspense account until the discrepancy is resolved.
- A control account is a summary of all the individual accounts within the ledger to which it relates. Control accounts are used to check the internal accuracy of a ledger. They also provide a quick way of obtaining a figure for the total of the account balances within a ledger.
- In a computer-based accounting system, the likelihood of data processing errors is minimal but the likelihood of data entry errors is high. Strict control must be exercised over the input of data to a computer-based system.

EXERCISES 9

9.1 (a) Identify the account books in which each of the following accounts would normally be held:

(i) Returns outwards
(ii) Cash
(iii) J Price (a customer)
(iv) Motor vehicles.

(b) Identify the subsidiary books in which each of the following transactions would normally be recorded:

(i) A purchase of goods on credit from a supplier.
(ii) A payment made by cheque.
(iii) The purchase of a fixed asset on credit.
(iv) A return of goods by a customer.

9.2 Keith began trading on 1 October 19X9. All of his payments and receipts are made by cheque and he has a manual book-keeping system. His transactions during the first month of trading were as follows:

1 October Keith opened a business bank account and paid £2,000 of his own money into this account. He also introduced equipment valued at £5,000 and a motor vehicle valued at £8,000.

2 October Bought stock on credit from S Singh for £3,200 and from R Shipley for £6,500.

3 October Paid rent of £1,200, paying by cheque.

5 October Bought stationery on credit from M Goodall for £500 and petrol on credit from Hodgkins Garage for £40.

6 October Sold stock on credit to M Mohindra for £1,500 and to R Griffin for £4,750.

8 October Returned damaged stock costing £200 to S Singh.

11 October Sold stock for £1,000, receiving immediate payment by cheque.

12 October Bought petrol on credit from Hodgkins Garage for £35.

13 October Bought equipment on credit from P Lomas Ltd for £2,500.

17 October Bought stock for £850, paying by cheque.

21 October Bought stock on credit from R Shipley for £3,000.

23 October Sold stock on credit to B Dean for £4,200.

24 October Bought petrol on credit from Hodgkins Garage for £45.

27 October Paid S Singh's account in full, less a 3% cash discount. Also paid £6,300 to R Shipley, in full satisfaction of the £6,500 invoice received on 2 October.

30 October Sold stock on credit to M Mohindra for £700.

31 October Received cheque from R Griffin for £4,650 in full satisfaction of his account.

Required:

Record the above transactions in Keith's books of prime entry, write up the relevant ledger accounts and extract a trial balance as at 31 October 19X9.

9.3 A business has extracted a trial balance at the end of an accounting period but the trial balance totals do not agree. For the purposes of preparing draft accounts, the discrepancy between the trial balance totals has been entered in a suspense account. Where in the draft accounts should the suspense account balance be shown, if:

(a) the balance on the account is a debit balance?

(b) the balance on the account is a credit balance?

9.4 Laura's trial balance on 31 December 19X7 shows total debit balances of £52,346 and total credit balances of £52,519. The difference is temporarily placed in a suspense account. A search of Laura's books reveals the following errors:

(a) A sales invoice has been recorded correctly as £225 in the sales daybook but has been posted to the sales ledger as £252.

(b) An amount of £50 drawn out of the business by Laura has been credited to her capital account.

(c) The discounts received column in the cashbook has been overcast by £100.

Required:

Prepare journal entries to correct these errors and write up the suspense account.

9.5 On 30 September 19X8, the balance on Michael's sales ledger control account is £24,768 (debit). The total of a list of balances extracted from the sales ledger on that date is £22,761. A search through Michael's accounting records reveals the following errors:

(a) A bad debt of £500 has been written off in the sales ledger but not shown in the control account.

(b) A sales invoice for £1,230 has been recorded correctly in the sales daybook but has been debited to the customer's account in the sales ledger as £123.

(c) The sales returns daybook has been overcast by £200.

(d) A £600 debtor has been omitted from the list of balances extracted from the sales ledger.

Required:

Prepare a reconciliation of the control account balance with the total of the list of individual balances. What is the correct figure for trade debtors at 30 September 19X8?

***9.6** Pamela's trial balance on 31 January 19X9 showed that total debit balances exceeded total credit balances by £1,350. This discrepancy was temporarily credited to a suspense account whilst draft accounts for the year to 31 January 19X9 were prepared (with the suspense account balance being shown on the balance sheet as a current liability). These accounts showed a net profit of £52,873. On investigation, the following errors were discovered in Pamela's accounting records:

(a) A credit sale of £1,050 had been recorded correctly in the sales daybook but debited to the customer's account as £1,500.

(b) A prepaid insurance premium on 31 January 19X8 of £240 had not been brought down in the insurance account in the nominal ledger.

(c) Wages of £340 had been debited to the purchases account.

(d) The purchase of a motor vehicle for £14,000 had been debited to the motor expenses account. (Pamela depreciates motor vehicles at 20% on the straight-line basis, with a full year's charge in the year of acquisition and none in the year of disposal).

(e) A motor vehicle which had been bought for £12,000 in July 19X5 had been sold for £5,000 and the sale proceeds had been credited to the sales account.

(f) The purchases daybook had been overcast by £1,000 (i.e. the daybook total had been calculated as £1,000 more than the correct figure).

(g) Accrued heating and lighting charges at 31 January 19X9 of £360 had not been recorded in Pamela's books at all.

(h) The credit side of a customer's account in the sales ledger had been undercast by £10.

(i) No adjustment had yet been made to the provision for doubtful debts, which should be calculated as 3% of trade debtors. The provision at 31 January 19X8 was £610 and the trial balance extracted on 31 January 19X9 showed trade debtors of £18,560.

(j) Bank interest received of £24 had been recorded in the cashbook only.

(k) A discount of £37 received from a supplier had been recorded on the wrong side of the supplier's account in the purchase ledger.

(l) The total at the bottom of page 38 of the sales daybook was £11,425. This had been carried forward to the top of page 39 as £11,245.

Required:

Prepare appropriate journal entries to rectify these errors and write up the suspense account. Also calculate Pamela's corrected net profit for the year to 31 January 19X9.

***9.7** The purchase ledger control account of a business for the year to 31 March 19X9 has been drawn up as follows:

Purchase ledger control account

	£		£
Purchases returns	2,438.65	Balance b/d	6,769.13
Cheques sent to suppliers	52,117.94	Purchases	59,432.77
Discounts received	3,443.80	Contras to the sales ledger	1,119.99
Balance c/d	8,321.50		
	67,321.89		67,321.89
		Balance b/d	8,321.50

A list of balances extracted from the purchase ledger on 31 March 19X9 shows total creditors of £7,418.49. On investigation, the following errors were discovered:

(a) Two glaringly obvious mistakes had been made when the control account was drawn up.

(b) A purchase invoice for £201.23 had been recorded correctly in the purchases daybook but had then been debited to the supplier's account in the purchase ledger.

(c) One supplier had refused to accept payment by cheque. Since the amount owing to this supplier was only £20, the payment was made out of petty cash. The payment was debited to the supplier's account in the purchase ledger but was not reflected in the control account.

(d) The purchases returns daybook had been undercast by £110.

(e) A £701.27 credit note received from a supplier had been recorded in the purchases daybook as a purchase invoice and had been credited to the supplier's account in the purchase ledger.

(f) A £10 discount received from a supplier had been posted to the purchase ledger as £100.

(g) One of the accounts in the purchase ledger has a debit balance of £124.87. This had been included on the list of ledger balances as a £124.78 credit balance.

(h) One of the sales ledger contras, amounting to £354.89, had been entered on the wrong side of the supplier's account in the purchase ledger. This contra is included in the total contras figure shown in the control account.

Required:

Draw up an amended purchase ledger control account and reconcile the balance on this account with the total of the list of balances extracted from the purchase ledger.

10

INCOMPLETE RECORDS

Chapter objectives

When you have finished this chapter, you should be able to:

- **Calculate the profit or loss for an accounting period by constructing a statement of affairs as at the beginning and end of the period.**
- **Prepare a trading, profit and loss account and balance sheet from a set of incomplete records.**
- **Estimate the value of assets lost or destroyed in cases where the available records provide incomplete information.**

1. INTRODUCTION

We have assumed so far that every business maintains a complete set of double-entry records. In practice, this is not the case. A small business usually cannot afford to employ book-keeping staff and so, unless the owner has book-keeping skills or the business uses a computer-based accounting system, the records maintained are likely to be limited in scope. Typically, these records might consist of little more than a cashbook and a file of suppliers' invoices. In an extreme case, there may be no records at all, either because none have been kept or because they have been destroyed or lost.

A limited set of records may be quite sufficient to meet the needs of the owner of a small business, who is usually also the manager of the business and is in day-to-day contact with its affairs. A lot of necessary management information can be obtained from sources other than the accounting records. For example, stock levels can be assessed by physical observation, the bank balance can be determined from bank statements, the amounts owed to suppliers can be ascertained from invoices. In these circumstances, the main reason for keeping any records at all is to comply with legal requirements (as imposed by tax law and, for a small company, by company law) and to provide data for the accountant who will be charged with the task of preparing year-end accounts.

It is essential to prepare annual accounts, whether or not the owner of the business has any great interest in them. The Inland Revenue need information on which to base their tax assessments and if the business is incorporated it is necessary to file accounts with the Registrar of Companies (see Chapter 14). The purpose of this chapter is to explain how the annual accounts can be prepared from a set of incomplete accounting records.

2. BUSINESSES WITH NO ACCOUNTING RECORDS AT ALL

As mentioned above, it is a legal requirement to keep accounting records sufficient to meet the needs of the tax authorities and therefore it is rather unlikely that a business will maintain no records at all. However, it is conceivable that the records may be stolen or destroyed or that the owner of a small business may be unaware of the need to keep records. In such a case, an accountant may be faced with the task of producing financial statements in the total absence of any accounting records. The situation will be made worse if the business has traded entirely on a cash basis, so that external evidence in the form of bank statements, suppliers' invoices etc. is also unavailable.

This task may appear at first to be impossible, but help is at hand in the form of the balance sheet equation (see Chapter 3). If the assets and liabilities of the business at the end of an accounting period can be ascertained, then a *statement of affairs* can be drawn up and the capital at the end of the period can be derived. If the capital introduced and the drawings for the period are known, the profit for the period can then be deduced from the following formula:

Profit = Closing capital – Capital intro. + Drawings – Opening capital

If this is the first accounting period for the business in question, the figure for opening capital will of course be zero.

Although it is not possible to draw up a detailed profit and loss account if no accounting records are available, this method does at least allow the derivation of a profit figure which may satisfy the needs of the tax authorities and other users. It is desirable that the profit should be calculated as soon as possible after the end of the accounting period, so that the figures for assets, liabilities, capital introduced and drawings can be ascertained whilst the events of the period are still fairly fresh in the mind of the owner of the business.

EXAMPLE

Ursula began trading on 1 November 19X8 and chose 31 October as her annual accounting date. She did not open a business bank account, preferring that all of her receipts and payments should be made in cash. A simple cashbook was maintained during her first year of trading but unfortunately this was stolen in early November 19X9 when her rented business premises were burgled. An interview with Ursula soon afterwards revealed the following information:

(a) She started the business on 1 November 19X8 with cash of £500 and a motor vehicle which was worth £4,000 at that time. The vehicle was still in Ursula's possession at the end of her first year and was expected to last for a further two years before being sold for an estimated £1,000.

(b) Ursula thinks that her cash box contained approximately £150 at the end of October 19X9 and that the cost of her stock on that date was about £2,500.

(c) On 31 October 19X9, Ursula owed £840 to her suppliers and was owed £320 by her customers. She had paid £100 rent in advance and she estimates that electricity charges of approximately £50 had accrued.

(d) Ursula introduced no further capital during the year to 31 October 19X9, but drew £120 per week out of the business to cover her personal living expenses. Her uncle lent £1,000 to the business on 1 May 19X9 at an interest rate of 5% per annum. No interest had yet been paid on this loan.

Draw up a statement of affairs as at 31 October 19X9 and estimate Ursula's profit for the year ended on that date.

SOLUTION

Ursula
Statement of Affairs as at 31 October 19X9

	£	£
Fixed assets		
Motor vehicle		3,000
Current assets		
Stock of goods for resale	2,500	
Trade debtors	320	
Prepayments	100	
Cash in hand	150	
	3,070	
Current liabilities		
Trade creditors	840	
Accruals	75	
	915	
Net current assets		2,155
Total assets less current liabilities		5,155
Long-term liabilities		
Loan		1,000
Capital as at 31 October 19X9		4,155

Notes:

1. It has been assumed that the vehicle is to be depreciated on the straight-line basis, with a cost of £4,000, a useful life of 3 years and a residual value of £1,000. This gives depreciation of £1,000 per annum and therefore a written-down value of £3,000 after the first year of trading.
2. Accruals consist of electricity £50 and interest £25 (5% x £1,000 for 6 months).

Ursula's opening capital was £nil and her closing capital was £4,155. Capital introduced was £4,500 and drawings were £6,240 (52 @ £120). Therefore the profit for the year was £4,155 – £4,500 + £6,240 = £5,895.

3. BUSINESSES WHICH MAINTAIN A CASHBOOK

If a business has kept records of cash received and paid, it will usually be possible to prepare a full set of accounts at the end of each accounting period. A systematic approach to the preparation of accounts in these circumstances is as follows:

(a) If the opening balance sheet is not given, prepare an opening statement of affairs from the information provided and calculate the opening capital figure.

(b) Prepare a summary cash account for the year. This may involve deriving a missing figure if the information given is incomplete.

(c) Prepare a summary bank account for the year. Even if the business has not maintained records of bank transactions, this account can always be prepared by referring to copy bank statements.

(d) If the business sells goods on credit terms, prepare a total debtors account.

(e) If the business buys goods on credit terms, prepare a total creditors account.

(f) Open a "T" account for each expense or revenue item for which there are opening and/or closing accruals/prepayments and use these "T" accounts to calculate the amount which should be shown in the profit and loss account for each item. If an expense or a revenue item has no accruals or prepayments, then the amount to be shown in the profit and loss account is equal to the amount actually paid/received in the year and there is no need to open "T" accounts for such items.

(g) Deal with any closing adjustments (e.g. depreciation, provisions for doubtful debts) using either workings or "T" accounts, depending upon the complexity of the adjustments required.

(h) Extract the profit and loss account and draw up the closing balance sheet.

EXAMPLE

Victor prepares accounts to 30 June each year. He does not maintain full double-entry records but he does keep a cashbook. The following information is available:

(a) Victor's sales are mainly cash sales (i.e. the customers pay immediately by cash or cheque). He pays certain expenses out of his takings and then banks most of the remainder at the end of each week, retaining only a small cash float. The expenses paid out of takings during the year to 30 June 19X9 were as follows:

   (i) wages of £350 per week (including £200 per week for Victor himself)

   (ii) sundry expenses totalling £1,120 for the year.

   All other payments were made by business cheque.

(b) Customers who buy goods on credit terms always pay by cheque and these cheques are banked weekly.

(c) A summary of Victor's bank account for the year to 30 June 19X9 is as follows:

	£
Cash at bank as at 1 July 19X8	1,830
Receipts during the year:	
Takings paid into the bank	48,220
Credit customers' cheques paid into the bank	11,760
Sale of motor vehicle	3,700
Payments during the year:	
Suppliers of goods bought on credit terms	37,880
Purchase of new motor vehicle	15,800
Rent, rates and insurance	7,590
Heating and lighting	1,630
Motor expenses	3,640

(d) The motor vehicle sold during the year was bought for £12,300 in October 19X5. Victor calculates depreciation at 25% per annum using the straight line method, with a full charge in the year of acquisition and none in the year of disposal.

(e) Apart from motor vehicles and cash at bank, Victor's assets and liabilities are:

	30 June 19X8	*30 June 19X9*
	£	£
Stock of goods for resale, at cost	11,370	12,540
Trade debtors	960	1,020
Prepaid rent, rates and insurance	950	1,130
Cash in hand	120	150
Trade creditors	14,540	13,670
Accrued heating and lighting	220	260

Prepare Victor's trading and profit and loss account for the year to 30 June 19X9 and a balance sheet as at that date. (Ignore accrued interest on Victor's bank overdraft).

SOLUTION

Victor

Statement of Affairs as at 30 June 19X8

	£	£	£
Fixed assets			
Motor vehicle			3,075
Current assets			
Stock of goods for resale		11,370	
Trade debtors		960	
Prepayments		950	
Cash at bank		1,830	
Cash in hand		120	
		15,230	
Current liabilities			
Trade creditors	14,540		
Accruals	220	14,760	470
Capital as at 30 June 19X8			3,545

Note:

The motor vehicle cost £12,300. Depreciation has been provided for at 25% of this cost in each of the years to 30 June 19X6, 19X7 and 19X8, leaving a WDV of £3,075.

Cash

		£			£
1.7.X8	Balance b/d	120	30.6.X9	Wages	7,800
30.6.X9	Sales (deduced)	67,570	30.6.X9	Drawings	10,400
			30.6.X9	Sundry expenses	1,120
			30.6.X9	Bank	48,220
			30.6.X9	Balance c/d	150
		67,690			67,690
1.7.X9	Balance b/d	150			

Bank

		£			£
1.7.X8	Balance b/d	1,830	30.6.X9	Trade creditors	37,880
30.6.X9	Cash	48,220	30.6.X9	Motor vehicle	15,800
30.6.X9	Trade debtors	11,760	30.6.X9	Rent, rates and ins.	7,590
30.6.X9	Vehicle disposal	3,700	30.6.X9	Heating and lighting	1,630
30.6.X9	Balance c/d	1,030	30.6.X9	Motor expenses	3,640
		66,540			66,540
			1.7.X9	Balance b/d	1,030

Total debtors

		£			£
1.7.X8	Balance b/d	960	30.6.X9	Bank	11,760
30.6.X9	Sales (deduced)	11,820	30.6.X9	Balance c/d	1,020
		12,780			12,780
1.7.X9	Balance b/d	1,020			

Total creditors

		£			£
30.6.X9	Bank	37,880	1.7.X8	Balance b/d	14,540
30.6.X9	Balance c/d	13,670	30.6.X9	Purchases (deduced)	37,010
		51,550			51,550
			1.7.X9	Balance b/d	13,670

Rent, rates and insurance

		£			£
1.7.X8	Prepayment b/d	950	30.6.X9	Profit and loss a/c	7,410
30.6.X9	Bank	7,590	30.6.X9	Prepayment c/d	1,130
		8,540			8,540
1.7.X9	Prepayment b/d	1,130			

Heating and lighting

		£			£
30.6.X9	Bank	1,630	1.7.X8	Accrual b/d	220
30.6.X9	Accrual c/d	260	30.6.X9	Profit and loss a/c	1,670
		1,890			1,890
			1.7.X9	Accrual b/d	260

Disposal of motor vehicle

		£			£
30.6.X9	Motor vehicles	12,300	30.6.X9	Provision for dep'n	9,225
30.6.X9	Profit and loss a/c	625	30.6.X9	Bank	3,700
		12,925			12,925

Victor

Trading and profit and loss account for the year to 30 June 19X9

	£	£
Sales (£67,570 + £11,820)		79,390
Cost of goods sold:		
Stock as at 1 July 19X8	11,370	
Purchases	37,010	
	48,380	
Less: Stock as at 30 June 19X9	12,540	35,840
Gross profit		43,550
Profit on sale of motor vehicle		625
		44,175
Wages	7,800	
Sundry expenses	1,120	
Rent, rates and insurance	7,410	
Heating and lighting	1,670	
Motor expenses	3,640	
Depreciation (25% x £15,800)	3,950	25,590
Net profit for the year		18,585

Victor
Balance sheet as at 30 June 19X9

	£	£
Fixed assets		
Motor vehicle at cost	15,800	
Less: Accumulated depreciation to date	3,950	11,850
Current assets		
Stock of goods for resale	12,540	
Trade debtors	1,020	
Prepayments	1,130	
Cash in hand	150	
	14,840	
Current liabilities		
Trade creditors	13,670	
Accruals	260	
Bank overdraft	1,030	
	14,960	
Net current liabilities		120
		11,730
Capital		
As at 1 July 19X8	3,545	
Net profit for the year	18,585	
	22,130	
Less: Drawings	10,400	11,730
		11,730

Note:

Simple "T" accounts could have been drawn up for sales, purchases, stock, cost of goods sold, wages, sundry expenses, motor expenses and depreciation. However, the trading and profit and loss account can be produced more quickly if these "T" accounts are omitted.

4. ASSETS WHICH HAVE BEEN STOLEN OR LOST

If a business which does not maintain detailed accounting records loses cash or stock (perhaps as a result of theft, fire etc) it may be necessary to estimate the value of the lost assets for insurance purposes. The amount of any lost cash is usually determined by drawing up a cash account and calculating the difference on this account. The amount of any lost stock may be more difficult to ascertain and the calculation will generally depend on knowing one or other of the following ratios:

(a) The average *markup* used by the business (i.e. the ratio of gross profit to the cost of goods sold).

(b) The average *profit margin* enjoyed by the business (i.e. the ratio of gross profit to sales).

Both of these ratios are usually expressed as percentages and the profit margin is often referred to as the *gross profit percentage.*

EXAMPLE

A business sells goods at a constant markup of 25%. The cost of the stock held on 1 January 19X9 was £2,400. Purchases and sales for the month of January 19X9 were £5,240 and £7,300 respectively. On the night of 31 January 19X9, all of the stock held by the business was stolen. Calculate the cost of this stolen stock.

SOLUTION

From the information given, the trading account for the month of January 19X9 can be set out as follows:

	£	£
Sales		7,300
Cost of goods sold:		
Stock as at 1 January 19X9	2,400	
Purchases	5,240	
	7,640	
Less: Stock as at 31 January 19X9	?	?
Gross profit		?

We know that markup is 25% on cost. For instance, goods costing £4 are sold at a £1 profit, giving a selling price of £5. Therefore gross profit is 1/5th of sales. This means that gross profit in January 19X9 was 1/5th x £7,300 = £1,460 and that the cost of goods sold for the month was £5,840 (£7,300 – £1,460). The closing stock figure must have been £1,800, as shown below:

	£	£
Sales		7,300
Cost of goods sold:		
Stock as at 1 January 19X9	2,400	
Purchases	5,240	
	7,640	
Less: Stock as at 31 January 19X9	1,800	5,840
Gross profit		1,460

EXAMPLE

A business sells goods at a constant gross profit margin of 10%. Stock is bought on credit terms from suppliers but all sales are for cash. On 1 March 19X8, the business held stock costing £3,400, owed £1,530 to its suppliers and had cash in hand of £830. The following information relates to the 3 weeks to 21 March 19X8:

	£
Cash sales	15,900
Expenses paid in cash	1,460
Cash paid into the business bank account	14,670
Cheques paid to suppliers	15,010

The business premises were broken into on 21 March 19X8. The intruders stole all of the cash in hand on that day together with some stock, but stock costing £850 was left behind. Calculate the amount of cash stolen and the cost of the stolen stock, given that the business owed £1,740 to its suppliers on 21 March 19X8.

SOLUTION

Cash

		£			£
1.3.X8	Balance b/d	830	21.3.X8	Expenses	1,460
21.3.X8	Sales	15,900	21.3.X8	Bank	14,670
			21.3.X8	Stolen cash (deduced)	600
		16,730			16,730

Total creditors

		£			£
21.3.X8	Bank	15,010	1.3.X8	Balance b/d	1,530
21.3.X8	Balance c/d	1,740	21.3.X8	Purchases (deduced)	15,220
		16,750			16,750
			22.3.X8	Balance b/d	1,740

Trading account for the period to 21 March 19X8

	£	£
Sales		15,900
Cost of goods sold:		
Stock as at 1 March 19X8	3,400	
Purchases	15,220	
	18,620	
Less: Stock as at 21 March 19X8 (deduced)	4,310	14,310
Gross profit (10% of £15,900)		1,590

The cash account shows that the amount of cash stolen was £600. The trading account shows that the cost of the stock held on 21 March 19X8 was £4,310, so that the cost of the stolen stock must have been £4,310 – £850 = £3,460.

5. SUMMARY

- Many small businesses do not maintain a complete set of double-entry accounting records.
- If a business maintains no records at all (or if the records are lost or destroyed) the profit for an accounting period can be estimated by comparing the opening and closing capital, adjusted to take account of capital injections and drawings.
- If a business keeps records of cash received and paid, it is usually possible to prepare a full set of accounts at the end of each accounting period.
- The value of assets which have been stolen or lost can often be estimated. Lost cash can be estimated by drawing up a cash account. Lost stock can be estimated by drawing up a trading account (so long as the average markup or margin used by the business is known).

EXERCISES 10

10.1 Arthur prepares accounts to 31 March each year. Despite advice to the contrary he has always refused to open a bank account and insists that all of his receipts and payments should be in cash. His balance sheet at 31 March 19X7 was as follows:

	£	£
Fixed assets		
Equipment at cost	3,800	
Less: Accumulated depreciation to date	2,400	1,400
Current assets		
Stock of goods for resale	950	
Trade debtors	640	
Prepaid rent	80	
Cash in hand	730	
	2,400	
Current liabilities		
Trade creditors	590	
Accrued heating and lighting	180	
	770	
Net current assets		1,630
		3,030
Capital		
As at 31 March 19X7		3,030

Arthur keeps a rudimentary cashbook but this was lost in the spring of 19X8.

An interview with Arthur yielded the following information:

(a) Arthur estimates that his stock of goods on 31 March 19X8 cost £1,000. On that date, his customers owed him a total of approximately £500 but this figure includes a £100 debt which Arthur believes to be irrecoverable. A review of his suppliers' statements suggests that he owed £720 to those suppliers on 31 March 19X8.

(b) Arthur occupies rented business premises. The rent used to be £80 per month (payable one month in advance) but this increased by 25% with effect from 1 January 19X8. The rent for April 19X8 was paid on 30 March 19X8.

(c) Accrued heating and lighting expenses on 31 March 19X8 are estimated to be £200.

(d) In January 19X8, Arthur replaced some of his business equipment. He bought new equipment costing £800 but received a part-exchange allowance of £180 in relation to equipment which he had bought for £600 in June 19X4. The balance due of £620 was paid out of Arthur's private funds.

(e) Depreciation is calculated at 20% p.a. on the straight-line basis, with a full year's charge in the year of acquisition and none in the year of disposal. None of Arthur's equipment was more than four years old on 31 March 19X8.

(f) Arthur withdraws £150 from the business each week to cover his personal living expenses. In December 19X7, he withdrew an extra £250 to pay for Christmas presents. He also takes an estimated £20 worth of stock from the business each week.

(g) There was approximately £500 cash in hand on 31 March 19X8.

Required:

Insofar as the above information permits, calculate Arthur's net profit for the year to 31 March 19X8.

10.2 On 1 July 19X7, Luna started running a small shop and decided to produce accounts to 30 June each year. She does not maintain a full set of double-entry books but she does record her receipts and payments. The following information is available in relation to the year ended 30 June 19X8:

(a) Luna used some of the takings from her shop to pay wages for herself and her assistant and to pay certain small expenses. Most of the remaining takings were banked every week, but some cash was left in the till so that customers could be provided with change. Wages and other expenses paid in cash during the year to 30 June 19X8 were as follows:

	£
Assistant's wages	7,320
Luna's wages	9,650
Postage and stationery	137
Window cleaning for the shop	156

In order to provide a cash float on the first day of trading, Luna put £300 of her own money into the till.

(b) Luna's business bank statements for the year to 30 June 19X8 show the following receipts and payments:

		£
Receipts:	Capital introduced by Luna on 1 July 19X7	5,000
	Loan from Luna's uncle on 1 November 19X7	7,500
	Takings paid into the bank	54,745
Payments:	Suppliers of goods for resale	48,659
	Shop fixtures and fittings	3,750
	Shop equipment	2,860
	Rent, rates and insurance	8,340
	Electricity	2,567
	Repair to damaged shop display window	430

Takings of £1,236 paid into the bank on 30 June 19X8 did not appear on the bank statements until early July.

(c) Luna lives in a flat above the shop. One-third of rent, rates and insurance costs and one-quarter of heating and lighting costs relate to the flat.

(d) Most sales are for cash but Luna does allow credit to some regular customers, who owed her a total of £1,263 on 30 June 19X8. Cash in the till at the close of business on 30 June 19X8 was £336.

(e) Some of Luna's suppliers offer discounts for prompt payment and she always takes advantage of these discounts. Discounts received during the year to 30 June 19X8 totalled £1,297. Luna owed her suppliers a total of £4,739 on 30 June 19X8. Her stock of goods on that date had cost her £6,238.

(f) Rent is paid monthly in advance on the first day of each month. The most recent rates payment of £1,200 was paid in April 19X8 and covered the six months to 30 September 19X8. An insurance premium of £1,140 was paid on 1 January 19X8, covering the year to 31 December 19X8. The electricity bill for the 3 months to 30 June 19X8 arrived in July 19X8 and was for £513.

(g) Depreciation on shop fixtures and fittings and on shop equipment is to be provided at 10% p.a. and 15% p.a. respectively, both on the straight-line basis and with a full year's charge in the year of acquisition.

(h) The loan from Luna's uncle attracts interest at 5% p.a. No interest was paid on this loan during the year to 30 June 19X8.

Required:

Prepare Luna's trading and profit and loss account for the year to 30 June 19X8 and a balance sheet as at that date.

***10.3** Brendan's assets and liabilities on 1 February 19X8 were as follows:

		£
Assets:	Plant and machinery (net book value)	7,175
	Stock of goods for resale	4,730
	Prepaid operating expenses	410
Liabilities:	Trade creditors	3,869
	Accrued operating expenses	763
	Bank overdraft	2,775

The following information relates to the year ended 31 January 19X9:

(a) Brendan's sales were all for cash. He took sufficient money out of each week's takings to cover his personal living expenses and then banked the remainder.

(b) Cheque payments made during the year were:

	£
Suppliers of goods for resale	34,870
Operating expenses	13,220
Purchase of plant and machinery	5,000

(c) Brendan's gross profit percentage during the year was a consistent 35%.

(d) Plant and machinery is depreciated at 25% per annum on the reducing balance basis with a full year's charge in the year of acquisition and none in the year of disposal. During the year, plant which had cost £1,600 in October 19X5 was sold to a scrap metal dealer for £300. Brendan spent this money on a present for his wife.

(e) Stock at 31 January 19X9 was £5,071. Trade creditors were £5,090, accrued operating expenses were £850 and the bank overdraft was £3,210. There were no prepaid expenses.

Required:

Prepare Brendan's trading and profit and loss account for the year to 31 January 19X9 and a balance sheet as at that date.

***10.4** Charlotte's assets and liabilities at 31 August 19X8 were as follows:

		£
Assets:	Motor van (net book value)	11,700
	Stock of goods for resale	17,935
	Cash in hand	350
	Cash at bank	7,328
Liabilities:	Trade creditor	11,650
	Accrued operating expenses	540

Charlotte's business premises were burgled on the night of 17 November 19X8. The intruders took her van, her entire stock and her cash in hand. They also (presumably by mistake) took her cashbook and other accounting records. Charlotte's van and cash were insured against theft but unfortunately her stock was not. The following information is available:

(a) The market value of the van on 17 November 19X8 is estimated to be £10,000.

(b) Charlotte buys all her goods from a single supplier and always takes advantage of the 4% discount which this supplier offers for prompt payment. She invariably pays for goods by cheque. She sells goods at a constant markup of 30% and all her customers pay immediately in cash or by cheque.

(c) At the end of each working day, Charlotte deposits all of the cheques and most of the cash received from customers that day into the night safe outside her bank. However, Charlotte always retains some cash in the till to act as a float and she is sure that this float stood at £400 on the night of the burglary.

(d) Copy statements obtained from the bank show that Charlotte paid takings of £20,711 into her business bank account during the period from 1 September 19X8 to 17 November 19X8. There were no other payments into the account during that period.

(e) Cheques totalling £16,512 were sent to Charlotte's supplier between 1 September 19X8 and 17 November 19X8. The only other payments made from the bank account during the period were operating expenses of £1,211 and drawings of £2,400.

(f) On 1 November 19X8, Charlotte took goods from the business for her own personal use. These goods had a selling price of £520.

(g) £9,235 was owed to Charlotte's supplier on 17 November 19X8 and her accrued operating expenses on that date were £280.

Required:

Prepare Charlotte's trading and profit and loss account for the period from 1 September 19X8 to 17 November 19X8 and a balance sheet showing her financial position after the burglary. (Ignore depreciation).

11

ACCOUNTING FOR CLUBS AND SOCIETIES

Chapter objectives

When you have finished this chapter, you should be able to:

- **Understand the accounting requirements of a club or society.**
- **Prepare a receipts and payments account.**
- **Prepare an income and expenditure account.**

1. INTRODUCTION

This chapter is concerned with the accounting requirements of clubs, societies and other non-profit making organisations which exist primarily so as to provide a service to their members. Typical examples of such organisations include sports clubs, social clubs, staff associations and so forth.

Organisations of this type are often fairly small and usually entrust their financial affairs to an unpaid, elected official known as a *treasurer* (often a club member who has some knowledge or experience of accounting). The main functions of the treasurer are as follows:

(a) to maintain records of the club's financial transactions (these records may be quite simple, possibly consisting of little more than a cashbook)

(b) to prepare an annual financial report, which is presented to the members at an annual general meeting.

Since organisations of this type do not exist for the purpose of making a profit, the annual financial report does not take the form of a profit and loss account. Instead, the treasurer will probably prepare either a *receipts and payments account* or an *income and expenditure account*. Each of these financial statements is explained below.

2. RECEIPTS AND PAYMENTS ACCOUNTS

A receipts and payments account is simply a summary of the cashbook for the period under review. Such an account is easy for the club's members to understand and may be perfectly adequate for very small clubs or societies, especially those which have no assets other than their cash and bank balances. However, the receipts and payments account suffers from a number of disadvantages which make it unsuitable for clubs and societies with more complex financial affairs. These disadvantages include the following:

(a) A receipts and payments account is prepared on a cash basis. No attempt is made to account for the (possibly significant) effects of debtors, creditors, accruals or prepayments.

(b) Non-cash items such as the depreciation of fixed assets are ignored.

(c) It is difficult or impossible to prepare an accompanying balance sheet, since this would involve the use of accruals accounting.

For these reasons, larger clubs and societies usually prepare an income and expenditure account (see later in this chapter) rather than a receipts and payments account.

EXAMPLE

The cash account and the bank deposit account of the Yellow Dot Squash Club for the year to 30 June 19X9 can be summarised as follows:

Cash account

	£		£
Balance b/d	53	Hire of squash courts	680
Subscriptions received	1,269	Coaching fees	354
Donations received	31	Affiliation fees	30
Sale of tickets for annual dinner	540	Annual dinner - restaurant bill	425
Sale of Christmas raffle tickets	215	Christmas raffle prizes	140
		Printing and stationery	23
		Donation to Comic Relief	100
		Paid into bank deposit account	300
		Balance c/d	56
	2,108		2,108
Balance b/d	56		

Bank deposit account

	£		£
Balance b/d	152	Balance c/d	471
Cash paid in	300		
Interest received	19		
	471		471
Balance b/d	471		

Prepare a receipts and payments account for the year to 30 June 19X9.

SOLUTION

Yellow Dot Squash Club
Receipts and payments account for the year to 30 June 19X9

Receipts		£	*Payments*		£
Balance at 1 July 19X8:			Hire of squash courts		680
Cash	53		Coaching fees		354
Bank deposit account	152	205	Affiliation fees		30
			Printing and stationery		23
Subscriptions received		1,269	Donation to Comic Relief		100
Donations received		31			
Annual dinner:					
Sale of tickets	540				
Restaurant bill	425	115			
Christmas raffle:					
Sale of tickets	215		Balance at 30 June 19X9:		
Prizes	140	75	Cash	56	
Deposit account interest		19	Bank deposit account	471	527
		1,714			1,714

Notes:

1. The receipts and payments account combines the cash account and the bank deposit account. No attempt is made to indicate which receipts or payments were in cash and which passed through the bank.
2. Related receipts and payments have been set against one another so that the surpluses arising on the annual dinner and the Christmas raffle are disclosed.
3. The account has been presented in a horizontal format but a vertical presentation would have been possible.

3. INCOME AND EXPENDITURE ACCOUNTS

The income and expenditure account prepared by a non-profit making organisation such as a club or society is similar in many ways to the profit and loss account prepared by a business. Note the following points:

(a) An income and expenditure account shows the organisation's revenue and expenses for the period in question, calculated in accordance with normal accounting principles. The effects of debtors, creditors, accruals, prepayments and non-cash items such as depreciation are taken into account.

(b) If the organisation has a trading operation in addition to its other activities, the revenue and expenses of this trading operation may be shown in a separate trading and profit and loss account. The profit or loss revealed by this account is then transferred to the income and expenditure account. An example of such a trading operation would be a members' bar operated by a social club.

(c) If the income and expenditure account shows revenue in excess of expenses, the excess is usually referred to as the *surplus of income over expenditure*. Similarly, any excess of expenses over revenue is referred to as the *surplus of expenditure over income*. The terms net profit and net loss are not used.

(d) The income and expenditure account is usually accompanied by a balance sheet detailing the assets and liabilities of the organisation. The capital of a club or society is generally referred to as the *accumulated fund*.

(e) The majority of clubs and societies maintain incomplete records. Therefore, the preparation of an income and expenditure account and balance sheet will usually involve use of the techniques described in Chapter 10 of this book.

(f) An income and expenditure account (plus a balance sheet) provides members with much more information than a receipts and payments account and helps members to make informed decisions regarding the financial affairs of the organisation.

Subscriptions in advance and in arrears

In general, much of the income of a club or society will take the form of members' annual subscriptions. Unless all members pay their subscriptions when due (which is rather unlikely) it is necessary to consider the accounting treatment of subscriptions paid in advance and subscriptions in arrears.

(a) **Subscriptions paid in advance**. Subscriptions which members have paid in advance for the following year are prepaid revenue. The amount involved should be shown as a current liability in the balance sheet and should appear as income in the *following* year's income and expenditure account.

(b) **Subscriptions in arrears**. Members who are behind with their subscriptions might pay eventually. On the other hand, such members may have left the club altogether without officially resigning their membership. Although subscriptions in arrears could be treated as debtors, the most prudent treatment is to ignore such subscriptions altogether when preparing a club's income and expenditure account and balance sheet.

There is no compulsion for a club or society to account for members' subscriptions in any particular way and various accounting treatments are possible. In an examination question on this topic, the club's accounting policy with regard to subscriptions will be described and it is essential that this policy should be observed when answering the question.

Life memberships

It is sometimes possible for a club member to pay a one-off fee so as to obtain life membership of the club. Such fees should be credited initially to a life membership account and should then be transferred to the income and expenditure account by instalments. Strictly speaking, the number of these instalments should be equal to the number of years for which the member concerned is likely to use the club's facilities. Given the difficulty of making this estimate, it is normal for a club to transfer life membership fees to the income and expenditure account over an arbitrary number of years (typically ten or twenty).

EXAMPLE

Life membership of the Norfolk Hill-Walking Society can be obtained by paying a fee of £300. It is the Society's policy to allocate life membership fees to the income and expenditure account over a ten-year period. On 1 May 19X8, the balance on the life membership account was £2,190, representing the unexpired portion of the fees paid by eleven life members during the previous nine years. In the year to 30 April 19X9, a further £900 was received from three new life members.

Write up the life membership account for the year to 30 April 19X9.

SOLUTION

Life membership subscriptions

		£			£
30.4.X9	I & E account	420	1.5.X8	Balance b/d	2,190
30.4.X9	Balance c/d	2,670	30.4.X9	Bank	900
		3,090			3,090
			1.5.X9	Balance b/d	2,670

Notes:

1. £30 must be transferred to the income and expenditure account in relation to each of the existing eleven life members (none of whom obtained life membership more than nine years before the current accounting period began).
2. £30 must also be transferred to the income and expenditure account in relation to each of the three new life members.
3. The total amount transferred to the income and expenditure account for the year is therefore £30 x 14 = £420.

Funds other than the accumulated fund

As explained above, the capital of a non-profit making organisation is usually known as the *accumulated fund*. Any surplus of income over expenditure is added to this fund and a surplus of expenditure over income is subtracted from it. The accumulated fund represents the sum of the members' claims on the assets of the organisation.

A further claim on those assets might take the form of a special fund, established with a specific purpose in mind. For example, a cricket club might establish a special fund for the acquisition of a new pavilion. The presence of a special fund on the balance sheet indicates that some portion of the organisation's assets has been earmarked for the specific purpose with which the special fund is associated. Note the following points:

(a) One way of establishing a special fund is to make a transfer from the accumulated fund. Further transfers may be made from time to time so as to increase the size of the special fund. The book-keeping entries required on such a transfer are to debit the accumulated fund and credit the special fund with the amount involved.

(b) Alternatively (or additionally) revenue received from fund-raising activities may be credited directly to the special fund and so not pass through the income and expenditure account at all.

(c) A special fund is a claim on the overall net assets of the organisation. However, the existence of such a fund does *not* ensure that liquid assets equal to the amount of the fund will always be available when required. One way of ensuring this is to open a separate bank account for the special fund and to transfer money into this bank account whenever a transfer is made to the credit of the special fund.

COMPREHENSIVE EXAMPLE

The treasurer of the Young Accountants' Rugby Club has produced the following receipts and payments account for the year to 31 July 19X8:

Young Accountants' Rugby Club
Receipts and payments account for the year to 31 July 19X8

Receipts		£	*Payments*		£
Balance at 1 Aug 19X7:			Bar purchases		10,739
Cash	12		Clubhouse repairs & insurance		1,140
Bank account	419	431	Affiliation to Rugby Union		100
			Groundsman's wages		1,040
Subscriptions received		5,122	Bar staff wages		3,669
Life membership fees		500	Disco hire for dinner dance		100
Donations received		2,200	Dinner dance catering costs		400
Bar takings		15,542	Bank charges		113
Sale of dinner dance tickets		720	Charitable donations		900
			New shirts/shorts for 1st team		1,750
			Printing and stationery		321
			Balance at 31 July 19X8:		
			Cash	27	
			Bank account	4,216	4,243
		24,515			24,515

The following information is also available:

(a) Apart from cash and bank balances, the only assets and liabilities of the club are as follows:

	31 July 19X7	*31 July 19X8*
	£	£
Clubhouse, at cost	25,000	25,000
Bar stocks, at cost	713	812
Subscriptions received in advance	220	250
Amount owed to brewery	1,218	1,004
Subscriptions in arrears	350	290

The clubhouse is being depreciated at 10% per annum on cost. This process began on 1 August 19X3.

(b) The cost of the new shirts and shorts bought during the year to 31 July 19X8 is to be written off immediately.

(c) One-half of the clubhouse repairs/insurance and one-half of the clubhouse depreciation is to be regarded as an expense of operating the bar.

(d) The club's policy is to ignore subscriptions in arrears when preparing its annual accounts.

(e) Life membership of the club can be obtained by paying a fee of £250. Such fees are allocated to the income and expenditure account over a five-year period. On 31 July 19X7, the balance on the life membership account was £850. This figure related to seven life members, all of whom had paid the life membership fee within the previous four years. During the year to 31 July 19X8, a further £500 was received from two new life members.

(f) It was decided on 1 January 19X8 that a special fund should be established for the purchase of a new clubhouse. The sum of £3,000 was to be transferred to this special fund from the accumulated fund. Furthermore, £1,000 of the donations received during the year to 31 July 19X8 were intended for the special fund.

Prepare a bar trading and profit and loss account for the year to 31 July 19X8, an income and expenditure account for the year to 31 July 19X8 and a balance sheet as at that date.

SOLUTION

Young Accountants' Rugby Club
Bar trading and profit and loss account for the year to 31 July 19X8

	£	£
Bar takings		15,542
Cost of goods sold:		
Stock as at 1 August 19X7	713	
Bar purchases	10,525	
	11,238	
Less: Stock as at 31 July 19X8	812	10,426
Gross profit		5,116
Bar staff wages	3,669	
Clubhouse repairs and insurance	570	
Clubhouse depreciation	1,250	5,489
Net loss for the year		373

Young Accountants' Rugby Club
Income and expenditure account for the year to 31 July 19X8

	£	£	£
Income			
Subscriptions			5,092
Life membership fees			450
Donations			1,200
Dinner dance:			
Sale of tickets		720	
Less: Catering costs	400		
Disco hire	100	500	220
			6,962
Expenditure			
Loss on operating the bar		373	
Clubhouse repairs and insurance		570	
Groundsman's wages		1,040	
Affiliation to Rugby Union		100	
Bank charges		113	
Printing and stationery		321	
Charitable donations		900	
New shirts & shorts for the 1st team		1,750	
Clubhouse depreciation		1,250	6,417
Surplus of income over expenditure			545

Young Accountants' Rugby Club
Balance sheet as at 31 July 19X8

	£	£	£
Fixed assets			
Clubhouse, at cost		25,000	
Less: Accumulated depreciation to date		12,500	12,500
Current assets			
Bar stocks		812	
Cash at bank		4,216	
Cash in hand		27	
		5,055	
Current liabilities			
Subscriptions received in advance	250		
Owed to brewery	1,004	1,254	3,801
			16,301
Long-term liabilities			
Life memberships			900
			15,401
Accumulated fund			
As at 1 August 19X7		13,856	
Surplus of income over expenditure		545	
		14,401	
Less: Transferred to new clubhouse fund		3,000	11,401
New clubhouse fund			
Transferred from accumulated fund		3,000	
Donations received		1,000	4,000
			15,401

Notes:

1. Bar purchases are £10,739 – £1,218 + £1,004 = £10,525.
2. Subscriptions are £5,122 + £220 – £250 = £5,092.
3. Life membership fees credited to income and expenditure account are £50 for each of 9 life members = £450. The balance on the life memberships account is £850 + £500 – £450 = £900.
4. The opening accumulated fund is £25,000 – £10,000 + £713 + £419 + £12 – £220 – £1,218 – £850 = £13,856.

4. SUMMARY

- The treasurer of a club, society or other non-profit making organisation is required to submit a financial report to the members at each annual general meeting. This report usually takes the form of a receipts and payments account or an income and expenditure account.
- A receipts and payments account is a summary of the cashbook for the period under review. This form of financial report is suitable only for the smallest of organisations, essentially those which have no assets other than cash and no liabilities.
- An income and expenditure account shows the organisation's revenue and expenses for the period in question, calculated in accordance with normal accounting principles. It is usually accompanied by a balance sheet.
- Subscriptions paid in advance should be accounted for as prepaid revenue. It is generally thought prudent to ignore subscriptions in arrears. Life membership subscriptions are usually allocated to the income and expenditure account over an arbitrary number of accounting periods.
- A club or society may establish special funds for a specific purpose.

EXERCISES 11

11.1 Explain the differences between a receipts and payments account and an income and expenditure account. Identify the types of organisation which might find each of these financial statements useful.

11.2 A social club was established on 1 January 19X5. The members agreed that accounts should be prepared to 31 December each year. Subscriptions were received as follows in the first four accounting years:

	Relating to 19X5	*Relating to 19X6*	*Relating to 19X7*	*Relating to 19X8*	*Relating to 19X9*
	£	£	£	£	£
Received during 19X5	1,950	90			
Received during 19X6	340	2,130	110		
Received during 19X7		250	2,250	130	
Received during 19X8			180	2,340	150

Required:

Calculate the amount of subscriptions that should be shown in the club's accounts for the years to 31 December 19X5, 19X6, 19X7 and 19X8, assuming that:

(a) the club prepares receipts and payments accounts

(b) the club prepares income and expenditure accounts and takes no credit for subscriptions which are in arrears at the end of an accounting period.

11.3 The cash and bank accounts of the Walford Chess Club for the year to 31 December 19X8 are as follows:

Cash account

	£		£
Balance b/d	14	Room hire	520
Subscriptions received for 19X8	129	Coffee, biscuits etc.	93
Donations received	50	Balance c/d	30
Cash withdrawn from bank	450		
	643		643
Balance b/d	30		

Bank account

	£		£
Balance b/d	219	Purchase of chess sets & boards	480
Subscriptions received for 19X7	14	Purchase of chess clocks	120
Subscriptions received for 19X8	923	Purchase of chess books	50
Subscriptions received for 19X9	30	Costs of annual outing	427
Receipts from annual outing	395	Cash withdrawn from bank	450
		Balance c/d	54
	1,581		1,581
Balance b/d	54		

Required:

Prepare a receipts and payments account for the year to 31 December 19X8.

***11.4** The treasurer of the Trentside cricket club has prepared the following receipts and payments account for the year to 31 March 19X7:

Trentside Cricket Club
Receipts and payments account for the year to 31 March 19X7

Receipts		£	*Payments*		£
Balance at 1 April 19X6:			Purchase of refreshments		1,128
Cash	88		Catering staff wages		520
Bank account	109	197	Heating and lighting		218
			Purchase of plates & glasses		120
Subscriptions received		2,110	Purchase of cricket clothing		
Life membership fees		300	and equipment for resale		2,530
Donations received		540	Lords Test - admission fees		380
Sales of refreshments		2,986	Lords Test - coach hire		105
Sales of cricket clothing			Lords Test - tip for driver		10
and equipment		3,107	Rent of indoor cricket		
Receipts from trip to Lords			practice facilities		1,670
Test match		650	Repairs		325
Bank interest received		23	Groundsman's wages		500
			Public liability insurance		500
			Purchase of new motor mower		630
			Balance at 31 March 19X7:		
			Cash	92	
			Bank account	1,185	1,277
		9,913			9,913

The following information is also relevant:

(a) The club owns its own ground and pavilion. The ground cost £2,000 and the pavilion was built at a cost of £1,400. Depreciation has not been charged on these assets in the past but it has now been decided that the pavilion should be depreciated at a rate of 5% per annum on the straight-line basis, beginning in the year to 31 March 19X7.

(b) The new mower was bought for £900, less a part-exchange allowance of £270 on the old mower. Mowers are depreciated at 20% per annum on the straight-line basis, with a full charge in the year of acquisition and none in the year of disposal. The old mower had a written-down value of £310 on 31 March 19X6.

(c) Apart from the ground, the pavilion, the mowers and the cash and bank balances, the only assets and liabilities of the club are as follows:

	31/3/X6	*31/3/X7*
	£	£
Stock of refreshments	75	82
Stock of cricket clothing and equipment	430	510
Accrued heating and lighting	25	32
Prepaid insurance premium	100	125
Subscriptions received in advance	110	60
Subscriptions in arrears (year to 31 March 19X6)	95	25
Subscriptions in arrears (year to 31 March 19X7)	—	85
Owing to suppliers of cricket clothing & equipment	210	184

(d) The policy of the club is to show subscriptions in arrears as an asset in the balance sheet so long as they relate to the accounting period which has just ended rather than to an earlier accounting period.

(e) Life membership of the club is available at a fee of £150. Life membership fees are transferred to the income and expenditure account over a period of ten years. As at 31 March 19X6, the club had nine life members, six of whom had become life members within the previous nine years. The balance on the life membership account at 31 March 19X6 was £420.

(f) It was decided on 1 April 19X6 that a special fund should be established so that the club could acquire its own indoor practice facilities. All bank interest and all profits from the sale of cricket clothing and equipment are to be credited to this special fund until further notice.

(g) 40% of heating and lighting costs and 60% of repairs relate to the preparation and sale of refreshments. The cost of the plates and glasses acquired during the year is to be written off immediately. None of the other expenses described above relate to the refreshments operation.

Required:

1. Prepare a refreshments trading and profit and loss account for the year to 31 March 19X7.
2. Prepare a cricket clothing and equipment trading account for the year to 31 March 19X7.
3. Prepare an income and expenditure account for the year to 31 March 19X7.
4. Prepare a balance sheet as at 31 March 19X7.

12

PARTNERSHIP ACCOUNTS

Chapter objectives

When you have finished this chapter, you should be able to:

- **Explain the advantages and disadvantages of forming a partnership.**
- **Prepare a profit and loss appropriation account for a partnership.**
- **Write up partners' capital accounts and current accounts.**
- **Make the necessary adjustments when a partner joins or leaves the partnership or when there is a change in the profit-sharing agreement.**
- **Make closing entries on the dissolution of a partnership.**

1. INTRODUCTION

A partnership is defined by the Partnership Act 1890 as "*the relation which subsists between persons carrying on a business in common with a view of profit*". In other words, a partnership exists if two or more people own a business jointly.

Partnerships are formed because they offer certain advantages when compared with sole ownership of a business. The main advantages of forming a partnership are as follows:

(a) An increased amount of capital is made available when two or more partners own a business together. It becomes feasible to establish larger businesses and to fund business expansion.

(b) Each of the partners may possess distinctive skills or qualities which usefully complement those of the other partners. For example, one partner may have great technical expertise whilst another may be a specialist in marketing or finance or may have excellent business contacts.

(c) The risks and responsibilities of business ownership are shared amongst the partners rather than falling on just one person.

On the other hand, partnerships suffer from a number of disadvantages. The business is no longer under the control of one person and the partners may disagree on policy matters. More fundamentally, each partner is legally bound by the acts of all the other partners and can be held individually responsible for all of the partnership's debts. It would obviously be unwise to enter into partnership with anyone other than the most trustworthy of fellow partners.

The 1890 Act specifies that a partnership cannot have more than twenty partners, although this limit does not apply to certain types of partnership (e.g. firms of accountants or solicitors). In general, the only way of increasing the number of co-owners of a business beyond twenty is to form a limited company. The accounts of limited companies are introduced in Chapter 13.

2. THE PARTNERSHIP AGREEMENT

A partnership agreement sets out the terms of the partnership and records the financial arrangements to which the partners have agreed. The agreement, which may be either written or oral, covers such matters as:

(a) the name of the partnership and the type of business to be conducted

(b) the amount of capital to be contributed by each partner

(c) the way in which profits and losses are to be shared amongst the partners

(d) any limit placed on the amount of drawings which a partner is entitled to make in the course of an accounting year

(e) arrangements for the introduction of new partners

(f) the procedure to be followed when a partner retires or dies

(g) rules for making changes to the partnership agreement.

The profit-sharing agreement

One of the most important parts of a partnership agreement is the part which sets out the way in which profits and losses are to be shared amongst the partners. This is frequently referred to as the *profit-sharing agreement*. A profit-sharing agreement may involve the following elements:

(a) **Interest on capital**. Each partner may be entitled to interest, calculated at a specified rate, on the amount of capital that he or she has contributed. This provides compensation to those partners (if any) who have provided more capital than their fellow partners.

(b) **Partners' salaries**. Each partner may be entitled to a salary. The amount of a partner's salary will be commensurate with the amount of work which the partner does on behalf of the business or the level of expertise that the partner possesses.

(c) **Profit-sharing ratio**. The agreement will specify the ratio in which partners will share any profits (or losses) which remain after interest on capital and partners' salaries have been deducted. Senior partners will usually receive a greater profit share than junior partners.

It is important to realise that interest on capital and partners' salaries are merely ways of appropriating profits fairly between the partners. They are *not* business expenses and are *not* taken into account when calculating net profit.

A profit-sharing agreement may also specify that partners should be charged interest on their drawings. Interest on drawings is a negative appropriation of profit and is intended to discourage partners from making excessive drawings early in the accounting year. The total interest charged on partners' drawings is added to net profit and the resulting total is then appropriated amongst the partners according to the other provisions of their profit-sharing agreement.

The PA1890 defaults

In the absence of a written or oral partnership agreement, the Partnership Act 1890 provides that the following profit-sharing rules should apply:

(a) Partners will receive no interest on capital.
(b) Partners will receive no salaries or other remuneration.
(c) Partners will not be charged interest on drawings.
(d) Partners will share profits and losses equally.
(e) Partners will be entitled to interest at 5% per annum on any loans made to the partnership in excess of agreed capital (see later in this chapter).

EXAMPLE

Peter, Paul and Mary are in partnership. Their profit-sharing agreement is as follows:

(a) Each partner is entitled to interest on capital calculated at 5% per annum.
(b) Interest on partners' drawings is charged at 7.5% per annum.
(c) Partners' salaries are Peter £5,000, Paul £8,000 and Mary £12,000.
(d) Remaining profits and losses are to be shared equally.

The amount of capital contributed by each partner is Peter £24,000, Paul £16,000 and Mary £9,000.

The net profit for the year to 31 December 19X8 is £74,230 and interest on drawings has been calculated as Peter £180, Paul £320 and Mary £570. Show how the net profit for the year will be appropriated between the partners.

SOLUTION

The amount of interest charged on drawings is £1,070. This is added to the net profit of £74,230, giving a total of £75,300 to be appropriated between the partners. Interest on capital takes £2,450 of this (Peter £1,200, Paul £800, Mary £450) and partners' salaries take a further £25,000. The remaining £47,850 is divided equally between the partners (£15,950 each). In summary:

	Peter	*Paul*	*Mary*	*Total*
	£	£	£	£
Interest on capital	1,200	800	450	2,450
Partners' salaries	5,000	8,000	12,000	25,000
Profit share	15,950	15,950	15,950	47,850
	22,150	24,750	28,400	75,300
Less: Interest on drawings	180	320	570	1,070
Profit allocated to each partner	21,970	24,430	27,830	74,230

3. ACCOUNTING FOR PARTNERSHIPS

The profit and loss account and balance sheet of a partnership are prepared and presented in a very similar way to those of a sole trader. The only significant differences are as follows:

(a) **The appropriation account**. An extra account known as the *appropriation account* is appended to the profit and loss account of a partnership. The purpose of this account is to show how the net profit (or loss) for the year has been allocated between the partners.

(b) **Capital accounts**. Each partner will have his or her own capital account. The partnership balance sheet will show the balance on each of these accounts.

(c) **Current accounts**. Partners may have current accounts (see below) as well as capital accounts. In this case the partnership balance sheet will list the partners' current account balances as well as their capital account balances.

It is common practice for a partner's capital account to record only the fixed capital contributed by that partner. If this practice is followed, each partner will also have a separate current account, which is credited each year with the partner's profit allocation and debited with his or her drawings. Capital accounts will always be in credit but a current account may have a debit balance. This will occur if a partner's accumulated drawings exceed that partner's accumulated profit entitlement.

The main reason for having separate capital and current accounts is that interest on capital is usually payable only on a partner's fixed capital. This figure is more easily ascertained if it is isolated in a separate account.

Note that the use of the term "fixed" does not mean that the balance on a partner's capital account will never change, only that this balance is not affected by the partner's drawings and profit allocations. Subject to the terms of the partnership agreement, partners might withdraw capital or introduce fresh capital from time to time. Such transactions will, of course, be recorded in their capital accounts.

EXAMPLE

The following information refers to the partnership of Peter, Paul and Mary for the year to 31 December 19X8 (see previous example):

	Peter	*Paul*	*Mary*
	£	£	£
Opening capital account balances	24,000	16,000	9,000
Opening current account balances (all in credit)	1,350	2,170	430
Drawings for the year	19,840	23,590	29,920

No fixed capital was introduced or withdrawn during the year. Prepare an appropriation account for the year to 31 December 19X8 and write up the partners' capital accounts and current accounts for the year.

SOLUTION

Peter, Paul and Mary
Appropriation account for the year to 31 December 19X8

	£	£
Net profit for the year		74,230
Add: Interest on drawings:		
Peter	180	
Paul	320	
Mary	570	1,070
		75,300
Less: Interest on capital:		
Peter (5% x £24,000)	1,200	
Paul (5% x £16,000)	800	
Mary (5% x £9,000)	450	2,450
		72,850
Less: Partners' salaries:		
Peter	5,000	
Paul	8,000	
Mary	12,000	25,000
		47,850
Less: Profit shares:		
Peter (1/3)	15,950	
Paul (1/3)	15,950	
Mary (1/3)	15,950	47,850

Partners' capital accounts

	Peter	Paul	Mary		Peter	Paul	Mary
	£	£	£		£	£	£
				Balances b/d	24,000	16,000	19,000

Partners' current accounts

	Peter	Paul	Mary		Peter	Paul	Mary
	£	£	£		£	£	£
Drawings	19,840	23,590	29,920	Balances b/d	1,350	2,170	430
Int. on drawings	180	320	570	Int. on capital	1,200	800	450
Balances c/d	3,480	3,010		Salaries	5,000	8,000	12,000
				Profit shares	15,950	15,950	15,950
				Balance c/d			1,660
	23,500	26,920	30,490		23,500	26,920	30,490
Balance b/d			1,660	Balances b/d	3,480	3,010	

Note:

The capital and current accounts have been prepared in columnar form so as to save space and time. However, each partner's capital account is entirely separate from the other partners' capital accounts and each partner's current account is entirely separate from the other partners' current accounts.

Partners' loans

If a partner lends money to the partnership, the interest on this loan is usually treated as a business expense and is shown in the profit and loss account. Any loan interest which is not paid over to the partner concerned as soon as it falls due is normally credited to the partner's current account. Alternatively, such interest could be credited to a separate account in the partner's name and shown as a liability in the partnership balance sheet.

4. CHANGES TO THE PROFIT-SHARING AGREEMENT

A partnership's profit-sharing agreement will change if any one of the following events occurs:

(a) The partners decide to change their profit-sharing arrangements.
(b) A new partner is admitted to the partnership.
(c) An existing partner dies or retires from the partnership.

These events can occur in combination. For example, a new partner might join the partnership as a replacement for a retiring partner. The accounting implications of a change in the profit-sharing agreement are as follows:

(a) **Apportionment of profit**. If the profit-sharing agreement is changed part-way through an accounting year, the profit for the year must be apportioned. The profit arising before the change is allocated according to the old profit-sharing agreement and the profit arising after the change is allocated according to the new agreement. Apportionment calculations are usually made on the assumption that profits have accrued evenly throughout the year. However, some businesses are affected by seasonal factors and it may be necessary to take these into account when performing apportionment calculations.

(b) **Revaluation of assets**. The book value of a partnership's assets on the date of a change in the profit-sharing agreement is often different from the current value of those assets. If so, a previously undisclosed profit or loss has arisen in relation to these assets. This is a pre-change profit or loss and must be allocated between the partners according to their old profit-sharing agreement. For this reason, a change in the partnership agreement will usually trigger a revaluation of the partnership's assets. This matter is considered in more detail below.

EXAMPLE

John and Paul are in partnership. Their profit-sharing agreement provides for annual salaries of £5,000 for John and £7,000 for Paul. Remaining profits are shared equally. There is no interest on capital and interest is not charged on partners' drawings.

On 1 July 19X7, George is admitted as a partner. The new profit-sharing agreement provides for annual salaries of £4,000 for John, £6,000 for Paul and £8,000 for George. Remaining profits are to be shared in the ratio 5:3:2.

The summarised profit and loss account of the partnership for the year to 30 September 19X7 is as follows:

	£	£
Sales		180,000
Cost of goods sold		100,000
		80,000
Selling expenses	12,000	
Administrative expenses	20,000	32,000
Net profit for the year		48,000

(50% of sales occur in the final three months of the accounting year).

Assuming that the cost of goods sold and the selling expenses should be apportioned on a turnover basis, but that the administrative expenses should be apportioned on a time basis, show how the profit for the year should be allocated between the partners.

SOLUTION

	9 months to 30/6/X7		*3 months to 30/9/X7*		*Total*	
	£	£	£	£	£	£
Sales		90,000		90,000		180,000
Cost of goods sold		50,000		50,000		100,000
Gross profit		40,000		40,000		80,000
Selling expenses	6,000		6,000		12,000	
Admin. expenses	15,000	21,000	5,000	11,000	20,000	32,000
Net profit		19,000		29,000		48,000
Less: Partners' salaries						
John	3,750		1,000		4,750	
Paul	5,250		1,500		6,750	
George	-	9,000	2,000	4,500	2,000	13,500
		10,000		24,500		34,500
Less: Profit shares						
John	5,000		12,250		17,250	
Paul	5,000		7,350		12,350	
George	-	10,000	4,900	24,500	4,900	34,500

Notes:

1. Cost of goods sold and selling expenses have been apportioned 50% to the first 9 months and 50% to the final 3 months, in line with sales.
2. Administrative expenses have been apportioned on a time basis, 75% to the first 9 months and 25% to the final 3 months.
3. Salaries due for the first 9 months have been calculated as 9/12ths of the annual salaries due under the old agreement. Salaries due for the final 3 months have been calculated as 3/12ths of the annual salaries due under the new agreement.
4. Remaining profits for the final 3 months are to be divided "in the ratio 5:3:2". The sum of these ratio parts is 10. Therefore John receives 5/10ths of the remaining profit, Paul receives 3/10ths and George receives 2/10ths.

5. REVALUATION ACCOUNTS

As stated earlier, it is usually necessary to revalue the partnership assets on a change in the profit-sharing agreement. If this were not done, the profit or loss arising on the subsequent sale of an asset would include a pre-change element. Since all profits and losses arising after the date of a change are automatically shared between the partners according to their new agreement, this would unfairly penalise some partners and enrich others. The revaluation procedure is as follows:

(a) If the current value of an asset is greater than its book value, the increase in value is debited to the relevant asset account and credited to an account known as the *revaluation account.*

(b) If the current value of an asset is less than its book value, the decrease in value is credited to the relevant asset account and debited to the revaluation account.

(c) The balance on the revaluation account represents the overall profit or loss on revaluation of the partnership's assets. This is allocated between the partners in their old (pre-change) profit-sharing ratio.

It should be noted that similar adjustments may occasionally be required in relation to the partnership's liabilities, but these are comparatively rare.

EXAMPLE

Debbie and Diana are in partnership sharing profits in the ratio 5:3. On 1 May 19X8, they agree to admit Damon as a partner. Damon will introduce capital of £20,000 and the new partnership of Debbie, Diana and Damon will share profits in the ratio 5:4:1. The partnership's balance sheet as at 30 April 19X8 is as follows:

	£	£
Fixed assets		
Land and buildings		45,000
Motor vehicles		23,500
c/f		68,500

	£	£
b/f		68,500
Current assets		
Stock of goods for resale	17,760	
Trade debtors	13,330	
Cash at bank	2,870	
	33,960	
Current liabilities		
Trade creditors	15,550	18,410
		86,910
Capital accounts		
Debbie	50,000	
Diana	30,000	80,000
Current accounts		
Debbie	4,280	
Diana	2,630	6,910
		86,910

On Damon's admission, the partnership assets are to be revalued as follows. Land and buildings £85,000, Motor vehicles £21,500, Stock £18,200 and Debtors £12,170.

Write up the revaluation account and the partners' capital accounts. Prepare a balance sheet for the partnership as at 1 May 19X8.

SOLUTION

Revaluation account

	£		£
Motor vehicles	2,000	Land and buildings	40,000
Trade debtors	1,160	Stock	440
Profit on revaluation:			
Debbie (5/8th)	23,300		
Diana (3/8th)	13,980		
	40,440		40,440

Partners' capital accounts

	Debbie	Diana	Damon		Debbie	Diana	Damon
	£	£	£		£	£	£
Balances c/d	73,300	43,980	20,000	Balances b/d	50,000	30,000	
				Revaluation	23,300	13,980	
				Bank			20,000
	73,300	43,980	20,000		73,300	43,980	20,000
				Balances b/d	73,300	43,980	20,000

Note:

The profit on revaluation has been divided between the partners in their old profit-sharing ratio and then credited to their *capital* accounts. A profit on revaluation is an unrealised profit and cannot be used to fund increased drawings, hence the decision to use the capital accounts rather than the current accounts.

Debbie, Diana and Damon
Balance sheet as at 1 May 19X8

	£	£
Fixed assets		
Land and buildings		85,000
Motor vehicles		21,500
		106,500
Current assets		
Stock of goods for resale	18,200	
Trade debtors	12,170	
Cash at bank	22,870	
	53,240	
Current liabilities		
Trade creditors	15,550	37,690
		144,190
Capital accounts		
Debbie	73,300	
Diana	43,980	
Damon	20,000	137,280
Current accounts		
Debbie	4,280	
Diana	2,630	6,910
		144,190

Revaluation and the accounting conventions

We have seen that it is essential to revalue assets when there is a change in the profit-sharing agreement of a partnership. However, the historic cost convention and the objectivity convention both require that assets should be shown in the balance sheet at original cost, not at a subjective valuation.

One way of resolving this conflict is to leave the assets at their historic cost but to make adjustments to the partners' capital account balances so as to maintain equity between the partners. The process is illustrated by the following example.

EXAMPLE

Bob and Bill are in partnership sharing profits equally. On 1 May 19X9, they admit Barry as a partner. Barry will introduce capital of £10,000 and the new partnership of Bob, Bill and Barry will share profits in the ratio 2:2:1.

None of the partnership's assets needs revaluing other than freehold premises. These have a current value of £100,000 but are shown in the balance sheet at their original cost of £72,000. The partners have agreed that the premises will continue to be shown at cost in the balance sheet. Show the adjustments which must be made on Barry's admission to the partnership.

SOLUTION

The difference between the book value of the freehold premises and their current value is £28,000. If the premises had been sold for £100,000 just *before* Barry's admission, Bob and Bill would each have been credited with a profit of £14,000. If the premises are sold for £100,000 at any time *after* Barry's admission, the profit on the sale will be credited to the partners as follows:

		£
Bob	(2/5th)	11,200
Bill	(2/5th)	11,200
Barry	(1/5th)	5,600

This means that Bob and Bill will each be credited with £2,800 less than their fair entitlement, whilst Barry will be credited with £5,600 to which he is not entitled at all. *Therefore Barry must purchase the right to receive his share of this profit by paying £2,800 each to Bob and Bill when he is admitted as a partner.* These payments can be achieved by debiting Barry's capital account with £5,600 and crediting Bob's and Bill's capital accounts with £2,800 each. It may seem unfair that Barry should lose £5,600 of his capital as soon as he joins the partnership. However, he has bought a 1/5th share in the difference between the book value and market value of the freehold premises and this share is worth the £5,600 of capital which he has sacrificed. An alternative (but equivalent) solution to this problem consists of the following two steps:

(a) The premises are temporarily revalued at their current value of £100,000 and the profit on revaluation is shared between the partners in their *old* profit-sharing ratio (Bob £14,000, Bill £14,000).

(b) The premises are then written back down to their original cost of £72,000 and the loss on this write-down is shared between the partners in their *new* profit-sharing ratio (Bob £11,200, Bill £11,200, Barry £5,600).

The net effect of these entries is precisely the same as before. Barry loses £5,600 from his capital account whilst Bob and Bill gain £2,800 each.

Some assets shown at current value and others shown at historic cost

When there is a change in profit-sharing agreement, the partners may decide that some of the partnership assets should be shown in the balance sheet at their current values whilst others should remain at historic cost. A typical approach is as follows:

(a) Minor changes to the values of current assets and any decreases in the values of fixed assets *are* reflected in the balance sheet. A revaluation account is used to calculate the overall profit or loss arising in connection with these assets, as explained earlier in this chapter.

(b) Increases in the values of fixed assets are *not* reflected in the balance sheet. Such assets remain at historic cost and the necessary adjustments are made through the partners' capital accounts, as described above.

This policy conforms with the prudence convention whilst over-riding the historic cost, objectivity and consistency conventions. In the end, it is up to the partners to decide how assets should be valued in their balance sheet. The approach to be adopted in any examination question on the topic will undoubtedly be explained in the question.

6. GOODWILL

There is one partnership asset which will almost certainly have a book value of less than its current value. In fact, the asset concerned is often omitted from the balance sheet altogether. This asset is *goodwill*, which may be defined as the difference between the total value of the partnership's assets (net of all liabilities) and the value of the partnership business as a whole. Goodwill arises as a result of a number of factors. These include the good reputation of the business, its established customer base and the skill of its workforce.

Goodwill may be a very important asset. In fact, for some businesses, it may be the most important asset of all. However, it is difficult to value with any precision and is often omitted from the balance sheet both for this reason and for reasons of prudence.

Goodwill valuation methods

As explained above, the assets of a partnership must be revalued whenever there is a change in the profit-sharing agreement. Goodwill is no exception to this rule, but goodwill valuation methods tend to be rather arbitrary. Valuation methods in common use include the following:

(a) **Based on average profit**. Goodwill is valued as the average net profit of the partnership in recent years, multiplied by an agreed factor. The number of years' profits which are averaged and the size of the multiplication factor are matters which have to be agreed between the partners. A variant on this method is to use a weighted average, so that the profits of later years weigh more heavily in the calculation than the profits of earlier years.

(b) **Based on average super-profit**. Goodwill is valued as the average *super-profit* of the partnership in recent years, multiplied by an agreed factor. Super-profit is defined as net profit, less the amount of interest which the partners could obtain if their capital were invested elsewhere, less the salaries which the partners could obtain if they worked elsewhere.

(c) **Based on average revenue**. Goodwill is valued as the average revenue or turnover of the partnership in recent years, multiplied by an agreed factor.

Accounting for goodwill

In general, goodwill is not shown in the partnership balance sheet and there is no goodwill account in the partnership books. On a change in the profit-sharing agreement it is necessary to value the goodwill in some way (see above) and then to make the following entries:

(a) Open a goodwill account and debit this account with the amount of the goodwill.

(b) Credit the partners' capital accounts with this amount, shared between them in their *old* profit-sharing ratio.

If the partners wish to continue the practice of not showing goodwill in the books, the following entries are also required:

(c) Close the goodwill account by crediting it with the amount of the goodwill.

(d) Debit the partners' capital accounts with this amount, allocated between them in their *new* profit-sharing ratio.

Alternatively, the required adjustments could be made entirely in the partners' capital accounts, without troubling to open and close a goodwill account. The process is exactly the same as that described earlier in this chapter in relation to assets other than goodwill.

EXAMPLE

(a) Charles and Carol are in partnership, sharing profits equally. No goodwill account appears in the books of the business and the partners wish to continue with this policy. They decide that, as from 1 June 19X8, profits should be shared between them in the ratio 3:2. Goodwill is valued at £60,000. Show the adjustments required on the change in profit-sharing ratio.

(b) Saeed, Simon, Sally and Susan are in partnership sharing profits in the ratio 4:3:2:1. No goodwill account appears in the books of the business and this policy is to continue. On 1 May 19X9, they agree to admit Sam into the partnership. He will pay £2,000 for his share of the goodwill. The partnership of Saeed, Simon, Sally, Susan and Sam will share profits in the ratio 3:2:2:2:1. Show the adjustments required on the admission of Sam.

SOLUTION

(a) A goodwill account is debited with £60,000 and Charles and Carol are credited with £30,000 each. The goodwill account is then credited with £60,000, Charles is debited with £36,000 (3/5th x £60,000) and Carol is debited with £24,000 (2/5th x £60,000).

The alternative is simply to debit Charles and credit Carol with £6,000. In effect, Charles is paying Carol £6,000 for the extra 10% of the goodwill which he now owns.

(b) Sam will own a 1/10th share in the partnership and he is paying £2,000 for "his share" of the goodwill. Therefore the goodwill must be valued at £20,000. The required entries may be summarised as follows:

	Saeed	*Simon*	*Sally*	*Susan*	*Sam*
	£	£	£	£	£
Credit to capital a/cs (in old ratio)	8,000	6,000	4,000	2,000	-
Debit to capital a/cs (in new ratio)	6,000	4,000	4,000	4,000	2,000

Saeed and Simon have each sold 10% of the goodwill and are £2,000 better off as a result. Susan and Sam have each bought 10% of the goodwill and are £2,000 worse off as a result. Sally's share of the goodwill has not altered and so neither has her capital account balance.

7. PARTNERSHIP DISSOLUTIONS

When a partnership is dissolved, the partnership assets are sold off (or *realised*) and any resulting profit or loss on realisation is shared between the partners in profit-sharing ratio. The partnership liabilities are paid off and then, finally, the partners are paid the amounts outstanding on their capital and current accounts. The necessary book-keeping entries are as follows:

(a) A realisation account is opened. The purpose of this account is to calculate the profit or loss arising on realisation of the partnership assets.

(b) All of the asset accounts (except cash and bank) are closed down by transferring the book value of each asset to the realisation account.

(c) As assets are sold, cash or bank is debited and the realisation account is credited with the sale proceeds. If any of the assets is taken over by one of the partners, the partner's capital account is debited and the realisation account is credited with the agreed value of the asset.

(d) Any costs of dissolution are debited to the realisation account and credited to the cash or bank account.

(e) As liabilities are paid off, liability accounts are debited and the cash or bank account is credited with the amounts paid. Any discounts received are debited to the relevant liability account and credited to the realisation account.

(f) When all of the assets have been sold and all the liabilities have been settled, the balance on the realisation account is the profit or loss on realisation. This is divided between the partners in their profit-sharing ratio.

(g) The partners' current account balances are transferred to their capital accounts.

(h) The partners are then paid the balances outstanding on their capital accounts and the dissolution is complete.

Overdrawn capital accounts

If there is a loss on realisation, it is possible that one or more of the partners' capital accounts may become overdrawn (i.e. show a debit balance). A partner with an overdrawn capital account should pay sufficient cash into the partnership to clear the debit balance. If he or she is unable to do so, the resulting loss must be borne by the remaining partners.

In the famous case of *Garner* v *Murray* (1904) it was held that such a loss should not be divided between the remaining partners in their usual profit-sharing ratio, but in the ratio of their capital account balances immediately prior to the dissolution. This rule applies unless the partnership agreement stipulates otherwise.

EXAMPLE

Jean, Jill and John are in partnership, sharing profits and losses equally. On 17 May 19X9 they decide to dissolve the partnership. Their balance sheet on that date can be summarised as follows:

	£	£	£
Fixed assets			
At cost, less accumulated depreciation			19,500
Current assets			
Stock of goods for resale		18,670	
Trade debtors		7,490	
		26,160	
Current liabilities			
Trade creditors	12,480		
Bank overdraft	9,220	21,700	4,460
			23,960
Capital accounts			
Jean		12,300	
Jill		8,200	
John		3,460	23,960
			23,960

The fixed assets and stock are auctioned for £12,750 and £8,000 respectively. The debtors realise £7,200 and discounts of £610 are received from the creditors. The costs of dissolution amount to £2,100. John is unable to meet his liability to the partnership. Write up the realisation account, the partners' capital accounts and the bank account.

SOLUTION

Realisation account

	£			£
Fixed assets	19,500	Bank - sale of fixed assets		12,750
Stock	18,670	Bank - sale of stock		8,000
Trade debtors	7,490	Bank - received from debtors		7,200
Bank - costs of dissolution	2,100	Discounts received		610
		Loss on realisation:		
		Jean	6,400	
		Jill	6,400	
		John	6,400	19,200
	47,760			47,760

Partners' capital accounts

	Jean	Jill	John		Jean	Jill	John
	£	£	£		£	£	£
Realisation a/c	6,400	6,400	6,400	Balances b/d	12,300	8,200	3,460
John's deficit	1,764	1,176		John's deficit			2,940
Bank	4,136	624					
	12,300	8,200	6,400		12,300	8,200	6,400

Bank

	£		£
Realisation of fixed assets	12,750	Balance b/d	9,220
Realisation of stock	8,000	Costs of dissolution	2,100
Realisation of debtors	7,200	Trade creditors	11,870
		Jean	4,136
		Jill	624
	27,950		27,950

Note:

John's deficit of £2,940 has been divided between Jean and Jill in the ratio 12,300:8,200. This ratio simplifies to 3:2.

Sale to a limited company

If a partnership is dissolved and the business is transferred to a limited company, all or part of the consideration received for the partnership's assets is likely to take the form of shares in the company. The accounting implications are as follows:

(a) An account must be opened to record the shares received from the company.

(b) The realisation account is credited and the shares account is debited with the agreed value of the shares received.

(c) When realisation is complete, the shares are divided between the partners in any way that they choose. Each partner's account is debited and the shares account is credited with the value of the shares taken over by that partner.

(d) Any closing balances on partner's capital accounts are then settled in cash, as usual.

8. SUMMARY

► A partnership is the relation which subsists between persons carrying on a business in common with a view of profit. A partnership agreement sets out the terms of the partnership and the financial arrangements to which the partners have agreed.

► A partner may be entitled to interest on capital, a partner's salary and a share in the remaining profits. Partners may also be charged interest on their drawings.

► An appropriation account shows how the net profit of the business has been allocated between the partners. Each partner has a capital account and may also have a current account.

► A change in the partners' profit-sharing agreement will occur if a new partner is admitted, if a partner dies or retires or if the existing partners decide to change their profit-sharing arrangements.

► A change in profit-sharing agreement triggers a revaluation of the partnership assets. The profit or loss arising on this revaluation must be shared between the partners in their old profit-sharing ratio.

► Goodwill is the difference between the total value of a partnership's net assets and the value of the partnership business as a whole. Goodwill is normally not shown in the partnership balance sheet but must be valued when there is a change in the profit-sharing agreement. There are various ways of arriving at a goodwill valuation.

► A realisation account is used to calculate the profit or loss arising on the dissolution of a partnership.

EXERCISES 12

12.1 Kevin, Kate and Kim are in partnership. Their partnership agreement states that:

(a) partners are entitled to 6% p.a. interest on their capital accounts

(b) interest is charged on partners' drawings at the rate of 8% p.a.

(c) partners' annual salaries are Kevin £4,000, Kate £7,000, Kim £11,000

(d) remaining profits and losses are shared in the ratio 8:7:5.

The partners' capital and current account balances at 1 July 19X8 and their drawings for the year to 30 June 19X9 were as follows:

	Capital a/c balances at 1 July 19X8	*Current a/c balances at 1 July 19X8*		*Drawings for year to 30 June 19X9*
	£	£		£
Kevin	30,000	1,235	(credit)	18,000
Kate	20,000	450	(debit)	15,000
Kim	10,000	1,202	(credit)	17,500

On 1 April 19X9, Kevin reduced his capital by £8,000. He withdrew only £3,000 of this sum, leaving the remainder as a loan to the partnership, bearing interest at 10% p.a. This loan interest is to be credited to his current account. On the same date, Kim increased her capital by a further £7,000.

The net profit for the year to 30 June 19X9, before interest, was £82,410.

Required:

Prepare an appropriation account for the year to 30 June 19X9 and write up the partners' capital accounts and current accounts for the year. (For the purposes of calculating interest on drawings, it is assumed that all drawings were made on a date falling exactly half-way through the accounting year).

12.2 Liam and Lorna have been in partnership for many years, sharing profits in the ratio 3:2. On 31 October 19X8 they agree to admit Len as a partner. Len will introduce capital of £15,000 and the new partnership of Liam, Lorna and Len will share profits in the ratio 4:3:1. The partnership balance sheet on 31 October 19X8 is as follows:

	£	£
Fixed assets		
Land and buildings		50,000
Plant and equipment		18,300
Motor vehicles		19,750
		88,050
Current assets		
Stock of goods for resale	12,450	
Trade debtors	17,210	
Bank balance	680	
	30,340	
Current liabilities		
Trade creditors	22,220	8,120
		96,170
Capital accounts		
Liam	60,000	
Lorna	30,000	90,000
Current accounts		
Liam	5,100	
Lorna	1,070	6,170
		96,170

It was agreed that the market values of the partnership's assets on 31 October 19X8 were Goodwill £40,000, Land & buildings £95,000, Plant & equipment £20,000, Motor vehicles £15,000, Stock £11,500 and Debtors £16,430.

The partners wish to continue the practice of not showing goodwill in the balance sheet. Land & buildings are to remain in the balance sheet at historic cost, but all of the other assets are to be shown at their revalued amounts.

Required:

Make the necessary entries to record Len's admission to the partnership and prepare a revised balance sheet for the partnership.

12.3 Edna, Enid and Eric are in partnership. Their profit-sharing agreement is:

(a) Partners' salaries are Edna £12,000, Enid £14,000, Eric £5,000.

(b) Each partner is entitled to interest on capital calculated at 4% per annum. The partners' fixed capitals are Edna £32,000, Enid £17,500, Eric £5,000.

(c) Remaining profits are to be shared in the ratio 4:3:1.

(d) Eric is guaranteed a minimum allocation of profit (including interest on capital and partner's salary) of £12,500 per annum. Any deficiency will be made up by the remaining partners in their profit-sharing ratio.

In the year to 31 December 19X9, the partnership net profit is £87,220. Show how this profit will be divided between the partners.

***12.4** Fiona and Frank have been in partnership for many years, sharing profits in the ratio 2:1. Fiona decides to retire from the partnership with effect from 31 August 19X8 and Fred is admitted as a partner on that date. The new partnership of Frank and Fred will share profits in the ratio 3:1.

The trial balance of the partnership as at 31 August 19X8, before Fiona's retirement and Fred's admission, is as follows:

	Dr balances £	*Cr balances* £
Capital accounts at 1 September 19X7:		
Fiona		23,000
Frank		29,000
Current accounts at 1 September 19X7:		
Fiona		1,540
Frank	1,210	
Freehold premises	55,000	
Motor cars - at written down value	13,850	
Bank overdraft		9,820
Stock at 1 September 19X7	5,440	
Purchases	43,750	
Sales		98,690
Operating expenses, including depreciation	21,860	
Drawings:		
Fiona	15,100	
Frank	10,300	
Trade debtors and creditors	7,270	11,730
	173,780	173,780

Further information:

1. Fred contributes capital of £16,000 on his admission as a partner.
2. On her retirement, Fiona takes her motor car at its book value of £7,150. She also withdraws £10,000 in cash. The remainder of the amount owed to her is left in the partnership as a long-term loan.
3. The partners have agreed that the value of the closing stock on 31 August 19X8 is £4,500 and that trade debtors of £550 should be written off.
4. The freehold premises are valued at £85,000 on 31 August 19X8 but should continue to be shown at cost in the balance sheet.
5. Goodwill is valued at £24,000 on 31 August 19X8 but should not be shown in the partnership balance sheet.

Required:

(a) Prepare a trading and profit and loss account and an appropriation account for the year to 31 August 19X8.

(b) Make the necessary entries to record Fiona's retirement and Fred's admission to the partnership.

(c) Prepare a balance sheet for the partnership of Frank and Fred after these entries have been made.

***12.5** Mary, Mark and Mike have been in partnership for many years, sharing profits in the ratio 3:2:1. Their balance sheet as at 31 December 19X9 is as follows:

	£	£
Fixed assets		
Goodwill		25,000
Tools and equipment		8,340
		33,340
Current assets		
Stock of goods for resale	7,910	
Trade debtors	13,170	
Bank balance	2,310	
	23,390	
Current liabilities		
Trade creditors	8,730	14,660
		48,000
Capital accounts		
Mary	36,000	
Mark	3,000	
Mike	9,000	48,000
		48,000

The partners decide to dissolve the partnership on 31 December 19X9 and to sell the business to MMM Ltd. The following information is available:

(a) The company agrees to buy all of the partnership's assets (apart from the bank balance) for £30,000 but does not take over the partnership's liabilities.

(b) The £30,000 consideration takes the form of £10,000 in cash together with 5,000 shares in MMM Ltd, valued at £4 each.

(c) Mary and Mike agree to divide the shares equally between them and to settle any remaining balance in cash.

(d) Mark is bankrupt and is unable to meet any of his liabilities.

Required:

Write up the realisation account, the partners' capital accounts, the "Shares in MMM Ltd" account and the bank account.

13

THE ACCOUNTS OF LIMITED COMPANIES

Chapter objectives

When you have finished this chapter, you should be able to:

- **Outline the main characteristics of a limited company.**
- **Explain the concept of share capital and make the necessary entries to record a simple share issue.**
- **Identify the main types of reserves.**
- **Prepare a profit and loss account for a limited company.**
- **Prepare an appropriation account for a limited company.**
- **Prepare a balance sheet for a limited company.**

1. INTRODUCTION

If a business is owned by a sole trader or partnership, the law draws no distinction between the business and its owner (or owners). This means that if the business runs into financial difficulties, the owners can be required to pay business debts out of their own private funds, to the point of personal bankruptcy if necessary.

Many people would be deterred from owning a business if there were no way of avoiding this risk of financial ruin. In particular, people would be very reluctant to invest their capital in a business unless they were personally involved in its day-to-day management. It would be especially difficult to establish very large businesses, since these must rely upon the combined contributions of many thousands of investors to supply the required amounts of capital.

The solution to these problems is provided by the type of business entity known as the "limited company". If a business takes the form of a limited company, there is a legal limit to the amount of money which the owners (or "shareholders") can be required to contribute in the event that the company cannot pay its debts. In other words, the shareholders of a limited company enjoy *limited liability*.

In return for the privilege of limited liability, limited companies must comply with company law, as laid out in the Companies Acts. From an accounting point of view, the most important legal stipulation is that the annual accounts of a company must be made available for public inspection and must satisfy certain requirements with regard to their content and format. These requirements are dealt with in Chapter 14 of this book. The purpose of the current chapter is to outline the main characteristics of limited companies and to introduce the basic principles of limited company accounts.

2. THE CHARACTERISTICS OF LIMITED COMPANIES

The main characteristics of a limited company are as follows:

(a) **Legal entity**. A limited company is a legal "person" in its own right, distinct from its owners. A company can enter into legal contracts in its own name and can be sued in its own name. As we have seen, *all* businesses are deemed to be distinct from their owners for accounting purposes (the business entity convention) but in the case of limited companies this is also true legally. The fact that a company is legally distinct from its owners means that a company has a potentially infinite lifespan.

(b) **Limited liability**. As explained above, the shareholders of a limited company benefit from the protection of limited liability. Shareholders cannot be required to provide funds beyond the capital which they have already contributed (plus any further capital which they have pledged themselves to contribute).

(c) **Share capital**. The capital of a limited company is divided into equal-sized units known as "shares". Someone wishing to become a shareholder may do so either by purchasing newly-issued shares directly from the company (if any such shares are available) or by purchasing previously-issued shares from existing shareholders who wish to dispose of them. It is usual for a part of the company's profits to be distributed to the shareholders each year in the form of payments known as "dividends". Share capital is discussed in more detail later in this chapter.

(d) **Separation of ownership from management**. Companies are owned by their shareholders but are managed by their "directors". Note that:

- The directors are employees of the company. They are appointed by the shareholders and can be dismissed by the shareholders.
- The directors may be shareholders themselves.
- In the case of a small private company (see below) it is quite possible that all or most of the shareholders will also be directors. But if a company has many thousands of shareholders, then only a few of them (if any) will also be directors.

(e) **Legal formalities**. A company is formed by filing certain documents with the Registrar of Companies and paying the appropriate fee. The two most important documents are:

- The "Memorandum of Association", which sets out the name of the company, the objects for which it was formed and the maximum amount of share capital which it is authorised to issue.

- The "Articles of Association", which set out the internal rules of the company, including such matters as the duties of the directors and the voting rights of shareholders.

Once formed, a company must file an annual return with the Registrar of Companies. The company must also file a copy of its annual accounts with the Registrar. Any member of the public can then inspect these accounts on payment of a small fee.

Advantages and disadvantages of limited companies

In summary, the main *advantages* of limited companies over other forms of business entity (i.e. sole traders and partnerships) are as follows:

(a) The shareholders enjoy limited liability.

(b) There is no upper limit on the number of shareholders, so it becomes feasible to raise very large sums of capital.

(c) Shares in a company can usually be transferred fairly easily from one person to another.

The main *disadvantages* of forming a limited company are:

(a) Compliance with the Companies Acts imposes an increased administrative burden on the company. For example, companies must maintain certain statutory books, including a Register of Members (which lists every shareholder's name, address and shareholding) and a Register of Directors.

(b) The annual accounts of a company must satisfy a number of requirements with regard to their content and format, and this adds to the cost of producing these accounts. Furthermore, if a company's turnover exceeds £350,000 per annum, the accounts must be audited by a qualified, independent person and the audit fee is an extra cost which the company must bear.

(c) A company's affairs are less private than those of a sole trader or partnership, since company accounts are made available for public inspection.

It is also worth noting that a company's profits are taxed in a different way from those of sole traders and partnerships. This can sometimes be an advantage and sometimes a disadvantage, depending upon the circumstances of each individual case.

Public companies and private companies

There are two main types of limited company:

(a) **Public companies.** A public limited company is one which:

- states in its Memorandum that it is a public limited company, and
- has a name ending with "plc", and
- has a minimum issued share capital of £50,000, and
- has at least two shareholders and at least two directors.

A public limited company may offer its shares for sale to the general public and will often obtain a Stock Exchange listing.

(b) **Private companies**. A private limited company is one which does not qualify as a public limited company. It may not offer its shares to the public and cannot obtain a Stock Exchange listing. The name of a private limited company ends with "Ltd".

3. SHARE CAPITAL

As mentioned above, a company's capital is divided into equal-sized units known as "shares". Note the following important points:

(a) **Authorised share capital**. The maximum amount of share capital which a company is authorised to issue is stated in its Memorandum of Association. This amount is known as the company's "authorised share capital".

(b) **Nominal value**. Each share must have a "nominal value" or "par value". A typical nominal value is £1 per share, but greater and lesser nominal values are often encountered. Note that the *market* value of a share will depend upon such matters as the profitability and future prospects of the company concerned and may be very different from the *nominal* value.

(c) **Share premium**. A company may issue shares at their nominal value ("at par"). However, if the shares are in demand, the company may be able to issue them at more than nominal value ("at a premium"). It is usually illegal to issue shares at less than their nominal value ("at a discount").

(d) **Issued share capital**. The total nominal value of all the shares issued by a company to date is known as the company's "issued share capital".

(e) **Called-up share capital**. A company might sometimes issue shares on the understanding that shareholders will pay by instalments. In these circumstances, that part of the issued share capital for which the company has so far requested payment is known as the "called-up share capital".

(f) **Paid-up share capital**. The term "paid-up share capital" refers to the amount of money which the company has actually received to date in return for the shares which it has issued (excluding any premium).

EXAMPLE

(a) A company is formed with an authorised share capital of 10,000 £1 shares. The first share issue made by the company consists of 2,000 shares at a price of £1.50 per share, payable in full on issue. After this issue has been made, state the amount of the company's:

(i) authorised share capital
(ii) issued share capital
(iii) called-up share capital
(iv) paid-up share capital

(b) The same company now issues a further 1,000 shares at par. 60p per share is payable on issue and the remaining 40p will be called-up at some future time, yet to be determined. So far, the company has received a total of £580 from the people to whom the shares were allotted. State the amount of the company's:

(i) authorised share capital
(ii) issued share capital
(iii) called-up share capital
(iv) paid-up share capital.

SOLUTION

(a) (i) Authorised share capital is 10,000 @ £1 = £10,000.

(ii) Issued share capital is 2,000 @ £1 = £2,000. The premium of £1,000 is *not* part of the share capital of the company, but is a "profit" achieved by selling shares at more than their nominal value. The treatment of share premiums is explained later in this chapter.

(iii) Called-up share capital is also £2,000.

(iv) Paid-up share capital is also £2,000.

(b) (i) Authorised share capital remains unchanged at £10,000.

(ii) Issued share capital is now 3,000 @ £1 = £3,000.

(iii) Called-up share capital increases by 1,000 @ 60p = £600, giving a total of £2,600.

(iv) Paid-up share capital increases by £580 to £2,580.

Accounting for a share issue

In accounting terms, an issue of share capital by a company is very similar to an injection of capital by a sole trader or partner. The required book-keeping entries can be summarised as follows:

(a) If shares are issued at par and paid for in full on the issue date, the bank account is debited and the share capital account is credited with the amount of the issue.

(b) If shares are issued at a premium and are paid for in full on the issue date, then:

- the bank account is debited with the total amount of money received
- the share capital account is credited with the nominal value of the issued shares
- an account known as the "share premium account" is credited with the premium received.

(c) If shares are issued (either at par or at a premium) and the issue price is payable by instalments, then the book-keeping entries required are slightly more complex and are not considered in this book.

It is important to appreciate that the entries described above are required only if a company makes a new issue of shares. No accounting entries whatsoever are needed if an existing shareholder sells previously-issued shares to someone else, since this has no direct financial effect on the company concerned. (All that the company has to do in these circumstances is to alter its Register of Members accordingly).

EXAMPLE

On 17 July 19X8, a company issued 5,000 £1 shares at par. On 12 June 19X9, the company issued a further 8,000 £1 shares at a premium of 30p per share. In both cases, the shares were paid for in full on the date of issue. Prepare journal entries to record these two share issues.

SOLUTION

		Dr	Cr
		£	£
17.7.X8	Bank	5,000	
	Share capital		5,000
	Being an issue of 5,000 £1 shares at par.		
12.6.X9	Bank	10,400	
	Share capital		8,000
	Share premium		2,400
	Being an issue of 8,000 £1 shares at a premium of 30p per share.		

Preference shares and ordinary shares

There are two main classes of share which a company might issue, if authorised to do so by its Memorandum of Association. These are "preference shares" and "ordinary shares". The rights attached to each class of share vary from company to company and are specified in the Articles of Association. The most important features of preference shares and ordinary shares are listed below.

Preference shares

(a) Preference shareholders are entitled to a fixed rate of dividend each year, before any dividends are paid to ordinary shareholders. The dividend rate is expressed as a percentage of the nominal value of the shares concerned. For example, a holding of "7% £1 preference shares" would entitle the holder to an annual dividend calculated at 7p per share.

(b) Preference shares may be "cumulative" or "non-cumulative". If a company cannot afford to pay the preference dividend in a given year, the holders of cumulative preference shares are entitled to receive the arrears out of future years' profits, before any dividends at all are paid to the ordinary shareholders. The holders of non-cumulative preference shares are not entitled to receive arrears of dividends.

(c) Preference shareholders cannot usually vote at shareholders' meetings.

(d) When a company is wound up, preference shareholders are usually entitled to repayment of their share capital in priority to ordinary shareholders.

(e) In most cases, preference shareholders are not entitled to any of the company's profits apart from their fixed dividend. Nor are they entitled to any of the company's assets on a winding-up, apart from the amount required to repay the nominal value of their shares.

Ordinary shares

(a) Ordinary shareholders own the remainder of the company's profits after any preference dividend has been paid. The rate of dividend paid to ordinary shareholders will vary from year to year and can be expressed either as a percentage of nominal value or as a number of pence per share.

(b) Ordinary shareholders rarely receive a dividend sufficient to absorb the entire profits of the company (less any preference dividend). Companies usually retain part of their profits each year and pay out only a portion of the profits in the form of dividends. Retained profits can be used to finance expansion of a company's business.

(c) It is common for an "interim" ordinary dividend to be paid part-way through an accounting year and for a "final" ordinary dividend to be paid when the year is over.

(d) Ordinary shareholders are entitled to vote at shareholders' meetings.

(e) When a company is wound up, the ordinary shareholders are entitled to the whole of the company's assets, after all of the liabilities and the preference shares (if any) have been repaid.

(f) Ordinary shares are sometimes referred to as "equity shares".

4. RESERVES

In the case of a sole trader or partnership, any profits which have not been drawn out of the business by its owner (or owners) form part of the capital (or current) account balances which are shown on the balance sheet. In the case of a company, profits or gains which have been retained within the company and not distributed to shareholders are shown separately on the balance sheet as "reserves". Reserves are simply part of the capital of a company and represent a claim on the company's assets by its ordinary shareholders. The main classes of reserve are as follows:

(a) **Revenue reserves**. Revenue reserves are those which consist of undistributed trading profits. The company could have paid out these profits as dividends (and might still do so at some time in the future) but, for the time being, has decided to retain them within the company. Revenue reserves might appear on the balance sheet in two guises:

- A company might explicitly transfer profits to a "general reserve". This indicates clearly that, in the opinion of the directors, those profits should not be distributed to the shareholders as dividends.
- Alternatively, the company might simply leave any undistributed profits as a balance on the profit and loss account. In the case of sole traders and partnerships, we are used to closing the profit and loss account each year and transferring the entire profit to the credit of the owners' capital/current accounts. But in the case of a company, it is normal to leave a balance of undistributed profits in the profit and loss account and to show this balance as one of the revenue reserves on the company's balance sheet.

(b) **Capital reserves**. Capital reserves represent profits and gains which cannot legally be distributed to shareholders in the form of dividends. Share premium accounts and revaluation reserves are the capital reserves most often encountered in practice. These arise as follows:

- As explained earlier in this chapter, any premium received on an issue of shares at a price exceeding their nominal value is credited to an account known as the "share premium account". The Companies Acts forbid the balance on this account to be distributed as dividends but it may be used to finance an issue of bonus shares (see later in this chapter).
- If a company (in contravention of the historic cost convention) decides to revalue one or more of its fixed assets, any increase on revaluation will be credited to a "revaluation reserve". This gain will not be realised until the assets concerned are sold and so the revaluation reserve cannot be paid out as dividends. Like the share capital account, the revaluation reserve can be used to finance an issue of bonus shares.

5. DEBENTURES

A company wishing to raise finance in the form of a long-term loan may make an issue of "debentures". Debentures are similar to preference shares in some ways:

(a) They are divided into equal-sized units (often of £1 each).

(b) They attract a fixed rate of interest.

(c) The debentures of a public company may be listed on the Stock Exchange, so facilitating their transfer from one person to another.

However, debentures are very different from shares in some fundamental ways:

(a) Debenture-holders are *not* part-owners of the company. They are *lenders* and the amount owed to them is one of the company's liabilities.

(b) Debenture interest is one of the company's expenses and is shown as such in the profit and loss account, whereas the dividends paid to preference shareholders are an appropriation of profit.

(c) The company has no choice but to pay the required amount of debenture interest on the due dates, whereas dividends will not be paid if profits are insufficient for the purpose.

Debentures may be secured or unsecured and are usually redeemable (i.e. repayable) on a specified date in the future. The terms and conditions of a debenture loan are laid out in a legal document known as a debenture trust deed.

6. COMPANY ACCOUNTS FOR INTERNAL USE

As explained earlier, the annual accounts of a limited company are filed with the Registrar of Companies and may be inspected by the public. These "published accounts" must comply with certain requirements, some of which are statutory (see Chapter 14) and some of which are non-statutory (see Chapter 15). For the remainder of this chapter, we will ignore these requirements and consider only the preparation of company accounts for *internal* purposes (i.e. *not* for publication).

The accounts of a limited company are similar in many ways to those of a sole trader or partnership. The main distinctive features of company accounts are described below.

The profit and loss account

A company's profit and loss account may include the following expenses (in addition to the usual expenses which would be found in the profit and loss account of any business organisation):

(a) directors' remuneration
(b) the audit fee (if applicable)
(c) debenture interest.

The profit and loss appropriation account

A company's profit and loss appropriation account shows how the profit for the accounting year has been allocated. This account is usually presented immediately beneath the profit and loss account itself. Profits are allocated in the following order:

(a) **Corporation tax**. A company must pay corporation tax on its profits. The estimated tax liability for the year is shown in the appropriation account and also as a current liability in the balance sheet (corporation tax is payable 9 months after the end of the accounting year). The estimated liability will usually turn out to be slightly higher or lower than the amount eventually paid. This will leave a small balance on the corporation tax account which will be written off to the following year's profit and loss appropriation account.

(b) **Transfers to reserves.** A part of the profit remaining after deduction of corporation tax may be transferred to a revenue reserve (e.g. the general reserve).

(c) **Dividends.** The profit remaining after transfers to reserves is available for distribution to the shareholders as dividends. The appropriation account will show dividends which have already been paid (e.g. the first half-year's preference dividend, the interim dividend on the ordinary shares) together with dividends which the directors are now proposing to pay (subject to shareholders' approval at an annual general meeting).

Any unappropriated profit remaining after dividends have been deducted is carried forward as a credit balance on the profit and loss account and is shown as a revenue reserve in the balance sheet. Each year, any unappropriated profit brought forward from the previous year is added to the current year's after-tax profit in the appropriation account, so increasing the amount available for transfers to reserves and for the payment of dividends.

The balance sheet

The main distinctions between a company balance sheet and the balance sheet of a sole trader or partnership are as follows:

(a) **Current liabilities.** These will include the estimated corporation tax liability for the year and the amount of any proposed dividends. Debentures which are within one year of their redemption date will also be shown as current liabilities.

(b) **Long-term liabilities.** A company's long-term liabilities will include any debentures which are redeemable more than 12 months after the balance sheet date.

(c) **Capital and reserves.** This section of the balance sheet will show the called-up share capital (analysed by class of share) and the balance on each of the company's reserves, including the profit and loss account balance.

EXAMPLE

Anstruther plc prepares accounts to 30 April each year. The following information relates to the year to 30 April 19X9:

(a) The net profit for the year is £234,530.

(b) The company has unappropriated profits brought forward of £78,250.

(c) The estimated corporation tax liability for the year is £59,000. The corporation tax liability for the previous year was estimated at £53,000 but the amount paid on 1 February 19X9 was only £52,400.

(d) The directors propose to transfer £100,000 to the general reserve and to pay a final ordinary dividend of 6p per share, in addition to the interim dividend of 3p per share which was paid on 1 January 19X9. The company has an issued share capital consisting of 800,000 fully paid £1 ordinary shares. There are no preference shares.

(e) The general reserve stood at £150,000 on 30 April 19X8. The company's only capital reserve arose on 1 January 19X3 as a consequence of issuing 200,000 ordinary shares at an issue price of £1.70p per share. This reserve has remained unchanged since that date.

Prepare the profit and loss appropriation account for the year to 30 April 19X9. Also prepare the capital and reserves section of the company's balance sheet as at 30 April 19X9.

SOLUTION

Anstruther plc

Profit and loss appropriation account for the year to 30 April 19X9

	£	£
Net profit for the year before tax		234,530
Less: Corporation tax		58,400
Net profit after tax		176,130
Unappropriated profit brought forward		78,250
		254,380
Less: Transfer to general reserve		100,000
		154,380
Less: Dividends paid and proposed		
Interim dividend paid of 3p per ordinary share	24,000	
Final dividend proposed of 6p per ordinary share	48,000	72,000
Unappropriated profit carried forward		82,380

Note:

The figure shown for corporation tax consists of £59,000 for the current year, less the £600 overestimate made in the previous year.

Anstruther plc

Balance sheet (extract) as at 30 April 19X9

	£	£
Capital and reserves		
Called-up share capital		
800,000 ordinary shares of £1 per share, fully paid		800,000
Reserves		
Share premium account	140,000	
General reserve	250,000	
Profit and loss account	82,380	472,380
		1,272,380

Notes:

1. The share premium account is 200,000 @ 70p per share = £140,000.
2. The general reserve is £150,000 + £100,000 = £250,000.

7. BONUS ISSUES AND RIGHTS ISSUES

Earlier in this chapter, we considered the concept of share capital and looked at the accounting entries normally required when shares are issued. But as well as issuing shares in the normal way, companies might make either a *bonus issue* or a *rights issue*. These special types of share issue are explained below.

Bonus issues

A bonus issue consists of an issue of shares to existing shareholders in proportion to their existing holdings. The most important feature of a bonus issue is that *no money changes hands* when such an issue is made. Instead of shares being exchanged for cash in the usual way, a bonus issue is financed out of the company's reserves.

The accounting entries required when a bonus issue is made are to debit the relevant reserve account and to credit the share capital account with the amount of the issue.

EXAMPLE

A company's share capital and reserves are as follows:

	£
£1 ordinary shares, fully paid	600,000
Share premium account	200,000
Revenue reserves	160,000

The directors of the company decide to use the share premium account to make a 1 for 3 bonus issue to the ordinary shareholders (i.e. shareholders will receive 1 bonus share for every 3 shares which they already hold).

(a) Identify the accounting entries which must be made to record this bonus issue.

(b) Show the company's share capital and reserves after the bonus issue has been made.

(c) Are the shareholders better off financially as a result of the bonus issue?

SOLUTION

(a) The share premium account is debited with £200,000 and the ordinary share capital account is credited with £200,000.

(b) The share capital and reserves after the bonus issue are as follows:

	£
£1 ordinary shares, fully paid	800,000
Revenue reserves	160,000

(c) The net assets of the company were £960,000 before the bonus issue, so each of the 600,000 ordinary shares had a claim on £1.60 worth of net assets. Net assets are still £960,000 after the bonus issue, so each of the 800,000 shares now has a claim on net assets of £1.20. The financial position of shareholders remains unchanged. For instance, a shareholder who had 3,000 shares before the bonus issue, representing net assets of 3,000 x £1.60 = £4,800, now has 4,000 shares which represent net assets of 4,000 x £1.20 = £4,800.

Reasons for making a bonus issue

As illustrated by the above example, a bonus issue is not made with the intention of increasing shareholders' wealth. The main reasons for making a bonus issue are as follows:

(a) If a company has retained substantial amounts of profits over the years and has used these retained profits to finance the expansion of the business (e.g. through the acquisition of fixed assets) there is little possibility that sufficient cash would ever be available to distribute the retained profits as dividends. A bonus issue financed out of the revenue reserves of the company gives official recognition to the fact that these reserves are now part of the permanent capital of the company.

(b) The reclassification of reserves as share capital increases the proportion of the company's capital which is permanent and cannot be repaid to shareholders in any circumstances until the company is wound up. This gives creditors additional protection and may make it easier for the company to obtain credit.

(c) A bonus issue increases the number of issued shares and reduces the market value of each share. Shares can be traded more easily if the value of each share is comparatively low.

Rights issues

A company making a rights issue offers existing shareholders the right to buy new shares in proportion to their existing holdings. The price at which the shares are offered is usually somewhat less than the current market value of the company's shares, so making the issue attractive to shareholders. A shareholder who is offered rights shares may do one of three things:

(a) ignore the offer completely

(b) buy the shares at the offer price

(c) sell the right to buy the shares to someone else (not necessarily an existing shareholder) who wishes to acquire shares in the company at a bargain price.

From the company's point of view, a rights issue is administratively cheaper than a normal share issue. Also, it may be much easier to find buyers for the company's shares amongst existing shareholders than amongst the general public.

The accounting entries required when shareholders buy rights shares from the company are precisely the same as those required for a normal share issue. Assuming that the shares must be paid for in full on the issue date, the nominal value of the issued shares is credited to the share capital account, any premium is credited to the share premium account and the proceeds of the issue are debited to the bank account.

8. SUMMARY

- A limited company is a legal entity in its own right. A company is owned by its shareholders, who enjoy limited liability, and is managed by its directors.
- A public company may offer its shares for sale to the general public and might obtain a Stock Exchange listing. A private company can do neither of these things.
- A company's capital is divided into units known as "shares". The maximum amount of share capital which a company is authorised to issue is known as its authorised share capital.
- Any premium received on the issue of shares must be credited to a capital reserve known as the share premium account.
- Revenue reserves consist of undistributed trading profits and may be used to finance the payment of dividends. Capital reserves represent profits and gains which cannot legally be distributed to shareholders.
- Debentures are a form of long-term loan. They are divided into equal-sized units and may be transferred from one person to another. Debentures may be secured or unsecured and are usually redeemable on a specified date.
- The first claim on a company's profit is the corporation tax liability. Part of the profit remaining after tax may be transferred to reserves and the balance paid out as dividends.
- A bonus issue is an issue of shares to existing shareholders in proportion to their existing holdings, funded out of the company's reserves. A rights issue is also an issue of shares to existing shareholders in proportion to their existing holdings but rights shares must be paid for.

EXERCISES 13

13.1 The trial balance of Carruthers & Co Ltd at 31 January 19X7 is as follows:

	Dr balances	*Cr balances*
	£	£
Land and buildings at cost	325,000	
Equipment at cost	84,290	
Prov'n for depreciation of equipment at 1/2/X6		37,940
Stock at 1/2/X6	91,180	
Debtors and creditors	42,760	35,410
Provision for doubtful debts at 1/2/X6		1,070
Bank balance		6,320
Purchases and sales	371,990	605,430
Operating expenses	95,680	
7% debentures		50,000
£10 ordinary shares, fully paid		200,000
5% preference shares of £1 each, fully paid		40,000
Profit and loss account at 1/2/X6		34,730
	1,010,900	1,010,900

Additional information:

1. Stock at 31 January 19X7 is valued at £83,710.
2. Depreciation of equipment for the year to 31 January 19X7 is £12,860.
3. The doubtful debts provision is to be reduced to £900.
4. Interest on the 7% debentures for the year to 31 January 19X7 has not yet been paid or provided for. The debentures are to be redeemed in 19X9.
5. The corporation tax liability for the year is estimated to be £45,000.
6. The directors propose that the preference dividend for the year should be paid and that an ordinary dividend of £3 per share should also be paid.

Required:

Prepare a trading and profit and loss account and an appropriation account for the year to 31 January 19X7 and a balance sheet as at that date.

13.2 The balance sheet of Boscastle plc as at 30 September 19X9 may be summarised as follows:

	£
Fixed assets	4,560,000
Net current assets	1,345,400
	5,905,400
Share capital	
2,000,000 £1 ordinary shares, fully paid	2,000,000
Reserves	
Share premium account	400,000
General reserve	3,000,000
Profit and loss account	505,400
	5,905,400

On 1 October 19X9, the company makes a 1 for 10 rights issue at a price of £2.50 per share. All of the company's shareholders take up their rights. The company then makes an immediate 1 for 2 bonus issue, financed as far as possible out of the share premium account, with any shortfall being financed out of the general reserve.

Required:

Assuming that no other transactions take place on 1 October 19X9, show the summarised balance sheet of the company as at that date.

***13.3** Amongst other things, a company balance sheet may include liabilities, provisions and reserves, all of which are represented by credit balances in the company's ledger. Explain the differences between these three types of credit balance and give an example of each.

***13.4** The trial balance of Devenish plc at 30 November 19X8 (in alphabetical order and shown to the nearest £1,000) is as follows:

	Dr balances	*Cr balances*
	£'000	£'000
Bank balance	121	
Carriage inwards	52	
Carriage outwards	73	
Corporation tax	6	
8% Debentures		60
Directors' remuneration	150	
Discounts allowed and received	103	86
Dividends paid	33	
Freehold property, at cost	650	
General reserve		200
Heating and lighting	76	
Motor expenses	42	
Motor vehicles, at cost	85	
Ordinary shares of 50p each, fully paid		300
Plant and machinery, at cost	100	
Postage, stationery and telephone	56	
6% Preference shares of £1 each, fully paid		100
Profit and loss account at 1/12/X7		134
Provisions for depreciation at 1/12/X7:		
Motor vehicles		32
Plant and machinery		43
Provision for doubtful debts at 1/12/X7		2
Purchases and sales	620	1,990
Rent, rates and insurance	92	
Repairs and renewals	23	
Returns inwards and outwards	74	21
Stock at 1/12/X7	254	
Suspense account		50
Trade debtors and creditors	152	93
Wages and salaries (other than directors)	349	
	3,111	3,111

The following information is also available:

1. Freehold property is to be revalued at £1,000,000.
2. One of the company's motor vehicles (which had been acquired in July 19X6 for £15,000) was part-exchanged for a new vehicle during the year. The new vehicle cost £23,000 and a part-exchange allowance of £10,000 was granted in relation to the old vehicle. The balance of £13,000 was paid by cheque and debited to motor vehicles account. No other entry has been made in relation to this transaction.
3. The company calculates depreciation on the straight-line basis at 10% p.a. for plant and machinery and at 20% p.a. for motor vehicles, with a full charge in the year of acquisition and none in the year of disposal. None of the plant and machinery or motor vehicles had been fully depreciated by 30 November 19X7.
4. Accrued electricity charges on 30 November 19X8 are estimated at £11,000 and accrued telephone charge are estimated to be £5,000. Rent of £3,000 has been paid in advance. The last rates bill paid during the year was for £12,000 and covered the six months to 31 March 19X9. Insurance premiums of £18,000 for the year to 31 May 19X9 were paid on 2 June 19X8.
5. Closing stock at 30 November 19X8 is valued at £282,000.
6. Bad debts of £2,000 are to be written off and the provision for doubtful debts is to be adjusted to 2% of the remaining trade debtors.
7. All of the 8% Debentures were issued on 1 July 19X8 and are redeemable after 10 years. No debenture interest has yet been paid or accounted for.
8. The audit fee for the year is estimated to be £10,000.
9. The balance of £6,000 on the corporation tax account is the difference between the estimated liability for the year to 30 November 19X7 and the amount actually paid on 1 September 19X8. The estimated liability for the year to 30 November 19X8 is £125,000.
10. 20,000 ordinary shares were issued in November 19X8 at an issue price of £2.50 per share. The proceeds of £50,000 were debited to the bank account and credited to a suspense account. No other entries were made in relation to this share issue.
11. £120,000 is to be transferred to the general reserve.
12. Dividends paid during the year consist of the first half-year's dividend on the preference shares and an interim dividend of 5p per share on the ordinary shares. The interim dividend was paid before the new issue (see above) was made. The directors propose that the remaining half-year's dividend should be paid on the preference shares and that a final dividend of 10p per share should be paid on the ordinary shares.

Required:

(a) Prepare a trading and profit and loss account and an appropriation account for the year to 30 November 19X8.

(b) Prepare a balance sheet as at 30 November 19X8.

14

COMPANY ACCOUNTS FOR PUBLICATION

Chapter objectives

When you have finished this chapter, you should be able to:

- **Outline the main statutory regulations which apply to the published accounts of limited companies and explain the purpose of these regulations.**
- **Prepare a limited company profit and loss account and balance sheet in a form suitable for publication.**
- **List the main contents of a directors' report.**
- **State the reporting exemptions which are available to small and medium-sized companies.**

1. INTRODUCTION

The previous chapter of this book was concerned with the preparation of limited company accounts for internal use. In this chapter (and in the following chapter) we turn our attention to the preparation of limited company accounts in a form suitable for publication to the shareholders and to the general public. The main influences on these *published accounts* of limited companies are:

(a) statute law, as embodied in the Companies Acts

(b) accounting standards issued by either the Accounting Standards Board (ASB) or its predecessor, the Accounting Standards Committee (ASC)

(c) for listed companies only, the requirements of the Stock Exchange.

The purpose of this chapter is to examine the *statutory* regulations relating to the published accounts of limited companies. Accounting standards and the requirements of the Stock Exchange are considered in Chapter 15.

Summary of the statutory regulations

The statutory regulations with which the published accounts of limited companies must comply are set out in the Companies Act 1985 (as amended by the Companies Act 1989). The main regulations are as follows:

(a) The directors of a limited company are responsible for the preparation of the company's annual accounts. These accounts must give a *true and fair view* of the company's results for the period covered by the accounts and of the financial position of the company at the end of that period.

(b) The accounts must be in an approved format and must comply with minimum disclosure requirements (see later in this chapter). They must also be prepared in accordance with four specific accounting conventions (going concern, consistency, matching and prudence).

(c) Two further accounting principles which must be observed are as follows:

- Each component of any category of assets or liabilities must be valued separately when arriving at a total to be shown in the accounts for that category. For example, the value of each stock item should be calculated individually at the lower of cost and NRV (see Chapter 7) and the resulting values should then be totalled to give the stock figure which appears in the accounts. It is not permissible to value stock at the lower of total cost and total NRV.
- Assets and liabilities must not be subtracted from one another to give a net figure which is then shown on the balance sheet. For example, the amount owing on a loan must be shown separately from the fixed asset which was bought with the proceeds of the loan. The same principle applies to items of income and expenditure shown in the profit and loss account.

However, any of the rules relating to format, content, accounting conventions and principles may be over-ridden if compliance with these rules would prevent the accounts from showing a true and fair view.

(d) The signature of at least one of the directors must appear on the balance sheet, as evidence that the accounts have been approved by the directors.

(e) For companies with a turnover exceeding £350,000 per annum, the accounts must be audited by an independent, qualified person. In practice, the shareholders will usually appoint a firm of professional accountants to act as auditors. The auditors' duty is to carry out an independent review of the company's published accounts and to form an opinion as to whether:

- the accounts show the required true and fair view
- the accounts comply with Companies Act requirements
- the accounts comply with relevant accounting standards
- the company has maintained adequate accounting records
- the directors' report (see below) is in agreement with the accounts.

The auditors must submit an audit report to the members of the company (i.e. to the shareholders). It is important to note that the auditors are appointed by and are responsible to the shareholders, *not* the directors.

(f) Each shareholder and each debenture-holder is entitled to receive a copy of the audited accounts and a copy must be laid before a general meeting of the company's members. The accounts must include:
   - a profit and loss account for the accounting period
   - a balance sheet as at the end of the accounting period
   - a set of *notes to the accounts*, providing information which is required by statute but which is not shown in the profit and loss account or on the balance sheet.

   The accounts must be accompanied by a directors' report and by the report of the auditors.

(g) When the members have adopted the accounts in a general meeting, a copy must be filed with the Registrar of Companies and thus made available for public inspection. Note that small and medium-sized companies are allowed to omit certain information from the copy of the accounts which is filed with the Registrar (see later in this chapter).

Purpose of the statutory regulations

The main purpose of the statutory regulations is to ensure that users have access to a sufficient quantity of reliable, relevant information and that this information is laid out in a clear, consistent format. The regulations prevent company directors from concealing important information (either by omitting the information from the accounts entirely or by formatting the accounts in such a way that users cannot follow them). The requirement that accounts must be presented in a standard format increases the likelihood that users will be able to find the information which they need and make comparisons between one company and another and between one year and another. Three main user groups benefit from the statutory regulations relating to company accounts:

(a) **Shareholders**. The shareholders of a limited company entrust their capital to the directors and rely upon the directors to manage the company competently and honestly. The annual accounts which the directors are statutorily compelled to produce should help shareholders to assess the directors' performance. This is particularly important in the case of larger companies, where it is likely that few (if any) of the shareholders will have day-to-day involvement in the company's management. Potential shareholders will also find the published accounts helpful when deciding whether or not to invest their capital in the company.

(b) **Creditors**. The fact that shareholders enjoy the protection of limited liability means that debenture-holders, banks and other creditors run the risk of losing their money if the company becomes insolvent. The information provided in the published accounts may help potential creditors to decide whether or not to lend money to the company.

(c) **The public**. The actions of large companies may have a significant effect on the local economy of the areas in which they operate. The largest companies of all may make a significant impact on the UK national economy. In these circumstances, it is reasonable that the general public should have access to information about a company's activities and that the right to this information should be enshrined in statute law. Smaller companies exercise less economic influence than their larger counterparts. This is why (as mentioned above) they are allowed to omit certain information from the accounts filed with the Registrar.

2. THE PUBLISHED PROFIT AND LOSS ACCOUNT

The published profit and loss account of a limited company must be laid out in one of four formats prescribed by the Companies Acts. These formats specify the information which must be shown in the profit and loss account and the order in which it must be given. Note the following points:

(a) Formats 1 and 2 are fairly similar. Both present the profit and loss account in vertical form, but Format 2 provides a more detailed analysis of the company's expenses. These formats are illustrated on the next two pages of this chapter.

(b) Formats 3 and 4 are simply horizontal equivalents of Formats 1 and 2 and are rarely encountered in practice.

(c) Format 1 is used by the large majority of companies and will therefore be used throughout the remainder of this book.

(d) Having chosen a format for the profit and loss account, a company is obliged to use the same format each year unless the directors are of the opinion that there are good reasons for changing to a different format. These reasons must be explained in a note to the accounts in the year that the change is made.

Published profit and loss account - Format 1

		£	£
1	Turnover		x
2	Cost of sales		x
3	Gross profit or loss		x
4	Distribution costs	x	
5	Administrative expenses	x	x
			x
6	Other operating income		x
			x
7	Income from shares in group undertakings		x
8	Income from participating interests		x
9	Income from other fixed asset investments		x
10	Other interest receivable and similar income		x
			x
11	Amounts written off investments	x	
12	Interest payable and similar charges	x	x
	Profit or loss on ordinary activities before taxation		x
13	Tax on profit or loss on ordinary activities		x
14	Profit or loss on ordinary activities after taxation		x
15	Extraordinary income	x	
16	Extraordinary charges	x	
17	Extraordinary profit or loss	x	
18	Tax on extraordinary profit or loss	x	x
			x
19	Other taxes not shown under the above items		x
20	Profit or loss for the financial year		x
	Transfers to or from reserves	x	
	Dividends paid and proposed	x	x
	Retained profit or loss for the financial year		x

Published profit and loss account - Format 2

			£	£	£
1	Turnover				x
2	Change in stocks of finished goods and in work in progress				x
3	Own work capitalised				x
4	Other operating income				x
					x
5	(a)	Raw materials and consumables	x		
	(b)	Other external charges	x	x	
6	Staff costs:				
	(a)	Wages and salaries	x		
	(b)	Social security costs	x		
	(c)	Other pension costs	x	x	
7	(a)	Depreciation and other amounts written off tangible and intangible fixed assets	x		
	(b)	Exceptional amounts written off current assets	x	x	
8	Other operating charges			x	x
					x
9	Income from shares in group undertakings				x
10	Income from participating interests				x
11	Income from other fixed asset investments				x
12	Other interest receivable and similar income				x
					x
13	Amounts written off investments			x	
14	Interest payable and similar charges			x	x
	Profit or loss on ordinary activities before taxation				x
15	Tax on profit or loss on ordinary activities				x
16	Profit or loss on ordinary activities after taxation				x
17	Extraordinary income			x	
18	Extraordinary charges			x	
19	Extraordinary profit or loss			x	
20	Tax on extraordinary profit or loss			x	x
					x
21	Other taxes not shown under the above items				x
22	Profit or loss for the financial year				x
	Transfers to or from reserves			x	
	Dividends paid and proposed			x	x
	Retained profit or loss for the financial year				x

Matters relating to the Format 1 profit and loss account

The following important matters should be borne in mind when preparing a Format 1 profit and loss account:

(a) The numbers (from 1 to 20) which appear in the standard format are for reference purposes only and do not need to be shown in an actual profit and loss account.

(b) The official format ends with the *profit or loss for the financial year.* However, the Companies Acts also require companies to show transfers to/from reserves and dividends paid/proposed on the face of the profit and loss account. Therefore it is customary to extend the format as shown in the above illustration.

(c) The format specifies only the *minimum* amount of information which must be shown in a profit and loss account. Companies are at liberty to provide further information if they wish.

(d) The illustration given above shows the format as specified by the Companies Acts 1985 and 1989. In 1992, the Accounting Standards Board issued Financial Reporting Standard 3 (FRS3) which made some changes to the format of the profit and loss account. These changes are considered in Chapter 17.

(e) Comparative figures for the previous financial year must be disclosed.

(f) If an item does not apply to a company (in either the current year or the previous year) it may be entirely omitted from the profit and loss account.

(g) *Distribution costs* are the costs incurred in selling and distributing goods or services (e.g. advertising, warehousing costs, delivery costs, the salaries of sales staff, shop rent and rates, shop heating and lighting etc).

(h) *Administrative expenses* include most of the other expenses that would normally be shown in a profit and loss account (e.g. office salaries, office rent and rates, office heating and lighting, telephone etc). Discounts allowed and bad/doubtful debts are normally shown as administrative expenses. Discounts received are normally deducted from administrative expenses. Note that *interest payable* is shown separately and so is *not* included in administrative expenses.

(i) Depreciation will be allocated to whichever heading is appropriate. For example, the depreciation of delivery vans is a distribution cost whilst the depreciation of office equipment is an administrative expense. (For a manufacturing company, it is normal to include the depreciation of factory buildings and machinery in cost of sales).

(j) *Other operating income* includes such income as rents receivable and royalties receivable.

(k) The items *income from shares in group undertakings* and *income from participating interests* apply only if the company is a member of a group or owns at least a 20% stake in another business (see Chapter 18).

(l) *Extraordinary items* are material items possessing a high degree of abnormality. They arise from events or transactions that fall outside the company's ordinary activities and that are not expected to recur. Extraordinary items are now rarely encountered in practice.

EXAMPLE

The trading and profit and loss account of Ponsonby plc for the year to 30 June 19X8 (for internal use) is shown below. Prepare a profit and loss account in a form suitable for publication.

Ponsonby plc

Trading and profit and loss account for the year to 30 June 19X8

		£	£
Sales			401,130
Cost of goods sold:			
Stock as at 1 July 19X7		47,250	
Purchases		183,290	
		230,540	
Less: Stock as at 30 June 19X8		43,170	187,370
Gross profit			213,760
Discounts received			6,440
Profit on disposal of delivery van			530
Reduction in provision for doubtful debts			110
Rents receivable			5,200
Bank interest received			250
			226,290
Less: Office staff wages		21,650	
Shop assistants' wages		33,290	
Directors' remuneration		45,000	
Rates, insurance, heat and light	- shop premises	8,760	
	- office premises	7,200	
Postage, stationery and telephone		6,070	
Motor expenses	- delivery van	4,320	
	- director's motor cars	5,110	
Depreciation of delivery van		3,320	
Depreciation of shop equipment		3,500	
Depreciation of director's motor cars		8,400	
Discounts allowed		3,430	
Bad debts written off		420	
Debenture interest		5,000	
Audit and accountancy fees		8,000	163,470
Net profit for the year			62,820

	£	£
Net profit for the year		62,820
Less: Corporation tax		15,300
Net profit after tax		47,520
Unappropriated profit brought forward		14,280
		61,800
Less: Transfer to general reserve		15,000
		46,800
Less: Dividends paid and proposed		
Paid, interim dividend of 5p per share	10,000	
Proposed, final dividend of 10p per share	20,000	30,000
Unappropriated profit carried forward		16,800

SOLUTION

Ponsonby plc

Profit and loss account for the year to 30 June 19X8

	£	£
Turnover		401,130
Cost of sales		187,370
Gross profit		213,760
Distribution costs	52,660	
Administrative expenses	98,730	151,390
		62,370
Other operating income		5,200
		67,570
Other interest receivable and similar income		250
		67,820
Interest payable and similar charges		5,000
Profit on ordinary activities before taxation		62,820
Tax on profit on ordinary activities		15,300
Profit on ordinary activities after taxation		47,520
Transfers to reserves	15,000	
Dividends paid and proposed	30,000	45,000
Retained profit for the financial year		2,520

Tutorial notes:

1. Distribution costs are £33,290 + £8,760 + £4,320 + £3,320 + £3,500 – £530 = £52,660.
2. Administrative expenses are £21,650 + £45,000 + £7,200 + £6,070 + £5,110 + £8,400 + £3,430 + £420 + £8,000 – £6,440 – £110 = £98,730.

3. THE PUBLISHED BALANCE SHEET

The published balance sheet of a limited company must be laid out in one of two prescribed formats. Note that:

(a) Format 1 presents the information is vertical form and is used almost exclusively in practice. Format 1 is illustrated on the next three pages of this chapter and will be used throughout the remainder of the book.

(b) Format 2 is a horizontal equivalent of Format 1 and is rarely used.

(c) The same provisions apply to a change of balance sheet format as apply to a change of profit and loss account format (see above).

Matters relating to the Format 1 balance sheet

The following important matters should be borne in mind when preparing a Format 1 balance sheet:

(a) The items listed in the official format are labelled with either letters of the alphabet (from A to K), roman numerals (from I to V) or arabic numbers (from 1 to 9). These letters and numbers appear for reference purposes only and are not shown in an actual balance sheet.

(b) Any item which is labelled with a letter of the alphabet or a roman numeral must be shown on the face of the balance sheet (unless it is not applicable to the company concerned). Items labelled with arabic numerals may be aggregated on the face of the balance sheet, in which case the individual items are shown in the notes to the accounts instead.

(c) As with the profit and loss account, the format specifies only the *minimum* amount of information which must be shown in a balance sheet. Companies may provide further information if they wish.

(d) Comparative figures for the previous financial year must be disclosed.

(e) If an item does not apply to a given company (in either the current year or the previous year) it may be entirely omitted from the balance sheet.

(f) A Format 1 balance sheet may seem rather formidable at first. However, a fairly straightforward structure emerges if non-applicable items are omitted and items labelled with arabic numbers are relegated to the notes. Useful points to remember are:

- *Called up share capital not paid* may be shown either as item A or as item 5 of debtors.
- *Prepayments and accrued income* may be shown either as item D or as item 6 of debtors.
- *Accruals and deferred income* may be shown either as item J or as item 9 of creditors.
- The items relating to *group undertakings* and *participating interests* are relevant only if the company is a member of a group of companies or owns at least a 20% stake in another business (see Chapter 18).

Published balance sheet - Format 1

			£	£	£
A	CALLED UP SHARE CAPITAL NOT PAID				x
B	FIXED ASSETS				
	I	Intangible assets			
	1.	Development costs	x		
	2.	Concessions, patents, licenses, trade-marks and similar rights and assets	x		
	3.	Goodwill	x		
	4.	Payments on account	x	x	
	II	Tangible assets			
	1.	Land and buildings	x		
	2.	Plant and machinery	x		
	3.	Fixtures, fittings, tools and equipment	x		
	4.	Payments on account and assets in course of construction	x	x	
	III	Investments			
	1.	Shares in group undertakings	x		
	2.	Loans to group undertakings	x		
	3.	Participating interests	x		
	4.	Loans to undertakings in which the company has a participating interest	x		
	5.	Other investments other than loans	x		
	6.	Other loans	x		
	7.	Own shares	x	x	x
C	CURRENT ASSETS				
	I	Stocks			
	1.	Raw materials and consumables	x		
	2.	Work in progress	x		
	3.	Finished goods and goods for resale	x		
	4.	Payments on account	x	x	
	II	Debtors			
	1.	Trade debtors	x		
	2.	Amounts owed by group undertakings	x		
	3.	Amounts owed by undertakings in which the company has a participating interest	x		
	4.	Other debtors	x		
	5.	Called up share capital not paid	x		
	6.	Prepayments and accrued income	x	x	
	c/f			x	x

Published balance sheet - Format 1 (continued)

			£	£	£
	b/f			x	x
	III	Investments			
	1.	Shares in group undertakings	x		
	2.	Own shares	x		
	3.	Other investments	x	x	
	IV	Cash at bank and in hand		x	
				x	
D	PREPAYMENTS AND ACCRUED INCOME			x	
				x	
E	CREDITORS: AMOUNTS FALLING DUE WITHIN ONE YEAR				
	1.	Debenture loans	x		
	2.	Bank loans and overdrafts	x		
	3.	Payments received on account	x		
	4.	Trade creditors	x		
	5.	Bills of exchange payable	x		
	6.	Amounts owed to group undertakings	x		
	7.	Amounts owed to undertakings in which the company has a participating interest	x		
	8.	Other creditors including taxation and social security	x		
	9.	Accruals and deferred income	x	x	
F	NET CURRENT ASSETS (LIABILITIES)				x
G	TOTAL ASSETS LESS CURRENT LIABILITIES				x
H	CREDITORS: AMOUNTS FALLING AFTER MORE THAN ONE YEAR				
	1.	Debenture loans	x		
	2.	Bank loans and overdrafts	x		
	3.	Payments received on account	x		
	4.	Trade creditors	x		
	5.	Bills of exchange payable	x		
	6.	Amounts owed to group undertakings	x		
	7.	Amounts owed to undertakings in which the company has a participating interest	x		
	8.	Other creditors including taxation and social security	x		
	9.	Accruals and deferred income	x	x	
	c/f			x	x

Published balance sheet - Format 1 (continued)

		£	£	£
	b/f		x	x
I	PROVISIONS FOR LIABILITIES AND CHARGES			
	1. Pensions and similar obligations	x		
	2. Taxation, including deferred taxation	x		
	3. Other provisions	x	x	
J	ACCRUALS AND DEFERRED INCOME		x	x
				x
K	CAPITAL AND RESERVES			
	I Called up share capital			x
	II Share premium account			x
	III Revaluation reserve			x
	IV Other reserves			
	1. Capital redemption reserve		x	
	2. Reserve for own shares		x	
	3. Reserves provided for by the articles of association		x	
	4. Other reserves		x	x
	V Profit and loss account			x
				x

Tutorial note:

The length of the format has made it necessary to spread the balance sheet over three pages and to show carry-forward and brought-forward figures to link the pages together. These carry-forward and brought-forward figures are *not* part of the format.

EXAMPLE

The balance sheet of J Postlethwaite & Co Ltd for the year to 30 April 19X5 (for internal use) is shown below. Prepare a balance sheet in a form suitable for publication.

J Postlethwaite & Co Ltd
Balance sheet as at 30 April 19X5

	£	£	£
Fixed assets			
Land and buildings, at cost			200,000
Factory machinery, at cost		106,850	
Less: Accumulated depreciation to date		69,540	37,310
Motor vehicles, at cost		42,180	
Less: Accumulated depreciation to date		11,150	31,030
c/f			268,340

	£	£	£
b/f			268,340
Office furniture and fittings, at cost		26,250	
Less: Accumulated depreciation to date		7,030	19,220
Patents and trademarks			20,000
Goodwill			50,000
			357,560
Current assets			
Stock of raw materials		27,830	
Work in progress		13,560	
Stock of finished goods		85,220	
Trade debtors	66,960		
Less: Provision for doubtful debts	2,500	64,460	
Prepayments		2,200	
Cash in hand		230	
		193,500	
Current liabilities			
Trade creditors	59,130		
Accruals	3,000		
Corporation tax	75,000		
Proposed dividends	40,000		
Bank overdraft	101,310	278,440	(84,940)
			272,620
Long-term liabilities			
7.5% Debentures redeemable in 19X9			80,000
			192,620
Capital and reserves			
Called-up share capital			
50,000 ordinary shares of £1 per share, fully paid			50,000
25,000 6% preference shares of £1 per share, fully paid			25,000
			75,000
Reserves			
Share premium account			30,000
Revaluation reserve			50,000
Profit and loss account			37,620
			192,620

SOLUTION

J Postlethwaite & Co Ltd
Balance sheet as at 30 April 19X5

	£	£	£
FIXED ASSETS			
Intangible assets			
Concessions, patents, licenses, trade-marks and similar rights and assets	20,000		
Goodwill	50,000	70,000	
Tangible assets			
Land and buildings	200,000		
Plant and machinery	68,340		
Fixtures, fittings, tools and equipment	19,220	287,560	357,560
CURRENT ASSETS			
Stocks			
Raw materials and consumables	27,830		
Work in progress	13,560		
Finished goods and goods for resale	85,220	126,610	
Debtors			
Trade debtors	64,460		
Prepayments and accrued income	2,200	66,660	
Cash at bank and in hand		230	
		193,500	
CREDITORS: AMOUNTS FALLING DUE WITHIN ONE YEAR			
Bank loans and overdrafts	101,310		
Trade creditors	59,130		
Other creditors including taxation and social security	115,000		
Accruals and deferred income	3,000	278,440	
NET CURRENT LIABILITIES			84,940
TOTAL ASSETS LESS CURRENT LIABILITIES			272,620
CREDITORS: AMOUNTS FALLING AFTER MORE THAN ONE YEAR			
Debenture loans			80,000
			192,620
CAPITAL AND RESERVES			
Called up share capital			75,000
Share premium account			30,000
Revaluation reserve			50,000
Profit and loss account			37,620
			192,620

4. THE NOTES TO THE ACCOUNTS

As well as being obliged to prepare and publish a profit and loss account and balance sheet in a prescribed format, companies are required to disclose certain additional information by way of a set of notes. These notes form an important and integral part of the company's published accounts. The main disclosures which must be made in the notes are as follows:

(a) **Accounting policies**. The notes to the accounts must include a statement of the accounting policies adopted by the company in relation to material items included in the balance sheet and profit and loss account (see Chapter 15).

(b) **Analysis of turnover and profit**. The required analyses are an analysis of turnover and pre-tax profit by class of business and an analysis of turnover by geographical market.

(c) **Directors' emoluments**. The notes must disclose the following information relating to directors' emoluments:

- the total of the directors' emoluments, including benefits in kind and pension contributions paid by the company, distinguishing between emoluments paid for services as a director and emoluments paid for other services
- the total pensions paid to former directors
- the total amount of any compensation for loss of office paid to directors and former directors.

The following further disclosures are required only if the total of the directors' emoluments exceeds £60,000:

- the chairman's emoluments and the emoluments of the highest-paid director, if this is not the chairman
- the number of directors who have waived any of their emoluments and the total amount waived
- the number of directors whose total emoluments (excluding pension contributions paid by the company) fall into each pay "band". The pay bands are £0 - £5,000, £5,001 - £10,000, £10,001 - £15,000 and so forth.

(d) **Employees other than directors**. The required disclosures in relation to employees other than directors are:

- the total of employees' wages and salaries
- the total social security costs paid by the company
- the total of other pension costs paid by the company
- the average number of persons employed by the company, analysed by category of work.

(e) **Charges for the year**. The following amounts charged to the profit and loss account must be disclosed:

- the total amount of depreciation charged in the year
- the auditors' remuneration, including expenses
- the total amount paid for the hire of plant and machinery.

(f) **Interest payable**. Interest payable must be analysed between interest on loans repayable within 5 years and interest on loans which are not repayable within 5 years.

(g) **Fixed assets**. For each category of fixed assets, the notes must disclose:

- the total cost (or valuation) at the beginning and end of the year and the effect on total cost (or valuation) of any acquisitions, disposals or revaluations made during the year
- the amount of depreciation provided for the year
- the accumulated depreciation at the beginning and end of the year and the effect on the accumulated depreciation of any disposals made during the year.

If assets (other than listed investments) are shown at a valuation, the notes must disclose the amount and date of the valuation. Furthermore, if assets have been revalued during the year, the notes must disclose the names and qualifications of the valuers and the basis of valuation used.

(h) **Land and buildings**. Land and buildings must be analysed into freeholds, long leaseholds and short leaseholds. A long lease is one which has at least 50 years to run from the balance sheet date. A short lease is any other lease.

(i) **Investments**. For each category of investments, the notes must disclose:

- the amount of any listed investments included within the category
- the total market value of the listed investments, if different from the amount shown in the balance sheet.

(j) **Debtors**. For each category of debtors, it is necessary to disclose the amount which falls due to be paid after more than one year.

(k) **Creditors**. For each category of creditors, the notes must disclose:

- the amount of any secured creditors and the nature of the security
- in the case of creditors payable after more than one year, the total amount payable after more than 5 years.

An analysis must be given of other creditors including taxation and social security and the amount of any proposed dividends must be disclosed.

(l) **Share capital and reserves**. The notes must disclose:

- the company's authorised share capital, analysed by class of share
- the company's issued share capital, analysed by class of share
- an analysis of any movements on reserves.

5. THE DIRECTORS' REPORT

The published accounts of a limited company must be accompanied by a directors' report. The main types of information contained in this report are:

(a) a statement of the *principal activities* of the company and any significant changes in these activities during the year under review

(b) a *review of developments* in the company's business during the year and an indication of plans for the future

(c) an indication of the company's *research and development* activities

(d) details of any significant *post-balance sheet events* i.e. events which have occurred since the end of the accounting year and which should be brought to the members' attention

(e) the amount which the directors propose transferring to/from *reserves* and details of any *proposed dividends*

(f) details of any significant changes in *fixed assets* during the year and the difference between the book value and the market value of land and buildings (if material)

(g) total *charitable donations* and total *political donations* made by the company during the year (only required if donations of all types exceed £200 in total) and the amount and the recipient of any individual political donation exceeding £200

(h) the names of those persons who have been *directors* at any time during the accounting year and details of the shares and debentures held by each director at the end of the year

(i) a statement regarding the health, safety and welfare at work of the *employees* of the company and (if there are more than 250 employees) the company's policy with regard to the employment of disabled people

(j) a statement to the effect that the *auditors* (who are appointed each year by the company's members) are seeking re-election or are not seeking re-election, as the case may be.

The directors' report should also disclose *any other material matter* necessary for the members' appreciation of the company's state of affairs.

6. SMALL AND MEDIUM-SIZED COMPANIES

Small and medium-sized companies are allowed certain exemptions with regard to the copy of their annual accounts which is filed with the Registrar of Companies. Public companies (regardless of size) can never qualify for these exemptions. Private companies qualify if they satisfy at least two of the following three criteria for both the current year and the previous year:

	Small	*Medium*
Total assets	£1.4 million or less	£5.6 million or less
Turnover	£2.8 million or less	£11.2 million or less
Average number of employees	50 or less	250 or less

A company's total assets for this purpose are the assets labelled A through to D in the statutory balance sheet. The exemptions available to small and medium-sized companies are listed below.

Small companies

(a) Small companies are not required to file a profit and loss account or a directors' report.

(b) The filed copy of the balance sheet need show only those items which are labelled with a letter of the alphabet or a roman numeral.

(c) The filed copy of the notes to the accounts need show only those notes which relate to:

- accounting policies
- movements in the totals of intangible fixed assets, tangible fixed assets and investments
- debtors which fall due to be paid after more than one year
- secured creditors
- creditors which are payable after more than 5 years
- share capital.

Medium-sized companies

(a) In the filed copy of the profit and loss account:

- it is not necessary to show turnover or cost of sales
- if Format 1 is used, items 1, 2, 3 and 6 may be combined into one figure
- if Format 2 is used, items 1 to 5 may be combined into one figure.

(b) The filed copy of the notes to the accounts need not provide the analyses of turnover and profit.

7. SUMMARY FINANCIAL STATEMENTS

A company which is listed on the Stock Exchange may offer each of its members a summary financial statement (SFS) in lieu of the full published accounts. This provision was introduced by the Companies Act 1989 in recognition of the fact that the full accounts may be of little interest or relevance to many shareholders. The main rules relating to SFS's are as follows:

(a) An SFS must be derived from the full accounts of the company and may not contain any information which is not shown in the full accounts. The content and format of an SFS is specified by statutory regulations.

(b) An SFS must state that it is only a summary of the full accounts and must contain a statement by the auditors to the effect that the SFS is consistent with the full accounts and complies with statutory requirements.

(c) The company must ask each of its members whether they would prefer to receive the full accounts or the SFS. Those who choose the SFS retain the right to change their minds at any time and demand the full accounts instead.

(d) The company must always file its full published accounts with the Registrar of Companies.

8. SUMMARY

- Companies must prepare their annual accounts in a form suitable for publication. The format and content of the published accounts are specified in the Companies Acts.
- A company's published accounts must be sent to each of the company's shareholders and debenture-holders. A copy must also be filed with the Registrar of Companies.
- The Companies Acts specify four formats for the published profit and loss account and two formats for the published balance sheet. Format 1 is the most popular format in each case.
- The published accounts must disclose certain information by means of a set of notes. These notes form an integral part of the published accounts.
- The published accounts must be accompanied by a directors' report. The contents of this report are specified in the Companies Acts.
- Small and medium-sized companies may omit certain information from the copy of their annual accounts which is filed with the Registrar of Companies.
- Listed companies may offer their members a summary financial statement in lieu of full published accounts.

EXERCISES 14

14.1 The trial balance of Fairweather Ltd as at 31 March 19X6 is as follows:

	Dr balances	*Cr balances*
	£	£
Goodwill at cost	150,000	
Land and buildings at cost	185,000	
Delivery vans at cost	40,100	
Warehouse plant and machinery at cost	8,300	
Directors' motor cars at cost	39,800	
Office equipment at cost	26,400	
Provisions for depreciation at 1/4/19X5:		
Delivery vans		20,120
Warehouse plant and machinery		3,650
Motor cars		10,200
Office equipment		11,650
Stock of goods for resale at 1/4/19X5	72,800	
Debtors and creditors	11,620	29,140
Prepayments and accruals	3,600	2,860
Provision for doubtful debts at 1/4/19X5		930
Cash in hand	520	
Bank balance		11,110
Purchases and sales	123,540	611,300
Returns inwards and outwards	23,760	1,650
Discounts allowed and received	12,530	3,370
Directors' remuneration	100,000	
Salaries of warehouse staff and van drivers	89,660	
Office salaries	56,530	
Delivery van expenses	18,330	
Motor car expenses	4,120	
Rates and insurance	37,200	
Heating and lighting	19,300	
Repairs and renewals	12,480	
Office stationery , telephone and sundries	7,220	
Bank interest payable	870	
Advertising	12,760	
Rent receivable		35,600
8% debentures		30,000
£1 ordinary shares, fully paid		100,000
6% preference shares of £1 each, fully paid		50,000
Share premium account		75,000
General reserve as at 1/4/19X5		50,000
Profit and loss account at 1/4/19X5		9,860
	1,056,440	1,056,440

Additional information:

1. Stocks at 31 March 19X6 are valued at £77,730.
2. Rates & insurance, heating & lighting and repairs & renewals are split equally between the warehouse and the offices.

3. Depreciation charges for the year to 31 March 19X6 are delivery vans £9,250, warehouse plant and machinery £2,800, motor cars £7,960 and office equipment £3,960.
4. The doubtful debts provision is to be increased by £100.
5. Interest on the 8% debentures for the year to 31 March 19X6 has not yet been paid or provided for. The debentures were issued several years ago and are redeemable in the year 19X9.
6. The corporation tax liability for the year is estimated at £30,000.
7. The directors propose to transfer £50,000 to the general reserve. They also propose that the preference dividend should be paid and that an ordinary dividend of 15p per share should also be paid.

Required:

Insofar as the information permits, prepare Fairweather Ltd's profit and loss account for the year to 31 March 19X6 and balance sheet as at that date in a form suitable for publication. Use Format 1 in each case. The notes to the accounts are not required.

14.2 (a) List the main types of information which must be disclosed in the notes which form part of a limited company's published accounts.

(b) List the main types of information which must be given in a directors' report.

14.3 Refer to your solution to the Fairweather Ltd exercise given above and then answer the following additional questions:

(a) Is the company small, medium-sized or neither for the purpose of filing its accounts with the Registrar of Companies?

(b) Prepare the accounts which would be filed with the Registrar if the company took full advantage of any exemptions to which it is entitled. (As before, the notes to the accounts are not required).

***14.4** The trial balance of Greenacre plc as at 30 September 19X8 (in alphabetical order) is as follows:

	Dr balances	*Cr balances*
	£'000	£'000
Bank balance	239	
Bank interest received		29
Calls in arrear	5	
Carriage inwards	142	
Cash in hand	17	
Corporation tax	14	
9% Debentures		1,100
Debenture interest paid	99	
Dividends received		16
Fixed asset investments at cost	140	
Freehold property at cost	1,200	
General administrative expenses	391	
General distribution costs	275	
General reserve as at 1/10/19X7		700
Goodwill at cost	200	
Hire of distribution equipment	78	
Interim dividends paid:		
Ordinary shares, at 10p per share	70	
Preference shares, half-year's dividend	4	
Leasehold property at cost	320	
Motor expenses	140	
Motor vehicles at cost	750	
Office equipment at cost	382	
Ordinary shares of 50p each		400
8% Preference shares of £1 each, fully paid		100
Prepayments and accruals	28	59
Profit and loss account at 1/10/19X7		42
Profit on sale of distribution vehicles		4
Provisions for depreciation:		
Leasehold property		120
Motor vehicles		212
Office equipment		92
Shop fixtures and fittings		128
Purchases and sales	3,515	6,930
Royalties received		50
Share premium account		300
Shop fixtures and fittings at cost	520	
Stock of goods for resale at 1/10/19X7	743	
Trade debtors and trade creditors	559	1,214
Wages and salaries	1,665	
	11,496	11,496

The following information is also available:

1. On 30 September 19X8, the freehold property was valued at £2,000,000 by W Atkinson & Co (a firm of Chartered Surveyors). The directors have decided to incorporate this valuation into the company's accounts.

2. The company has a 40-year lease on the leasehold property.
3. Motor vehicles costing £85,000 were purchased during the year and vehicles costing £80,000 (accumulated depreciation to 30/9/X7 £32,000) were sold during the year for £52,000. Office equipment was bought during the year for £72,000. There were no other fixed asset acquisitions or disposals during the year. All of the acquisitions and disposals were properly accounted for *before* extracting the above trial balance.
4. Depreciation charges for the year to 30 September 19X8 have *not* yet been calculated. Depreciation rates are as follows:

Leasehold property	2.5% per annum straight line
Motor vehicles	20% per annum straight line
Office equipment	40% per annum reducing balance
Shop fixtures and fittings	25% per annum straight line

   It is company policy to charge a full year's depreciation in the year of acquisition and none in the year of disposal. None of the fixed assets had been fully depreciated by 30 September 19X7.
5. The leasehold property is used entirely for administrative purposes. The motor vehicles (and the motor expenses) are split 60:40 between distribution and administration.
6. All of the investments are listed on the Stock Exchange. Their market value at 30 September 19X8 was £172,000.
7. Closing stock on 30 September 19X8 is valued at £727,000.
8. Trade debtors include £20,000 which is not payable until 31 October 19X9. All of the trade creditors are payable within 30 days.
9. The debentures are redeemable in 7 years' time and are secured by a charge on the company's freehold property.
10. The audit fee of £14,000 is included in "General administrative expenses".
11. Wages and salaries may be analysed as follows:

	£'000	*Number of staff*
B Greenacre (Managing director)	312	1
S Greenacre (Chairman)	100	1
W Greenacre (Director)	147	1
J Adams (Director)	79	1
R Yeomans (Director)	76	1
Wages of distribution staff	411	29
Office salaries	540	41
	1,665	75

12. The company issued 100,000 50p ordinary shares on 31 August 19X8 at an issue price of £2.50 per share. These new shares were not eligible for any dividends declared for the year to 30 September 19X8. A total of £245,000 had been received in relation to this issue by 30 September 19X8. No preference shares were issued during the year.
13. The balance on the corporation tax account represents an underprovision in the year to 30 September 19X7. The corporation tax liability for the year to 30 September 19X8 is estimated to be £95,000.

14. The directors propose to transfer £100,000 from the general reserve, to pay the remaining half-year's dividend on the preference shares and to pay a final ordinary dividend of 25p per share.

Required:

Insofar as the information permits, prepare Greenacre plc's profit and loss account for the year to 30 September 19X8 and balance sheet as at that date in a form suitable for publication (using Format 1). The accounts should be accompanied by a set of formal notes but a statement of accounting policies is not required.

15

ACCOUNTING STANDARDS

Chapter objectives

When you have finished this chapter, you should be able to:

- **Explain the purpose of accounting standards.**
- **Outline the functions of each of the bodies involved in the standard setting process.**
- **Summarise the main points of the accounting standards which are currently in force.**
- **Summarise the ASB Statement of Principles.**
- **State the Stock Exchange rules which relate to the published accounts of listed companies.**

1. INTRODUCTION

The statutory regulations described in Chapter 14 ensure that a company discloses at least a minimum of important financial information in its published accounts and does so in a standard format. However, compliance with these statutory regulations does not prevent companies from employing a wide variety of accounting treatments for many of the items shown in their accounts. For example, the statutory regulations insist that a company discloses the amount set aside for depreciation each year but do not require that a specific depreciation method should be used.

Of course, it is quite right that accountants should be allowed to exercise their professional judgement when selecting an accounting treatment for a financial item. On the other hand, if accountants were totally free to choose any treatment they wished, this would inevitably result in significant variations between the accounts of different companies and hinder the comparability of company accounts. Total freedom of choice would also facilitate the deliberate distortion of information so as to make a company's accounts appear as favourable as possible.

For these reasons, the published accounts of limited companies must comply with all *relevant accounting standards* issued by the Accounting Standards Board (ASB) or its predecessor, the Accounting Standards Committee (ASC). Some of the standards are relevant to all companies whilst others are relevant only to certain types of company. Each standard addresses a different accounting matter and provides guidance on the way in which that matter should be dealt with in company accounts.

The legal status of accounting standards

The accounting standards are not embedded in the Companies Acts and are not part of the law of the land. However, three factors combine to ensure that the standards will have the force of law in most cases:

(a) The Companies Act 1989 requires public companies and large private companies to state in their accounts whether or not accounting standards have been complied with and to explain any material departures.

(b) The professional accounting bodies require their members to comply with the accounting standards when preparing company accounts and to report on any significant departures from the standards when auditing company accounts. (This last requirement is overridden if the auditor is of the opinion that compliance with a given standard would prevent the accounts from showing a true and fair view).

(c) A body known as the Financial Reporting Review Panel examines the published accounts of limited companies. If accounting standards have not been complied with and the company concerned refuses to comply, the FRRP may seek a court order requiring the accounts to be revised. The courts usually hold that company accounts cannot show a true and fair view unless accounting standards have been complied with and will therefore make the order.

In summary, a company cannot hide the fact that it has contravened accounting standards and will almost certainly be required to revise its accounts if standards have not been complied with. In effect, therefore, the accounting standards have a quasi-legal impact on company accounts.

2. BODIES INVOLVED IN THE STANDARD-SETTING PROCESS

There are four bodies involved in the process of setting standards and monitoring adherence to standards, as shown in the following diagram:

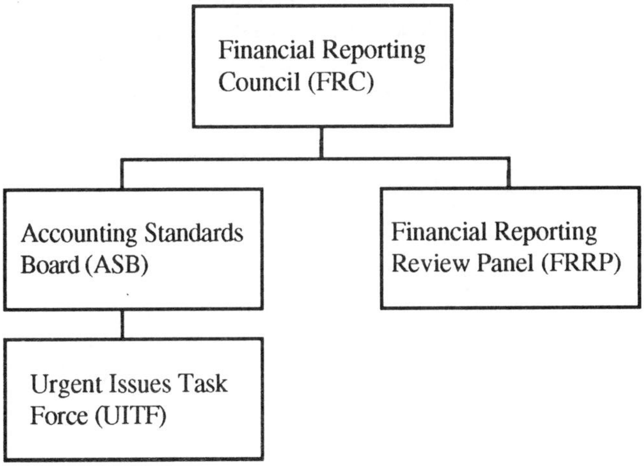

(a) **Financial Reporting Council**. The FRC, which consists of approximately 25 members drawn from the accounting profession, industry and commerce, is in overall charge of the accounting standards system. The FRC's role is:

- to make suggestions to the government for improvements in the law relating to accounting
- to appoint members to the ASB and the FRRP and to obtain funding for their work
- to set the direction in which accounting standards should develop and guide the Accounting Standards Board in its work.

(b) **Accounting Standards Board**. The ASB consists of approximately 10 qualified accountants, including a full-time Chairman. The role of the ASB is to write and issue accounting standards, which are now known as Financial Reporting Standards (FRS's). When a new standard is first being considered, a document known as a Discussion Draft (DD) may be circulated to interested parties to elicit preliminary views on the matter concerned. A Financial Reporting Exposure Draft (FRED) may then be circulated for further consultation before the FRS finally emerges.

(c) **Financial Reporting Review Panel**. The FRRP has approximately 15 members and its role (as explained earlier) is to monitor the published accounts of limited companies and to look into cases in which accounting standards have been contravened. The FRRP will try to persuade a non-compliant company to revise its accounts but, if necessary, the FRRP may apply to the courts for an order requiring the company to comply.

(d) **Urgent Issues Task Force**. The UITF is a sub-committee of the ASB. Its main role is to deal with urgent matters for which the normal standard-setting process would be impracticably slow.

3. THE ACCOUNTING STANDARDS

A complete list of the accounting standards in force at the time of writing (January 1997) is shown below. The standards issued by the now-defunct Accounting Standards Committee are known as Statements of Standard Accounting Practice (SSAP's) and have been adopted by the ASB. As stated earlier, the standards produced by the ASB itself are known as Financial Reporting Standards (FRS's). Standards missing from the list have either been withdrawn or superseded by later standards.

Standard	*Title*	*Year issued or revised*
SSAP 1	Accounting for the results of associated companies	1982
SSAP 2	Disclosure of accounting policies	1971
SSAP 3	Earnings per share	1974
SSAP 4	The accounting treatment of government grants	1990
SSAP 5	Accounting for value added tax	1974
SSAP 8	The treatment of taxation under the imputation system in the accounts of companies	1977
SSAP 9	Stocks and long-term contracts	1988
SSAP 12	Accounting for depreciation	1987
SSAP 13	Accounting for research and development	1989
SSAP 15	Accounting for deferred taxation	1985
SSAP 17	Accounting for post balance sheet events	1980
SSAP 18	Accounting for contingencies	1980
SSAP 19	Accounting for investment properties	1981
SSAP 20	Foreign currency translation	1983
SSAP 21	Accounting for leases and hire purchase agreements	1984
SSAP 22	Accounting for goodwill	1989
SSAP 24	Accounting for pension costs	1988
SSAP 25	Segmental reporting	1990
FRS 1	Cash flow statements	1996
FRS 2	Accounting for subsidiary undertakings	1992
FRS 3	Reporting financial performance	1992
FRS 4	Capital instruments	1993
FRS 5	Reporting the substance of transactions	1994
FRS 6	Acquisitions and mergers	1994
FRS 7	Fair values in acquisition accounting	1994
FRS 8	Related party disclosures	1995

Some of the standards deal with rather advanced technical topics and it is beyond the scope of this book to explain all of them in great detail. However a summary of each standard, with more emphasis on those which are usually of interest to students studying financial accounting at an introductory level, is given below.

Accounting for the results of associated companies (SSAP1)

This standard applies only to companies which have a significant influence over the financial and operating policy decisions of another company (see Chapter 18).

Disclosure of accounting policies (SSAP2)

This standard is concerned with the accounting policies adopted by companies when preparing their annual accounts. The standard uses the terms "fundamental accounting concepts", "accounting bases" and "accounting policies". These terms are defined as follows:

(a) Fundamental accounting concepts are the "*broad basic assumptions which underlie the periodic financial accounts of business enterprises*". The standard states that four such concepts have general acceptability. These are the going concern concept, the accruals (or matching) concept, the consistency concept and the prudence concept. These concepts are explained in Chapter 2 of this book, where they are referred to as accounting conventions.

(b) Accounting bases are "*the methods developed for applying fundamental accounting concepts to financial transactions and items*". These methods are used to identify the periods in which revenue and expenditure are shown in the profit and loss account and the values at which assets and liabilities are shown in the balance sheet. For example, the matching convention requires that fixed assets should be depreciated, but a company might adopt any one of several different bases when performing depreciation calculations (e.g. straight-line, reducing-balance).

(c) Accounting policies are "*the specific accounting bases selected and consistently followed by a business enterprise*". For example, a company might decide to use the straight-line basis for the depreciation of its plant and machinery.

SSAP2 requires companies to explain any departure from the four fundamental accounting concepts and to disclose their accounting policies in relation to material items included in the profit and loss account and balance sheet. (As we saw in Chapter 14, these requirements have received statutory backing in the Companies Acts).

Earnings per share (SSAP3)

This standard requires companies whose shares are listed on the Stock Exchange to show an earnings per share figure on the face of the profit and loss account. This figure is widely used as a means of assessing company performance and is often used:

(a) to compare a company's results in different accounting periods, and
(b) to compare a company's results with those of other companies.

Such comparisons are invalid unless the earnings per share figure is calculated on a consistent basis and therefore SSAP3 provides a standard definition of the term. This definition was revised by FRS3 in 1992. The revised definition is:

> "*the profit in pence attributable to each equity share, based on the consolidated profit of the period after tax, minority interests, extraordinary items and preference dividends, divided by the number of equity shares in issue and ranking for dividend in respect of the period*".

The words "consolidated" and "minority interests" in this definition apply only if the company is a parent company (see Chapter 18).

The accounting treatment of government grants (SSAP4)

In certain circumstances, companies may receive government grants to help them to acquire assets or pay expenses. SSAP4 requires that these grants should be credited to the profit and loss account in such a way that they are matched against the expenditure to which they relate. The consequences of this rule are as follows:

(a) A grant made towards a company's revenue expenditure should be credited to the profit and loss account in the same period as the expenditure itself is shown.

(b) A grant made towards the acquisition of a fixed asset should be credited to the profit and loss account over the useful life of the asset. The preferred method is to credit the grant initially to a deferred income account and then to transfer an appropriate portion of this to the profit and loss account each year.

Accounting for value added tax (SSAP5)

The main points of this fairly straightforward standard are as follows:

(a) The turnover figure given in a company's accounts should exclude any VAT charged to customers.

(b) If a company can recover the VAT paid on the purchase of goods or services, the amounts shown in the accounts in relation to those goods or services should exclude the VAT paid.

(c) If a company cannot recover the VAT paid on the purchase of goods or services, then this VAT forms part of the purchase price of the items concerned and should be treated as such in the accounts.

(d) Any amount of VAT owing to or from the Customs and Excise at the end of an accounting year should be included in creditors or debtors and need not be disclosed separately.

The treatment of taxation under the imputation system in the accounts of companies (SSAP8)

Before explaining this standard, it is necessary to describe (in outline) the workings of the UK taxation system with regard to companies. The main features of this system are as follows:

(a) Companies pay corporation tax on their profits. This tax is payable 9 months after the end of the accounting year.

(b) When a company pays a dividend, it must also pay an amount of advance corporation tax (ACT) calculated as a specified fraction of that dividend. ACT is payable 14 days after the end of the quarter in which the dividend is paid.

(c) The ACT paid in relation to a dividend is usually recovered by set-off against the company's corporation tax liability for the accounting year in which the dividend is paid. However, there is an upper limit on the amount of ACT which may be offset in this way and so it is possible that some of the ACT paid by a company may become irrecoverable.

(d) When a company receives a dividend from another UK company, this dividend comes with an attached tax credit. In effect, the dividend is received net of tax and the receiving company has no further tax liability with respect to the dividend.

The main requirements of SSAP8 are:

(a) Dividends paid and proposed should be shown in the profit and loss appropriation account without including the related ACT.

(b) Any irrecoverable ACT suffered by a company should be included as part of the tax charge shown in the profit and loss account but disclosed separately in the notes to the accounts if material.

(c) Dividends received should be "grossed-up" in the profit and loss account (i.e. the profit and loss account should show the amount actually received plus the attached tax credit). The total tax credits relating to the dividends received in an accounting year should be shown as part of the tax charge for that year.

(d) The ACT payable on proposed dividends should be treated in the balance sheet both as a current liability and (if recoverable) as a deferred asset. The reason that recoverable ACT is a *deferred* asset is that the recovery will not take effect until the corporation tax liability for the *following* year is settled (i.e. the year in which the dividends are eventually paid).

Stocks and long-term contracts (SSAP9)

This standard requires that stocks and work in progress (apart from long-term contracts) should be valued at the lower of cost and net realisable value. If possible, the cost and NRV of each stock item should be considered separately, but it is permissible to group items if it would be impracticable to deal with them on an individual basis. It is *not* permissible to value stock at the lower of total cost and total NRV. The following definitions are given:

(a) The cost of a stock item is the expenditure incurred in bringing the item to its present location and condition. If stock items are not uniquely identifiable, the standard regards FIFO and AVCO as acceptable methods of ascertaining cost but rejects LIFO (see Chapter 7).

(b) The net realisable value of a stock item is the estimated selling price of the item less all costs to completion and less all costs relating to the sale of the item.

A *long-term contract* is a contract entered into for the design, manufacture or construction of an asset or for the provision of a service, where the time taken to complete the contract is such that it falls into more than one accounting period. If there were no special rules regarding long-term contracts, an incomplete contract would be treated as ordinary work in progress and would be valued at the lower of cost and NRV. In effect, companies would be unable to take credit for any of the profit arising on such contracts until completion. The accounting treatment established by SSAP9 as a solution to this problem is rather complex, but the main principles involved are as follows:

(a) If a long-term contract is incomplete at the end of an accounting period and it is reasonably certain that the contract will yield an overall profit, the portion of that profit which is attributable to the work done to date may be recognised in the profit and loss account. This is achieved by:

  (i) crediting profit and loss account with the recorded turnover to date (this will typically be an amount which has been certified by an architect or engineer as being the value of the work done so far), and

  (ii) debiting profit and loss account with the related costs (i.e. the costs incurred to date which relate to the recorded turnover).

  Any remaining costs incurred to date are shown as work in progress on the balance sheet.

(b) If a long-term contract is incomplete at the end of an accounting period and the contract is expected to yield an overall loss, the whole of this loss should be provided for immediately. This is achieved by deducting the amount of the anticipated loss when calculating the value of work in progress at the end of the period.

Accounting for depreciation (SSAP12)

SSAP12 defines depreciation as "*the measure of the wearing out, consumption or other reduction in the useful economic life of a fixed asset whether arising from use, effluxion of time or obsolescence through technological or market changes*". The standard's basic requirement is that *all* fixed assets having a finite useful economic life should be the subject of a provision for depreciation. However, the following types of fixed asset are outside the scope of SSAP12:

(a) Investment properties, which are the subject of SSAP19
(b) Goodwill, which is the subject of SSAP22
(c) Development costs, which are dealt with in SSAP13
(d) Investments.

SSAP12 states that depreciation charges should be computed by allocating the cost of fixed assets (less estimated residual value) as fairly as possible to the periods which are expected to benefit from their use. The standard does not dictate or even advise any specific depreciation methods but does require that the chosen methods should be appropriate to the types of asset concerned and should be used consistently. A change in depreciation method is permitted only if it would give a fairer presentation of the company's results and its financial position. Further requirements of SSAP12 are as follows:

Charged to the profit and loss account

The whole of the depreciation charge for an accounting period should be shown in the profit and loss account. It is not permissible to debit all or part of the depreciation charge to a reserve.

Revision of useful life

The useful economic lives of fixed assets should be estimated realistically and should be reviewed on a regular basis. If the estimated useful life of an asset is revised, then the net book value of the asset should be depreciated over the remainder of its revised useful life. In extreme cases, this may lead to a material distortion of future results, in which case an adjustment to the accumulated depreciation in previous years should be made.

EXAMPLE

A fixed asset with an expected useful life of 10 years and no residual value was acquired for £6,000 on 1 January 19X3 and depreciated using the straight-line method. On 31 December 19X5, it was estimated that the remaining useful life of the asset was only one year. Calculate the amount of depreciation charged in each of the four years to 31 December 19X6.

SOLUTION

Depreciation of £600 would be charged in the year to 31 December 19X3 and the same sum would be charged in the year to 31 December 19X4, leaving a written down value of £4,800 on 1 January 19X5. This would then be written off over the remaining two years of the asset's revised useful life, giving a charge of £2,400 in the year to 31 December 19X5 and another £2,400 in the year to 31 December 19X6.

If it is considered that these charges would lead to a material distortion of the results for the years to 31 December 19X5 and 19X6, the accumulated depreciation of £1,200 brought forward on 1 January 19X5 should be adjusted to £3,000 (i.e. the figure which would have accumulated by 1 January 19X5 if the original estimate of the asset's useful life had been four years instead of ten). The profit and loss accounts for each of the two years to 31 December 19X6 should then be charged with depreciation of £1,500.

The adjustment described above involves debiting profit and loss account with an extra £1,800 in the year to 31 December 19X5. This is an exceptional item as defined by FRS3 and would be treated as such in the accounts (see Chapter 17).

Change in method

If there is a change in depreciation method, the net book value of the assets concerned should be written off on the new basis over the remainder of their useful lives. If this would lead to a material distortion of future results, accumulated depreciation in previous years should be adjusted.

Revaluations

If an asset is revalued, the revalued amount should be depreciated over the remainder of the asset's useful life.

Land and buildings

The useful life of most buildings is finite and therefore buildings should be depreciated in the same way as other fixed assets. Freehold land normally has an infinite useful life and will only be depreciated if it is subject to depletion (e.g. by the extraction of mineral deposits).

Disclosures

The following disclosures are required for each major class of depreciable asset:

(a) the depreciation method used

(b) the average useful lives or depreciation rates used

(c) the total amount of depreciation charged in the accounting period

(d) the gross amount of the assets and the accumulated depreciation to date

(e) the reason for and the effect on the depreciation charge for the year of any change in depreciation method (if material)

(f) the effect on the depreciation charge for the year of any revaluations made in the period (if material).

Accounting for research and development (SSAP13)

In principle, expenditure on research and development (R & D) could be treated in one of two ways:

(a) The expenditure might be capitalised and written off over the accounting periods in which revenues arise in the future as a consequence of the expenditure. This accounting treatment conforms with the matching convention.

(b) The expenditure might be written off immediately, on the grounds that it is impossible to predict with any certainty whether or not the expenditure will generate revenues in the future. This accounting treatment conforms with the prudence convention.

SSAP13 attempts to resolve this dilemma by classifying R & D expenditure into three types. These are:

(a) **Pure research**. This is experimental or theoretical work which is undertaken primarily to acquire new scientific or technical knowledge and is not directed towards any specific application.

(b) **Applied research**. This is work undertaken in order to gain new scientific or technical knowledge and which is directed towards a specific practical aim.

(c) **Development**. This is the use of existing scientific or technical knowledge in order to produce new or substantially improved products, services etc.

The standard requires that expenditure on pure or applied research should be written off immediately. As regards development expenditure, companies may choose between writing off the expenditure immediately or (subject to certain conditions) capitalising the expenditure and writing it off over its useful life. The same accounting policy must be applied to *all* development expenditure. The conditions which must be satisfied before development expenditure may be capitalised (or "deferred") are as follows:

(a) There must be a clearly defined development project.

(b) The expenditure concerned must be separately identifiable.

(c) There must be reasonable certainty that the project is technically feasible and commercially viable.

(d) Adequate resources must be available to complete the project (or there must be a reasonable expectation that such resources will become available).

(e) There must be a reasonable expectation that future revenues from the project will be sufficient to cover the total development costs to date, plus any further development costs, plus the costs of production, selling and administration.

All deferred development expenditure must be reviewed each year to ensure that the above conditions are still satisfied and should be written off immediately if this is not the case.

SSAP13 requires companies to state their accounting policy with regard to development expenditure and to disclose movements on the deferred development expenditure account during the year, together with the opening and closing balances on the account. Public companies and certain large private companies are also required to disclose the total amount of R & D expenditure charged to the profit and loss account for the year, analysed between current year expenditure and depreciation of previous years' expenditure.

Accounting for deferred taxation (SSAP15)

The amount of profit which is shown in a company's profit and loss account is often very different from the amount of profit which is charged to tax. This discrepancy arises because of two types of differences:

(a) **Permanent differences**. Some classes of income received by a company and credited to the profit and loss account may not be chargeable to tax. Similarly, some classes of expenditure incurred by a company and debited to the profit and loss account may not be deductible for tax purposes.

(b) **Timing differences**. Certain items of income or expenditure which are shown in the profit and loss account for a given accounting period may be dealt with in the taxation computation for a different period. For instance, the depreciation charges shown in a company's profit and loss account are disallowed for tax purposes and replaced by standardised capital allowances. Total depreciation will equal total capital allowances over the entire lifespan of the company but there may be a sizeable difference between the two figures in any one accounting period.

Permanent differences have no accounting implications but timing differences can lead to material distortion of a company's after-tax profit figures. In turn, this can lead to material distortion of the all-important earnings per share figures.

EXAMPLE

A company with an issued share capital of 10,000 ordinary shares has the following results for the three years to 31 March 19X9:

	31/3/X7	*31/3/X8*	*31/3/X9*
	£	£	£
Net profit after depreciation	5,000	5,000	5,000
Depreciation for the year	1,000	1,000	1,000
Capital allowances available	2,000	750	250

Assuming that there are no other permanent or timing differences and that the rate of corporation tax rate is 24% throughout, calculate the company's profit after tax and earnings per share for each of the three years.

SOLUTION

	31/3/X7	*31/3/X8*	*31/3/X9*
	£	£	£
Net profit before depreciation	6,000	6,000	6,000
Less: Capital allowances	2,000	750	250
Taxable profit	4,000	5,250	5,750
Net profit per accounts	5,000	5,000	5,000
Tax @ 24% of taxable profit	960	1,260	1,380
Profit after tax	4,040	3,740	3,620
Earnings per share	40.4p	37.4p	36.2p

The company's earnings per share figures appear to be on a downward trend (which may deter investors) and yet the company's profits have been a consistent £5,000 per year over the three-year period. Total depreciation and total capital allowances are both £3,000 but timing differences have resulted in distortion of the EPS figures.

The problems caused by timing differences are usually resolved in the following way:

(a) Profits are transferred to a provision for deferred taxation account in the years in which taxable profits are *lower* than accounting profits.

(b) Profits are then transferred back out of this account in the years in which taxable profits are *higher* than accounting profits.

These transfers have the effect of smoothing out the overall tax charge so that after-tax profits and earnings per share are not distorted by timing differences.

EXAMPLE

Rework the above example, given that the company maintains a provision for deferred taxation.

SOLUTION

		31/3/X7		31/3/X8		31/3/X9
		£		£		£
Net profit per accounts		5,000		5,000		5,000
Tax @ 24% of taxable profit	960		1,260		1,380	
Transfer to deferred tax a/c	240		-		-	
Transfer from deferred tax a/c	-	1,200	(60)	1,200	(180)	1,200
Profit after tax		3,800		3,800		3,800
Earnings per share		38.0p		38.0p		38.0p

£240 is transferred from profit and loss account to the provision for deferred taxation in the year to 31 March 19X7. £60 of this is transferred back in the year to 31 March 19X8 and the other £180 is transferred back in the year to 31 March 19X9. These transfers have the effect of maintaining the overall tax charge at a level percentage of the company's profits, so avoiding misleading fluctuations in after-tax profits and earnings per share.

SSAP15 lists the main types of timing differences and requires that deferred tax should be accounted for so long as it is probable that these differences will eventually be reversed. Disclosure requirements are as follows:

(a) In the profit and loss account, transfers to/from the deferred tax account should be shown separately as part of the tax charge for the year and the company should disclose the amount of any unprovided deferred tax for the year.

(b) The balance on the deferred tax account should be disclosed in the balance sheet or in the notes to the accounts. The notes should also disclose the total amount of any unprovided deferred tax.

Accounting for post balance sheet events (SSAP17)

SSAP17 defines post balance sheet events as "*those events, both favourable and unfavourable, which occur between the balance sheet date and the date on which the financial statements are approved by the board of directors*". The standard distinguishes between two types of post balance sheet event:

(a) **Adjusting events**. These provide new or additional evidence of conditions existing at the balance sheet date. Typical examples of adjusting events include:

- the insolvency of a debtor who owed money to the company at the year-end
- events which provide evidence of the net realisable value of closing stocks

- the announcement of tax rates applicable to the accounting year
- a property valuation which indicates a permanent diminution in the value of property existing at the balance sheet date (unless the decline in value took place after the year-end).

SSAP17 requires that the effects of adjusting events *should* be reflected in the accounts.

(b) **Non-adjusting events**. These are concerned with conditions which did not exist at the balance sheet date. Typical examples of non-adjusting events are:

- a fire, flood or other catastrophe which destroys company assets
- an industrial dispute
- mergers and acquisitions
- issues of shares or debentures.

SSAP17 requires that the effects of non-adjusting events *should not* be reflected in the accounts but that material non-adjusting events should be disclosed in the notes to the accounts.

Accounting for contingencies (SSAP18)

SSAP18 defines a contingency as a "*condition which exists at the balance sheet date, where the outcome will be confirmed only on the occurrence of one or more uncertain future events*". A typical example of a contingency is a legal case in which a company is involved at the balance sheet date but which will not be decided until after the accounts are approved by the directors.

A contingency will result in either a contingent gain or a contingent loss at some future date. SSAP18 requires contingencies to be dealt with as follows:

(a) **Contingent losses**.

- A material contingent loss should be provided for in the accounts so long as it is *probable* that the loss will occur and the amount of the loss can be estimated with reasonable accuracy. If the amount of a probable contingent loss cannot be estimated, the contingency should be disclosed in a note to the accounts.
- If it is only *possible* (but not probable) that a material contingent loss will occur, the contingency should be disclosed in a note to the accounts.
- If there is only a *remote possibility* that a material contingent loss will occur, the contingency need not be disclosed at all.

(b) **Contingent gains**.

- A material contingent gain should be disclosed in a note to the accounts so long as it is *probable* that the gain will occur.
- Contingent gains which are anything *less than probable* should not be disclosed at all.

If a contingent gain or loss is disclosed in a note to the accounts, the note should disclose the nature of the contingency, a summary of the uncertainties which will affect the final outcome of the contingency and a prudent estimate of the amount of the contingent gain or loss. If such an estimate cannot be made, the note should include a statement to that effect.

Accounting for investment properties (SSAP19)

An investment property is defined as "*an interest in land and/or buildings*" which is "*held for its investment potential*". The main requirements of SSAP19 are:

(a) Investment properties should not be depreciated in accordance with SSAP12 (apart from leasehold properties held on a lease of less than 20 years).

(b) Instead, investment properties should be shown in the balance sheet at their open market value. Surpluses and deficits on revaluation should be credited and debited respectively to a revaluation reserve. A debit balance on this reserve should normally be written off to the profit and loss account.

(c) The names and/or the qualifications of the valuers should be disclosed in a note to the accounts, along with the basis of valuation. If a valuer is also an employee or officer of the company, the notes to the accounts must disclose this fact.

Foreign currency translation (SSAP20)

A full coverage of this very complex topic is beyond the scope of this book, but a brief summary of the main provisions of SSAP20 is as follows:

(a) **Individual companies**.

- In the accounts of individual companies, foreign currency items should usually be translated into sterling using historical exchange rates. In other words, each item should be translated at the exchange rate which was in force when the transaction occurred which gave rise to that item. For instance, if a fixed asset was bought abroad some years ago, the price of the asset should be converted into sterling at the exchange rate which was in force when the asset was bought.
- However, all monetary items shown in the balance sheet should instead be translated at the closing rate i.e. at the exchange rate in force on the balance sheet date. Monetary items consist mainly of cash and bank balances held in foreign currency and amounts which are due to be received or paid in foreign currency (i.e. foreign debtors and creditors).
- Any surpluses or deficits arising on foreign currency translation should usually be shown in the profit and loss account.

(b) **Group companies**. If a company has a foreign subsidiary, the accounts of that subsidiary should normally be translated into sterling at the closing rate when preparing consolidated accounts (see Chapter 18).

Accounting for leases and hire purchase agreements (SSAP21)

A lease is an agreement whereby the owner of an asset (the lessor) allows someone else (the lessee) to use that asset for a period of time at an agreed rent. SSAP21 is concerned with the accounting problems which arise when companies use leasing as a means of acquiring fixed assets such as plant and machinery. The standard classifies leases into two types:

(a) **Finance leases**. A finance lease is "*a lease that transfers substantially all the risks and rewards of ownership of an asset to the lessee*". The substance of such a lease (though not the legal form) is that the lessee acquires the asset permanently and agrees to pay for it by instalments. Most hire purchase agreements are very similar in nature to finance leases.

(b) **Operating leases**. An operating lease is "*a lease other than a finance lease*". The substance of an operating lease is that the lessee is simply renting the asset from the lessor and will return it at the end of the lease agreement.

SSAP21 takes the view that the substance of a transaction is more important than its legal form. Accordingly, assets acquired via finance leases (or hire purchase agreements) should be shown as assets in the lessee's balance sheet. The lessee's obligation to make rental payments in the future should be shown as a liability in the balance sheet.

By contrast, the rental payments relating to an operating lease should be written off in the year to which they relate and the leased assets should *not* be shown in the lessee's balance sheet.

Accounting for goodwill (SSAP22)

Goodwill is defined as "*the difference between the value of a business as a whole and the aggregate of the fair values of its separable net assets*". Goodwill may arise for a variety of reasons. For example, a successful business may enjoy a good local reputation and have an established customer base. This would make the business worth more than the total of the net assets listed on the balance sheet (assuming that goodwill is not shown on the balance sheet). SSAP22 distinguishes between two categories of goodwill:

(a) **Purchased goodwill**. This is goodwill which has been established as a result of the purchase of a business. For example, a new owner may take over the business of a retiring sole trader or one company may acquire the business of another company. In each case the acquirer might pay for the goodwill of the acquired business.

(b) **Non-purchased goodwill**. This is any goodwill other than purchased goodwill. For example, a company might simply estimate the value of its own goodwill and wish to show this as an asset on the company's balance sheet.

SSAP22 states that non-purchased goodwill may not be shown on a company balance sheet. Purchased goodwill should normally be written off immediately on acquisition but the standard permits purchased goodwill to be capitalised and amortised over its estimated useful life. The main disclosure requirements of SSAP22 are as follows:

(a) The company's accounting policy with regard to goodwill should be disclosed in the notes to the accounts.

(b) The notes should also show the movements on the goodwill account during the year, the amount of goodwill written off in the year and the amortisation period for each major acquisition of purchased goodwill.

(c) If a material acquisition has been made during the year, the notes should disclose the fair values of the assets and liabilities acquired, the value of the consideration given and the amount of the purchased goodwill. The accounting treatment of this goodwill should also be revealed.

If negative goodwill arises on the acquisition of a business, SSAP22 suggests that the fair values of the assets acquired should be reviewed in case they have been overstated. Negative goodwill which remains after this review must be credited to reserves. Accounting standard FRS7 (see later in this chapter) provides guidance on the measurement of fair values when one company acquires another.

Accounting for pension costs (SSAP24)

The basic principle of SSAP24 is that an employer's accounts should recognise the cost of providing employees' pensions on a systematic and rational basis over the period during which the employer benefits from the employees' services. The standard distinguishes between two types of pension schemes:

Defined contribution schemes

In a defined contribution scheme, the employer makes agreed contributions to the scheme in each accounting period and has no further liability beyond the amount of these contributions. These schemes cause no accounting difficulties. The pension cost shown in the profit and loss account for an accounting period is simply the amount of the employers' agreed contributions for that period.

Defined benefit schemes

In a defined benefit scheme, the benefits to be paid to an employee on retirement are defined (usually as a proportion of final salary) but the employer's contributions are not. It is up to the employer to make contributions which are sufficient (together with related investment income) to ensure that funds are available to cover benefit payments when they fall due.

These schemes are much less straightforward than defined contribution schemes, since the level of contributions required over the working life of an employee in order to fund that employee's retirement benefits can only be estimated. The main requirements of SSAP24 in relation to defined benefit schemes are as follows:

(a) The pension cost for an accounting period should be calculated using approved actuarial valuation methods. These methods involve making estimates of such factors as future rates of inflation, future pay increases, future investment income, life expectancy of employees etc.
(b) The valuation method used should be such that the pension cost charged in each accounting period should be a substantially level percentage of the pensionable payroll.
(c) If the contributions actually made in an accounting period are not equal to the pension cost shown in the accounts, the difference should be treated as a provision or a prepayment.

Regardless of the type of pension scheme in operation, SSAP24 requires that certain information relating to pension costs should be disclosed in the notes to the accounts. The main disclosures required are:

(a) whether the pension scheme is on a defined contribution or defined benefit basis
(b) the company's accounting policy with regard to pension costs
(c) the pension cost charged to the profit and loss account for the accounting period
(d) the amount of any accruals, provisions or prepayments in the balance sheet which relate to pension costs.

Segmental reporting (SSAP25)

As we saw in Chapter 14, the Companies Acts require companies to analyse turnover by class of business and geographical market and to analyse pre-tax profit by class of business. SSAP25 extends these requirements for public companies, for banking or insurance companies and for certain large private companies. If such a company has more than one class of business or operates in more than one geographical segment, then it must report for each class and for each segment:

(a) turnover, distinguishing between sales to external customers and internal sales to other segments of the company
(b) pre-tax profits
(c) net assets.

Cash flow statements (FRS1)

FRS1 is the subject of Chapter 16 of this book.

Accounting for subsidiary undertakings (FRS2)

FRS2 provides guidance on the preparation of group accounts. This subject is dealt with in Chapter 18 of this book.

Reporting financial performance (FRS3)

FRS3 is the subject of Chapter 17 of this book.

Capital instruments (FRS4)

FRS4 is a complex standard dealing with the accounting treatment of sophisticated company financing mechanisms. It is beyond the scope of an introductory accounting textbook and is considered no further here.

Reporting the substance of transactions (FRS5)

FRS5 is concerned with the accounting treatment of certain specialised financial arrangements which companies have used in the past as a means of borrowing money without showing a corresponding liability in their accounts. An example is the sale of stock to a financier on the understanding that the stock will be bought back on a future date at an enhanced price. The legal form of this transaction is that there has been a sale of stock. The actual substance of the transaction is that the company has borrowed money from the financier, which it must eventually repay with interest. An accounting treatment based solely on the legal form of the transaction would not reflect its true substance.

FRS5 establishes a set of principles for dealing with such transactions so as to ensure that companies report the substance of transactions rather than their legal form.

Acquisitions and mergers (FRS6)

FRS6 distinguishes between the situation in which one company acquires another and the situation in which two companies merge together. The standard establishes rules for determining whether a given business combination comprises an acquisition or a merger and specifies the form of accounting which should be used in each case. The accounting rules of FRS6 can be summarised as follows:

(a) Any business combination which does not qualify as a merger must be accounted for by "acquisition accounting". This is the form of accounting used in the preparation of consolidated accounts (see Chapter 18).

(b) A business combination which does qualify as a merger may be accounted for by a form of accounting known as "merger accounting". Merger accounting is beyond the scope of this book.

Fair values in acquisition accounting (FRS7)

When one company acquires another, it is necessary to calculate the fair value of the identifiable assets and liabilities of the acquired company (see Chapter 18). FRS7 provides definitions of the terms "fair value" and "identifiable assets and liabilities" and establishes a set of rules for the calculation of fair values in acquisition accounting.

Related party disclosures (FRS8)

FRS8 requires disclosure of all material transactions between the reporting company and a related party. Parties are related for this purpose if:

(a) one party has direct or indirect control over the other party, or

(b) the parties are subject to common control from the same source, or

(c) one party can influence the financial and operating policies of the other party, to the extent that the other party might be inhibited from pursuing its own separate interests, or

(d) the parties are subject to influence from the same source to such an extent that one of the parties has subordinated its own separate interests.

4. THE ASB STATEMENT OF PRINCIPLES

In November 1995, the ASB published an Exposure Draft of its Statement of Principles for Financial Reporting. This is not an accounting standard and will not become one. Rather, the Statement of Principles is intended to act as a framework within which standard-setters will do their work. The following quotation is taken from an ASB progress paper:

"*A statement of principles is designed to provide a coherent frame of reference, including a set of definitions, to be used by the Board ... during the course of the standard-setting process. Having an interrelated set of fundamental principles should ensure consistency in the Board's standards and minimise the need to reinvent fundamental concepts in the course of every project. Such a statement will also provide assistance to preparers, auditors and others in assessing alternatives when the law and accounting standards do not provide sufficient guidance*".

The Statement of Principles was briefly introduced in Chapter 2 of this book but is now considered in more detail. The Statement consists of the following seven chapters:

Chapter 1 The objective of financial statements.
Chapter 2 The qualitative characteristics of financial information.
Chapter 3 The elements of financial statements.
Chapter 4 Recognition in financial statements.
Chapter 5 Measurement in financial statements.
Chapter 6 Presentation of financial information.
Chapter 7 The reporting entity.

The content of each chapter is summarised below.

The objective of financial statements

According to Chapter 1 of the Statement, the objective of financial statements is "*to provide information about the financial position, performance and financial adaptability of an enterprise that is useful to a wide range of users for assessing the stewardship of management and for making economic decisions*".

The suggestion that financial statements should provide information about financial position and performance comes as no surprise. However, the reference to financial adaptability is less expected. Financial adaptability is defined as "*the ability of an enterprise to take effective action to alter the amount and timing of its cash flows so that it can respond to unexpected events and opportunities*".

The Statement recognises that financial statements are subject to certain limitations and therefore cannot provide all of the information which users may need. The main limitations of financial statements are seen as their historic nature, the lack of non-financial information and the need to incorporate estimates. However, it is stressed that financial statements do provide a great deal of useful information, despite these limitations.

The main users of financial statements are listed as owners/investors, employees, lenders, suppliers and other creditors, customers, governments and their agencies and the public. The information needs of each user group are also identified (see Chapter 1 of this book).

The qualitative characteristics of financial information

Chapter 2 of the Statement explains that qualitative characteristics are those characteristics which make financial information useful. The main characteristics relating to the *content* of financial information are identified as materiality, relevance and reliability.

(a) **Materiality**. Materiality is described as a "threshold quality". Information is regarded as material if it could influence the decisions taken by users on the basis of the financial statements.

(b) **Relevance**. Information cannot be useful unless it is relevant to user needs.

- Relevant information may have either predictive value (by helping users to predict future events) or confirmatory value (by helping users to assess the accuracy of past predictions).
- It is important that financial statements should report those attributes of a financial item which are most relevant to user needs. For instance, three attributes associated with any asset are its historic cost, its replacement cost and its net realisable value. The preparer of financial statements must choose which of these attributes to report and this choice should be made on the basis of relevance.

(c) **Reliability**. To be useful, information must also be reliable. Reliable information is free from any material error or bias.

- Reliable information faithfully represents the effects of transactions and other events. This implies that the substance of transactions must be reflected in financial statements rather than the legal form.

- Reliable information possesses the characteristic of neutrality. Financial statements cannot be neutral if they contain information which has been selected or presented in such a way that users are steered towards predetermined decisions.
- Prudence is essential when preparing financial statements but this does not mean that financial statements should be prepared on a pessimistic basis. Information which is over-pessimistic can be just as unreliable as information which is over-optimistic.
- Reliable information will be complete information (subject to materiality and cost constraints).

The main characteristics relating to the *presentation* of financial information are identified as comparability and understandability.

(d) **Comparability**. Comparability means that users are able to make meaningful comparisons between financial statements drawn up by different entities and between financial statements drawn up by the same entity in different accounting periods.

- Comparability cannot be achieved unless similar transactions are treated in a consistent way from one entity to another and from one period to another.
- Comparability also requires disclosure of the accounting policies adopted in the preparation of financial statements.

(e) **Understandability**. It is obviously essential that users should understand the information presented to them in financial statements.

- The way in which items are aggregated and classified in the financial statements has an effect on understandability.
- Understandability is dependent upon users' abilities.

Finally, the main *constraints* which may limit the application of the qualitative characteristics are identified as the balance between the characteristics, timeliness and cost/benefit.

(f) **Balance between the characteristics**. It may not be possible to achieve all of the qualitative characteristics simultaneously because of conflict between them. For instance, information which is more relevant may be less reliable (and vice-versa). Therefore it is necessary to achieve an appropriate balance between the characteristics, bearing in mind the objectives of the financial statements.

(g) **Timeliness**. The need to produce timely financial statements may make it difficult to achieve some of the characteristics (e.g. completeness, reliability).

(h) **Cost/benefit**. The cost of producing financial statements which possess all of the desired characteristics may exceed the benefits of doing so.

The elements of financial statements

Chapter 3 of the Statement lists the elements of financial statements as assets, liabilities, ownership interest, gains, losses, contributions from owners and distributions to owners. Any item which does not fall within one of these categories should not be included in financial statements. The Statement also provides a definition of each of the seven elements:

(a) The definitions of assets, liabilities and ownership interest are given in Chapter 3 of this book.

(b) Gains and losses are defined as "*increases and decreases in the ownership interest, other than those relating to contributions from owners or distributions to owners*".

(c) Contributions from owners are defined as "*increases in the ownership interest resulting from investments made by owners in their capacity as owners*".

(d) Distributions to owners are defined as "*decreases in the ownership interest resulting from transfers made to owners in their capacity as owners*".

Recognition in financial statements

Chapter 4 of the Statement sets out the criteria for recognising an element in the financial statements. Recognition "*involves depiction of the element both in words and by a monetary amount and the inclusion of that amount in the statement totals*". There are three stages in the recognition of an asset or liability:

(a) **Initial recognition**. An asset or liability should be recognised if there is sufficient evidence that the asset or liability exists and if it can be measured at a monetary amount with sufficient reliability.

(b) **Subsequent remeasurement**. A change in the amount of an asset or liability should be recognised if there is sufficient evidence that the amount of the asset or liability has changed and if the new amount can be measured with sufficient reliability.

(c) **Derecognition**. An asset or liability should cease to be recognised if there is no longer sufficient evidence of its existence.

If, at any of these three stages, a change in total assets is not matched by a change in total liabilities, then a gain or loss has occurred and this should be recognised in the financial statements.

Measurement in financial statements

Chapter 5 of the Statement is concerned with the values at which assets and liabilities should be shown in financial statements. The question is whether an asset (or liability) should continue to be recognised at its initial value or whether it should be remeasured at its current value. Essentially, this is a choice between conventional historic cost accounting and non-conventional current cost accounting.

The subsequent remeasurement stage of the recognition process (see above) seems to imply that current values should be recognised so long as they can be reliably measured. Indeed, the ASB has stated its belief that current values should be used in situations where historic costs are clearly ineffective. This is not as controversial a view as it may seem, since many companies are already in the habit of showing certain assets (particularly land and buildings) in their balance sheets at current value.

However, the ASB has been at pains to point out that it has no intention of imposing a system of current cost accounting. It is accepted that many businesses will continue to use a mix of historic and current measures for the forseeable future and Chapter 5 of the Statement of Principles tries only to suggest what that mix should be.

The relative merits of historic cost accounting and current cost accounting are discussed in Chapter 20 of this book.

Presentation of financial information

Chapter 6 of the Statement deals with the way in which information should be presented in financial reports. The chapter states that the information should be structured into a set of interlocking financial statements and identifies the main financial statements as:

(a) the profit and loss account

(b) the statement of total recognised gains and losses (see Chapter 17 of this book)

(c) the balance sheet

(d) the cash flow statement (see Chapter 16 of this book).

These four primary statements may be accompanied by a set of notes which amplify or explain items in the statements and provide any necessary additional information.

The need to aggregate information so as to make the financial statements more manageable is accepted, but the Statement takes the view that a given item should be reported separately if its disclosure is likely to be significant.

The reporting entity

The final chapter of the Statement is concerned with the accounting treatment of investments made by one business entity in another business entity. The appropriate accounting treatment depends upon the degree of influence which the investing entity has over the other entity. Four degrees of influence are identified:

(a) **No significant influence**. The investment should simply be shown in the investing entity's balance sheet at cost or at a valuation. Any income received in relation to the investment should be shown in the profit and loss account.

(b) **Significant influence but not control.** The investment should be dealt with in a similar way as that required by SSAP1 for investments in associated companies (see Chapter 18 of this book).

(c) **Shared control with other entities.** In most cases, the investment should be dealt with in the same way as an investment which gives significant influence (see above).

(d) **Control.** If the investing entity has complete control over the other entity, then full consolidated accounts should be prepared (see Chapter 18 of this book).

5. STOCK EXCHANGE REQUIREMENTS

Companies which are listed on the Stock Exchange must comply with certain Stock Exchange rules relating to their accounts (as well as complying with Companies Acts requirements and accounting standards). The main Stock Exchange rules are as follows:

(a) Listed companies must prepare a half-yearly report and either send this report to the shareholders and debenture-holders or publish the report in at least two of the leading daily newspapers.

(b) Listed companies must issue their annual accounts within six months of the end of the accounting period to which they relate.

(c) The annual accounts of listed companies must provide several items of additional information. The required information includes:

- the names of the principal countries in which the company operates
- an explanation of the reasons for any significant departure from accounting standards
- an explanation of any significant discrepancies between the company's trading results and any published forecasts of those results.

A full list of all the required information is beyond the scope of this book.

6. SUMMARY

► The published accounts of limited companies must comply with all relevant accounting standards issued by the Accounting Standards Board (ASB) or by its predecessor, the Accounting Standards Committee (ASC).

► The accounting standards do not form part of the Companies Acts but have quasi-legal status, since company accounts cannot show a true and fair view unless accounting standards have been complied with.

- Accounting standards are issued by the Accounting Standards Board, which reports to the Financial Reporting Council. Urgent matters are dealt with by the Urgent Issues Task Force.
- The Financial Reporting Review Panel monitors the published accounts of limited companies and looks into cases in which accounting standards have been contravened.
- At the time of writing, there are 18 extant Statements of Standard Accounting Practice (SSAP's) and 8 extant Financial Reporting Standards (FRS's).
- The ASB Statement of Principles is an attempt to provide a coherent frame of reference for use by the Board when devising accounting standards.
- Listed companies must comply with Stock Exchange accounting regulations as well as complying with the Companies Acts and with accounting standards.

EXERCISES 15

15.1 A company's issued share capital consists of 15,000 ordinary shares of 50p each and 20,000 7% preference shares of £1 each. The company's pre-tax profit on ordinary activities for the year to 31 July 19X8 is £8,900 and the corporation tax liability for the year is £2,200. The company paid an extraordinary charge during the year of £800 (after deducting tax relief).

Required:

Calculate the company's earnings per share for the year to 31 July 19X8 in accordance with SSAP3 (as amended by FRS3).

15.2 On 1 June 19X4, a company buys an item of plant costing £12,000 and receives a government grant of £3,000 towards this cost. The plant is to be written off on the straight-line basis over five years, with an estimated residual value of £nil. The company's annual accounting date is 31 May.

Required:

Prepare ledger accounts showing how the plant and the government grant will be accounted for (in accordance with SSAP4) during the two years to 31 May 19X6. How will the government grant be reflected in the company's balance sheet?

15.3 On 1 January 19X0, a company which prepares annual accounts to 31 December paid £10,000 to acquire a fixed asset with an expected useful life of 4 years and no residual value. The asset was to be depreciated by the straight-line method. On 1 January 19X2 the remaining useful life of the asset was revised to 8 years and the residual value was revised to £2,000.

Required:

Calculate the amount of depreciation which should be charged in each of the ten years to 31 December 19X9 (in accordance with SSAP12).

15.4 Distinguish between pure research, applied research and development expenditure as defined in SSAP13. Explain how these three types of expenditure may be treated in the accounts of a limited company.

15.5 Explain how the following post balance sheet events should be dealt with in the accounts of a limited company (in accordance with SSAP17):

(a) the takeover of another company

(b) the sale of stock for £21,400 (the stock had cost £20,000 and was shown in the draft balance sheet at its estimated net realisable value of £18,000)

(c) a valuation of one of the company's properties, indicating that the true value of the property on the balance sheet date was less than the figure shown in the draft balance sheet

(d) the destruction of one of the company's factory buildings by fire.

***15.6** (a) Explain the purpose of accounting standards and describe the relationship between accounting standards and the Companies Acts.

(b) Outline the role of each of the main bodies involved in the standard-setting process.

***15.7** Harrington plc (a food manufacturer) is finalising its accounts for the year to 31 August 19X8. The accounts are due to be approved by the directors of the company on 20 November 19X8. Explain how (and whether) each of the following items should be dealt with in these accounts:

(a) A customer became ill after eating one of the company's products in June 19X8 and is suing the company for damages of £20,000. The case will not be heard until mid-19X9. Harrington's lawyers think that there is a 30% chance that the company will lose the case.

(b) On 1 September 19X2, the company acquired land and buildings at a cost of £180,000 (including £40,000 for the land). The buildings were thought to have a useful life of 50 years with no residual value and were depreciated accordingly on the straight-line basis. On 1 September 19X7, the land was valued at £65,000 and the buildings at £135,000 and it has been decided that these valuations should be incorporated into the company's accounts. The original estimates of the useful life and residual value of the buildings remain unchanged.

(c) On 31 August 19X8, the value of the goodwill of Harrington plc is estimated by its directors to be approximately £5 million. This goodwill has arisen gradually over the years as a consequence of the growing reputation of the company's products.

(d) On 31 August 19X8, the company was owed 7 million Italian lire by an overseas customer and owned property abroad which it had bought on 11 December 19X7 for 300,000 US dollars.

(e) Harrington plc is suing another company for breach of contract and is claiming damages of £50,000. Legal opinion is that the court will definitely find in favour of Harrington plc and that the full damages will be awarded.

(f) The company's research and development expenditure during the year amounted to £730,000. Of this sum, £290,000 was spent on an attempt (unsuccessful so far) to synthesise an ingredient which it is becoming difficult to obtain from natural sources. The remaining £440,000 was spent on the development of a new product which is to be launched in early 19X9.

(g) A customer who owed the company £25,000 on 31 August 19X8 became bankrupt in early October 19X8. Indications are that the customer's debts will be settled at the rate of only 20p in the £.

(h) On 1 October 19X8, Harrington plc acquired a 55% shareholding in R Knight & Co Ltd.

(i) Harrington plc has guaranteed a bank loan of £100,000 granted to Macintyre plc. This company is currently in financial trouble and it seems quite likely that Harrington plc will be obliged to meet its guarantee.

(j) After making all necessary adjustments in relation to the matters listed above, the company's pre-tax profit shown in the accounts exceeds the taxable profit by £80,000. This difference is caused by two factors. Firstly, the company's accounts show expenses of £45,000 which are not deductible for tax purposes. Secondly, the available capital allowances are £125,000 more than the depreciation shown in the accounts. The company's corporation tax rate is 33%.

16

CASH FLOW STATEMENTS

Chapter objectives

When you have finished this chapter, you should be able to:

- **Explain the purpose of a cash flow statement.**
- **Define the terms "cash" and "liquid resources".**
- **List the main categories of cash inflow and cash outflow.**
- **Summarise the requirements of FRS1.**
- **Prepare a cash flow statement and relevant notes in accordance with the requirements of FRS1.**

1. INTRODUCTION

Until the mid-1970's, the profit and loss account and the balance sheet were the only financial statements which companies were required to publish. This situation changed in 1975 with the introduction of accounting standard SSAP10, which obliged most companies to publish a statement of sources and applications of funds (commonly known as a "funds flow statement") in addition to the traditional financial statements.

The purpose of a funds flow statement was to show the sources from which a company had obtained funds during an accounting period and the uses to which those funds had been put. This information was intended to be helpful when assessing the company's ability to generate sufficient funds to finance its operations in the future. But SSAP10 attracted a number of criticisms:

(a) The term "funds" (which was usually taken to mean a company's net current assets or working capital) was not well defined and was open to a variety of interpretations.

(b) The accounting standard did not prescribe a fixed format for the funds flow statement and therefore companies laid out the statement in different ways. This lack of uniformity made it very difficult to compare funds flow statements produced by different companies.

(c) Many users of financial accounts did not understand funds flow statements and so simply ignored them.

As a result of these criticisms, SSAP10 was replaced in 1991 by FRS1, which shifted the emphasis from flows of funds to flows of cash (a more widely understood concept). The fact that the then newly-formed Accounting

Standards Board selected cash flows as the subject of its very first standard is an indication of the importance attached to this topic.

A revised version of FRS1 was issued in 1996 and took effect for accounting periods ending on or after 23 March 1997. This chapter explains the requirements of the revised standard.

Introduction to FRS1

FRS1 aims to ensure that companies "*provide information that assists in the assessment of their liquidity, solvency and financial adaptability*". The main requirements of FRS1 are as follows:

(a) Companies must publish a *cash flow statement* for each accounting period, showing the sources from which cash has been received and the ways in which cash has been used.

(b) The statement must be accompanied by a number of reconciliations and explanatory notes.

(c) The statement must be published in a prescribed format.

For this purpose, cash is defined as "*cash in hand and deposits repayable on demand with any qualifying financial institution, less overdrafts from any qualifying financial institution repayable on demand*". In straightforward cases this boils down to cash in hand, plus cash at bank, less bank overdrafts.

Compliance with the standard is mandatory for most companies, the main exception being those companies regarded as small for financial reporting purposes (see Chapter 14). Even small companies are recommended to prepare cash flow statements and such statements could be prepared for any form of business entity.

2. PURPOSE OF A CASH FLOW STATEMENT

When a company publishes its financial statements, the figure which attracts most attention is undoubtedly the profit for the accounting period. In fact, the keen interest with which a company's profit figure is greeted can give the impression that profit is the only important measure of a company's success. But the attention paid to profit should not distract users from the fact that even the most profitable of companies can fail simply for lack of cash.

Cash is the "lifeblood" of a company. A company which is starved of cash will be unable to meet its financial obligations as they fall due and will eventually be forced to cease trading, no matter how profitable it might be.

Cash and the profit and loss account

It may seem odd that a profitable company could run out of cash, but the reasons for this apparent paradox lie mainly in the accounting conventions on which the profit calculation is based. Two conventions are especially relevant:

(a) The *realisation convention* allows revenue to be shown in the profit and loss account before that revenue is actually received. For example, if an increase in turnover is achieved by offering customers extended credit terms, the amount of cash collected from customers during an accounting period may fall well short of the turnover shown in the profit and loss account for that period.

(b) The *matching convention* states that expenses should be matched against the revenues to which they relate, regardless of the dates on which the expenses are actually paid. Consequently, an expense may be paid in one accounting period but not appear in the profit and loss account until a future accounting period. Such timing differences are particularly significant in the case of capital expenditure, which is usually transferred to the profit and loss account by instalments (in the form of depreciation charges) over several years.

It should also be noted that the calculation of a company's profit does not take into account any appropriations of that profit. Substantial payments of taxation and/or dividends will therefore drain the cash resources of the company without affecting its reported profit in any way.

Cash and the balance sheet

Although a company's profit figure can be an unreliable indicator of its cash situation, more dependable information on the matter can be gleaned from the balance sheet. The cash available at the balance sheet date can be compared with the company's financial commitments on that date and the results of the comparison can be used to assess the company's solvency. But a balance sheet suffers from a number of shortcomings which prevent it from providing a comprehensive analysis of the company's cash position. These are:

(a) A balance sheet shows only a snapshot of the financial position at the end of an accounting period. The cash resources existing on the balance sheet date may not be typical of the accounting period as a whole and may provide a misleading indication of the likely extent of those resources in the future.

(b) A balance sheet does not give information on the sources of cash or the uses of cash during the accounting period. This is the information which is provided by a cash flow statement.

The cash flow statement

In simple terms, a cash flow statement is nothing more than a summary of a company's cash book for the accounting period under review. The statement reconciles the opening cash balance with the closing cash balance, showing the sources and uses of cash during the period. Although a cash flow statement shows only historic data, it should help users to assess a company's ability to:

(a) generate sufficient cash to fund its day-to-day operations

(b) repay loans as they fall due and make payments of loan interest
(c) replace and improve fixed assets as necessary.
(d) make the required payments of corporation tax and maintain an acceptable level of dividend

A cash flow statement provides information which is both *reliable* (since preparation of the statement involves little, if any, subjectivity) and also *relevant* to the needs of many users. The information provided is fairly easy to understand and it is generally agreed that the cash flow statement is a worthy and useful addition to a company's published accounts.

3. FORMAT OF A CASH FLOW STATEMENT

FRS1 requires companies to analyse cash inflows and cash outflows for each accounting period under the following eight headings:

(a) **Operating activities**. The amount shown under this heading is the net cash inflow or outflow which has been generated by the company's "operations" or trading activities. This figure must be reconciled with the operating profit in the profit and loss account (see later in this chapter).

(b) **Returns on investments and servicing of finance**. This heading covers interest received, dividends received, interest paid and dividends paid to non-equity shareholders (e.g. preference dividends).

(c) **Taxation**. This heading shows the amount of corporation tax and other taxes paid during the accounting period.

(d) **Capital expenditure and financial investment**. The cash flows to be shown under this heading relate to:

- the purchase and sale of tangible fixed assets, intangible fixed assets and fixed asset investments, other than those which are required to be included in "acquisitions and disposals" (see below)
- the purchase and sale of any current asset investments not classed as "liquid resources" (see below).

The words "and financial investment" can be omitted from the heading if there are no cash flows relating to financial investment.

(e) **Acquisitions and disposals**. The cash flows to be shown under this heading relate to the acquisition or disposal of a trade or business, or of an investment in an associated undertaking or subsidiary undertaking (see Chapter 18).

(f) **Equity dividends paid**. In most cases, these consist of dividends paid to the company's ordinary shareholders.

(g) **Management of liquid resources**. This heading covers cash flows in respect of "liquid resources". Liquid resources are "*current asset investments held as readily disposable stores of value*". A readily disposable investment is one which is disposable without curtailing or disrupting the company's business and which is either readily convertible into known amounts of cash or traded in an active market. Examples of liquid resources are treasury bills and money held on short-term deposit.

(h) **Financing**. The main items appearing under this heading are cash received on an issue of shares or debentures, cash paid on the redemption of debentures and any expenses incurred in connection with these items.

The first six headings must be shown in the order given above. The cash flows relating to management of liquid resources and financing can be combined into a single heading so long as the cash flows for each are shown separately and separate subtotals are provided.

It is permissible to show only the total for each heading in the cash flow statement itself and then to provide details of the cash inflows and outflows arising under each heading in a set of notes. Alternatively, the details may be given on the face of the cash flow statement.

EXAMPLE

An example of a cash flow statement prepared in accordance with the requirements of FRS1 is given below. It is conventional to show cash outflows in parentheses and this convention has been followed in the example.

Alpha plc
Cash flow statement for the year to 31 March 19X7

	£'000	£'000
Net cash inflow from operating activities		987
Returns on investments and servicing of finance		
Interest received	3	
Dividends received	17	
Interest paid	(129)	
Preference dividend paid	(100)	(209)
Taxation		(220)
Capital expenditure and financial investment		
Purchase of tangible fixed assets	(586)	
Sales of tangible fixed assets	43	
Purchase of investment securities	(150)	(693)
Acquisitions and disposals		
Sale of investment in subsidiary undertaking		150
Equity dividends paid		(212)
Management of liquid resources		
Cash placed on 7 day deposit		(120)
Financing		
Issue of ordinary share capital	500	
Repayment of debenture loans	(100)	400
Increase in cash during the period		83

4. PREPARATION OF A CASH FLOW STATEMENT

As explained earlier in this chapter, a cash flow statement begins by stating the net cash flow generated by the company's operating activities. FRS1 allows this figure to be calculated by either the direct method or the indirect method:

(a) The *direct* method involves analysing the company's underlying accounting records for the period in question and ascertaining the amounts of cash received from customers, paid to suppliers, paid to employees and paid for other expenses. These figures are listed at the start of the cash flow statement and are then aggregated to give the net cash flow from operating activities.

(b) The *indirect* method takes as its starting point the company's operating profit for the accounting period and then makes a number of adjustments to this profit so as to calculate the net cash flow from operating activities (see below). If a profit and loss account is prepared using Format 1, operating profit is the figure shown as a subtotal after other operating income.

Although the direct method is undoubtedly the more obvious approach it has not proved popular in practice. This is probably because, whichever method is used, FRS1 also requires companies to provide a reconciliation between operating profit and net cash flow from operating activities. It therefore makes sense to adopt the indirect method and so satisfy two requirements simultaneously. For this reason, the indirect method will be used for the remainder of this chapter.

Calculation of the net cash flow from operating activities using the indirect method

The adjustments which must be made to operating profit so as to derive a company's net cash flow from operating activities may be summarised as follows:

(a) *Add back* any non-cash items which have been debited to the profit and loss account but which have not resulted in a cash outflow e.g. depreciation, losses on the disposal of fixed assets and increases in the provision for doubtful debts.

(b) *Subtract* any non-cash items which have been credited to the profit and loss account but which have not resulted in a cash inflow e.g. profits on the disposal of fixed assets and decreases in the provision for doubtful debts.

(c) *Adjust* for increases or decreases in any of the following items between the start and end of the accounting period:

	Add	*Subtract*
Debtors and prepayments	Decreases	Increases
Stocks	Decreases	Increases
Creditors and accruals	Increases	Decreases

The effect of the adjustments relating to debtors, prepayments, stocks, creditors and accruals is to convert the revenue and expenses shown in the profit and loss account onto a cash basis. For instance, the cash received from customers during an accounting period and the turnover for that period are related in the following way:

Cash received = Opening debtors + Turnover – Closing debtors

Depending upon whether debtors have increased or decreased during the period, this can be rewritten in one of two ways:

either Cash received = Turnover – Increase in debtors
or Cash received = Turnover + Decrease in debtors

Therefore, an increase in debtors must be *subtracted* from operating profit and a decrease in debtors must be *added* to operating profit when calculating the net cash flow from operating activities. A similar argument applies to increases and decreases in prepayments, stocks, creditors and accruals.

A simple way of remembering the correct adjustment for each of the increases and decreases listed above is to ask what effect the increase or decrease would have on the company's cash position, if everything else on the balance sheet (apart from cash) remained unchanged. For example, a decrease in debtors would generate extra cash (as customers paid their debts) and therefore this decrease should be *added* to operating profit when calculating the net cash flow from operating activities.

Note that adjustments should be made only for those increases and decreases which have had an impact on operating profit. Increases and decreases which have not affected operating profit (e.g. changes in the creditors for taxation and dividends) do *not* require an adjustment.

EXAMPLE

The summarised profit and loss account of Beta plc for the year to 31 March 19X8 is given below, together with the company's balance sheets as at 31 March 19X7 and 31 March 19X8.

Beta plc
Profit and loss account for the year to 31 March 19X8

	£'000
Operating profit	323
Interest paid	12
Profit on ordinary activities before taxation	311
Tax on profit on ordinary activities	90
Profit on ordinary activities after taxation	221
Retained profits brought forward	406
	627
Dividends paid and proposed	200
Retained profits carried forward	427

Beta plc
Balance sheets as at 31 March

		19X7		*19X8*
	£'000	£'000	£'000	£'000
Fixed assets				
Tangible fixed assets at cost		605		808
Less: Accumulated depreciation		265		328
		340		480
Current assets				
Stocks	205		345	
Trade debtors and prepayments	403		509	
Cash at bank and in hand	8		-	
	616		854	
Current liabilities				
Trade creditors and accruals	60		84	
Bank overdraft	-		183	
Taxation	70		90	
Dividends	120		150	
	250		507	
Net current assets		366		347
		706		827
Debenture loans		100		80
		606		747
Financed by				
Ordinary share capital		200		320
Profit and loss account		406		427
		606		747

Required:

Prepare a cash flow statement for the year to 31 March 19X8. (No fixed assets were disposed of during the year).

SOLUTION

The first task is to calculate the company's net cash flow from operating activities, beginning with the operating profit for the year and then making the necessary adjustments. This calculation is known as the "reconciliation of operating profit to net cash flow from operating activities". The cash flow statement itself can then be prepared. (Note that the workings shown alongside certain items in this solution are shown for tutorial purposes only and would not appear in the published cash flow statement).

BETA PLC
CASH FLOW STATEMENT FOR THE YEAR TO 31 MARCH 19X8

Reconciliation of operating profit to net cash inflow from operating activities

	£'000	£'000
Operating profit		323
Depreciation charges (328 – 265)		63
Increase in stocks (345 – 205)		(140)
Increase in trade debtors and prepayments (509 – 403)		(106)
Increase in trade creditors and accruals (84 – 60)		24
Net cash inflow from operating activities		164

Cash flow statement

Net cash inflow from operating activities		164
Returns on investments and servicing of finance		
Interest paid		(12)
Taxation		(70)
Capital expenditure		
Purchase of tangible fixed assets (808 – 605)		(203)
Equity dividends paid		(170)
Financing		
Issue of ordinary share capital (320 – 200)	120	
Repayment of debenture loans (80 – 100)	(20)	100
Decrease in cash during the period		(191)

Tutorial notes:

1. The depreciation charge was calculated by comparing the accumulated depreciation charge at 31 March 19X7 with the corresponding figure at 31 March 19X8. This task was made easier by the fact that there had been no fixed asset disposals during the year. In practice, the depreciation charge would be ascertained by examining the detailed profit and loss account.
2. The figures for dividends paid and tax paid are derived as follows:

	Dividends	*Tax*
	£'000	£'000
Opening creditor	120	70
Charged to P & L account for the year	200	90
	320	160
Less: Closing creditor	150	90
Paid during the year	170	70

3. The cash flow statement shows that, despite a profitable year, the cash resources of Beta plc have fallen by £191,000 (from a favourable bank balance of £8,000 to a bank overdraft of £183,000). An initial analysis of the information provided by the

cash flow statement suggests that this fall is the consequence of substantial increases in stocks and debtors, coupled with a sizeable investment in the acquisition of tangible fixed assets. The fall would have been worse if it had not been for the share issue made during the year.

5. RECONCILIATIONS REQUIRED BY FRS1

FRS1 requires two reconciliations to be given, either adjoining the cash flow statement or in the form of notes accompanying the statement. If the reconciliations are shown adjoining the cash flow statement they must be clearly labelled and kept separate from the statement itself. The reconciliations are as follows:

(a) **Reconciliation of operating profit to net cash flow from operating activities**. This reconciliation (see above) is required by FRS1 in all cases, even if the direct method is used.

(b) **Reconciliation of net cash flow to movement in net debt**. The term "net debt" means the company's total borrowings less cash and liquid resources. If the total of cash and liquid resources exceeds total borrowings, the term "net funds" is used rather than "net debt". If several balance sheet headings have to be combined to arrive at a figure for net debt, sufficient detail should be given to enable the components of the figure to be traced back to the company's balance sheets. Changes in net debt resulting from the following causes should be shown separately:

- cash flows
- changes in market values
- other non-cash changes (e.g. a movement between debt due after more than one year and debt due within one year, caused simply by the passage of time).

EXAMPLE

Show how the cash flow statement of Beta plc for the year to 31 March 19X8 would appear in the company's published accounts, complete with all required reconciliations and notes.

SOLUTION

The full cash flow statement consists of the reconciliation of operating profit to net cash flow from operating activities, followed by the cash flow statement itself, followed by the reconciliation of net cash flow to movement in net debt. Since net debt is composed of several balance sheet items, it is also necessary to attach a note to the cash flow statement, showing the composition of the opening and closing net debt figures.

BETA PLC
CASH FLOW STATEMENT FOR THE YEAR TO 31 MARCH 19X8

Reconciliation of operating profit to net cash inflow from operating activities

	£'000	£'000
Operating profit		323
Depreciation charges		63
Increase in stocks		(140)
Increase in trade debtors and prepayments		(106)
Increase in trade creditors and accruals		24
Net cash inflow from operating activities		164

Cash flow statement

Net cash inflow from operating activities		164
Returns on investments and servicing of finance		
Interest paid		(12)
Taxation		(70)
Capital expenditure		
Purchase of tangible fixed assets		(203)
Equity dividends paid		(170)
Financing		
Issue of ordinary share capital	120	
Repayment of debenture loans	(20)	100
Decrease in cash during the period		(191)

Reconciliation of net cash flow to movement in net debt (note 1)

Decrease in cash during the period	(191)	
Cash used to redeem debentures	20	
Change in net debt		(171)
Net debt at 1 April 19X7		(92)
Net debt at 31 March 19X8		(263)

Note 1 - Analysis of changes in net debt

	At 1 April 19X7	*Cash flows*	*At 31 March 19X8*
	£'000	£'000	£'000
Cash at bank	8	(8)	-
Overdrafts	-	(183)	(183)
Decrease in cash		(191)	
Debenture loans	(100)	20	(80)
Total	(92)	(171)	(263)

6. SUMMARY

- Most companies are required by FRS1 to publish a cash flow statement for each accounting period. The statement must be accompanied by a number of reconciliations and explanatory notes and must appear in a prescribed format.
- A cash flow statement shows the sources from which cash has been obtained and the ways in which cash has been used during the accounting period under review.
- The main purpose of a cash flow statement is to help users to assess a company's ability to meet its financial obligations as they fall due.
- FRS1 requires companies to analyse cash flows over eight headings. These are operating activities, returns on investments and servicing of finance, taxation, capital expenditure and financial investment, acquisitions and disposals, equity dividends paid, management of liquid resources and financing.
- For FRS1 purposes, the term "cash" usually includes cash in hand, bank balances and bank overdrafts.
- A cash flow statement may be prepared by either the direct method or the indirect method. The indirect method appears to be more popular in practice.
- The reconciliations which must accompany a cash flow statement are a reconciliation of operating profit to net cash flow from operating activities and a reconciliation of net cash flow to movement in net debt.

EXERCISES 16

16.1 Classify each of the following as either a cash inflow, a cash outflow or neither.

(a) sale of a fixed asset for more than book value
(b) sale of a fixed asset for less than book value
(c) repayment of a debenture loan
(d) increasing the provision for doubtful debts
(e) making a bonus issue of shares.

16.2 Explain the effect (if any) which each of the following transactions will have on a company's operating profit and on its cash flows.

(a) purchase of a fixed asset and depreciating that asset over its useful life
(b) paying a supplier's invoice
(c) accounting for accrued rent at the end of an accounting period
(d) investing spare cash in a bank deposit account (repayable on demand).

16.3 (a) Identify the eight main headings under which a company's cash flows must be analysed when preparing an FRS1 cash flow statement.

(b) Define the term "liquid resources".

(c) Identify the two reconciliations which must accompany a cash flow statement drawn up in accordance with FRS1.

16.4 (a) Distinguish between the direct method and the indirect method of calculating a company's net cash flow from operating activities.

(b) If the indirect method is used, explain the adjustments required in relation to increases or decreases in a company's stocks.

16.5 The summarised profit and loss account of Gamma Ltd for the year to 30 June 19X7 is given below, together with the company's balance sheets as at 30 June 19X6 and 30 June 19X7.

Gamma Ltd
Profit and loss account for the year to 30 June 19X7

		£
Operating profit		170,200
Income from fixed asset investments		7,100
Interest paid		(6,120)
Profit on ordinary activities before taxation		171,180
Tax on profit on ordinary activities		37,870
Profit on ordinary activities after taxation		133,310
Retained profits brought forward		2,540
		135,850
Transfer to general reserve	30,000	
Dividends paid	20,000	
Dividends proposed	80,000	130,000
Retained profits carried forward		5,850

Gamma Ltd
Balance sheets as at 30 June

		19X6		*19X7*
	£	£	£	£
Fixed assets				
Tangible fixed assets at cost	210,000		369,300	
Less: Accumulated depr'n	107,340	102,660	151,650	217,650
Investments at cost		120,000		120,000
		222,660		337,650
Current assets				
Stocks	97,430		86,220	
Trade debtors	58,100		82,610	
Prepayments	7,000		7,200	
	162,530		176,030	
Current liabilities				
Trade creditors	44,310		40,920	
Accruals	8,250		9,130	
Taxation	32,300		37,870	
Proposed dividends	65,000		80,000	
Bank overdraft	2,790		34,910	
	152,650		202,830	
Net current assets/(liabilities)		9,880		(26,800)
		232,540		310,850
Debenture loans		50,000		75,000
		182,540		235,850
Financed by				
Ordinary share capital		100,000		120,000
General reserve		80,000		110,000
Profit and loss account		2,540		5,850
		182,540		235,850

There were no disposals of fixed assets during the year to 30 June 19X7.

Required:

(a) Prepare a cash flow statement for the year to 30 June 19X7 in accordance with the requirements of FRS1 (using the indirect method) together with the accompanying reconciliations and notes.

(b) Comment on the significance of the information provided by this cash flow statement.

***16.6** An extract from the profit and loss account of Delta Ltd for the year to 31 May 19X9 is given below, together with the company's balance sheets as at 31 May 19X8 and 31 May 19X9.

Delta Ltd
Profit and loss account (extract) for the year to 31 May 19X9

		£
Profit on ordinary activities before taxation		205,600
Tax on profit on ordinary activities		46,980
Profit on ordinary activities after taxation		158,620
Retained profits brought forward		19,990
		178,610
Transfer to general reserve	90,000	
Dividends:		
Paid - preference shares	5,000	
- ordinary shares	45,000	
Proposed ordinary dividend	10,000	150,000
Retained profits carried forward		28,610

Delta Ltd
Balance sheets as at 31 May

		19X8		*19X9*
	£	£	£	£
Fixed assets				
Plant and machinery at cost	183,000		285,000	
Less: Accumulated depr'n	95,160	87,840	151,650	133,350
Investments at cost		10,000		12,000
		97,840		145,350
Current assets				
Stocks	133,330		171,220	
Trade debtors and prepayments	86,500		121,630	
Cash at bank and in hand	-		710	
Treasury bills	-		5,000	
	219,830		298,560	
Current liabilities				
Trade creditors and accruals	61,530		89,370	
Taxation	42,660		45,930	
Proposed dividends	20,000		10,000	
Bank overdraft	23,490		-	
	147,680		145,300	
Net current assets		72,150		153,260
		169,990		298,610
11% Debenture stock		-		30,000
		169,990		268,610

	19X8	19X9
	£	£
Financed by		
Preference share capital	50,000	50,000
Ordinary share capital	100,000	100,000
General reserve	-	90,000
Profit and loss account	19,990	28,610
	169,990	268,610

Additional information:

1. The 11% debentures were issued on 1 December 19X8 and the first half-year's interest was paid on 31 May 19X9.
2. Bank overdraft interest paid during the year amounted to £1,320.
3. Dividends received for the year were £930.
4. No investments were sold during the year.
5. During the year, plant and machinery which had cost the company £22,000 was sold for £7,000. The accumulated depreciation on this plant and machinery was £16,230.
6. Proposed dividends at 31 May 19X8 and 31 May 19X9 consist entirely of ordinary dividends.
7. The Treasury bills rank as liquid resources for FRS1 purposes.

Required:

Prepare a cash flow statement for the year to 31 May 19X9 in accordance with the requirements of FRS1 (using the indirect method) together with the accompanying reconciliations and notes.

***16.7** The balance sheets of Epsilon plc as at 31 July 19X7 and 19X8 are shown below.

Epsilon plc
Balance sheets as at 31 July

			19X7			*19X8*
		£'000	£'000		£'000	£'000
Fixed assets						
Tangible fixed assets at cost		450			490	
Less: Accumulated depr'n		330	120		370	120
Investments at cost			44			19
			164			139
Current assets						
Stocks		176			289	
Trade debtors	106			231		
Less: Prov'n for bad debts	4	102		26	205	
Prepayments		12			13	
Cash on 7-day deposit		50			-	
Cash at bank and in hand		59			-	
		399			507	
Current liabilities						
14% Debenture stock		-			40	
Trade creditors		55			60	
Accruals		8			9	
Creditors re purchase of fixed assets		-			20	
Taxation		47			9	
Proposed dividends		80			50	
Bank overdraft		-			40	
		190			228	
Net current assets			209			279
			373			418
Long-term liabilities						
14% Debenture stock			40			-
12% Debenture stock			-			30
			333			388
Financed by						
10% Preference shares of £1			20			20
Ordinary shares of £1			180			230
Share premium account			-			30
General reserve			120			100
Profit and loss account			13			8
			333			388

Additional information:

1. Tangible fixed assets which had cost £30,000 during the year to 31 July 19X5 were sold in February 19X8 for £10,000. The company depreciates tangible fixed assets at 20% per annum on cost, with a full charge in the year of acquisition and none in the year of disposal. (Some of the tangible fixed assets were over 5 years old on 31 July 19X8).
2. Fixed asset investments which had cost £25,000 some years previously were sold during the year for £21,000.
3. Dividends received during the year amounted to £5,000. No interest was received during the year but interest payments (including debenture interest) totalled £8,000.
4. The 14% debentures were issued many years ago and are due to be redeemed on 1 January 19X9. A fresh issue of 12% debentures was made on 31 July 19X8.
5. An interim ordinary dividend of £20,000 was paid during the year.
6. The proposed dividends at 31 July 19X7 and 31 July 19X8 both include preference dividends of £2,000.
7. The taxation and proposed dividends shown as liabilities as at 31 July 19X7 were paid during the year to 31 July 19X8 at the amounts stated.
8. In January 19X8, the company issued 50,000 £1 shares at an issue price of £1.60 per share.

Required:

(a) Prepare a cash flow statement for the year to 31 July 19X8 in accordance with the requirements of FRS1 (using the indirect method) together with the accompanying reconciliations and notes.

(b) Comment on the significance of the information provided by this cash flow statement.

17

REPORTING FINANCIAL PERFORMANCE

Chapter objectives

When you have finished this chapter, you should be able to:

- **Prepare a profit and loss account in accordance with the requirements of FRS3.**
- **Deal correctly with exceptional items, extraordinary items and prior period adjustments.**
- **Prepare a statement of total recognised gains and losses.**
- **Prepare a reconciliation of movements in shareholders' funds.**
- **Explain the purpose of preparing a note of historical cost profits and losses.**

1. INTRODUCTION

The purpose of this chapter is to summarise the requirements of accounting standard FRS3 (Reporting Financial Performance). FRS3 was issued in 1992 in an attempt to improve the quality of the performance information provided to the users of financial statements. The main problems which FRS3 set out to resolve were as follows:

(a) **Performance comparisons**. Many companies (especially larger ones) derive their profits from a number of separate operations. From time to time, new operations may commence or existing operations may cease. In these circumstances, it is impossible to make valid performance comparisons between one year and another (or to forecast performance in future years) unless the profit and loss account analyses the company's results between new operations, continuing operations and discontinued operations. FRS3 requires such an analysis.

(b) **Unusual items**. Prior to the introduction of FRS3, the accounting treatment of unusual items in the profit and loss account was governed by SSAP6. The definition of extraordinary items given in SSAP6 was rather broad and this encouraged companies to move some of their expenses from the main part of the profit and loss account to the extraordinary section, thereby increasing the figure for profit on ordinary activities.

FRS3 (which superseded SSAP6) introduced much tighter rules relating to the treatment of unusual items in the profit and loss account.

(c) **Earnings per share**. The original definition of earnings per share was provided by SSAP3 and excluded extraordinary items from the calculation. This provided a further incentive for companies to relegate as many expenses as possible to the extraordinary section of the profit and loss account. As explained in Chapter 15, FRS3 amended the definition of earnings per share so that extraordinary items *are* now included in the calculation.

(d) **Unrealised gains and losses**. A company's profit and loss account shows *realised* profits and losses, but certain *unrealised* profits or losses may be reflected somewhere else in the accounts. For example, a surplus on the revaluation of a freehold property may be credited to a revaluation reserve. Before FRS3, there was no financial statement which brought together *all* of a company's profits and losses (whether realised or unrealised) and therefore it was difficult for users to obtain an overall picture of a company's performance. FRS3 rectified this omission by requiring companies to prepare a *statement of total recognised gains and losses* in addition to the conventional financial statements. In fact, FRS3 introduced three new financial statements into the published accounts of limited companies, as explained later in this chapter.

2. ANALYSIS OF PROFIT AND LOSS ACCOUNT ITEMS

FRS3 requires that a company's profit and loss account, down to the figure for operating profit, should be analysed between *continuing operations*, *acquisitions* (i.e. new operations) and *discontinued operations*. Note the following points:

(a) Turnover and operating profit must be analysed on the face of the profit and loss account. As explained in Chapter 16, operating profit is the figure shown as a subtotal after other operating income in a Format 1 profit and loss account.

(b) Cost of sales, distribution costs, administrative expenses and other operating income may be analysed either on the face of the profit and loss account or in a note to the accounts.

(c) FRS3 permits companies (if they so wish) to combine distribution costs, administrative expenses and other operating income into a single line in the profit and loss account, known as *net operating expenses*. If this is done, the analysis of net operating expenses between distribution costs, administrative expenses and other operating income must be shown in a note to the accounts.

EXAMPLE

The following is an extract from the profit and loss account of P Fanshawe Ltd for the year to 31 October 19X8:

P Fanshawe Ltd
Profit and loss account for the year to 31 October 19X8

	£'000	£'000
Turnover		673
Cost of sales		189
Gross profit		484
Distribution costs	96	
Administrative expenses	211	307
		177
Other operating income		10
Operating profit		187

On 1 December 19X7, the company acquired a business operation which contributed £129,000 of the year's turnover. The costs of this operation in the year were cost of sales £37,000, distribution costs £12,000 and administrative expenses £49,000.

On 31 March 19X8, the company disposed of one of its business operations. This operation generated turnover of £77,000 in the year to 31 October 19X8. Related costs for the year were cost of sales £41,000, distribution costs £13,000 and administrative expenses £28,000.

Other operating income relates entirely to the company's continuing operations.

Required:

Insofar as the information given permits, prepare a profit and loss account for the year to 31 October 19X8, in accordance with the minimum disclosure requirements of FRS3.

Also prepare a note to the accounts providing the further analysis required by FRS3.

SOLUTION

P Fanshawe Ltd
Profit and loss account for the year to 31 October 19X8

	£'000	£'000
Turnover:		
Continuing operations	467	
Acquisitions	129	
	596	
Discontinued operations	77	673
Cost of sales		(189)
Gross profit		484
Net operating expenses		(297)
Operating profit		
Continuing operations	161	
Acquisitions	31	
	192	
Discontinued operations	(5)	187

P Fanshawe Ltd
Notes to the accounts (extract) for the year to 31 October 19X8

	Continuing operations	*Acquisitions*	*Discontinued operations*	*Total*
	£'000	£'000	£'000	£'000
Cost of sales	111	37	41	189
Net operating expenses:				
Distribution costs	71	12	13	96
Administrative expenses	134	49	28	211
Other operating income	(10)	-	-	(10)
	195	61	41	297

3. EXCEPTIONAL ITEMS AND EXTRAORDINARY ITEMS

FRS3 distinguishes between two categories of unusual item which might need to be shown in a profit and loss account. These are:

(a) **Exceptional items.** Exceptional items are material items which are derived from the company's ordinary activities but which are so large that they must be disclosed separately if the accounts are to give a true and fair view. A typical example of an exceptional item is a very large bad debt. In general, FRS3 requires that exceptional items should be included under the appropriate heading in the profit and loss account but should then be disclosed in the notes to the accounts. However, the following exceptional items must be shown separately on the face of the profit and loss account and allocated between continuing and discontinued operations:

- profits or losses on the disposal of fixed assets
- profits or losses on the sale or termination of an operation
- the costs of a fundamental reorganisation or restructuring of the company.

(b) **Extraordinary items**. Extraordinary items are material items possessing a high degree of abnormality which are not derived from the company's ordinary activities and which are not expected to recur. In view of the all-embracing definition of ordinary activities given in FRS3, it appears that extraordinary items will occur very rarely indeed, if at all. However, if such items do appear in a company's profit and loss account, they should be shown as extraordinary income or charges and explained in a note to the accounts.

4. PRIOR PERIOD ADJUSTMENTS

Every profit and loss account is affected to a slight extent by adjustments relating to a previous accounting period. These adjustments arise from the need to make estimates when preparing financial statements. For instance, if the estimated amount of an accrued expense at the end of an accounting period turns out to be £10 greater than it should have been, then the following period's profit will be £10 greater as a result.

These adjustments are usually immaterial and do not need to be disclosed separately in the profit and loss account. However, FRS3 requires a special accounting treatment of any "*material adjustments applicable to prior periods arising from changes in accounting policies or from the correction of fundamental errors*". Such prior period adjustments should be accounted for as follows:

(a) The opening balance on the profit and loss account should be altered to take account of the adjustment.

(b) The reason for making the adjustment should be disclosed in a note to the accounts.

(c) The effect of the adjustment should be noted at the foot of the statement of total recognised gains and losses.

(d) The comparative figures for the preceding accounting period should be restated.

EXAMPLE

Greatorex plc prepares accounts to 31 March each year. During the year to 31 March 19X6, the company began to develop a new product and was confident that this product would be a commercial success. Accordingly, the development costs of £423,000 were capitalised (as permitted by SSAP13).

Further development costs of £295,000 were incurred during the year to 31 March 19X7. However, the directors of the company opted for a change in accounting policy and decided to write off all of the development costs to date. Therefore, the draft profit and loss account for the year to 31 March 19X7 was debited with development costs totalling £718,000.

The profit and loss account balance at 31 March 19X6 was £517,000 and the retained profit for the year to 31 March 19X7 (as shown in the draft accounts, after accounting for development costs of £718,000) was £118,000.

How would the change in accounting policy be dealt with in the published profit and loss account of the company for the year to 31 March 19X7?

SOLUTION

Greatorex plc
Profit and loss account (extract) for the year to 31 March 19X7

	£'000	£'000
Retained profit for the year		541
Retained profit brought forward		
As previously reported	517	
Prior year adjustment	(423)	94
Retained profit carried forward		635

Tutorial notes:

1. The retained profit for the year is £118,000 + £423,000 = £541,000.
2. The prior year adjustment would be explained in a note to the accounts.
3. The comparative figures for the year to 31 March 19X6 would be restated to show development costs written off in the year of £423,000.

5. NEW FINANCIAL STATEMENTS REQUIRED BY FRS3

FRS3 requires companies to produce three new financial statements. These new statements are:

(a) a statement of total recognised gains and losses
(b) a reconciliation of movements in shareholders' funds
(c) a note of historical cost profits and losses.

Statement of total recognised gains and losses

This statement (as explained earlier) draws together all of the gains and losses recognised in an accounting period. The statement begins with the profit or loss for the financial year and then shows any unrealised gains or losses which have been credited or debited directly to reserves. FRS3 describes this statement as a *primary* statement, equal in importance to the profit and loss account, the balance sheet and the cash flow statement. A typical statement of total recognised gains and losses is shown below.

Statement of total recognised gains and losses
for the year to 31 December 19X9

	£'000
Profit for the financial year	837
Unrealised surplus on revaluation of properties	112
Unrealised loss on trade investment	(37)
Total recognised gains and losses relating to the year	912
Prior year adjustment	(108)
Total gains and losses recognised since last annual report	804

Reconciliation of movements in shareholders' funds

This statement lists the various items which have caused shareholders' funds to change during the accounting period and provides a reconciliation of the total funds at the start of the period with the total funds at the end of the period. For this purpose, the term "shareholder's funds" refers to the total of share capital and reserves. A typical reconciliation of movements in shareholders' funds is shown below.

Reconciliation of movements in shareholders' funds
for the year to 31 December 19X9

		£'000
Profit for the financial year		126
Dividends paid and proposed		(40)
		86
Other recognised gains and losses		(9)
New share capital subscribed		100
Goodwill written off		(50)
Net addition to shareholders' funds		127
Opening shareholders' funds:		
As previously reported	294	
Prior year adjustment	(25)	269
Closing shareholders' funds		396

Tutorial note:

Goodwill written off against reserves is not usually regarded as a real loss but merely as an accounting adjustment. Therefore goodwill written off does not appear in the statement of recognised gains and losses and must be shown separately (if it occurs) in the reconciliation of movements in shareholders' funds.

Note of historical cost profits and losses

If a company revalues any of its fixed assets, the company's profit and loss account will be affected in two ways:

(a) The depreciation charged in the profit and loss account will be based upon the revalued amount (as required by SSAP12) rather than on original cost.

(b) The profit or loss shown in the profit and loss account when the asset is sold will be the difference between the sale proceeds and the written down revalued amount. Without a revaluation, the profit or loss would have been the difference between the sale proceeds and the written down cost of the asset.

FRS3 requires companies to calculate what the profit or loss for the accounting period would have been if historical cost accounting had been in force and (if the difference between the reported profit and the historical cost profit is material) to provide a *note of historical cost profits and losses*. A typical example of such a note is shown below.

Note of historical cost profits and losses
for the year to 31 December 19X9

	£'000
Reported profit on ordinary activities before taxation	175
Realisation of property revaluation gains of previous years	50
Difference between an historical cost depreciation charge and the actual charge for the year calculated on the revalued amount	12
Historical cost profit on ordinary activities before taxation	237

6. SUMMARY

- The purpose of FRS3 is to improve the quality of the performance information provided to the users of financial statements.
- FRS3 requires that profit and loss account items down as far as the operating profit should be analysed between continuing operations, acquisitions and discontinued operations.
- An exceptional item is a material item derived from the company's ordinary activities which, by virtue of its size, must be disclosed separately. Such items should normally be included under the appropriate heading in the profit and loss account and disclosed in the notes to the accounts.
- Three types of exceptional item must be shown on the face of the profit and loss account. These are profits or losses on the sale or termination of an operation, costs of a fundamental reorganisation or restructuring and profits or losses on the disposal of fixed assets.
- An extraordinary item is a material item possessing a high degree of abnormality which is not derived from the company's ordinary activities and which is not expected to recur. Such items are very rare. If they do occur, they should be shown in the extraordinary section of the profit and loss account and explained in a note to the accounts.

- Material adjustments applicable to prior periods, if arising from changes in accounting policies or from the correction of fundamental errors, should be accounted for by adjusting the opening balance on the profit and loss account.
- The statement of total recognised gains and losses draws together all of the gains and losses recognised in an accounting period (whether or not these gains and losses have been realised).
- The reconciliation of movements in shareholders' funds provides a reconciliation of the total shareholders' funds at the start of the period with the total shareholders' funds at the end of the period.
- The note of historical cost profits and losses shows the amount of the company's profit or loss as it would have been if historical cost accounting had been used.
- FRS3 has changed the definition of earnings per share so that extraordinary items are included within the definition.

EXERCISES 17

17.1 An extract from the profit and loss account of J Harrison Ltd for the year to 30 April 19X8 (before considering the requirements of FRS3) is shown below.

J Harrison Ltd
Profit and loss account (extract) for the year to 30 April 19X8

	£'000	£'000
Turnover		558
Cost of sales		204
Gross profit		354
Distribution costs	119	
Administrative expenses	148	267
		87
Other operating income		12
Operating profit		99

Further information:

1. During the year, the company sold off one of its business operations, incurring a loss on sale of £27,000 (which is included in administrative expenses). Up until the date of the sale, the operation concerned had yielded turnover of £53,000 for the year and related costs had been cost of sales £38,000, distribution costs £2,000 and administrative expenses £20,000.
2. The company also began a new business operation during the year, generating turnover of £193,000 and incurring cost of sales £71,000, distribution costs £42,000 and administrative expenses £45,000.

3. None of the other operating income was generated by the sold-off operation or by the new operation.
4. Administrative expenses on continuing operations include an unusually large bad debt of £22,000.

Required:

Insofar as the information given permits, prepare a profit and loss account for the year to 30 April 19X8, in accordance with the minimum disclosure requirements of FRS3, together with related notes to the accounts.

17.2 Distinguish between exceptional items and extraordinary items. Describe the required accounting treatment of each type of item.

17.3 Accounting standard FRS3 requires companies to prepare three new financial statements in addition to the profit and loss account, balance sheet and cash flow statement. Identify the three new financial statements and briefly explain the purpose and content of each statement.

***17.4** Jerome plc prepares accounts to 31 July each year. An extract from the profit and loss account for the year to 31 July 19X9 and extracts from the balance sheets as at 31 July 19X8 and 19X9 are given below.

Jerome plc
Profit and loss account (extract) for the year to 31 July 19X9

	£'000	£'000
Profit for the financial year		429
Transferred to reserves	100	
Dividends paid and proposed	250	350
Retained profit for the year		79
Retained profit brought forward		
As previously reported	112	
Prior year adjustment	(15)	97
Retained profit carried forward		176

Jerome plc
Balance sheets (extract) as at 31 July

	19X8	*19X9*
	£'000	£'000
Share capital	1,100	1,300
Share premium account	100	180
Revaluation reserve	-	50
Other reserves	400	500
Profit and loss account	112	176
	1,712	2,206

Further information:

1. The balance sheet extract at 31 July 19X8 shows the figures which were reported when the accounts for that year were finalised. The figures have

not been restated to take into account the prior year adjustment shown in the 19X9 accounts.

2. The company's freehold properties were revalued during the year to 31 July 19X9, giving rise to a surplus on revaluation of £50,000.

Required:

Insofar as the information given permits, prepare a statement of total recognised gains and losses and a reconciliation of movements in shareholders' funds for the year to 31 July 19X9.

18

INTRODUCTION TO GROUP ACCOUNTS

Chapter objectives

When you have finished this chapter, you should be able to:

- **Define the terms "parent company" and "subsidiary company".**
- **Explain the purpose of group accounts.**
- **Prepare a simple consolidated balance sheet and profit and loss account, in accordance with the requirements of the Companies Acts and FRS2.**
- **Define the term "associated company" and outline the requirements of SSAP1 in relation to associated companies.**

1. INTRODUCTION

The Companies Acts distinguish between three ways in which a company may invest in the shares of another company:

(a) **Investments in subsidiary companies**. A company may own so many of another company's shares that it is able to control that company's financial and operating policy decisions. Control is usually achieved by acquiring over 50% of the other company's ordinary share capital. In these circumstances, the investing company is known as a *parent company* and the other company is known as its *subsidiary company*. The term *group* is often used to refer to a parent company together with all of its subsidiaries.

(b) **Participating interests**. A company may own too few of another company's shares to achieve control but it may still own sufficient shares to exercise significant influence over that company's policy decisions. Significant influence is usually assumed to exist if the investing company owns at least 20% of the other company's shares. In this case, the investing company is said to have a *participating interest* in the other company.

(c) **Other investments**. Finally, a company may own a comparatively small proportion of another company's shares, insufficient to exercise any significant influence over its policy decisions.

In the accounts of the investing company, all three of these types of investment are treated in much the same way. The investment is usually shown at cost in the balance sheet (though some companies may show investments at market value) and any dividends received in relation to the investment are shown as income in the profit and loss account. Different headings are used for each type of investment, as follows:

(a) Shares in a subsidiary company are shown in the balance sheet as *shares in group undertakings* and the related dividends are shown in the profit and loss account as *income from shares in group undertakings*. The use of the word "undertakings" rather than "companies" reflects the fact that a company might own a controlling interest in an unincorporated business (e.g. a partnership).

(b) Shares which comprise a participating interest are shown in the balance sheet as *participating interests* and the related dividends are shown in the profit and loss account as *income from participating interests*.

(c) Other shares are shown in the balance sheet as *other investments other than loans* and the related dividends are shown in the profit and loss account as *income from other fixed asset investments*.

The need for group accounts

Indirectly, the shareholders of a parent company own all or part of the net assets of the company's subsidiaries and are entitled to receive all or part of the subsidiaries' profits. Information relating to the assets, liabilities, profits and losses of subsidiary companies would therefore be of relevance to the shareholders of a parent company, but this information is not provided in the parent company's own accounts. Accordingly, parent companies are required to prepare and publish a set of accounts for the group as a whole, in recognition of the fact that the parent company and its subsidiaries are, in effect, a single economic unit. It is important to appreciate that these *group accounts* are intended only for the shareholders of the parent company and are of little use to anyone else.

The requirement to produce group accounts is laid down in the Companies Acts, but much of the fine detail relating to the preparation of group accounts in contained in accounting standard FRS2. The main purpose of this chapter is to provide an introduction to the preparation of group accounts in accordance with statutory requirements and the provisions of FRS2.

Associated companies

Accounting standard SSAP1 is concerned with the accounting treatment of investments in *associated companies*. The definition of an associated company is broadly similar to the definition of a participating interest (see above). The requirements of SSAP1 are considered towards the end of this chapter.

2. PARENT AND SUBSIDIARY UNDERTAKINGS

As mentioned earlier, a parent company usually achieves control over the policy decisions of a subsidiary company by acquiring more than 50% of its ordinary share capital. However, there are other ways of achieving control and these are listed in FRS2. In summary, FRS2 states that an undertaking is a parent undertaking of another undertaking if any of the following conditions are satisfied:

(a) It holds a majority of the voting rights in the other undertaking. (In practice, this normally means holding more than 50% of another company's ordinary shares).

(b) It is a member of the other undertaking and has the right to appoint or remove directors holding a majority of the voting rights at board meetings.

(c) It has the right to exercise a dominant influence over the other undertaking.

(d) It is a member of the other undertaking and controls alone (pursuant to an agreement with other members) a majority of the voting rights in the undertaking.

(e) It has a participating interest in the other undertaking and:

    (i) it exercises a dominant influence over the undertaking, or
    (ii) the two undertakings are managed on a unified basis.

(f) It is the parent undertaking of a parent undertaking of the other undertaking.

For the remainder of this chapter, we will assume that we are dealing exclusively with companies (rather than with undertakings in the broader sense) and that the parent company has achieved control by acquiring over 50% of the subsidiary's ordinary shares. Note that if a parent company owns the whole of a subsidiary's share capital, the subsidiary is said to be *wholly-owned*. If the parent owns only part of the subsidiary's share capital, the subsidiary is said to be *partly-owned*.

3. THE CONSOLIDATED BALANCE SHEET

The preparation of a group balance sheet is basically a matter of adding together (line by line) the individual balance sheets of all of the companies in the group. This process is known as *consolidation* and therefore a group balance sheet is often referred to as a *consolidated balance sheet*.

When carrying out a consolidation it is necessary to cancel out any items which appear both as an asset in the balance sheet of one group company and as a liability in the balance sheet of another group company. This ensures that the consolidated balance sheet shows only the true assets and liabilities of the group as a whole. The main examples of such *intra-group balances* are as follows:

(a) A parent company's balance sheet will show (as an asset) the cost of its investment in the shares of each subsidiary. Each subsidiary's balance sheet will show its own share capital and reserves, representing the subsidiary's liability to its shareholders. In the case of a wholly-owned subsidiary, this asset and this liability should be cancelled out when preparing the consolidated balance sheet. (Partly-owned subsidiaries are considered later in this chapter).

(b) If one group company owes money to another group company, the creditor shown in the balance sheet of the first company should be cancelled out with the corresponding debtor shown in the balance sheet of the other company.

It is important to appreciate that the cancellation of intra-group balances does *not* take place in the books of the individual companies concerned. The entire consolidation process takes place on a set of *consolidation working papers* and the books of the group companies are completely unaffected by this process.

EXAMPLE

On 31 July 19X7, A Ltd paid £35,000 to acquire the entire share capital of B Ltd. The balance sheets of the two companies at close of trading on 31 July 19X7 were as follows:

	A Ltd	B Ltd
	£	£
Fixed assets		
Tangible assets	200,000	27,000
Investments		
Shares in group undertaking	35,000	
	235,000	
Net current assets	73,000	8,000
	308,000	35,000
Capital and reserves		
Called-up share capital	250,000	30,000
Profit and loss account	58,000	5,000
	308,000	35,000

Prepare a consolidated balance sheet as at 31 July 19X7.

SOLUTION

A Ltd
Consolidated balance sheet as at 31 July 19X7

	£
Fixed assets	
Tangible assets	227,000
Net current assets	81,000
	308,000
Capital and reserves	
Called-up share capital	250,000
Profit and loss account	58,000
	308,000

Notes:

1. The £35,000 paid by A Ltd has been cancelled out with the £35,000 share capital and reserves of B Ltd. The two balance sheets have then been consolidated, line by line.
2. In effect, the asset "Shares in group undertaking" shown in the balance sheet of A Ltd has been replaced in the consolidated balance sheet by the underlying net assets of the subsidiary company.

Goodwill arising on consolidation

In the above example, the amount paid by the parent company to acquire the shares of the subsidiary was precisely equal to the book value of the subsidiary's net assets. However, parent companies are often willing to pay more than book value to acquire a controlling interest in a subsidiary, for two main reasons:

(a) The fair value of the assets shown in the subsidiary's balance sheet may exceed the book value of those assets (accounting standard FRS7 provides guidance on how to measure fair values when one company acquires another).

(b) The parent company may be paying for the subsidiary's goodwill (which is probably not shown on the balance sheet at all).

When preparing consolidated accounts, the disparity between the cost of the parent company's investment in a subsidiary and the book value of the subsidiary's net assets is dealt with as follows:

(a) Each of the subsidiary's assets and liabilities is adjusted to its fair value on the date that the parent company acquired the subsidiary's shares. Any profit on this revaluation process is credited to a revaluation reserve. (A loss on revaluation would usually be debited to the subsidiary's revenue reserves).

(b) If the parent company has paid more than fair value to acquire the shares of a subsidiary, the excess is known as *goodwill arising on consolidation* and is shown as an asset on the consolidated balance sheet.

(c) If the parent company has paid less than fair value to acquire the shares of a subsidiary, the difference is *negative goodwill*. In this situation, SSAP22 (see Chapter 15) suggests that the fair values attributed to the assets acquired should be reviewed to see if they have been overstated. If the negative goodwill remains, it should be credited to reserves.

Once again, it is very important to appreciate that all of these adjustments relating to fair value and goodwill are made only in the consolidation working papers and not in the books of the companies concerned. As mentioned earlier, the books of the parent company and its subsidiaries are entirely unaffected by the consolidation process.

EXAMPLE

On 30 June 19X7, C Ltd paid £60,000 to acquire the entire share capital of D Ltd. The balance sheets of the two companies at close of trading on 30 June 19X7 were as follows:

	C Ltd	D Ltd
	£	£
Fixed assets		
Tangible assets	410,000	30,000
Investments		
Shares in group undertaking	60,000	
	470,000	
Net current assets	117,000	12,000
	587,000	42,000
Capital and reserves		
Called-up share capital	400,000	25,000
Profit and loss account	187,000	17,000
	587,000	42,000

The fair value of D Ltd's tangible fixed assets on 30 June 19X7 was £40,000. Prepare a consolidated balance sheet as at 30 June 19X7.

SOLUTION

C Ltd
Consolidated balance sheet as at 30 June 19X7

	£
Fixed assets	
Tangible assets	450,000
Goodwill arising on consolidation	8,000
Net current assets	129,000
	587,000
Capital and reserves	
Called-up share capital	400,000
Profit and loss account	187,000
	587,000

Notes:

1. In the consolidation working papers, D Ltd's tangible fixed assets are revalued at £40,000 and the £10,000 profit on revaluation is credited to a revaluation reserve.
2. The goodwill arising on consolidation is the difference between the price paid by C Ltd (£60,000) and the fair value of the net assets of D Ltd (£52,000).
3. After deducting the amount paid for goodwill, the balance of the price paid by C Ltd (£52,000) is cancelled against the share capital and reserves of D Ltd (£25,000 + £17,000 + revaluation reserve £10,000).
4. None of these adjustments have the slightest effect on the books of either C Ltd or D Ltd.

Amortisation of goodwill

Goodwill arising on consolidation is an example of *purchased goodwill*, as defined in SSAP22 (see Chapter 15). This standard allows two possible accounting treatments of purchased goodwill. It may be written off to reserves immediately on acquisition or it may be capitalised and then amortised over its estimated useful life.

EXAMPLE

Rework the above example concerning C Ltd and D Ltd, assuming that both companies prepare accounts to 30 June each year and that either:

(a) goodwill arising on consolidation is written off immediately against reserves, or

(b) goodwill arising on consolidation is amortised at 25% per annum on the straight-line basis, with a full year's charge in the year of acquisition.

SOLUTION

C Ltd
Consolidated balance sheet as at 30 June 19X7

	(a) £	(b) £
Fixed assets		
Tangible assets	450,000	450,000
Goodwill arising on consolidation	-	6,000
Net current assets	129,000	129,000
	579,000	585,000
Capital and reserves		
Called-up share capital	400,000	400,000
Profit and loss account	179,000	185,000
	579,000	585,000

Notes:

1. If goodwill is written off immediately against reserves, the profit and loss account balance shown in the consolidated balance sheet (the only reserve available in this case) is reduced by £8,000 to £179,000.
2. If goodwill is amortised at 25% per annum, the profit and loss account balance shown in the consolidated balance sheet is reduced by £2,000 to £185,000.

Post-acquisition changes in the reserves of a subsidiary company

All of the examples given so far in this chapter have been concerned with the balance sheet on the date that a parent company first acquires control of a subsidiary. In subsequent years, the situation is complicated by the fact that the reserves of the subsidiary company may have changed since acquisition. Such changes should be dealt with as follows:

(a) A post-acquisition increase in the reserves of a subsidiary company represents an increase in the value of the investment made by the parent company in the shares of the subsidiary. This increase in value belongs ultimately to the members of the parent company and should therefore be added to consolidated reserves (i.e. the reserves shown in the consolidated balance sheet).

(b) Similarly, any post-acquisition decrease in the reserves of a subsidiary company should be subtracted from consolidated reserves.

EXAMPLE

On 1 January 19X6, E Ltd paid £70,000 to acquire the entire share capital of F Ltd. On that date, the unappropriated profit of F Ltd was £14,000 and all of its assets and liabilities were shown in the books at fair values. The balance sheets of E Ltd and F Ltd as at 31 December 19X8 are as follows:

	E Ltd	F Ltd
	£	£
Fixed assets		
Tangible assets	620,000	47,000
Investments		
Shares in group undertaking	70,000	
	690,000	
Net current assets	203,000	19,000
	893,000	66,000
Capital and reserves		
Called-up share capital	500,000	40,000
Profit and loss account	393,000	26,000
	893,000	66,000

The share capital of F Ltd has remained unchanged since 1 January 19X6. Goodwill arising on consolidation is written off in the year of acquisition. Prepare a consolidated balance sheet as at 31 December 19X8.

SOLUTION

E Ltd
Consolidated balance sheet as at 31 December 19X8

	£
Fixed assets	
Tangible assets	667,000
Net current assets	222,000
	889,000
Capital and reserves	
Called-up share capital	500,000
Profit and loss account	389,000
	889,000

Notes:

1. On 1 January 19X6, the net assets of F Ltd must have been £54,000 (£40,000 + £14,000). Therefore the goodwill arising on consolidation is £70,000 – £54,000 = £16,000.
2. The consolidated profit and loss account balance consists of the profit and loss account balance of E Ltd (£393,000), plus the post acquisition increase in the reserves of F Ltd (£26,000 – £14,000 = £12,000), less the goodwill written off (£16,000), giving a total of £389,000.

Partly-owned subsidiaries

If a subsidiary is only partly-owned by the parent company, the remainder of its shares are held by *minority shareholders.* In these circumstances, FRS2 requires that the consolidated balance sheet should include *all* of the subsidiary's net assets (exactly as if the subsidiary were wholly-owned) but should then show as a liability the part of those assets which is owned by the minority shareholders. This liability is known as the *minority interest.*

EXAMPLE

The balance sheets of G Ltd and H Ltd as at 31 March 19X9 are as follows:

	G Ltd	H Ltd
	£	£
Fixed assets		
Tangible assets	527,000	39,000
Investments		
Shares in group undertaking	48,000	
	575,000	
Net current assets	173,000	15,000
	748,000	54,000
Capital and reserves		
Called-up share capital	600,000	32,000
Profit and loss account	148,000	22,000
	748,000	54,000

On 1 April 19X7, G Ltd paid £48,000 to acquire 75% of the shares in H Ltd. On that date, the unappropriated profit of H Ltd was £10,000 and the fair value of the company's fixed assets was £8,000 more than their book value. This revaluation has not been reflected in the books of H Ltd.

H Ltd has issued no shares since being acquired by G Ltd. Goodwill arising on consolidation is amortised at 20% per annum on the straight-line basis. Prepare a consolidated balance sheet as at 31 March 19X9.

SOLUTION

G Ltd

Consolidated balance sheet as at 31 March 19X9

	£
Fixed assets	
Tangible assets	574,000
Goodwill arising on consolidation	6,300
Net current assets	188,000
	768,300

	£
Capital and reserves	
Called-up share capital	600,000
Profit and loss account	152,800
	752,800
Minority interest	15,500
	768,300

Notes:

1. The net assets of H Ltd on the date of acquisition were £32,000 + £10,000 + £8,000 = £50,000. G Ltd acquired 75% of these assets at a cost of £48,000, so the goodwill arising on consolidation is £48,000 – 75% x £50,000 = £10,500.
2. This is the second year since the date of acquisition, so amortisation of goodwill to date is 2 x 20% x £10,500 = £4,200 and the written down value of the goodwill is the remaining £6,300.
3. The post-acquisition increase in the reserves of H Ltd is £22,000 – £10,000 = £12,000. G Ltd owns a 75% share of this i.e. £9,000.
4. The consolidated profit and loss account balance is calculated as follows:

	£
G Ltd profit and loss account	148,000
75% of post acquisition increase in reserves of H Ltd	9,000
	157,000
Less: Amortisation of goodwill	4,200
	152,800

5. The minority interest is 25% x (£54,000 + revaluation reserve £8,000) = £15,500.

Preference shares

As explained in Chapter 13, a company's reserves normally belong entirely to the ordinary shareholders. If the company were wound up, the preference shareholders (if any) would be entitled to receive only assets equal to the nominal value of their preference shares. This fact must be borne in mind when preparing the consolidated balance sheet of a group if one or more of the subsidiary companies has issued preference shares.

EXAMPLE

On 30 September 19X6, J Ltd paid £40,000 to acquire 60% of the ordinary shares and 25% of the preference shares of K Ltd. On that date, the unappropriated profit of K Ltd was £4,000 and all of its assets and liabilities were shown at fair values. The balance sheets of J Ltd and K Ltd as at 30 September 19X9 are as follows:

	J Ltd	K Ltd
	£	£
Fixed assets		
Tangible assets	438,000	47,000
Investments		
Shares in group undertaking	40,000	
	478,000	
Net current assets	241,000	22,000
	719,000	69,000
Capital and reserves		
Called-up share capital		
Ordinary shares of £1	600,000	50,000
Preference shares of £1		10,000
Profit and loss account	119,000	9,000
	719,000	69,000

K Ltd has issued no shares since being acquired by J Ltd. Goodwill arising on consolidation is written off in the year of acquisition. Prepare a consolidated balance sheet as at 30 September 19X9.

SOLUTION

J Ltd
Consolidated balance sheet as at 30 September 19X9

	£
Fixed assets	
Tangible assets	485,000
Net current assets	263,000
	748,000
Capital and reserves	
Called-up share capital	600,000
Profit and loss account	116,900
	716,900
Minority interest	31,100
	748,000

Notes:

1. J Ltd acquired 60% of the ordinary share capital and reserves of K Ltd, plus 25% of the preference share capital. Therefore the goodwill arising on consolidation is equal to £40,000 – 60% x (£50,000 + £4,000) – 25% x £10,000 = £5,100.
2. The minority interest is 40% x (£50,000 + £9,000) + 75% x £10,000 = £31,100.

3. The post-acquisition increase in the reserves of K Ltd is £5,000 and J Ltd owns 60% of this i.e. £3,000. The consolidated profit and loss account balance is therefore £119,000 + £3,000 – £5,100 = £116,900.

Elimination of intra-group balances

As mentioned earlier, it is necessary to cancel intra-group debtors and creditors when preparing a consolidated balance sheet. Such debtors and creditors may arise in any of the following circumstances:

(a) One group company may lend money to another group company. In this case, the loan will be shown as an asset in the lending company's balance sheet and as a liability in the borrowing company's balance sheet. The asset and the liability will be cancelled out when the consolidated balance sheet is prepared.

(b) One group company may buy goods or services on credit from another group company. In this case, the trade debtor shown in the balance sheet of the supplier company will be cancelled against the trade creditor shown in the balance sheet of the customer company.

(c) A group company may have a *current account* with another group company. A current account is used to record movements of goods, services and money between the two companies and the balance on the account will appear as a debtor in one company's balance sheet and as a creditor in the other company's balance sheet. The debtor and the creditor will be cancelled out when the consolidated balance sheet is prepared.

If items are in transit from one company to another at the balance sheet date, it may be that the relevant debtor and creditor are not equal in amount. In this case it will be necessary to show the value of the in-transit items as an asset in the consolidated balance sheet.

EXAMPLE

L Ltd is the parent company of M Ltd. The following balances appeared in the books of the two companies on their balance sheet date:

	In the books of L Ltd	*In the books of M Ltd*
	£	£
M Ltd current account (debit balance)	26,750	
L Ltd current account (credit balance)		14,600

The discrepancy between these two balances is caused by the fact that M Ltd sent a cheque for £12,150 to L Ltd on the very last day of the accounting year. L Ltd did not receive this cheque until the third day of the following accounting year. Explain how this matter will be dealt with in the consolidated balance sheet.

SOLUTION

The two current account balances will be cancelled against each other, leaving a net debit balance of £12,150. This will be shown on the consolidated balance sheet as cash in transit.

Unrealised profit on assets transferred between group companies at more than cost

The assets shown on the individual balance sheet of a group company may well include assets acquired from another member of the same group. If such assets have been transferred between the two companies at a price in excess of original cost, then their valuation includes an element of *unrealised profit* and this must be provided for when the consolidated balance sheet is prepared. If this were not done, a group could artificially increase the values of its assets simply by passing them from one member of the group to another at inflated prices.

FRS2 requires that profits or losses on intra-group transactions must be eliminated in full on consolidation, irrespective of whether the subsidiary companies involved are wholly-owned or partly-owned.

EXAMPLE

P Ltd owns 80% of the share capital of Q Ltd. The stocks of Q Ltd on 31 December 19X8 include goods purchased from P Ltd for £15,000. These goods had cost P Ltd £10,000. Explain how the goods should be dealt with in the consolidated balance sheet at 31 December 19X8.

SOLUTION

The unrealised profit of £5,000 must be subtracted when calculating the consolidated stock figure and must also be subtracted from the consolidated profit and loss account balance. It might be thought that 20% of the profit has in fact been realised (since 20% of the goods in question are now owned by the minority interest, who are not part of the group) but FRS2 insists that the full £5,000 should be provided for.

4. THE CONSOLIDATED PROFIT AND LOSS ACCOUNT

The purpose of the consolidated profit and loss account is to show the profit or loss of the group as a whole. It is prepared by adding together (line by line) the individual profit and loss accounts of all of the companies in the group, cancelling out any intra-group items. Note the following points:

(a) Intra-group sales are included in the turnover of the selling company and in the cost of sales of the buying company. Therefore intra-group sales are deducted from both group turnover and group cost of sales when preparing the consolidated profit and loss account.

(b) As we saw above, any element of unrealised profit must be deducted from the stock figure shown in the consolidated balance sheet. A reduction in closing stock causes an increase in cost of sales, so the group cost of sales figure must be increased by the amount of any unrealised profit.

(c) If the group includes one or more partly-owned subsidiaries, part of the after-tax profit is attributable to the minority shareholders and this amount is deducted in the consolidated profit and loss account. The balance of the after-tax profit is attributable to the members of the parent company.

(d) Any dividends paid (or payable) by a subsidiary company to its parent company are cancelled against the dividends received (or receivable) shown in the parent company's profit and loss account.

(e) Any dividends paid or payable to the minority shareholders should be entirely ignored when preparing the consolidated profit and loss account. This is because the amount of profit attributable to the minority shareholders has already been deducted in full (see above).

(f) The only dividends shown in the consolidated profit and loss account are those paid or payable to the shareholders of the parent company. This is logical, since the consolidated accounts are prepared solely for the benefit of these shareholders.

(g) The retained profit brought forward in the consolidated profit and loss account is the profit and loss account balance which was shown on the previous year's consolidated balance sheet. Similarly, the retained profit carried forward is the amount of the profit and loss account balance which is shown on the current year's consolidated balance sheet.

EXAMPLE

R Ltd acquired 70% of the share capital of S Ltd on 1 July 19X6. On that date, the unappropriated profit of S Ltd was £2,000. The profit and loss accounts of R Ltd and S Ltd for the year to 30 June 19X9 are as follows:

	R Ltd	S Ltd
	£	£
Turnover	624,000	109,000
Cost of sales	267,400	65,300
Gross profit	356,600	43,700
Distribution costs	(71,370)	(5,100)
Administrative expenses	(101,430)	(10,500)
Operating profit	183,800	28,100
Income from shares in group undertakings	14,000	-
Profit on ordinary activities before taxation	197,800	28,100
Tax on profit on ordinary activities	51,200	7,100
Profit on ordinary activities after taxation c/f	146,600	21,000

	R Ltd	S Ltd
	£	£
Profit on ordinary activities after taxation b/f	146,600	21,000
Dividends		
Paid	(40,000)	(5,000)
Proposed	(80,000)	(15,000)
Retained profit for the financial year	26,600	1,000
Retained profit brought forward	54,900	7,000
Retained profit carried forward	81,500	8,000

During the year, R Ltd sold goods to S Ltd for £8,000. These goods had cost R Ltd £5,000. At the year end, one-half of these goods were still held by S Ltd. Prepare a consolidated profit and loss account for the year to 30 June 19X9.

SOLUTION

R Ltd
Consolidated profit and loss account for the year to 30 June 19X9

	£	£
Turnover		725,000
Cost of sales		326,200
Gross profit		398,800
Distribution costs	76,470	
Administrative expenses	111,930	188,400
Profit on ordinary activities before taxation		210,400
Tax on profit on ordinary activities		58,300
Profit on ordinary activities after taxation		152,100
Minority interest		6,300
		145,800
Dividends		
Paid	40,000	
Proposed	80,000	120,000
Retained profit for the financial year		25,800
Retained profit brought forward		58,400
Retained profit carried forward		84,200

Notes:

1. Group turnover is £624,000 + £109,000 – £8,000 = £725,000.
2. Group cost of sales is £267,400 + £65,300 – £8,000 + £1,500 (unrealised profit on intra-group transfer) = £326,200.
3. The minority interest is 30% of the after-tax profits of S Ltd (30% x £21,000 = £6,300).

4. The group retained profit brought forward is equal to the retained profit brought forward of R Ltd (£54,900), plus 70% of the post-acquisition retained profits brought forward of S Ltd (70% of (£7,000 – £2,000) = £3,500).
5. The group retained profit carried forward is equal to the retained profit carried forward of R Ltd (£81,500), plus 70% of the post-acquisition retained profits carried forward of S Ltd (70% of (£8,000 – £2,000) = £4,200), less the unrealised profit included in the stock of S Ltd (£1,500).

5. ASSOCIATED COMPANIES

As mentioned earlier, accounting standard SSAP1 is concerned with the accounting treatment of *associated companies*. Broadly speaking, X Ltd is considered to be an associate company of Y Ltd (an *investing company*) if:

(a) it is not a subsidiary of Y Ltd, but
(b) Y Ltd is in a position to exercise significant influence over its financial and operating policy decisions.

Significant influence is usually deemed to accompany ownership of at least 20% of a company's share capital. The main requirements of SSAP1 in relation to associated companies are as follows:

(a) The consolidated profit and loss account of the investing company should include the group's share of the profits of associated companies. However, the turnover and expenses of associated companies are *not* aggregated with those of the group. Instead, the group's share of the profits of associated companies is shown as a separate line in the consolidated profit and loss account.
(b) The consolidated profit and loss account should also disclose the group's share of the taxation charge, extraordinary items and retained profits of associated companies.
(c) In the consolidated balance sheet, the investment in an associated company should be shown at original cost plus the group's share of the post-acquisition retained profits of the associated company.

6. SUMMARY

- A parent company is one which can control the financial and operating policy decisions of another company, known as its subsidiary company. Control usually accompanies ownership of 50% of the subsidiary's ordinary share capital.
- A parent company together with its subsidiaries is known as a group. The Companies Acts require the parent company to prepare and publish accounts for the group as a whole.
- The group balance sheet is prepared by consolidating the balance sheets of the group members and cancelling out intra-group items. The group

balance sheet should show the extent to which the assets of the group members are attributable to the minority interest.

- If a parent company has paid more than fair value to acquire the shares of a subsidiary, the excess is treated as goodwill arising on consolidation. This may either be written off immediately or amortised over its estimated useful life.
- Post-acquisition increases in the reserves of a subsidiary company are added to consolidated reserves.
- Any unrealised profit on assets transferred between group companies at more than cost must be provided for when preparing the group accounts.
- The group profit and loss account is prepared by consolidating the profit and loss accounts of the group members and cancelling out intra-group items. The group profit and loss account should show the amount of after-tax profit which is attributable to the minority interest.
- Accounting standard SSAP1 is concerned with the treatment of associated companies in group accounts.

EXERCISES 18

18.1 The balance sheets of AA Ltd and BB Ltd as at 30 April 19X9 are as follows:

	AA Ltd	**BB Ltd**
	£'000	£'000
Fixed assets		
Tangible assets	2,265	345
Investments		
Shares in group undertaking	800	
	3,065	
Net current assets	964	228
	4,029	573
Capital and reserves		
Called-up share capital	3,000	350
Profit and loss account	1,029	223
	4,029	573

The following information is relevant:

(a) AA Ltd acquired the entire share capital of BB Ltd on 30 April 19X5. There have been no changes in the share capital of BB Ltd since that date.

(b) On 30 April 19X5, the fair value of BB Ltd's fixed assets was £500,000, as compared with their book value on that date of £320,000. This revaluation has not been reflected in the books of BB Ltd.

(c) On 30 April 19X5, the balance on the profit and loss account of BB Ltd was £195,000.

(d) Goodwill arising on consolidation is written off in the year of acquisition.

Required:

Prepare a consolidated balance sheet as at 30 April 19X9.

18.2 The balance sheets of CC Ltd and its two subsidiaries DD Ltd and EE Ltd as at 31 December 19X8 are as follows:

		CC Ltd		**DD Ltd**		**EE Ltd**
		£'000		£'000		£'000
Fixed assets						
Tangible assets		4,761		521		411
Investments						
Shares in DD Ltd		600				
Shares in EE Ltd		575				
		5,936		521		411
Current assets						
Stocks	1,532		222		187	
Debtors	1,947		258		202	
Bank	239		30		13	
	3,718		510		402	
Current liabilities						
Creditors	1,607		211		163	
Net current assets		2,111		299		239
		8,047		820		650
Capital and reserves						
Called-up share capital		5,000		500		300
Capital reserves		2,500		-		100
Profit and loss account		547		320		250
		8,047		820		650

The following information is also available:

(a) CC Ltd acquired 60% of the share capital of DD Ltd on 1 January 19X7, when the profit and loss account balance of DD Ltd was £280,000. The fair value of DD Ltd's fixed assets on that date was £30,000 more than their book value. This revaluation has not been reflected in the books of DD Ltd.

(b) CC Ltd acquired 90% of the share capital on EE Ltd on 1 January 19X8, when DD Ltd had a balance of £60,000 on capital reserves and £230,000 on its profit and loss account. The fair value of EE Ltd's fixed assets on that date was equal to their book value.

(c) Neither DD Ltd nor EE Ltd have issued any shares since being acquired by CC Ltd.

(d) Goodwill arising on consolidation is amortised at a rate of 25% per annum on the straight line basis.

(e) The following intra-group debts exist on 31 December 19X8:

- DD Ltd owes CC Ltd £15,000.
- EE Ltd owes CC Ltd £25,000.
- EE Ltd owes DD Ltd £8,000.

(f) Goods purchased for £8,000 from CC Ltd are included in DD Ltd's stock at 31 December 19X8. CC Ltd had invoiced these goods to DD Ltd at cost plus 60%.

Required:

Prepare a consolidated balance sheet as at 31 December 19X8.

18.3 FF Ltd acquired 80% of the share capital of GG Ltd on 1 April 19X4. On that date, the unappropriated profit of GG Ltd was £18,260. The profit and loss accounts of FF Ltd and GG Ltd for the year to 31 March 19X8 are as follows:

	FF Ltd	**GG Ltd**
	£	£
Turnover	359,800	154,600
Cost of sales	102,600	55,550
Gross profit	257,200	99,050
Distribution costs	(36,120)	(7,730)
Administrative expenses	(82,360)	(11,570)
Operating profit	138,720	79,750
Income from shares in group undertakings	28,000	-
Profit on ordinary activities before taxation	166,720	79,750
Tax on profit on ordinary activities	40,000	20,000
Profit on ordinary activities after taxation	126,720	59,750
Dividends		
Paid	(30,000)	(10,000)
Proposed	(60,000)	(25,000)
Retained profit for the financial year	36,720	24,750
Retained profit brought forward	66,090	41,110
Retained profit carried forward	102,810	65,860

On 4 March 19X8, FF Ltd sold goods to GG Ltd for £10,000. These goods had cost FF Ltd £6,000. One-quarter of these goods were included in GG Ltd's stock at the year end.

Required:

Prepare a consolidated profit and loss account for the year to 31 March 19X8.

***18.4** The balance sheets of JJ Ltd and KK Ltd as at 30 June 19X9 and the profit and loss accounts of these two companies for the year ended on that date are shown below:

Balance sheets as at 30 June 19X9

	JJ Ltd		KK Ltd	
		£'000		£'000
Fixed assets				
Tangible assets		5,961		2,667
Investments				
Shares in KK Ltd		3,153		
		9,114		
Current assets				
Stocks	2,215		1,052	
Debtors	1,823		829	
Bank	101		5	
	4,139		1,886	
Current liabilities				
Trade creditors	1,004		315	
Taxation	1,500		450	
Proposed dividends	800		300	
	3,304		1,065	
Net current assets		835		821
		9,949		3,488
Capital and reserves				
Called-up share capital				
Ordinary shares of £1		7,000		2,500
10% Preference shares of £1		800		400
Capital reserves		200		100
Profit and loss account		1,949		488
		9,949		3,488

Profit and loss accounts for the year to 30 June 19X9

	JJ Ltd	KK Ltd
	£'000	£'000
Turnover	21,545	5,328
Cost of sales	13,335	3,552
Gross profit	8,210	1,776
Distribution costs	(1,662)	(199)
Administrative expenses	(2,427)	(211)
Operating profit c/f	4,121	1,366

	JJ Ltd	KK Ltd
	£'000	£'000
Operating profit b/f	4,121	1,366
Income from shares in group undertakings	379	-
Profit on ordinary activities before taxation	4,500	1,366
Tax on profit on ordinary activities	1,500	450
Profit on ordinary activities after taxation	3,000	916
Dividends paid		
Ordinary shares	(1,000)	(200)
Preference shares	(80)	(40)
Dividends proposed		
Ordinary shares	(800)	(300)
Retained profit for the financial year	1,120	376
Retained profit brought forward	829	112
Retained profit carried forward	1,949	488

The following information is relevant:

(a) On 1 July 19X5, JJ Ltd paid £3,153,000 to acquire 75% of the ordinary shares and 10% of the preference shares of KK Ltd. On that date, the unappropriated profit of KK Ltd was £684,000 and its capital reserves were £20,000.

(b) The fair value of KK Ltd's fixed assets on 1 July 19X5 was £600,000 more than their book value. This revaluation has not been reflected in the books of KK Ltd.

(c) KK Ltd has issued no shares since being acquired by JJ Ltd.

(d) Goodwill arising on consolidation is written off in the year of acquisition.

(e) JJ Ltd sells goods to KK Ltd at cost plus 60%. During the year to 30 June 19X9, these sales totalled £2,400,000, of which £216,000 was still owing to JJ Ltd at the end of the year. The stock of KK Ltd at 30 June 19X9 includes goods bought from JJ Ltd for £512,000.

Required:

Prepare a consolidated profit and loss account for the year to 30 June 19X9 and a consolidated balance sheet as at that date.

19

ACCOUNTING RATIOS

Chapter objectives

When you have finished this chapter, you should be able to:

- **Appreciate the role of accounting ratios in the analysis and interpretation of accounting information.**
- **Define each of the most commonly-used accounting ratios.**
- **Use accounting ratios to analyse accounting information.**
- **Explain the limitations of ratio analysis.**

1. INTRODUCTION

So far, this book has been concerned almost exclusively with the preparation of financial statements. In this chapter, we turn our attention to the *interpretation* of the information contained in these statements.

As was explained in Chapter 1, the purpose of preparing financial statements is to provide users with information which will help them to make better economic decisions. Confronted with a set of financial statements, a user will need to *analyse* the information provided and draw some conclusions about the financial performance and position of the business concerned.

There are several ways in which financial statements might be analysed. In practice, one of the most important methods is the technique known as *ratio analysis*, which involves the calculation of a number of *accounting ratios*. The main purpose of this chapter is to introduce some of the most commonly-used accounting ratios and to explain the significance of each ratio.

2. RATIO ANALYSIS

An accounting ratio is a measure of the relationship which exists between two figures shown in a set of financial statements. For example, the gross profit margin (see Chapter 10) measures the relationship between gross profit and sales. The usefulness of accounting ratios in the analysis and interpretation of accounting information can be illustrated by means of the following example.

Suppose that a company makes a profit of £110,000 in 19X9, as opposed to £100,000 in 19X8. A shareholder seeking to assess the company's performance might ask whether the company has done better in 19X9 than it did in 19X8. The obvious answer to this question is "Yes" but obvious answers can be wrong. For instance, it may be that the company raised substantial amounts of extra capital at the start of 19X9, in which case a 10% increase in profit might actually represent a deterioration in financial performance. The problem is that we are trying to compare two years which may not be directly comparable and this problem becomes even worse if we try to compare one business with another.

In general, the problems of comparability are reduced or eliminated if we calculate and compare accounting ratios rather than comparing absolute figures. In the above example, the ratio of profit to capital in 19X9 should be calculated and compared with the equivalent figure for 19X8. This will give a much better indication of the company's performance than can be obtained by comparing the absolute profit figures for the two years.

Ratios as a means of comparison

It should be emphasised at this point that performing a ratio analysis on a single set of accounts is usually a fairly pointless exercise. Most of the ratios mean very little in absolute terms and only become meaningful when used as a basis for comparison. In general, ratios are used for making the following comparisons:

(a) **Comparing one year with another**. The financial performance of a business for a given accounting year and its financial position at the end of that year may be judged by calculating a set of ratios and comparing the results with the equivalent figures for the same business in previous years. Any perceived trends might be extrapolated into the future and used as a basis for making economic forecasts.

(b) **Comparing one business with another**. Similarly, the ratios calculated for a business in a given accounting year may be compared with those calculated for other businesses in the same year (though this comparison would usually be invalid unless all of the businesses were in the same trade).

When used as a means of comparison, accounting ratios are undoubtedly a valuable tool for the analysis of financial statements. However, ratio analysis does suffer from a number of limitations and the user should be aware of these before basing important economic decisions on the results of such an analysis. The limitations of ratio analysis are discussed at the end of this chapter.

Types of accounting ratio

In theory, it would be possible to calculate literally hundreds of accounting ratios from a given set of financial statements. Some of these ratios would not mean very much but many of them might serve a useful purpose. In practice, however, it is usually sufficient to calculate a fairly small number of key ratios and each of these ratios is described in this chapter. They can be classified into four main groups:

(a) **Profitability ratios**. The profitability ratios are used to assess whether the business has succeeded in making an acceptable level of profit.

(b) **Liquidity ratios**. The liquidity ratios are a measure of the ability of the business to pay its debts as they fall due.

(c) **Efficiency ratios**. The efficiency ratios (which are sometimes referred to as the "activity" ratios) provide some indication of the extent to which the assets of the business have been efficiently managed.

(d) **Investment ratios**. The investment ratios are mainly of interest to investors or potential investors and may help these users to decide whether or not a business represents a worthwhile investment. However, some of the investment ratios may be of interest to other user groups.

Most of the accounting ratios could be calculated for any kind of business entity (sole trader, partnership or limited company) but some of them are relevant only to companies. Since ratio analysis is most frequently applied to company accounts, it is assumed for the remainder of this chapter that the business for which ratios are being calculated is a limited company.

3. PROFITABILITY RATIOS

The main profitability ratios are:

(a) Return on capital employed
(b) Gross profit margin
(c) Net profit margin.

Return on capital employed (ROCE)

This important ratio expresses the company's net profit as a percentage of the amount of capital invested in the company. Unfortunately, there are several different ways of calculating ROCE, each using a different definition of the words "profit" and "capital employed". Two fairly common definitions are as follows:

(a) **Return on total capital**

$$\text{ROCE} = \frac{\text{Net profit before long-term loan interest and tax}}{\text{Share capital and reserves plus long-term loans}} \times 100\%$$

This version of the ratio interprets "capital" as the *total* amount of money invested in the company in the long term (regardless of whether that money has been supplied by shareholders or lenders). This amount is then compared with the return achieved on that capital. Since the denominator used in the calculation is equal to the total assets of the company less its current liabilities, this ratio is sometimes referred to as the *return on net assets*.

(b) **Return on equity capital**

$$\text{ROCE} = \frac{\text{Net profit after interest, tax and preference dividend}}{\text{Ordinary share capital and reserves}} \times 100\%$$

This version is calculated from the point of view of the ordinary shareholders and compares their capital with the amount of profit which has been earned on their behalf.

Ideally, any ROCE calculation should be based upon the *average* amount of capital employed in the company during the year and this can be approximated by averaging the opening and closing capital figures. However, the calculation of ROCE is often based upon closing capital only, since opening capital may not be known for all of the accounting years under review.

One way of judging the adequacy of a company's ROCE is to compare it with the return which could be expected from a risk-free investment such as a bank or building society deposit. If the company is seen as a high-risk investment, a comparatively high ROCE might be expected as compensation for this risk.

Gross profit margin

This ratio (which is sometimes referred to as the *gross profit percentage*) expresses a company's gross profit as a percentage of its sales revenue. The ratio is calculated as follows:

$$\text{Gross profit margin} = \frac{\text{Gross profit}}{\text{Sales}} \times 100\%$$

It would be very misleading to compare the gross profit margin of two totally dissimilar businesses (e.g. a jeweller and a supermarket) but a comparison between two companies in the same line of trade should be meaningful and might throw some light on the pricing policies adopted by each of the companies concerned.

Net profit margin

The net profit margin expresses a company's net profit as a percentage of its sales revenue. The ratio is calculated as follows:

$$\text{Net profit margin} = \frac{\text{Net profit before tax}}{\text{Sales}} \times 100\%$$

A year-on-year comparison of a company's net profit margin may reveal the extent to which the company's expenses are under control. For example, if the net profit margin has increased whilst the gross profit margin has remained stable, this might indicate that the company has been successful in trimming its overhead costs.

4. LIQUIDITY RATIOS

The main liquidity ratios are:

(a) The current ratio
(b) The quick assets ratio.

The current ratio

The purpose of the current ratio is to measure the company's ability to meet its short-term financial obligations out of its current assets. The current ratio is usually expressed as an actual ratio (e.g. 3:1) and is calculated as follows:

$$\text{Current ratio} = \frac{\text{Current assets}}{\text{Current liabilities}}$$

What is perceived as an acceptable level of current ratio will vary from one type of business to another. For example, a ratio of 1:1 may be perfectly adequate for a supermarket chain which has virtually no debtors and which rapidly converts its stocks into cash. On the other hand, a ratio of at least 2:1 might be seen as necessary for a manufacturing company which holds stocks for a longer period and then sells them on credit terms.

The quick assets ratio

In many cases, a company's stocks cannot be converted into cash at short notice and therefore the current ratio (which takes all current assets into account) may give an over-optimistic view of the company's liquidity. The quick assets ratio provides a more severe test of liquidity by omitting stocks from the calculation. The ratio is calculated as follows:

$$\text{Quick assets ratio} = \frac{\text{Current assets less stocks}}{\text{Current liabilities}}$$

Although a quick assets ratio of at least 1:1 might be seen as desirable, it should be borne in mind that some of the current liabilities shown in a company's balance sheet might not be payable immediately. For instance, the corporation tax liability does not fall due until nine months after the end of the accounting year. In these circumstances, a ratio of less than 1:1 might be acceptable. Note that the quick assets ratio is also known as the *acid test.*

5. EFFICIENCY RATIOS

The main efficiency ratios are:

(a) Fixed asset turnover
(b) Stock holding period
(c) Debtor collection period
(d) Creditor payment period.

Fixed asset turnover

This ratio measures the efficiency with which the company's fixed assets have been used to generate sales revenue. The ratio is usually calculated as follows:

$$\text{Fixed asset turnover} = \frac{\text{Sales}}{\text{Net book value of fixed assets}}$$

The use of net book value in the calculation means that the ratio is strongly affected by the company's depreciation policy. This should be borne in mind when comparing the fixed asset turnover of different companies (which may have different depreciation policies). If a company makes substantial acquisitions or disposals of fixed assets, the ratio should be calculated with reference to the *average* fixed assets held during the year (if this figure is available).

Stock holding period

The stock holding period is a measure of the average number of days which elapse between acquiring an item of stock and selling that item. The ratio is calculated as follows:

$$\text{Stock holding period (in days)} = \frac{\text{Average stock}}{\text{Cost of sales}} \times 365$$

The average stock for the year is usually approximated by averaging the opening and closing stock figures. If opening stock is not known, then there is no option but to base the calculation on closing stock only.

The stock-holding period (when compared with other businesses in the same trade) provides an indication of the efficiency with which a company manages its stocks. An efficient company will maintain as little stock as possible whilst ensuring that sufficient stock is always available to satisfy customer demand. Excessive stocks will be avoided since these tie up the company's money unnecessarily and may require costly warehousing.

Debtor collection period

The debtor collection period measures the average number of days which elapse between making a credit sale and receiving payment from the customer. The ratio is calculated as follows:

$$\text{Debtor collection period (in days)} = \frac{\text{Average trade debtors}}{\text{Credit sales}} \times 365$$

Closing debtors are sometimes substituted for average debtors if it is not possible to derive an average debtors figure.

The debtor collection period provides an insight into the credit terms offered to a company's customers. An increase in this period might indicate that the company is deliberately offering longer credit so as to attract more customers. Alternatively, an increase might suggest that the company's credit control system is not operating as efficiently as in previous years.

Creditor payment period

The creditor payment period measures the average number of days which elapse between the date of a credit purchase and the date on which payment is made to the supplier. The ratio is calculated as follows:

$$\text{Creditor payment period (in days)} = \frac{\text{Average trade creditors}}{\text{Credit purchases}} \times 365$$

If average creditors cannot be ascertained, the ratio might be based upon closing creditors instead. A substantial increase in a company's creditor payment period when compared with previous years might suggest that the company is experiencing difficulty in paying its creditors and is in danger of being refused further credit.

6. INVESTMENT RATIOS

The main investment ratios are:

(a) Earnings per share
(b) Price earnings ratio
(c) Dividend cover
(d) Dividend yield
(e) Capital gearing ratio
(f) Interest cover.

Earnings per share (EPS)

Earnings per share (EPS) is the amount of profit (in pence) which has been earned for each ordinary share. This ratio is frequently used as an indicator of financial performance and is calculated as follows:

$$\text{EPS} = \frac{\text{Net profit after tax and preference dividends}}{\text{Number of ordinary shares in issue}} \times 100\text{p}$$

The importance attached to EPS is attested by the fact that it is the subject of accounting standard SSAP3 (see Chapter 15).

Price earnings (P/E) ratio

The P/E ratio compares earnings per share with the market price of an ordinary share and calculates the number of years which it would take to recover the market price paid for a share if earnings remained constant in future years. The ratio is calculated as follows:

$$\text{Price earnings ratio} = \frac{\text{Market price per ordinary share}}{\text{Earnings per share}}$$

It might appear that shares with a low P/E ratio would be regarded as an attractive investment. In fact, high P/E ratios are usually viewed more favourably than low ones. This is because the market price of a share reflects the stock market's expectations of the company's *future* performance.

Therefore a high P/E ratio is seen as an indication that the company's shares will perform well in the future.

Dividend cover

Dividend cover is a measure of the number of times that the ordinary dividend for a year could have been paid out of the available profits. The ratio is calculated as follows:

$$\text{Dividend cover} = \frac{\text{Net profit after tax and preference dividends}}{\text{Ordinary dividends}}$$

A high dividend cover indicates that the company is retaining a substantial part of its profits. This policy might not be popular with the ordinary shareholders but at least the high level of cover means that profits are more than adequate to fund the dividends paid. On the other hand, a low dividend cover might indicate that the company is having difficulty in maintaining an acceptable level of dividend.

Dividend yield

The dividend yield expresses the dividend per ordinary share as a percentage of the market price per ordinary share. The calculation is as follows:

$$\text{Dividend yield} = \frac{\text{Dividends per ordinary share}}{\text{Market price per ordinary share}} \times 100\%$$

This ratio acts as an indicator of the cash return received on the investment made by an ordinary shareholder. Whilst a low dividend yield might deter an investor who views the shares primarily as a source of income, a dividend yield of even 0% might not deter an investor whose main concern is capital growth.

Capital gearing ratio

The capital gearing ratio measures the proportion of a company's long-term funds which have been provided by lenders. There are several different ways of calculating this ratio, but a frequently-used method of calculation is as follows:

$$\text{Gearing} = \frac{\text{Preference share capital plus long-term loans}}{\text{Share capital and reserves plus long-term loans}} \times 100\%$$

The reason for regarding preference shares as a form of borrowing for this purpose is that preference shares attract a fixed rate of dividend in much the same way as a loan attracts a fixed rate of interest. No dividend can be paid to the ordinary shareholders until loan interest and the preference dividend have both been paid.

A company with a high gearing ratio is known as a "high-geared" company and such a company represents a high-risk investment for the ordinary shareholder. In a difficult year, the need to pay the loan interest and preference dividend may mean that the ordinary shareholders will receive no dividend at all. Furthermore, if the company runs into financial trouble and is forced into liquidation, there may be insufficient funds to repay the ordinary share capital after the loans and preference shares have been repaid. Conversely, a low-geared company represents a comparatively low-risk investment for the ordinary shareholder.

The words "high" and "low" cannot be defined in absolute terms and a company's gearing ratio must be judged in context. For instance, a gearing ratio which might be regarded as perfectly acceptable in the case of a sound company with steadily rising profits and excellent prospects might be judged as worryingly high if it applied to a less successful company.

Interest cover

Interest cover is a measure of the number of times that the loan interest payable for a year could have been paid out of the available profits. The ratio is calculated as follows:

$$\text{Interest cover} = \frac{\text{Net profit before long-term loan interest and tax}}{\text{Long-term loan interest payable}}$$

This ratio is especially significant to the providers of long-term loans. A high figure for interest cover indicates that lenders are in a relatively secure position and that the company's profits could fall substantially before there was any likelihood that interest payments could not be met. On the other hand, lenders (and potential lenders) might lose confidence in the company if interest cover is low.

COMPREHENSIVE EXAMPLE

Quantock plc is a trading company which makes all of its sales and purchases on credit terms. The company's profit and loss accounts for the years to 31 December 19X8 and 19X9, together with the company's balance sheets on those dates, are shown below.

Quantock plc
Profit and loss accounts for the year to 31 December

	19X8	*19X9*
	£'000	£'000
Turnover	4,550	5,000
Cost of sales	3,330	3,660
Gross profit	1,220	1,340
Net operating expenses	400	380
Operating profit	820	960
Interest payable	100	80
Profit on ordinary activities before taxation	720	880
Tax on profit on ordinary activities	210	250
Profit on ordinary activities after taxation c/f	510	630

	19X8	19X9
	£'000	£'000
Profit on ordinary activities after taxation b/f	510	630
Proposed dividends	300	330
Retained profit for the financial year	210	300
Retained profit brought forward	420	630
Retained profit carried forward	630	930

Quantock plc
Balance sheets as at 31 December

		19X8		19X9
		£'000		£'000
Fixed assets				
Tangible assets		1,820		1,730
Current assets				
Stocks (*19X7 £670,000*)	690		740	
Trade debtors	760		820	
Cash at bank and in hand	340		560	
	1,790		2,120	
Creditors: Amounts falling due within one year				
Trade creditors	470		540	
Taxation	210		250	
Dividends	300		330	
	980		1,120	
Net current assets		810		1,000
Total assets less current liabilities		2,630		2,730
Creditors: Amounts falling due after more than one year				
Debenture loans		1,000		800
		1,630		1,930
Capital and reserves				
Called-up share capital				
Ordinary shares of £1		1,000		1,000
Profit and loss account		630		930
		1,630		1,930

The market price of the company's ordinary shares was 275p per share on 31 December 19X8 and 350p per share on 31 December 19X9.

Calculate a set of accounting ratios (for each of the two years) which may be used to judge the company's profitability, liquidity, efficiency and investment potential.

SOLUTION

Profitability	*19X8*	*19X9*
Return on total capital	$\frac{820}{2,630} \times 100\% = 31.2\%$	$\frac{960}{2,730} \times 100\% = 35.2\%$
Return on equity capital	$\frac{510}{1,630} \times 100\% = 31.3\%$	$\frac{630}{1,930} \times 100\% = 32.6\%$
Gross profit margin	$\frac{1,220}{4,550} \times 100\% = 26.8\%$	$\frac{1,340}{5,000} \times 100\% = 26.8\%$
Net profit margin	$\frac{720}{4,550} \times 100\% = 15.8\%$	$\frac{880}{5,000} \times 100\% = 17.6\%$

These ratios indicate that the business was more profitable in 19X9 than it was in 19X8. Both versions of ROCE show an improvement and although the gross profit margin was the same in both years, the net profit margin in 19X9 was much better than in 19X8. This was partly due to the fact that the company managed to reduce its operating expenses in 19X9 despite increasing its turnover.

Note:
For the sake of simplicity and to avoid making too many assumptions, the ROCE calculations have been based upon the closing capital in each year.

Liquidity	*19X8*	*19X9*
Current ratio	$\frac{1,790}{980} = 1.8$ to 1	$\frac{2,120}{1,120} = 1.9$ to 1
Quick assets ratio	$\frac{1,630 - 690}{980} = 1.1$ to 1	$\frac{2,120 - 740}{1,120} = 1.2$ to 1

Both of these ratios show a small improvement in 19X9 and the company does not seem to have any liquidity problems, despite having repaid £200,000 of debenture loans during 19X9.

Efficiency	*19X8*	*19X9*
Fixed asset turnover	$\frac{4,550}{1,820} = 2.5$	$\frac{5,000}{1,730} = 2.9$
Stock holding period	$\frac{680}{3,330} \times 365 = 75$ days	$\frac{715}{3,660} \times 365 = 71$ days
Debtor collection period	$\frac{760}{4,550} \times 365 = 61$ days	$\frac{820}{5,000} \times 365 = 60$ days
Creditor payment period	$\frac{470}{3,350} \times 365 = 51$ days	$\frac{540}{3,710} \times 365 = 53$ days

The fixed asset turnover highlights the fact that the company has managed to achieve an increase in sales without increasing its fixed assets. The stock holding period (based on the average stock in each year) shows a small reduction for 19X9 which may indicate a more efficient stock control policy. The debtor collection and creditor payment periods both show small improvements.

Note:
The purchases figures used in the calculation of the creditor payment period are derived by adjusting cost of sales to take account of opening and closing stocks.

Investment	*19X8*	*19X9*
Earnings per share	$\frac{510}{1,000} = 51p$	$\frac{630}{1,000} = 63p$
Price earnings ratio	$\frac{275}{51} = 5.4$	$\frac{350}{63} = 5.6$
Dividend cover	$\frac{510}{300} = 1.7$	$\frac{630}{330} = 1.9$
Dividend yield	$\frac{30}{275} \times 100\% = 10.9\%$	$\frac{33}{350} \times 100\% = 9.4\%$
Capital gearing ratio	$\frac{1,000}{2,630} \times 100\% = 38\%$	$\frac{800}{2,730} \times 100\% = 29\%$
Interest cover	$\frac{820}{100} = 8.2$	$\frac{960}{80} = 12$

Virtually all of these ratios indicate that the company is a good investment. Earnings per share increased in 19X9 and the stock market's regard for the shares (as indicated by the P/E ratio) also increased. The dividend yield went down but the dividend itself increased by 10% and dividend cover was adequate. The company is becoming more low-geared as the debentures are redeemed and the interest cover gives no cause for concern.

7. LIMITATIONS OF RATIO ANALYSIS

Although ratio analysis is an extremely useful and powerful tool for the analysis and interpretation of financial statements, it is subject to a number of limitations. Some of the more important limitations of ratio analysis are as follows:

(a) **Lack of standard definitions**. As we have seen, some accounting ratios may be defined in more than one way. This makes it difficult to compare ratios calculated by different accountants, each of whom might have used different definitions for the same ratios. It is very important that users should be aware of this problem when basing important economic decisions on information provided in the form of a ratio analysis.

(b) **Unrepresentative balance sheet figures**. A balance sheet shows only a snapshot of a company's financial position on a single date, whereas a profit and loss account covers an entire accounting year. Therefore, if the company's assets and liabilities on the balance sheet date are not typical of the year as a whole, any ratio which combines a balance sheet figure with a figure drawn from the profit and loss account might produce a misleading result. The usual solution to this problem is to average the figures shown in the opening and closing balance sheets, but this will be of little help if the company's balance sheet is affected every year by recurring seasonal factors.

(c) **Accounting policies**. A company's accounting policies with regard to such matters as depreciation and the valuation of stock might be very different to those of another company. These differences in policy may have a significant impact on accounting ratios and can make it difficult to effect a meaningful comparison between the companies concerned.

(d) **Misinterpretation**. Accounting ratios are open to misinterpretation unless all available evidence is taken into account. For example, a reduction in a company's gross profit margin might be interpreted as a bad sign, when in fact the company has deliberately dropped prices so as to boost sales. Similarly, a small increase in return on capital employed might be regarded as encouraging until it is discovered that most companies in the same sector have achieved a much larger increase. It is essential that ratios are judged collectively rather than singly, that a given company's ratios are compared with those of other companies in the same field and that anyone performing a ratio analysis is aware of background factors such as the overall economic climate, the rate of inflation, trends in interest rates etc.

8. SUMMARY

- Ratio analysis is a technique for the analysis and interpretation of the information contained in financial statements.
- Accounting ratios may be used to compare one year with another for the same business or to compare one business with another.
- The most commonly-used accounting ratios can be classified into four main groups. These are profitability ratios, liquidity ratios, efficiency ratios and investment ratios.
- Ratio analysis is subject to a number of limitations which should be borne in mind when basing economic decisions upon the results of a ratio analysis.

EXERCISES 19

19.1 The summarised accounts of Roscoe Ltd for the year to 30 April 19X9 are shown below.

Roscoe Ltd
Profit and loss account for the year to 30 April 19X9

		£'000
Turnover		410
Cost of sales		235
Gross profit		175
Net operating expenses		115
Operating profit		60
Interest payable		15
Profit on ordinary activities before taxation		45
Tax on profit on ordinary activities		10
Profit on ordinary activities after taxation		35
Proposed dividends:		
Preference shares	1	
Ordinary shares	20	21
Retained profit for the year		14
Retained profit brought forward		5
Retained profit carried forward		19

Roscoe Ltd
Balance sheet as at 30 April 19X9

	£'000	£'000
Fixed assets		208
Current assets		
Stocks	82	
Trade debtors	58	
Cash at bank	7	
	147	
Current liabilities		
Trade creditors	45	
Taxation	10	
Proposed dividends	21	
	76	
Net current assets		71
		279
10% Debentures		150
		129

	£'000
Financed by	
10% Preference shares of £1	10
Ordinary shares of £1	100
Profit and loss account	19
	129

Required:

Insofar as the information given permits, calculate the following ratios for Roscoe Ltd for the year to 30 April 19X9, stating any assumptions made:

(a) Return on total capital employed
(b) Return on equity capital
(c) Gross profit margin
(d) Net profit margin
(e) Current ratio
(f) Quick assets ratio
(g) Stock holding period
(h) Debtor collection period
(i) Creditor payment period
(j) Capital gearing ratio
(k) Interest cover
(l) Dividend cover
(m) Earnings per share.

19.2 Company X is an old-established clothing retailer. The company operates from expensive city centre premises and offers a high standard of customer service. The company's customers are willing to pay top prices so as to shop in comfort and many of them take advantage of the generous credit terms available.

Company Y is a recently-established clothing retailer. The company operates from a self-service store on the outskirts of the city and employs as few staff as possible. The company's "no frills" approach appeals to customers who wish to buy clothes as cheaply as possible. In general, customers are encouraged to pay for their purchases immediately, but certain regular customers have a monthly account with the company.

Required:

Explain how these differences between Company X and Company Y might be reflected in their accounting ratios.

19.3 The issued share capital of Sorensen plc consists of 1,000,000 ordinary shares of 50p each and 250,000 6% preference shares of £1 each. The preference dividend is payable half-yearly.

In the year to 31 March 19X9, the company's net profit after tax was £90,000. Interim dividends paid during the year consisted of the first half-year's preference dividend and an ordinary dividend amounting to £25,000. Proposed dividends at the end of the year comprised the remainder of the preference dividend and an ordinary dividend of £30,000. The market price of the company's ordinary shares on 31 March 19X9 was 70p per share.

Required:

Calculate the following ratios for Sorensen plc:

(a) Earnings per share
(b) Dividend cover
(c) Dividend yield
(d) Price earnings ratio.

***19.4** During the year to 31 December 19X9, Timberlake Ltd has attempted to stimulate sales and increase its profits by reducing selling prices, holding larger stocks and giving customers longer credit. All of the company's purchases and sales are on credit terms. The summarised accounts for the years to 31 December 19X8 and 19X9 are as follows:

Timberlake Ltd
Profit and loss accounts for the year to 31 December

	19X8	*19X9*
	£'000	£'000
Turnover	3,725	5,327
Cost of sales	2,905	4,420
Gross profit	820	907
Net operating expenses	75	87
Operating profit	745	820
Interest payable	20	130
Profit on ordinary activities before taxation	725	690
Tax on profit on ordinary activities	225	215
Profit on ordinary activities after taxation	500	475
Dividends	400	400
Retained profit	100	75

Timberlake Ltd
Balance sheets as at 31 December

		19X8		*19X9*
		£'000		£'000
Fixed assets		5,100		5,520
Current assets				
Stocks	730		1,334	
Debtors	596		1,278	
Bank	400		11	
	1,726		2,623	
Current liabilities				
Trade creditors	618		1,020	
Taxation	225		215	
Dividends	400		400	
	1,243		1,635	
Net current assets		483		988
		5,583		6,508
Long term liabilities				
Debenture loans		150		1,000
		5,433		5,508

	19X8	19X9
	£'000	£'000
Capital and reserves		
Ordinary shares of £1	2,000	2,000
Profit and loss account	3,433	3,508
	5,433	5,508

Required:

Calculate the following ratios for Timberlake Ltd for each of the two years concerned and comment on your results:

(a) Return on total capital employed

(b) Return on equity capital

(c) Gross profit margin

(d) Net profit margin

(e) Current ratio

(f) Quick assets ratio

(g) Stock holding period

(h) Debtor collection period

(i) Capital gearing ratio.

20

ACCOUNTING FOR INFLATION

Chapter objectives

When you have finished this chapter, you should be able to:

- **Recognise the main limitations of historic cost accounting in times of inflation.**
- **Explain briefly how current purchasing power (CPP) accounting attempts to overcome the limitations of historic cost accounting.**
- **Explain briefly how current cost accounting (CCA) attempts to overcome the limitations of historic cost accounting.**

1. INTRODUCTION

One of the accounting conventions introduced in Chapter 2 of this book was the *stable monetary unit* convention, which allows changes in the purchasing power of money to be neglected when financial statements are prepared. In other words, the effects of inflation are ignored.

The stable monetary unit convention certainly makes accounting easier. However, the purchasing power of money does decline over time and there is no doubt that financial statements which disregard this fact suffer from a number of limitations. The purpose of this final chapter is to assess the validity of conventional financial statements and to consider alternative ways of preparing financial statements so as to take inflation into account.

2. LIMITATIONS OF HISTORIC COST ACCOUNTING

The term *historic cost accounting* refers to the traditional method of accounting whereby expenditure is recorded at historic cost and no attempt is made to adjust recorded costs so as to take account of inflation. Although this approach is used almost exclusively in practice, the traditional profit and loss account and balance sheet both have serious weaknesses, as explained below.

Overstated profits

It is fairly obvious that the main objective of preparing a profit and loss account is to calculate the amount of profit earned by a business during an accounting period. It is less obvious that a conventional profit and loss account (which ignores the effects of inflation) does not really achieve this objective. It might be helpful to define what we mean by the term "profit". The following definition is based upon one which was coined by Sir John Hicks in 1930:

> The profit for an accounting period is "*the amount which the owner of a business can consume and still be as well off at the end of the period as he or she was at the start of the period*".

Another way of putting this is to say that profit is equal to the net amount which could be withdrawn from a business whilst maintaining its capital intact. This means that the measurement of profit depends upon being able to measure and compare the capital (or net assets) of a business at the beginning and end of an accounting period. There are essentially three different approaches to this problem:

(a) **Money capital maintenance**. This approach measures capital in money terms with no regard to changes in the purchasing power of money. A business which has capital of £x at the start of an accounting period and £y at the end of that period is assumed to have made a profit of £y – £x. This is, of course, the conventional approach to profit measurement.

(b) **General purchasing power maintenance**. This approach measures the capital of a business in terms of its general purchasing power (using the Retail Prices Index as a guide) and regards profit as the amount by which the general purchasing power of the business has increased during an accounting period.

(c) **Specific purchasing power maintenance**. This approach measures the capital of a business in terms of its purchasing power with regard to the specific items which the business needs to buy. Profit is defined as the increase in the specific purchasing power of the business during an accounting period.

In times of inflation, a conventional profit and loss account (which adopts the money capital maintenance approach) actually overstates the amount of profit earned by a business, as illustrated by the following example.

EXAMPLE

At the beginning of an accounting period, a business had cash of £1,000 and capital of £1,000. The cash was spent on acquiring stock which was all sold during the accounting period for £1,250. There were no other transactions.

(a) Calculate the profit for the period in money terms.

(b) If the Retail Prices Index (RPI) stood at 100 on the first day of the accounting period and at 110 on the last day of the period, calculate the profit for the period in terms of the general purchasing power of the business.

(c) If it would cost £1,130 at the end of the accounting period to replace the sold stock, calculate the profit in terms of the power of the business specifically to acquire stock for resale.

SOLUTION

	Money capital	*General purchasing power*	*Specific purchasing power*
	£	£	£
Assets at the end of the accounting period	1,250	1,250	1,250
Assets required at the end of the accounting period to be as well off as at the beginning of the period:			
(a) in money terms	1,000		
(b) general purchasing power (£1,000 x 110/100)		1,100	
(c) specific purchasing power			1,130
Net profit for the period	250	150	120

(a) In money terms, the business is £250 better off at the end of the accounting period. This is the profit figure which would be shown in a conventional profit and loss account.

(b) £1,100 is needed at the end of the accounting period to give the same general purchasing power as was given by £1,000 at the start of the period. Since the business has capital of £1,250 at the end of the period, its profit is calculated as £1,250 – £1,100 = £150.

(c) £1,130 is needed at the end of the accounting period to buy the same stocks as could be bought for £1,000 at the start of the period. Since the business has capital of £1,250 at the end of the period, its profit is calculated as £1,250 – £1,130 = £120.

As predicted, the conventional approach has overstated the profit figure. In fact, no more than £150 can be withdrawn from the business without reducing its general purchasing power and no more than £120 can be withdrawn without reducing the power of the business to replace its stocks. If conventionally-calculated profits were withdrawn in full each year, the business would suffer depletion of its capital. This would lead to a reduction in the operating capability of the business and, in the long run, to its eventual closure.

Inadequate depreciation charges

The sole purpose of depreciation in conventional accounting is to allocate the historic cost of a fixed asset to the profit and loss account over its useful life. However, a desirable side-effect of charging depreciation is that reported profits are reduced. This may act as a restraint on the amount of money drawn out of the business by its owner(s) and so make it more likely that funds will be available to replace fixed assets when necessary (though there is no guarantee that sufficient funds will be available in liquid form). The fact that inflation is usually ignored when calculating depreciation causes a number of problems:

(a) In the profit and loss account, sales revenue measured in current £'s is matched against depreciation charges calculated in historical £'s. If elderly fixed assets are still being depreciated or if inflation is running at a high rate (or both) there may be a great disparity between the value of these £'s and this must throw doubt on the validity and usefulness of the profit figure.

(b) The total amount of depreciation charged over the years in relation to a fixed asset will be less than its replacement cost. Profits will be overstated and may be over-distributed, so causing capital depletion.

EXAMPLE

A business starts trading with capital of £10,000. This is spent upon the acquisition of a fixed asset with a useful life of five years and no residual value. Depreciation is charged at 20% per annum on cost. The owner of the business withdraws the profits in full at the end of each accounting year. Will the business be able to replace the fixed asset at the end of its useful life, given that its replacement cost is £12,000?

SOLUTION

At the end of five years, the balance sheet will show capital of £10,000 and net assets of £10,000. Even if these net assets are entirely in liquid form, the business will not be able to replace the fixed asset without a capital injection (or loan) of £2,000. The conventional profit and loss accounts have overstated profits for the last five years and, as a consequence, the capital of the business (measured in specific purchasing power terms) has been depleted by £2,000.

Gains and losses on monetary items not disclosed

Monetary items are assets or liabilities which are fixed in monetary terms. Common examples of monetary items are debtors, creditors, loans and cash. In a period of inflation, a business loses purchasing power by holding monetary assets but gains purchasing power by holding monetary liabilities. However, these gains and losses are not revealed at all in a conventional profit and loss account. It can be argued that this is another shortcoming of the conventional approach to financial accounting.

EXAMPLE

At the start of an accounting year (when the RPI is 100) a business borrows £5,000 at an interest rate of 12% per annum. The loan is still outstanding at the end of the year (when the RPI has increased to 108).

(a) How will this loan be dealt with in the conventional profit and loss account drawn up for the year?

(b) Calculate the real cost of the loan to the business for the accounting year.

SOLUTION

(a) The profit and loss account will be debited with interest of £600.

(b) If the loan were fixed in terms of general purchasing power, the business would owe £5,400 (£5,000 x 108/100) at the end of the accounting year. However, as the loan is fixed in monetary terms, the business still owes only £5,000 and has gained purchasing power of £400 during the year. The real cost of the loan is only £200 (£600 – £400).

Holding gains on stocks not identified

During a period of inflation, any stock of goods held by a business for an appreciable amount of time will increase in monetary value. Such an increase is known as a *holding gain*. In a conventional profit and loss account, holding gains are not shown separately but are simply treated as part of the gross profit arising on the sale of goods. It has been suggested that the profit and loss account would be more useful if the gross profit were analysed so that holding gains were clearly identified.

Unrealistic fixed asset values

A combination of the historic cost convention and the realisation convention means that fixed assets are normally shown in a balance sheet at historic cost and that any increases in fixed asset values are not recognised until they are realised. As a consequence, a conventional balance sheet often fails to show the true financial position of a business, especially if the business owns assets (such as freehold land) which have been subject to substantial price increases since acquisition.

Furthermore, the historic costs of all the fixed assets owned by a business are added together in a conventional balance sheet, regardless of the fact that these costs have been incurred in different years. Adding together the £3,000 paid for a freehold property in 1960 and the £100,000 paid for a similar property in 1997 seems to serve no useful purpose and yet the system of historic cost accounting requires that these two figures should be aggregated.

Because of these problems, some businesses have now adopted the policy of showing land and buildings in the balance sheet at current value rather than at historic cost.

Misleading accounting ratios

As explained in Chapter 19, accounting ratios are often used as a tool for the analysis and interpretation of financial statements. However, the limitations of historic cost accounting suggest that it may be unwise to base economic decisions on a ratio analysis of figures shown in a conventional set of accounts.

EXAMPLE

A company's profit and loss account shows a pre-tax profit of £100,000. The average net assets employed by the company are shown in the balance sheet as £500,000. The company's financial statements are prepared on the historic cost basis.

(a) Calculate the company's return on capital employed (ROCE).

(b) When the financial statements are amended to take account of inflation, it transpires that the pre-tax profit has been overstated and the company's net assets have been understated. The revised figures are £60,000 and £1,200,000 respectively. Recalculate ROCE.

SOLUTION

(a) ROCE = 100,000/500,000 x 100% = 20%.

(b) The revised ROCE is 60,000/1,200,000 x 100%, which is only 5%. Clearly, anyone conducting a ratio analysis of conventional financial statements should be very mindful of the limitations of historic cost accounting.

Misleading comparisons over time

One way of assessing the progress made by a business is to compare its most recent results with those achieved in previous years. However, comparisons of this nature can be misleading if the effects of inflation are neglected. For instance, a 10% increase in sales from one year to the next might be seen as encouraging, but if this occurs against a background of 12% inflation, the sales revenue of the business has declined in real terms.

3. ALTERNATIVES TO HISTORIC COST ACCOUNTING

Despite its limitations, historic cost accounting has some distinct strengths. It is a comparatively simple accounting system that all accountants understand. It is also well-established, having served the needs of users for several centuries. Furthermore, it possesses the important characteristic of objectivity, in that the historic cost of an asset is an objective fact (though it must be admitted that some of this objectivity is lost when depreciation calculations are performed).

However, the limitations described above are sufficiently serious to have fuelled the search for alternative accounting systems. Not surprisingly, this search was at its most intense in the 1970's and 1980's (when inflation was running at record levels) but the various proposals put forward at that time generated more controversy than agreement and all of them were eventually abandoned. The comparatively low levels of inflation experienced in the 1990's have lessened the urgency of the search and no new proposals seem to be forthcoming at present. A brief summary of the most important proposals to date is given below.

Current purchasing power accounting and current cost accounting

Proposed alternatives to historic cost accounting can be classified into two main categories. These are *current purchasing power* accounting and *current cost* accounting.

(a) **Current purchasing power (CPP) accounting**. CPP accounting adopts the approach known as general purchasing power maintenance (see earlier in this chapter). Basically, each transaction shown in the historic cost accounts is adjusted to reflect the change in the general purchasing power of money since the transaction took place, as measured by the Retail Prices Index. The CPP accounts emerge as the result of this process.

CPP accounting is fairly straightforward but suffers from the disadvantage that the RPI (in common with other general inflation indices) does not measure the effects of inflation on the specific business for which accounts are being prepared.

(b) **Current cost accounting (CCA)**. CCA adopts the approach referred to earlier in this chapter as specific purchasing power maintenance. The basic principle of current cost accounting is that assets should be shown in the balance sheet at their *current value*, which is usually their replacement cost.

Current cost accounting was the subject of accounting standard SSAP16, which was issued in 1980. SSAP16 attempted to resolve most of the problems caused by the effects of inflation and required that a complex series of adjustments should be made to the historic cost accounts. The standard met fierce resistance, partly from a theoretical standpoint and partly because of its practical complexity. SSAP16 was finally withdrawn in 1988.

With the abandonment of SSAP16, attempts to remedy the limitations of historic cost accounting in times of inflation seem to have ground to a halt. The vast majority of businesses still prepare historic cost accounts, though some businesses show land and buildings in the balance sheet at current value, as was mentioned earlier.

The Exposure Draft of the ASB Statement of Principles, issued in November 1995, lends its support to the use of current values in certain circumstances but this Statement is not an accounting standard and has no mandatory application. Indeed, the ASB has made it very clear that it has no plans to impose a mandatory system of current cost accounting and has stated that "*current cost accounting is not on the agenda*".

In these circumstances, it is extremely important that the users of conventional financial statements should be aware of the limitations of historic cost accounting and should bear these limitations in mind when basing economic decisions on the information provided in those statements.

4. SUMMARY

- The stable monetary unit convention, which underlies conventional financial accounting, allows changes in the purchasing power of money to be ignored when preparing financial statements.

- Conventional financial accounting is often referred to as historic cost accounting, since expenditure is recorded at historic cost and no attempt is made to adjust costs to take account of inflation.
- Financial statements prepared in accordance with the historic cost convention suffer from a number of limitations, especially at a time of rapid inflation. Profits are generally overstated, gains and losses on monetary items are not disclosed and holding gains on stocks are not separately identified. Accounting ratios and comparisons made between one year and another may both be misleading.
- The search for an agreed alternative to historic cost accounting has not yet been successful. Neither current purchasing power (CPP) accounting nor current cost accounting (CCA) has attracted widespread support.

EXERCISES 20

20.1 Summarise the main limitations of financial statements which have been prepared on the historic cost basis at a time of rising prices.

***20.2** Explain the meaning of the following terms in relation to the problem of measuring the profit of a business:

(a) money capital maintenance

(b) general purchasing power maintenance

(c) specific purchasing power maintenance.

***20.3** Briefly distinguish between current purchasing power (CPP) accounting and current cost accounting (CCA).

ANSWERS TO EXERCISES

Chapter 1

1.1

In summary, the main users of accounting information are as follows (further detail can be found in the text of Chapter 1):

- Management, who need highly detailed and frequent information relating to the past, present and projected future activities of the business. Examples might be a sales forecast, an expenditure analysis, a report on the cost of manufacturing a product.
- Owners, investors, potential owners/investors, business analysts, banks, lenders, suppliers, customers, employees, competitors, the Government and the general public, all of whom require information about the financial performance and financial position of the business. In some cases, information which takes the form of forecasts for the future is just as important as historical information.

One set of accounting information is unlikely to meet the needs of all user groups for a number of reasons. Some of these reasons are:

- The information needs of management are very different from the needs of all other user groups.
- Some users need historical information (e.g. the tax authorities) whilst others need forecast information (e.g. banks).
- Some users can cope with complex financial reports (business analysts) whilst others may need fairly simple information (employees and many company shareholders).

1.2

(a) The purpose of management accounting is to provide information to support planning and control decisions made by managers. The purpose of financial accounting is to provide financial statements which help support the decisions made by owners, investors and other external users.

(b) Management accounting information is detailed, required frequently, for internal use, specified by management and often incorporates forecasts/projections.

Financial accounting information is summarised, produced annually, for external use, to some extent specified by legal requirements and mainly historical.

1.3

The main desirable qualities are:

- **Relevance**. Accounting information should be relevant to user needs. Relevance may be either predictive or confirmatory.
- **Reliability**. Accounting information should be complete, free from error or bias, prepared and presented neutrally and (as far as possible) objectively.
- **Comparability**. Accounting information should be prepared and presented in a consistent manner so as to facilitate comparisons.

- **Understandability**. Accounting information should be pitched at a level which the intended users will understand.

Information might not possess all of these qualities for a number of reasons. Firstly, the deadlines by which the information must be produced may make it necessary to estimate some figures, so reducing reliability. Secondly, the cost of producing high-quality information might be prohibitive. Finally, the desirable qualities may conflict, making it necessary to strike an appropriate balance between them.

Chapter 2

2.1

(a) Accounting standards provide guidance on the correct treatment of specific accounting problems. They are published by the Accounting Standards Board in the UK and it is obligatory for most companies to adhere to most of the standards.

(b) Accounting conventions are derived from the accumulated experience gained over centuries of accounting practice. In the absence of a proper conceptual framework, the conventions provide a set of accounting rules which underpin the work of financial accountants.

2.2

See the text of Chapter 2.

2.3

(a) The matching convention requires that the profit and loss account for the year to 30 September should include an estimate of the accrued telephone charges for the final month of the accounting year. The prepaid insurance premium (i.e. the part of the premium which relates to the period from 1 October to 31 December) should be shown as an expense in the following year's profit and loss account.

(b) The value of the reputation and goodwill of a business cannot reliably be expressed in money terms. Therefore, the money measurement convention requires that this asset is not shown in the financial statements. Even if a valuation could be obtained, the prudence convention would probably dictate that this asset should be ignored.

(c) The historic cost convention requires that the land is shown in the balance sheet at its historic cost of £10,000. The increased market value is ignored.

(d) The prudence convention requires that the potential bankruptcy is taken into account and that the balance sheet is adjusted to reflect this. The likelihood is that the business will make a provision for doubtful debts (see Chapter 7).

(e) Strict application of the matching convention requires that the stock of unused clips is measured and that their cost is shown as an expense in the following year's profit and loss account, not the current year's profit and loss account. However, the materiality convention will overrule this treatment and the cost of the entire box of clips will be shown as an expense in the current year's accounts.

(f) The business entity convention states that this transaction should be totally ignored when preparing the financial statements of the business.

(g) The business entity convention implies that a business may owe money to its owner and vice-versa. In this case, the owner owes money to the business and this fact should be reflected in the financial statements.

(h) The realisation convention requires the sale to be recognised in the accounting period in which the goods are passed to the customer, regardless of when payment takes place.

(i) The realisation convention ensures that the sale is recognised when the goods are passed to the customer and that the anticipated income from the sale is shown as revenue in the profit and loss account. The bad debt represents an expense which must be charged to the profit and loss account (see Chapter 7).

(j) The duality convention requires that the dual effect of this transaction is reflected in the financial statements. The liabilities of the business and its bank balance are both reduced as a consequence of the loan repayment.

Chapter 3

3.1

(a) This is an item of stock for resale (a current asset) and should be included at £1,500 (its historic cost) in the stock figure which is shown on the balance sheet at 31 December 19X9. To value the computer at its selling price of £2,000 would anticipate the profit on the sale, which has not yet been realised.

(b) This computer is not owned and controlled by the business and therefore falls outside the definition of an asset. It should not be shown on the balance sheet.

(c) This computer can provide no future economic benefit to the business. Therefore it cannot be regarded as an asset and should not be shown on the balance sheet.

(d) This computer has passed out of the control of the business and should not be shown on the balance sheet. When Ian took the computer, his capital should have been reduced by £800 and stock should have been reduced by £800.

(e) The premises should be shown as a fixed asset at their historic cost of £50,000.

(f) This is a long-term liability and should be shown on the balance sheet as such.

(g) Ian's home has not arisen as the result of a past business transaction, it is not under the control of the business and it will provide no future economic benefit to the business. It is not a business asset and it should be omitted from the balance sheet.

(h) This is a £27,400 trade creditor (a current liability).

(i) This is a £1,800 trade debtor (a current asset).

(j) Bank overdrafts are (at least in principle) repayable on demand. Therefore the overdraft of £13,750 should be shown as a current liability.

3.2

Assets are £12,670 + £35 + £21,950 + £54,000 + £3,500 = £92,155.

Liabilities are £17,850 + £4,800 = £22,650.

Therefore capital must be £92,155 – £22,650 = £69,505.

3.3

On 1 May 19X7, capital was £23,560 – £11,650 = £11,910.

On 30 April 19X8, capital was £25,880 – £9,890 = £15,990.

Closing capital = opening capital + capital injections + profit – drawings. In this case £15,990 = £11,910 + £0 + profit – £15,600 . Therefore profit must be £19,680.

3.4

Jill
Balance sheet as at 6 January 19X8

	£	£
Fixed assets		
Equipment		2,500
Motor van		7,200
		9,700
Current assets		
Stock of goods for resale (£6,200 – £2,200 – £2,800)	1,200	
Trade debtors	2,960	
Cash at bank (£20,000 – £7,200 – £3,100 + £3,880)	13,580	
	17,740	
Current liabilities		
Trade creditors	3,100	
Net current assets		14,640
Total assets less current liabilities		24,340
Capital		
Capital introduced (£20,000 + £2,500)	22,500	
Profit for the period (£760 + £1,080)	1,840	24,340
		24,340

Chapter 4

4.1

Trading account for the year to 30 June 19X9

	£	£	£
Sales			37,850
Less: Returns inwards			1,830
			36,020
Cost of goods sold:			
Stock as at 1 July 19X8		2,950	
Purchases	23,870		
Carriage inwards	370		
	24,240		
Less: Returns outwards	560	23,680	
		26,630	
Less: Stock as at 30 June 19X9		3,190	23,440
Gross profit			12,580

Note:

Carriage outwards is a distribution expense and is shown in the profit and loss account.

4.2

The sale to a regular customer would be recorded at £2,800 and included at that figure in the sales figure for the year. The £200 trade discount would not be mentioned anywhere at all in Sylvia's accounts.

The £78 cash discount allowed to a customer would be shown as an expense in the profit and loss account.

4.3

The insurance relating to 19X7 is 11/12 x £840 + 1/12 x £960 = £850. Therefore, this is the figure which should be shown in the profit and loss account for the year to 31 December 19X7. Similarly, the profit and loss account for the year to 31 December 19X8 should show insurance of 11/12 x £960 + 1/12 x £1,020 = £965.

The accruals and prepayments are as follows:

31 December 19X6	prepayment	11/12 x £840 = £770
31 December 19X7	accrual	1/12 x £960 = £80
31 December 19X8	prepayment	11/12 x £1,020 = £935.

The profit and loss account figures are related to the balance sheet figures as follows:

y/e 31/12/X7	£nil paid this year + £770 paid last year + £80 accrued = £850.
y/e 31/12/X8	£1,980 paid this year – £80 for last year – £935 prepaid = £965.

4.4

Terry
Trading and profit and loss account for the year to 31 May 19X8

	£	£
Sales		34,990
Cost of goods sold:		
Purchases	23,670	
Less: Stock as at 31 May 19X8	2,560	21,110
Gross profit		13,880
Discounts received		211
		14,091
Rent	2,650	
Staff wages	9,600	
Electricity	1,860	
Telephone	1,210	
Advertising	1,100	
Bank interest	500	16,920
Net loss for the year		2,829

Notes:

1. Rent is £1,400 + 5/12 x £3,000 = £2,650.
2. Discounts received are 1% of (£23,670 – £2,570) = £211.
3. Advertising is 11/12 x £1,200 = £1,100.
4. The van was not used during the year to 31 May 19X8. Therefore no depreciation is charged in the profit and loss account for the year.

Chapter 5

5.1

	Debit	*Credit*
(a)	Land and buildings	Bank
(b)	Rent	Cash
(c)	Purchases	J Calvert Ltd
(d)	J Calvert Ltd	Returns outwards
(e)	J Calvert Ltd	Bank
(f)	Motor vehicles	ABC Motors Ltd
(g)	Motor expenses	Bank
(h)	Cash	Sales
(i)	Bank	D Bentley
(j)	D Bentley	Sales
(k)	Returns inwards	D Bentley
(l)	Bank	Interest received

5.2

Capital

		£			£
			Nov 1	Cash	10,000

Equipment

		£			£
Nov 2	Bank	3,400			

Cash

		£			£
Nov 1	Capital	10,000	Nov 1	Bank	9,500
			Nov 1	Rent	350
			Nov 16	Sundry expenses	37

Bank

		£			£
Nov 1	Cash	9,500	Nov 2	Equipment	3,400
Nov 6	Sales	3,670	Nov 24	G McNab	8,673
Nov 28	M Hall	4,680	Nov 30	Wages	550
			Nov 30	Drawings	1,200

Purchases

		£			£
Nov 2	G McNab	8,950			
Nov 25	K Shaw	6,200			

Sales

		£			£
			Nov 6	Bank	3,670
			Nov 14	M Hall	5,000
			Nov 14	H Reynolds	300

Returns outwards

		£			£
			Nov 9	G McNab	100

Returns inwards

		£			£
Nov 18	M Hall	200			

Rent

		£			£
Nov 1	Cash	350			

Sundry expenses

		£			£
Nov 16	Cash	37			

Wages

		£			£
Nov 30	Bank	550			

Drawings

		£			£
Nov 30	Bank	1,200			

Discounts allowed

		£			£
Nov 28	M Hall	120			

Discounts received

		£			£
			Nov 24	G McNab	177

G McNab

		£			£
Nov 9	Returns outwards	100	Nov 2	Purchases	8,950
Nov 24	Bank	8,673			
Nov 24	Discounts received	177			

M Hall

		£			£
Nov 14	Sales	5,000	Nov 18	Returns inwards	200
			Nov 28	Bank	4,680
			Nov 28	Discounts allowed	120

H Reynolds

		£			£
Nov 14	Sales	300			

K Shaw

		£			£
			Nov 25	Purchases	6,200

Trial balance as at November 30

	Dr balances	Cr balances
	£	£
Capital		10,000
Equipment	3,400	
Cash	113	
Bank	4,027	
Purchases	15,150	
Sales		8,970
Returns outwards		100
Returns inwards	200	
Rent	350	
Sundry expenses	37	
Wages	550	
Drawings	1,200	
Discounts allowed	120	
Discounts received		177
H Reynolds	300	
K Shaw		6,200
	25,447	25,447

5.3

Capital

		£			£
Nov 30	Drawings	1,200	Nov 1	Cash	10,000
Nov 30	Balance c/d	9,620	Nov 30	Profit for the month	820
		10,820			10,820
			Dec 1	Balance b/d	9,620

Equipment

		£			£
Nov 2	Bank	3,400	Nov 30	Balance c/d	3,400
Dec 1	Balance b/d	3,400			

Cash

		£			£
Nov 1	Capital	10,000	Nov 1	Bank	9,500
			Nov 1	Rent	350
			Nov 16	Sundry expenses	37
			Nov 30	Balance c/d	113
		10,000			10,000
Dec 1	Balance b/d	113			

Bank

		£			£
Nov 1	Cash	9,500	Nov 2	Equipment	3,400
Nov 6	Sales	3,670	Nov 24	G McNab	8,673
Nov 28	M Hall	4,680	Nov 30	Wages	550
			Nov 30	Drawings	1,200
			Nov 30	Balance c/d	4,027
		17,850			17,850
Dec 1	Balance b/d	4,027			

Stock of goods for resale

		£			£
Nov 30	Trading a/c	7,980	Nov 30	Balance c/d	7,980
Dec 1	Balance b/d	7,980			

Purchases

		£			£
Nov 2	G McNab	8,950	Nov 30	Trading a/c	15,150
Nov 25	K Shaw	6,200			
		15,150			15,150

Sales

		£			£
Nov 30	Trading a/c	8,970	Nov 6	Bank	3,670
			Nov 14	M Hall	5,000
			Nov 14	H Reynolds	300
		8,970			8,970

Returns outwards

		£			£
Nov 30	Trading a/c	100	Nov 9	G McNab	100

Returns inwards

		£			£
Nov 18	M Hall	200	Nov 30	Trading a/c	200

Rent

		£			£
Nov 1	Cash	350	Nov 30	Profit and loss a/c	350

Sundry expenses

		£			£
Nov 16	Cash	37	Nov 30	Profit and loss a/c	37

Wages

		£			£
Nov 30	Bank	550	Nov 30	Profit and loss a/c	550

Drawings

		£			£
Nov 30	Bank	1,200	Nov 30	Capital	1,200

Discounts allowed

		£			£
Nov 28	M Hall	120	Nov 30	Profit and loss a/c	120

Discounts received

		£			£
Nov 30	Profit and loss a/c	177	Nov 24	G McNab	177

G McNab

		£			£
Nov 9	Returns outwards	100	Nov 2	Purchases	8,950
Nov 24	Bank	8,673			
Nov 24	Discounts received	177			
		8,950			8,950

M Hall

		£			£
Nov 14	Sales	5,000	Nov 18	Returns inwards	200
			Nov 28	Bank	4,680
			Nov 28	Discounts allowed	120
		5,000			5,000

H Reynolds

		£			£
Nov 14	Sales	300	Nov 30	Balance c/d	300
Dec 1	Balance b/d	300			

K Shaw

		£			£
Nov 30	Balance c/d	6,200	Nov 25	Purchases	6,200
			Dec 1	Balance b/d	6,200

Damon
Trading and profit and loss account for the month to 30 November

	£	£	£
Sales			8,970
Less: Returns inwards			200
			8,770
Cost of goods sold:			
Purchases	15,150		
Less: Returns outwards	100	15,050	
Less: Stock as at 30 November		7,980	7,070
Gross profit			1,700
Discounts received			177
			1,877
Rent		350	
Sundry expenses		37	
Wages		550	
Discounts allowed		120	1,057
Net profit for the month			820

Damon
Balance sheet as at 30 November

	£	£
Fixed assets		
Equipment		3,400
Current assets		
Stock of goods for resale	7,980	
Trade debtors	300	
Bank	4,027	
Cash	113	
	12,420	
Current liabilities		
Trade creditors	6,200	
Net current assets		6,220
Total assets less current liabilities		9,620
Capital		
Capital introduced	10,000	
Profit for the month	820	
	10,820	
Less: Drawings	1,200	9,620
		9,620

5.4

Emma
Trading and profit and loss account for the year to 31 March 19X9

	£	£	£
Sales			32,868
Less: Returns inwards			420
			32,448
Cost of goods sold:			
Stock as at 1 April 19X8		2,445	
Purchases	11,510		
Less: Returns outwards	50	11,460	
		13,905	
Less: Stock as at 31 March 19X9		3,480	10,425
Gross profit			22,023
Rent (£1,100 + £100)		1,200	
Heating and lighting (£1,630 + £340)		1,970	
Insurance (£1,350 – £210)		1,140	
Staff wages		6,540	
Bank overdraft interest		350	11,200
Net profit for the year			10,823

Emma
Balance sheet as at 31 March 19X9

	£	£
Fixed assets		
Motor van		6,500
Current assets		
Stock of goods for resale	3,480	
Trade debtors	3,720	
Prepayments	210	
	7,410	
Current liabilities		
Trade creditors	2,870	
Accruals	440	
Bank overdraft	3,777	
	7,087	
Net current assets		323
Total assets less current liabilities		6,823
Capital		
As at 1 April 19X8	8,000	
Profit for the year	10,823	
	18,823	
Less: Drawings	12,000	6,823

Chapter 6

6.1

Expenditure can be divided into two classes. Capital expenditure is expenditure on the acquisition of fixed assets, whilst revenue expenditure is expenditure on the acquisition of current assets (stock) or on the day-to-day running costs of a business. Expenditure becomes an expense and is transferred to the profit and loss account when the benefits obtained by reason of that expenditure are used up. This process is fairly immediate for revenue expenditure but is normally prolonged over several accounting periods in the case of capital expenditure. The amount of capital expenditure transferred to the profit and loss account in an accounting period is known as depreciation.

6.2

Providing for depreciation reduces the profit of a business but has no effect on the business bank account. It certainly does not ensure that an amount of money equal to the depreciation provision is "saved up" in readiness for the replacement of fixed assets. It might be suggested that lower profits will result in lower drawings by the owner of the business, thereby resulting in a build-up of cash which could be used to replace fixed assets, but there is no guarantee that this will occur.

A business wishing to ensure that funds are available to replace fixed assets must consciously set money aside for this purpose and the amount of money set aside should take into account the likelihood that replacement assets will cost more than their predecessors. None of this has anything to do with depreciation, which is concerned solely with the fair allocation of the cost of existing fixed assets to the accounting periods in which they are used.

6.3

(a) and (b)	*Straight-line* £	*Reducing-balance* £
Year to 30 September 19X6:		
Cost	138,600	138,600
Depreciation 1/4 x (£138,600 – £50,000)	22,150	
Depreciation 22.5% x £138,600		31,185
WDV	116,450	107,415
Year to 30 September 19X7:		
Depreciation 1/4 x (£138,600 – £50,000)	22,150	
Depreciation 22.5% x £107,415		24,168
WDV	94,300	83,247
Year to 30 September 19X8:		
Depreciation 1/4 x (£138,600 – £50,000)	22,150	
Depreciation 22.5% x £83,247		18,731
WDV	72,150	64,516
Year to 30 September 19X9:		
Depreciation 1/4 x (£138,600 – £50,000)	22,150	
Depreciation 22.5% x £64,516		14,516
WDV	50,000	50,000

(c) The straight-line method is certainly easier to operate and is often adopted for this reason. However, the only acceptable motive for choosing one method or the other is that the chosen method most closely matches the usage pattern of the asset. If the benefits obtained from the asset are spread fairly uniformly over its useful life, the straight-line method seems more appropriate. If these benefits diminish as the asset ages, the reducing-balance method would seem preferable. However, if repair costs are also taken into account, the reducing-balance method might be chosen even for assets with a uniform usage pattern (see text).

6.4

Motor vehicles

		£			£
1.6.X8	Balance b/d	18,320	1.9.X8	Disposal a/c	7,200
1.9.X8	Bank	9,400	31.5.X9	Balance c/d	20,520
		27,720			27,720
1.6.X9	Balance b/d	20,520			

Provision for depreciation of motor vehicles

		£			£
1.9.X8	Disposal a/c	3,960	1.6.X8	Balance b/d	11,540
31.5.X9	Balance c/d	11,574	31.5.X9	Profit and loss a/c	3,994
		15,534			15,534
			1.6.X9	Balance b/d	11,574

Disposal of motor vehicles

		£			£
1.9.X8	Motor vehicles	7,200	1.9.X8	Prov'n for dep'n	3,960
31.5.X9	Profit and loss a/c	110	1.9.X8	Bank	3,350
		7,310			7,310

Notes:

1. We are not told how Katherine treats vehicles bought and sold during an accounting year, so it is best to assume that she calculates a part-year's depreciation in the year of acquisition or disposal.
2. The vehicle sold on 1 September 19X8 had been owned by Katherine for 2 years and 9 months i.e. 2.75 years. The accumulated depreciation on this vehicle was therefore £7,200 x 20% x 2.75 = £3,960.
3. The depreciation charge for the year to 31 May 19X9 is made up as follows:

	£
Vehicles owned all year (£18,320 – £7,200) x 20%	2,224
Vehicle sold during the year £7,200 x 20% x 0.25	360
Vehicle bought during the year £9,400 x 20% x 0.75	1,410
	3,994

Chapter 7

7.1

	Cost	*Selling price*	*Costs of prep'n*	*Comm'n*	*NRV*	*Lower of cost and NRV*
	£	£	£	£	£	£
Lorry A	12,500	15,000	420	750	13,830	12,500
Lorry B	15,700	18,000	870	900	16,230	15,700
Lorry C	22,800	21,000	1,120	1,050	18,830	18,830
Lorry D	19,600	22,000	950	1,100	19,950	19,600
	70,600	76,000	3,360	3,800	68,840	66,630

7.2

(a) **FIFO**

	No of tons			*Cost (£)*
Sold 10 April	900	900 @ £8		7,200
Sold 23 April	1,100	300 @ £8	2,400	
		500 @ £8.50	4,250	
		300 @ £8.30	2,490	9,140
Stock 30 April	700	100 @ £8.30	830	
		600 @ £8.10	4,860	5,690

(b) **LIFO**

	No of tons			*Cost (£)*
Sold 10 April	900	500 @ £8.50	4,250	
		400 @ £8	3,200	7,450
Sold 23 April	1,100	600 @ £8.10	4,860	
		400 @ £8.30	3,320	
		100 @ £8	800	8,980
Stock 30 April	700	700 @ £8		5,600

(c) **AVCO**

	No of tons		*Total cost (£)*	*Weighted average cost*	*Cost of stock sold (£)*
Opening stock	1,200	@ £8	9,600		
Bought 3 April	500	@ £8.50	4,250		
	1,700		13,850	£8.15	
Sold 10 April	900	@ £8.15	7,335		7,335
Balance 10 April	800		6,515		
Bought 14 April	400	@ £8.30	3,320		
Bought 18 April	600	@ £8.10	4,860		
	1,800		14,695	£8.17	
Sold 23 April	1,100	@ £8.17	8,987		8,987
Stock 23 April	700		5,708		

7.3

Bad debts

		£			£
21.11.X7	P Gardiner	75	30.6.X8	Profit and loss a/c	177
18.5.X8	B Williams	102			
		177			177
29.10.X8	F Scott	43	30.6.X9	Profit and loss a/c	109
12.5.X9	L Turner	66			
		109			109

Provision for doubtful debts

		£			£
30.6.X8	Balance c/d	159	1.7.X7	Balance b/d	153
			30.6.X8	Profit and loss a/c	6
		159			159
30.6.X9	Profit and loss a/c	13	1.7.X8	Balance b/d	159
30.6.X9	Balance c/d	146			
		159			159
			1.7.X9	Balance b/d	146

Ronald
Profit and loss accounts for the years to 30 June (extracts)

	£
19X8	
Bad debts written off	177
Increase in provision for doubtful debts	6
19X9	
Bad debts written off	109
Decrease in provision for doubtful debts	(13)

Ronald
Balance sheets as at 30 June (extracts)

	£	£
19X8		
Current assets		
Trade debtors	7,950	
Less: Provision for doubtful debts	159	7,791
19X9		
Current assets		
Trade debtors	7,300	
Less: Provision for doubtful debts	146	7,154

7.4

Bank

		£			£
31.5.X9	P Jarvis	45	31.5.X9	Balance b/d	3,229
	Balance c/d	3,721		Bank charges	37
				J Giles	500
		3,766			3,766
			1.6.X9	Balance b/d	3,721

Bank reconciliation as at 31 May 19X9

	£
Overdrawn balance, per bank statement	1,351
Add: Unpresented cheques	2,820
	4,171
Less: Outstanding lodgements	450
Overdrawn balance, per bank account	3,721

Chapter 8

8.1

(a) Indirect manufacturing cost

(b) Selling and distribution expense

(c) Direct manufacturing cost

(d) Direct manufacturing cost

(e) Selling and distribution expense

(f) Indirect manufacturing cost

(g) Direct manufacturing cost

(h) Indirect manufacturing cost

(i) Indirect manufacturing cost

(j) Indirect manufacturing cost (to the extent that the computer is used for production planning and control work)

(k) Finance cost

(l) Direct manufacturing cost.

8.2

Stewart
Manufacturing account for the year to 31 March 19X8

	£	£
Stock of raw materials as at 1 April 19X7		53,210
Purchases of raw materials		151,490
		204,700
Less: Stock of raw materials as at 31 March 19X8		55,190
Direct materials consumed		149,510
Direct labour	68,220	
Direct expenses	13,550	81,770
Prime cost c/f		231,280

	£	£
Prime cost b/f		231,280
Indirect manufacturing costs		
Indirect wages and salaries	21,000	
Factory power	11,500	
Factory repairs	1,170	
Rent and rates	6,130	
Depreciation of factory machines	4,500	44,300
Total manufacturing costs incurred during the year		275,580
Add: Work in progress as at 1 April 19X7		11,650
		287,230
Less: Work in progress as at 31 March 19X8		13,220
Production cost of goods completed		274,010

Stewart
Trading and profit and loss account for the year to 31 March 19X8

	£	£
Sales		391,380
Cost of goods sold:		
Stock as at 1 April 19X7	49,420	
Completed goods transferred from manufacturing	274,010	
	323,430	
Less: Stock as at 31 March 19X8	47,150	276,280
Gross profit		115,100
Carriage outwards	6,230	
Office rent and rates	6,130	
Office salaries	36,800	
Office heating and lighting	2,540	
Other office expenses	5,660	
Depreciation of office equipment	2,400	59,760
Net profit		55,340

8.3

Provision for unrealised profit

		£			£
31.12.X8	Balance c/d	1,290	31.12.X7	Profit and loss a/c	1,210
			31.12.X8	Profit and loss a/c	80
		1,290			1,290
31.12.X9	Profit and loss a/c	70	1.1.X9	Balance b/d	1,290
31.12.X9	Balance c/d	1,220			
		1,290			1,290
			1.1.X0	Balance b/d	1,220

Chapter 9

9.1

(a) (i) Nominal ledger (ii) Cashbook
(iii) Sales ledger (iv) Nominal ledger

(b) (i) Purchases daybook (ii) Cashbook
(iii) Journal (or purchases daybook if this has the appropriate analysis columns)
(iv) Sales returns daybook.

9.2

Sales daybook

Date	*Name*	*Amount*
		£
Oct 6	M Mohindra	1,500
Oct 6	R Griffin	4,750
Oct 23	B Dean	4,200
Oct 30	M Mohindra	700
Total sales for the month		11,150

Purchases daybook

Date	*Name*	*Total*	*Purchases*	*Stationery*	*Motor Exp.*
		£	£	£	£
Oct 2	S Singh	3,200	3,200		
Oct 2	R Shipley	6,500	6,500		
Oct 5	M Goodall	500		500	
Oct 5	Hodgkins Garage	40			40
Oct 12	Hodgkins Garage	35			35
Oct 21	R Shipley	3,000	3,000		
Oct 24	Hodgkins Garage	45			45
Totals for the month		13,320	12,700	500	120

Purchases returns daybook

Date	*Name*	*Total*	*Purchases*	*Stationery*	*Motor Exp.*
		£	£	£	£
Oct 8	S Singh	200	200		

Cashbook

Oct		Disc. Allow'd £	Bank £	Oct		Disc. Rec'd £	Bank £
1	Capital		2,000	3	Rent		1,200
11	Sales		1,000	17	Purchases		850
31	R Griffin	100	4,650	27	S Singh	90	2,910
31	Balance c/d		3,610	27	R Shipley	200	6,300
		100	11,260			290	11,260
				Nov 1	Balance c/d		3,610

Journal

		Dr	Cr
		£	£
Oct 1	Equipment	5,000	
	Motor vehicles	8,000	
	Capital		13,000
	Being assets introduced by Keith on commencement of trade.		
Oct 13	Equipment	2,500	
	P Lomas Ltd		2,500
	Being a purchase of equipment on credit terms from P Lomas Ltd.		

Nominal ledger

Capital

		£			£
			Oct 1	Bank	2,000
			Oct 1	Equipment	5,000
			Oct 1	Motor vehicles	8,000

Equipment

		£			£
Oct 1	Capital	5,000			
Oct 13	P Lomas Ltd	2,500			

Motor vehicles

		£			£
Oct 1	Capital	8,000			

Sales

		£			£
			Oct 11	Bank	1,000
			Oct 31	Sales daybook	11,150

Purchases

		£			£
Oct 17	Bank	850			
Oct 31	Purchases daybook	12,700			

Purchases returns

		£			£
			Oct 31	Purch. returns daybook	200

Stationery

		£			£
Oct 31	Purchases daybook	500			

Motor expenses

		£			£
Oct 31	Purchases daybook	120			

Rent

		£			£
Oct 3	Bank	1,200			

Discounts allowed

		£			£
Oct 31	Cashbook	100			

Discounts received

		£			£
			Oct 31	Cashbook	290

Sales ledger
M Mohindra

		£			£
Oct 6	Sales	1,500			
Oct 30	Sales	700			

R Griffin

		£			£
Oct 6	Sales	4,750	Oct 31	Bank	4,650
			Oct 31	Discounts allowed	100

B Dean

		£			£
Oct 23	Sales	4,200			

Purchase ledger
S Singh

		£			£
Oct 8	Purchases returns	200	Oct 2	Purchases	3,200
Oct 27	Bank	2,910			
Oct 27	Discounts received	90			

R Shipley

		£			£
Oct 27	Bank	6,300	Oct 2	Purchases	6,500
Oct 27	Discounts received	200	Oct 21	Purchases	3,000

M Goodall

		£			£
			Oct 5	Stationery	500

Hodgkins Garage

	£			£
		Oct 5	Motor expenses	40
		Oct 12	Motor expenses	35
		Oct 24	Motor expenses	45

P Lomas Ltd

	£			£
		Oct 13	Equipment	2,500

Trial balance as at October 31

	Dr balances	Cr balances
	£	£
Bank		3,610
Capital		15,000
Equipment	7,500	
Motor vehicles	8,000	
Sales		12,150
Purchases	13,550	
Purchases returns		200
Stationery	500	
Motor expenses	120	
Rent	1,200	
Discounts allowed	100	
Discounts received		290
M Mohindra	2,200	
B Dean	4,200	
R Shipley		3,000
M Goodall		500
Hodgkins Garage		120
P Lomas Ltd		2,500
	37,370	37,370

Note:

The purchases daybook could have contained an analysis column for the purchase of equipment. This would have avoided the need for the second of the two journal entries.

9.3

(a) A debit balance can be shown either as an asset in the balance sheet or as an expense in the profit and loss account. The balance should therefore be shown as an extra expense in the profit and loss account (prudence convention).

(b) A credit balance can be shown either as a liability in the balance sheet or as revenue in the profit and loss account. The balance should therefore be shown as an extra liability in the balance sheet (prudence convention).

9.4

			Dr	Cr
			£	£
(a)	31.12.X7	Suspense account	27	
		Trade debtors		27
		Being the correction of an error. £225 sales invoice posted to sales ledger as £252.		
(b)	31.12.X7	Capital	100	
		Suspense account		100
		Being the correction of an error. Drawings of £50 incorrectly credited to capital a/c.		
(c)	31.12.X7	Discounts received	100	
		Suspense account		100
		Being the correction of an error. Discounts received overstated by £100.		

Suspense account

		£			£
31.12.X7	Balance b/d	173	31.12.X7	Capital	100
31.12.X7	Trade debtors	27	31.12.X7	Discounts received	100
		200			200

9.5

Sales ledger control account

		£			£
Sept 30	Total debtors b/d	24,768	Sept 30	Bad debt w/off	500
Sept 30	Sales returns	200	Sept 30	Total debtors c/d	24,468
		24,968			24,968
Oct 1	Total debtors b/d	24,468			

The correct figure for trade debtors at 30 September 19X8 is £24,468. This reconciles as follows with the list of debtor balances taken from the sales ledger:

	£
Original total	22,761
Add: Sales invoice incorrectly posted (£1,230 – £123)	1,107
Debtor omitted from list	600
	24,468

Chapter 10

10.1

Arthur
Statement of affairs as at 31 March 19X8

	£	£	£
Fixed assets			
Equipment at cost		4,000	
Less: Accumulated depreciation to date		2,840	1,160
Current assets			
Stock of goods for resale		1,000	
Trade debtors		400	
Prepaid rent		100	
Cash in hand		500	
		2,000	
Current liabilities			
Trade creditors	720		
Accrued heating and lighting	200	920	1,080
			2,240
Capital			
As at 31 March 19X8			2,240

Notes:

1. Equipment at cost is £3,800 + £800 – £600 = £4,000.
2. Accumulated depreciation on the sold equipment was 20% of £600 for 3 years = £360. Depreciation for the year to 31 March 19X8 is 20% of £4,000 = £800. Therefore the accumulated depreciation at 31 March 19X8 is £2,400 – £360 + £800 = £2,840.
3. Arthur's opening capital was £3,030 and his closing capital is estimated to be £2,240. Capital introduced during the year was £620. Drawings for the year were £7,800 + £250 + £1,040 = £9,090. Therefore the estimated profit for the year was £2,240 – £620 + £9,090 – £3,030 = £7,680.

10.2

Cash

		£			£
1.7.X7	Capital	300	30.6.X8	Assistant's wages	7,320
30.6.X8	Sales (deduced)	73,280	30.6.X8	Drawings	9,650
			30.6.X8	Postage & stationery	137
			30.6.X8	Window cleaning	156
			30.6.X8	Bank	55,981
			30.6.X8	Balance c/d	336
		73,580			73,580
1.7.X8	Balance b/d	336			

Bank

		£			£
1.7.X7	Capital	5,000	30.6.X8	Trade creditors	48,659
1.11.X7	Loan	7,500	30.6.X8	Fixtures and fittings	3,750
30.6.X8	Cash	55,981	30.6.X8	Equipment	2,860
			30.6.X8	Rent, rates and ins.	8,340
			30.6.X8	Heating and lighting	2,567
			30.6.X8	Repairs	430
			30.6.X8	Balance c/d	1,875
		68,481			68,481
1.7.X8	Balance b/d	1,875			

Total creditors

		£			£
30.6.X8	Bank	48,659	30.6.X8	Purchases (deduced)	54,695
30.6.X8	Discounts received	1,297			
30.6.X8	Balance c/d	4,739			
		54,695			54,695
			1.7.X8	Balance b/d	4,739

Rent, rates and insurance

		£			£
30.6.X8	Bank	8,340	30.6.X8	Drawings	2,390
			30.6.X8	Profit and loss a/c	4,780
			30.6.X8	Rates prepayment c/d	600
			30.6.X8	Ins. prepayment c/d	570
		8,340			8,340
1.7.X8	Prepayments b/d	1,170			

Heating and lighting

		£			£
30.6.X8	Bank	2,567	30.6.X8	Drawings	770
30.6.X8	Accrual c/d	513	30.6.X8	Profit and loss a/c	2,310
		3,080			3,080
			1.7.X8	Accrual b/d	513

Luna
Trading and profit and loss account for the year to 30 June 19X8

	£	£
Sales (£73,280 + £1,263)		74,543
Cost of goods sold:		
Purchases	54,695	
Less: Stock as at 30 June 19X8	6,238	48,457
Gross profit c/f		26,086

	£	£
Gross profit b/f		26,086
Discounts received		1,297
		27,383
Wages	7,320	
Postage and stationery	137	
Window cleaning	156	
Heating and lighting	2,310	
Rent, rates and insurance	4,780	
Repairs	430	
Loan interest	250	
Depreciation	804	16,187
Net profit for the year		11,196

Luna
Balance sheet as at 30 June 19X8

	£	£	£
Fixed assets			
Fixtures and fittings, at cost		3,750	
Less: Accumulated depreciation to date		375	3,375
Equipment, at cost		2,860	
Less: Accumulated depreciation to date		429	2,431
			5,806
Current assets			
Stock of goods for resale		6,238	
Trade debtors		1,263	
Prepayments		1,170	
Cash at bank		1,875	
Cash in hand		336	
		10,882	
Current liabilities			
Trade creditors	4,739		
Accruals (£513 + £250)	763	5,502	5,380
Total assets less current liabilities			11,186
Long-term liabilities			
Loan from uncle			7,500
			3,686
Capital			
Capital introduced (£5,000 + £300)		5,300	
Profit for the year		11,196	
		16,496	
Less: Drawings (£9,650 + £2,390 + £770)		12,810	3,686
			3,686

Notes:

1. Takings paid into the bank consist of £54,745 shown on the bank statements, plus the outstanding lodgement of £1,236, giving a total of £55,981.
2. After allowing for prepayments, rent, rates and insurance costs for the year are £7,170. One-third (£2,390) is private. The remainder is a business expense.
3. After allowing for accruals, the heating and lighting costs for the year are £3,080. One-quarter of this (£770) is private and the remainder is a business expense.
4. Depreciation is 10% x £3,750 + 15% x £2,860 = £804.
5. Accrued loan interest is £7,500 x 5% for 8 months = £250.

Chapter 11

11.1

See text.

11.2

(a) If the club prepares receipts and payments accounts, subscriptions are accounted for on a cash basis. The amounts shown for each of the four years are:

year to 31 December 19X5	£1,950 + £90	= £2,040
year to 31 December 19X6	£340 + £2,130 + £110	= £2,580
year to 31 December 19X7	£250 + £2,250 + £130	= £2,630
year to 31 December 19X8	£180 + £2,340 + £150	= £2,670

(b) If the club prepares income and expenditure accounts, subscriptions paid in advance should be regarded as prepaid revenue. The subscriptions which should be shown in the income and expenditure account for each of the four years are:

year to 31 December 19X5	£1,950	= £1,950
year to 31 December 19X6	£90 + £340 + £2,130	= £2,560
year to 31 December 19X7	£110 + £250 + £2,250	= £2,610
year to 31 December 19X8	£130 + £180 + £2,340	= £2,650

11.3

Walford chess club
Receipts and payments account for the year to 31 December 19X8

Receipts		£	**Payments**		£
Balance at 1 Jan. 19X8:			Purchase of chess sets/boards		480
Cash	14		Purchase of chess clocks		120
Bank account	219	233	Purchase of chess books		50
			Room hire		520
Subscriptions received		1,096	Coffee, biscuits etc.		93
Donations received		50	Annual outing:		
			Costs	427	
			Receipts	395	32
			Balance at 31 Dec. 19X8:		
			Cash	30	
			Bank account	54	84
		1,379			1,379

Chapter 12

12.1

Kevin, Kate and Kim
Appropriation account for the year to 30 June 19X9

	£	£
Net profit for the year before interest		82,410
Less: Loan interest (10% x £5,000 x 3/12)		125
Corrected net profit for the year		82,285
Add: Interest on drawings:		
Kevin (8% x £18,000 x 6/12)	720	
Kate (8% x £15,000 x 6/12)	600	
Kim (8% x £17,500 x 6/12)	700	2,020
		84,305
Less: Interest on capital:		
Kevin (6% x (£30,000 x 9/12 + £22,000 x 3/12))	1,680	
Kate (6% x £20,000)	1,200	
Kim (6% x (£10,000 x 9/12 + £17,000 x 3/12))	705	3,585
		80,720
Less: Partners' salaries:		
Kevin £4,000, Kate £7,000, Kim £11,000		22,000
		58,720
Less: Profit shares:		
Kevin (8/20)	23,488	
Kate (7/20)	20,552	
Kim (5/20)	14,680	58,720

Partners' capital accounts

	Kevin	Kate	Kim		Kevin	Kate	Kim
	£	£	£		£	£	£
Bank	3,000			Balances b/d	30,000	20,000	10,000
Loan account	5,000			Bank			7,000
Balances c/d	22,000	20,000	17,000				
	30,000	20,000	17,000		30,000	20,000	17,000
				Balances b/d	22,000	20,000	17,000

Partners' current accounts

	Kevin	Kate	Kim		Kevin	Kate	Kim
	£	£	£		£	£	£
Balance b/d		450		Balances b/d	1,235		1,202
Drawings	18,000	15,000	17,500	Loan interest	125		
Int. on drawings	720	600	700	Int. on capital	1,680	1,200	705
Balances c/d	11,808	12,702	9,387	Salaries	4,000	7,000	11,000
				Profit shares	23,488	20,552	14,680
	30,528	28,752	27,587		30,528	28,752	27,587
				Balances b/d	11,808	12,702	9,387

12.2

Revaluation account

	£		£
Motor vehicles	4,750	Plant and equipment	1,700
Stock	950	Loss on revaluation:	
Trade debtors	780	Liam (3/5th)	2,868
		Lorna (2/5th)	1,912
	6,480		6,480

Partners' capital accounts

	Liam	Lorna	Len		Liam	Lorna	Len
	£	£	£		£	£	£
Revaluation	2,868	1,912		Balances b/d	60,000	30,000	
Goodwill	20,000	15,000	5,000	Goodwill	24,000	16,000	
Land/buildings	22,500	16,875	5,625	Land/buildings	27,000	18,000	
Balances c/d	65,632	30,213	4,375	Bank			15,000
	111,000	64,000	15,000		111,000	64,000	15,000
				Balances b/d	65,632	30,213	4,375

Note:
Goodwill has been credited to the partners in their old ratio (3:2) and then debited to them in their new ratio (4:3:1). The same treatment has been applied to the difference between the book value and the market value of the land and buildings.

Liam, Lorna and Len
Balance sheet as at 31 October 19X8

	£	£	£	£
Fixed assets				
Land and buildings				50,000
Plant and equipment				20,000
Motor vehicles				15,000
				85,000
Current assets				
Stock of goods for resale			11,500	
Trade debtors			16,430	
Bank balance			15,680	
			43,610	
Current liabilities				
Trade creditors			22,220	21,390
				106,390
Capital accounts	Liam	Lorna	Len	
Balance at 31 October 19X8	65,632	30,213	4,375	100,220
Current accounts				
Balance at 31 October 19X8	5,100	1,070		6,170
				106,390

12.3

	Edna	*Enid*	*Eric*	*Total*
	£	£	£	£
Partners' salaries	12,000	14,000	5,000	31,000
Interest on capital	1,280	700	200	2,180
Profit share (4:3:1)	27,020	20,265	6,755	54,040
	40,300	34,965	11,955	87,220
Eric's deficiency	(311)	(234)	545	
Profit allocated to each partner	39,989	34,731	12,500	87,220

Note:
Eric's deficiency has been borne by Edna and Enid in the ratio 4:3.

Chapter 13

13.1

Carruthers & Co Ltd
Trading and profit and loss account for the year to 31 January 19X7

	£	£
Sales		605,430
Cost of goods sold:		
Stock as at 1 February 19X6	91,180	
Purchases	371,990	
	463,170	
Less: Stock as at 31 January 19X7	83,710	379,460
Gross profit		225,970
Reduction in provision for doubtful debts		170
		226,140
Operating expenses	95,680	
Depreciation of equipment	12,860	
Debenture interest	3,500	112,040
Net profit for the year		114,100
Less: Corporation tax		45,000
Net profit after tax		69,100
Unappropriated profit brought forward		34,730
		103,830
Less: Proposed dividends		
5% Preference shares	2,000	
Ordinary shares at £3 per share	60,000	62,000
Unappropriated profit carried forward		41,830

Note:

The ordinary shares have a nominal value of £10 per share, so 20,000 of these shares have been issued. A proposed dividend of £3 per share amounts to £3 x 20,000 = £60,000.

Carruthers & Co Ltd
Balance sheet as at 31 January 19X7

	£	£	£
Fixed assets			
Land and buildings, at cost			325,000
Equipment, at cost		84,290	
Less: Accumulated depreciation to date		50,800	33,490
			358,490
Current assets			
Stock of goods for resale		83,710	
Trade debtors	42,760		
Less: Provision for doubtful debts	900	41,860	
		125,570	
Current liabilities			
Trade creditors	35,410		
Corporation tax	45,000		
Proposed dividends	62,000		
Accrued debenture interest	3,500		
Bank overdraft	6,320	152,230	(26,660)
			331,830
Long-term liabilities			
7% Debentures			50,000
			281,830
Capital and reserves			
Called-up share capital			
20,000 ordinary shares of £10 per share, fully paid			200,000
40,000 5% preference shares of £1 per share, fully paid			40,000
			240,000
Reserves			
Profit and loss account			41,830
			281,830

13.2

Boscastle plc
Summarised balance sheet as at 1 October 19X9

	£
Fixed assets	4,560,000
Net current assets	1,845,400
	6,405,400
Called-up share capital	
3,300,000 £1 ordinary shares, fully paid	3,300,000
Reserves	
General reserve	2,600,000
Profit and loss account	505,400
	6,405,400

Notes:

1. The proceeds of the rights issue are 200,000 @ £2.50 = £500,000. Therefore net current assets increase by £500,000 to £1,845,400.
2. The 1 for 10 rights issue increased the number of issued shares by 200,000 to 2,200,000. The subsequent 1 for 2 bonus issue increases the number of issued shares by a further 50% to 3,300,000.
3. The premium received on the rights issue was 200,000 @ £1.50 = £300,000. This increased the balance on the share premium account to £700,000. However, the bonus issue of 1,100,000 £1 shares used up the whole of the share premium account together with £400,000 of the general reserve (reducing the general reserve to £2,600,000).

Chapter 14

14.1

Fairweather Ltd
Profit and loss account for the year to 31 March 19X6

	£	£
Turnover		587,540
Cost of sales		116,960
Gross profit		470,580
Distribution costs	167,290	
Administrative expenses	223,540	390,830
		79,750
Other operating income		35,600
		115,350
Interest payable and similar charges		3,270
Profit on ordinary activities before taxation		112,080
Tax on profit on ordinary activities		30,000
Profit on ordinary activities after taxation		82,080
Transfers to reserves	50,000	
Dividends paid and proposed	18,000	68,000
Retained profit for the financial year		14,080
Retained profit brought forward from previous year		9,860
Retained profit carried forward to next year		23,940

Tutorial notes:

1. Turnover is £611,300 – £23,760 = £587,540.
2. Cost of sales is £72,800 + £123,540 – £1,650 – £77,730 = £116,960.
3. Distribution costs and administrative expenses are made up of the following components:

Distribution costs:	£	*Administrative expenses:*	£
Salaries	89,660	Discounts allowed	12,530
Van expenses	18,330	Discounts received	(3,370)
Rates and insurance	18,600	Directors' remuneration	100,000
Heating and lighting	9,650	Office salaries	56,530
Repairs and renewals	6,240	Car running expenses	4,120
Advertising	12,760	Rates and insurance	18,600
Van depreciation	9,250	Heating and lighting	9,650
Warehouse plant depr'n	2,800	Repairs and renewals	6,240
		Stationery, telephone etc.	7,220
		Car depr'n	7,960
		Office equipment depr'n	3,960
		Doubtful debts prov'n	100
	167,290		223,540

Fairweather Ltd
Balance sheet as at 31 March 19X6

	£	£	£
FIXED ASSETS			
Intangible assets			
Goodwill		150,000	
Tangible assets			
Land and buildings	185,000		
Plant and machinery	34,220		
Fixtures, fittings, tools and equipment	10,790	230,010	380,010
CURRENT ASSETS			
Stocks			
Finished goods and goods for resale		77,730	
Debtors			
Trade debtors	10,590		
Prepayments and accrued income	3,600	14,190	
Cash at bank and in hand		520	
		92,440	
CREDITORS: Amounts falling due within one year			
Bank loans and overdrafts	11,110		
Trade creditors	29,140		
Other creditors including taxation and social security	48,000		
Accruals and deferred income	5,260	93,510	
NET CURRENT LIABILITIES			1,070
TOTAL ASSETS LESS CURRENT LIABILITIES			378,940
CREDITORS: Amounts falling after more than one year			
Debenture loans			30,000
			348,940

	£
CAPITAL AND RESERVES	
Called up share capital	150,000
Share premium account	75,000
Other reserves	100,000
Profit and loss account	23,940
	348,940

Tutorial notes:

1. Plant and machinery is:

	£
Delivery vans (£40,100 – £20,120 – £9,250)	10,730
Warehouse plant (£8,300 – £3,650 – £2,800)	1,850
Motor cars (£39,800 – £10,200 – £7,960)	21,640
	34,220

2. Fixtures, fittings etc. are £26,400 – £11,650 – £3,960 = £10,790.
3. Trade debtors are £11,620 – £930 – £100 = £10,590.
4. Other creditors are £30,000 + £18,000 = £48,000.
5. Accruals are £2,860 + debenture interest £2,400 = £5,260.

14.2

(a) See text.

(b) See text.

14.3

A comparison of Fairweather Ltd's figures in the year to 31 March 19X6 with the criteria for small and medium-sized companies is as follows:

	Fairweather Ltd	*Small*	*Medium*
	£	£	£
Total assets (£380,010 + £92,440)	472,450	£1,400,000	£5,600,000
Turnover	587,540	£2,800,000	£11,200,000

On both criteria, Fairweather Ltd is a small company. No information is available about the company's number of employees but this unimportant, since it is necessary to satisfy only two out the three criteria to be regarded as a small or medium-sized company.

Assuming that the company also satisfied at least two of the three criteria in the year to 31 March 19X5, it need not file a profit and loss account with the Registrar and may file the following abbreviated balance sheet:

Fairweather Ltd
Abbreviated balance sheet as at 31 March 19X6

	£	£
FIXED ASSETS		
Intangible assets	150,000	
Tangible assets	230,010	380,010
CURRENT ASSETS		
Stocks	77,730	
Debtors	14,190	
Cash at bank and in hand	520	
	92,440	
CREDITORS: Amounts falling due within one year	93,510	
NET CURRENT LIABILITIES		1,070
TOTAL ASSETS LESS CURRENT LIABILITIES		378,940
CREDITORS: Amounts falling after more than one year		30,000
		348,940
CAPITAL AND RESERVES		
Called up share capital		150,000
Share premium account		75,000
Other reserves		100,000
Profit and loss account		23,940
		348,940

Chapter 15

15.1

The company's profit after tax, extraordinary items and preference dividend is £4,500 (£8,900 – £2,200 – £800 – £1,400). Therefore EPS is 30p per ordinary share.

15.2

Plant at cost

		£			£
1.6.X4	Bank	12,000	31.5.X5	Balance c/d	12,000
1.6.X5	Balance b/d	12,000	31.5.X6	Balance c/d	12,000
1.6.X6	Balance b/d	12,000			

Provision for depreciation of plant

		£			£
31.5.X5	Balance c/d	2,400	31.5.X5	Profit and loss a/c	2,400
31.5.X6	Balance c/d	4,800	1.6.X5	Balance b/d	2,400
			31.5.X6	Profit and loss a/c	2,400
		4,800			4,800
			1.6.X6	Balance b/d	4,800

Government grant

		£			£
31.5.X5	Profit and loss a/c	600	1.6.X4	Bank	3,000
31.5.X5	Balance c/d	2,400			
		3,000			3,000
31.5.X6	Profit and loss a/c	600	1.6.X5	Balance b/d	2,400
31.5.X6	Balance c/d	1,800			
		2,400			2,400
			1.6.X6	Balance b/d	1,800

The balance on the government grant account should be shown in the balance sheet as deferred income (under the heading "accruals and deferred income").

15.3

Depreciation of £2,500 would be charged in the year to 31 December 19X0 and in the year to 31 December 19X1, leaving a WDV of £5,000 on 1 January 19X2. This amount (less the revised residual value of £2,000) should then be written off over the next eight years, giving a depreciation charge of £375 per annum.

If this procedure results in a material distortion of the company's results for the eight years to 31 December 19X9, the accumulated depreciation of £5,000 brought forward on 1 January 19X2 should be adjusted to £1,600 and depreciation of £800 per annum should be charged in each of the following eight years. The profit and loss account for the year to 31 December 19X2 would be credited with exceptional income of £3,400 as a consequence of this adjustment.

15.4

See text.

15.5

(a) This is a non-adjusting event and (if material) should be noted in the accounts.

(b) This is an adjusting event. Assuming that no further costs or selling expenses were incurred in relation to this stock between the balance sheet date and the date of the sale, the NRV of the stock is £21,400. Therefore it should be shown in the balance sheet at £20,000 (i.e. the lower of cost and NRV).

(c) If the drop in value is permanent, then this is an adjusting event and the balance sheet should show the property at the reduced valuation.

(d) This is a non-adjusting event and (if material) should be noted in the accounts.

Chapter 16

16.1

(a/b) The sale of a fixed asset yields a cash inflow, regardless of whether it is sold for more or less than book value.

(c) Cash outflow.

(d) Neither a cash inflow nor a cash outflow.

(e) No money changed hands when a bonus issue is made. Therefore a bonus issue yields neither a cash inflow nor a cash outflow.

16.2

(a) The purchase of a fixed asset has no effect on operating profit but gives rise to a cash outflow when the asset is paid for. The depreciation charges reduce operating profit but have no cash flow implications.

(b) Payment of a supplier's invoice has no effect on operating profit but gives rise to a cash outflow in the accounting period in which the payment is made.

(c) Accounting for accrued rent reduces operating profit but has no cash flow effect.

(d) No effect on operating profit or on cash flow.

16.3/4

See text.

16.5

(a)

GAMMA LTD
CASH FLOW STATEMENT FOR THE YEAR TO 30 JUNE 19X7

Reconciliation of operating profit to net cash inflow from operating activities

	£	£
Operating profit		170,200
Depreciation charges		44,310
Decrease in stocks		11,210
Increase in trade debtors		(24,510)
Increase in prepayments		(200)
Decrease in trade creditors		(3,390)
Increase in accruals		880
Net cash inflow from operating activities		198,500

Cash flow statement

	£	£
Net cash inflow from operating activities		198,500
Returns on investments and servicing of finance		
Dividends received	7,100	
Interest paid	(6,120)	980
Taxation		(32,300)
Capital expenditure		
Purchase of tangible fixed assets		(159,300)
Equity dividends paid		(85,000)
Financing		
Issue of ordinary share capital	20,000	
Issue of debentures	25,000	45,000
Decrease in cash during the period		32,120

Reconciliation of net cash flow to movement in net debt (note 1)

	£	£
Decrease in cash during the period	(32,120)	
Cash inflow from debenture issue	(25,000)	
Change in net debt		(57,120)
Net debt at 1 July 19X6		(52,790)
Net debt at 30 June 19X7		(109,910)

Note 1 - Analysis of changes in net debt

	At 1 July 19X6	*Cash flows*	*At 30 June 19X7*
	£	£	£
Bank overdraft	(2,790)	(32,120)	(34,910)
Decrease in cash		(32,120)	
Debenture loans	(50,000)	(25,000)	(75,000)
Total	(52,790)	(57,120)	(109,910)

(b) The cash flow statement explains why the company's bank overdraft increased by £32,120 in the year, despite the fact that an additional £45,000 was raised by the issue of shares and debentures.

The main problem is that the cash generated by the company's operating activities, after the payment of taxation and dividends, fell far short of the amount required to fund the very large investment in additional tangible fixed assets. This problem was compounded by a material increase in trade debtors (perhaps the company has been allowing longer credit) but was partly alleviated by a reduction in stocks.

The company's cash position at the end of June 19X7 is far worse than a year previously and it would appear that the company has invested more than it can really afford on additional fixed assets.

Chapter 17

17.1

J Harrison Ltd
Profit and loss account (extract) for the year to 30 April 19X8

	£'000	£'000
Turnover:		
Continuing operations	312	
Acquisitions	193	
	505	
Discontinued operations	53	558
Cost of sales		(204)
Gross profit		354
Net operating expenses		(228)
Operating profit		
Continuing operations	98	
Acquisitions	35	
	133	
Discontinued operations	(7)	126
Loss on disposal of discontinued operations		(27)

Notes to the accounts

1. **Analysis of expenses**

	Continuing operations	*Acquisitions*	*Discontinued operations*	*Total*
	£'000	£'000	£'000	£'000
Cost of sales	95	71	38	204
Net operating expenses:				
Distribution costs	75	42	2	119
Administrative expenses	56	45	20	121
Other operating income	(12)	-	-	(12)
	119	87	22	228

2. **Exceptional item**

   Administrative expenses on continuing operations include an exceptionally large bad debt amounting to £22,000.

17.2

See text

17.3

See text

Chapter 18

18.1

AA Ltd
Consolidated balance sheet as at 30 April 19X9

	£'000
Fixed assets	
Tangible assets	2,790
Net current assets	1,192
	3,982
Capital and reserves	
Called-up share capital	3,000
Profit and loss account	982
	3,982

Notes:

1. The profit on revaluation of fixed assets is £180,000.
2. On 30 April 19X5, the net assets of BB Ltd were £725,000 (£350,000 + £195,000 + £180,000). Therefore the goodwill arising on consolidation is £800,000 – £725,000 = £75,000.
3. The consolidated profit and loss account balance consists of the profit and loss account balance of AA Ltd (£1,029,000), plus the post acquisition increase in the reserves of BB Ltd (£223,000 – £195,000 = £28,000), less the goodwill written off (£75,000), giving a total of £982,000.

18.2

CC Ltd
Consolidated balance sheet as at 31 December 19X8

		£'000
Fixed assets		
Tangible assets		5,723
Goodwill arising on consolidation		90
		5,813
Current assets		
Stocks	1,938	
Debtors	2,359	
Bank	282	
	4,579	
Current liabilities		
Creditors	1,933	2,646
		8,459
Capital and reserves		
Called-up share capital		5,000
Capital reserves		2,536
Profit and loss account		518
		8,054
Minority interest		405
		8,459

Notes:

1. Goodwill for DD Ltd is £600,000 – 60% x (£500,000 + £280,000 + £30,000) = £114,000. Two years of amortisation reduces this by £57,000 to £57,000.
2. Goodwill for EE Ltd is £575,000 – 90% x (£300,000 + £60,000 + £230,000) = £44,000. One year of amortisation reduces this by £11,000 to £33,000.
3. The minority interests are DD Ltd 40% x (£820,000 + £30,000) = £340,000 and EE Ltd 10% x £650,000 = £65,000, giving a total for the group of £405,000.
4. The goods bought by DD Ltd from CC Ltd for £8,000 had an original cost of £5,000. Unrealised profit of £3,000 is subtracted from the group stock figure.
5. £48,000 of intra-group debts is subtracted from group debtors and creditors.
6. Capital reserves are £2,500,000 plus 90% of the £40,000 post acquisition increase for EE Ltd, giving £2,536,000.
7. Group profit and loss account balance is:

		£'000
CC Ltd		547
DD Ltd (60% x £40,000)		24
EE Ltd (90% x £20,000)		18
Amortisation of goodwill	- DD Ltd	(57)
	- EE Ltd	(11)
Unrealised profit in stock		(3)
		518

18.3

FF Ltd
Consolidated profit and loss account for the year to 31 March 19X8

		£
Turnover		504,400
Cost of sales		149,150
Gross profit		355,250
Distribution costs	43,850	
Administrative expenses	93,930	137,780
Profit on ordinary activities before taxation		217,470
Tax on profit on ordinary activities		60,000
Profit on ordinary activities after taxation		157,470
Minority interest		11,950
		145,520
Dividends		
Paid	30,000	
Proposed	60,000	90,000
Retained profit for the financial year		55,520
Retained profit brought forward		84,370
Retained profit carried forward		139,890

Notes:

1. Group turnover is £359,800 + £154,600 – £10,000 = £504,400.
2. Group cost of sales is £102,600 + £55,550 – £10,000 + £1,000 (unrealised profit) = £149,150.
3. The minority interest is 20% x £59,750 = £11,950.
4. Retained profit brought forward is £66,090 plus 80% of (£41,110 – £18,260) = £84,370.
5. Retained profit carried forward is £102,810 plus 80% of (£65,860 – £18,260) less unrealised profit £1,000 = £139,890.

Chapter 19

19.1

The main assumptions made when calculating the ratios for Roscoe Ltd are:

1. The year-end figures shown in the balance sheet are representative of the year as a whole and can therefore be used instead of average figures (which are not available for most items).
2. All sales and purchases are made on credit terms.
3. Cost of sales can be used as a reasonable approximation to purchases when calculating the creditor payment period.

Profitability ratios

Return on total capital employed	$\frac{60}{279} \times 100\%$	= 21.5%
Return on equity capital	$\frac{35-1}{119} \times 100\%$	= 28.6%
Gross profit margin	$\frac{175}{410} \times 100\%$	= 42.7%
Net profit margin	$\frac{45}{410} \times 100\%$	= 11.0%

Liquidity ratios

Current ratio	$\frac{147}{76}$	= 1.9 to 1
Quick assets ratio	$\frac{147-82}{76}$	= 0.9 to 1

Efficiency ratios

Stock holding period	$\frac{82}{235} \times 365$	= 127 days
Debtor collection period	$\frac{58}{410} \times 365$	= 52 days
Creditor payment period	$\frac{45}{235} \times 365$	= 70 days

Investment ratios

Capital gearing ratio	$\frac{150}{279} \times 100\%$	= 53.8%
Interest cover	$\frac{60}{15}$	= 4
Dividend cover	$\frac{35-1}{20}$	= 1.7
Earnings per share	$\frac{35-1}{100} \times 100p$	= 34p

19.2

Company X will have a high gross profit margin but much of the gross profit will be absorbed by overhead expenses so that the net profit margin might be disappointingly low. The stock holding period and the debtor collection period will both be comparatively long. The company will often have to pay for supplies of clothing well before the clothing is sold to customers and this may cause some liquidity problems. As a consequence, the company may have needed to obtain a source of long-term finance. This would be reflected in the capital gearing ratio and might depress the return obtained on equity capital.

Company Y will have a low gross profit margin but the lack of overhead costs may result in a surprisingly high net profit margin. The stock holding period and the debtor collection period will both be short. The company will often be able to sell goods and receive payment for them before having to pay its own suppliers, so that liquidity should not be a major problem.

19.3

Earnings per share	$\frac{90{,}000 - 15{,}000}{1{,}000{,}000}$ x 100p	= 7.5p
Dividend cover	$\frac{90{,}000 - 15{,}000}{25{,}000 + 30{,}000}$	= 1.4
Dividend yield	$\frac{5.5}{70}$ x 100%	= 7.9%
Price earnings ratio	$\frac{70}{7.5}$	= 9.3

Chapter 20

20.1

See text.

INDEX